The Role of Prosody in Affective Speech

Linguistic Insights

Studies in Language and Communication

Edited by Maurizio Gotti,
University of Bergamo

Volume 97

PETER LANG
Bern · Berlin · Bruxelles · Frankfurt am Main · New York · Oxford · Wien

Sylvie Hancil (ed.)

The Role of Prosody in Affective Speech

PETER LANG
Bern · Berlin · Bruxelles · Frankfurt am Main · New York · Oxford · Wien

Bibliographic information published by Die Deutsche Bibliothek
Die Deutsche Bibliothek lists this publication in the Deutsche Nationalbibliografie; detailed bibliographic data is available on the Internet at ‹http://dnb.ddb.de›.

British Library and Library of Congress Cataloguing-in-Publication Data:
A catalogue record for this book is available from *The British Library,* Great Britain.

Library of Congress Cataloging-in-Publication Data

The role of prosody in affective speech / Sylvie Hancil (ed.).
p. cm. – (Linguistic insights ; v. 97)
Includes bibliographical references.
ISBN 978-3-03911-696-6 (alk. paper)
1. Language and emotions. 2. Emotive (Linguistics)
3. English language–Versification. 4. French language–Versification.
I. Hancil, Sylvie.
BF582.R65 2009
401'.9–dc22

2009016419

ISSN 1424-8689
ISBN 978-3-03911-696-6

Hochfeldstrasse 32, CH-3012 Bern, Switzerland
info@peterlang.com, www.peterlang.com, www.peterlang.net

Printed in Germany

Contents

SYLVIE HANCIL

Introduction

At the centre of the relationship between 'langue', defined as "the underlying system shared by all speakers of a given language" (Culioli 1995: 4), and 'langage', defined as "speech activity as well as an evolving mass of individual speech events" (Culioli 1995: 4), lies the speaker, as was already acknowledged by Lyons (1982: 102), who associates the role of the speaker with the origin of enunciation. Here the speaking subject, to paraphrase Benveniste (1966), is understood as the one that is at the origin of enunciation.

In everyday conversational speech, the speaker will go through different types of affective states, all of which will reflect the interaction between his inner state and his environment in discourse. The complex manifestation of the various subjective states of a speaker, including attitudes and emotions, in discourse defines what will be the focus of our attention in this volume, namely affective speech, which cannot be reduced to a purely physiological phenomenon. Despite being a still new, emerging field, affective speech has been the object of significant, fruitful research over the last few years, especially with the official launching by Roddy Cowie of the HUMAINE Association at the end of the last plenary session organized with much success by Laurence Devillers and Jean-Claude Martin in June 2007 at the CNRS, Paris. The goal of this volume is to present a collection of review papers and research reports illustrating state-of-the-art research on prosody and affective speech, especially emotions.

The first part of this volume focusses on the sociolinguistic variables that are likely to influence the manifestation and the interpretation of affective speech in prosody. The first three analyses discuss the impact of culture on the manifestation of affective speech from various points of view. On the basis of ethology, which mainly explains behaviour in terms of phylogenetic adaptations, John J.

Ohala, provides a critical analysis of the various theoretical accounts underlining the connections between sounds and meanings and applies these principles to another level, involving the cross-cultural use of other emotional signals, namely kinesic elements such as eyes and eyebrows in non-verbal communication, where a gaze into the eyes of another individual can be interpreted as a threat or not. The novelty of his argumentation, which is borne out by biological and ethological evidence, contributes to shed more light on the richness of emotional communication. Takaaki Shochi, Albert Rilliard, Véronique Aubergé and Donna Erickson emphasize the interrelation of language with culture in the expression and perception of affects. More especially, their study focusses on the perception of the attitudes of twelve Japanese by groups of American English and French-speaking listeners unfamiliar with Japanese language and culture. The experiments show the cross-cultural manifestations and interpretations of affective speech that different cultures might have in common, along with the differences that can be a source of misunderstanding. Sophie de Abreu, Catherine Mathon and Alessandra Mosca offer a comparison of prosodic features of anger in three Romance languages, namely French, Italian and Portuguese. They also show that in the expression of this affective burst, the pragmatic context plays a key role in the strategic use of the acoustic parameters of fundamental frequency, intensity and speech rate, whether they are taken separately or together.

The next two contributions take into consideration the age criterion in their research, one being cross-generational, the other centering around senior citizens. Relying on the Code of Effort elaborated by Carlos Gussenhoven, Geneviève Caelen-Haumont's study explores in detail a specific emotional state, which reflects the personal involvement of the speaker, in a corpus of spontaneous conversations involving four female speakers from four different generations in the same family in the Bordeaux region. She analyzes the internal structure of the melodic prominences, coined *melisms*, along with the group duration, pauses and speech flow rates. The statistical findings clearly demonstrate that there is an underlying structure behind the apparent chaos of the F_0 values and that melodic subjectivity is not manifested by the speaker at random but under specific laws. Likewise, the analysis also takes into account a comparison between melisms and sequences of joy. The second contribution interested in the role of age is by Brigitte Zellner-Keller, who examines the relation of speech with aging, a still unexplored domain. The age factor affects various aspects of speech among senior citizens. The decrease of complexity in syntactic structures is correlated with a slowdown process in articulation and tempo, a decrease in fundamental frequency and intensity, an alteration of voice quality, along with an increasing difficulty in grasping emotional prosody.

The volume includes two neurobiological studies that underline the importance of sex differences in the expression of emotional prosody. The first one is by D. Erik Everhart, Amy J. Shiply and Heath A. Demaree. The article demonstrates that even though the right-hemisphere hypothesis of emotion processing is well supported in data, the results need to be refined since recent research indicates variation within this model as a function of sex. The differences observed are explained in relation to arguments elaborated in social cognitive neuroscience, a promising, emerging field. The second study pointing to the relevance of sex differences in the neurophysiological response to emotional expressions is by Annett Schirmer and Qingyang Li. It investigates the processing of attended and unattended vocal emotional expressions in men and women by measuring event-related brain potentials. The results show that unattended speech is more likely to attract attention when it is produced with emotional as compared to neutral prosody. Moreover, in women emotional vocalizations seem to capture attention more efficiently than neutral vocalizations, whereas in men attention capture seems largely unaffected by speaker emotion.

The second part of the volume pertains to the way emotion recognition is implemented in synthesis systems and how machine applications can contribute to a better description of emotion(s). Roddy Cowie and Ellen Douglas-Cowie focus on what they call ‘conversational emotion’, a still highly unstudied emotion encountered in everyday conversation, which is characterized as moderate. Relying on the ‘Sensitive Artificial Listener’ scenario to arouse a whole spectrum of emotions, they recorded a corpus of this type of emotion within two European projects, ERMIS and HUMAINE, and in this volume they present an analysis of the underlying speech patterns, a research that has not been carried out yet. In order to analyze the mass of information in a coherent and efficient way, they offer a stimulating model, which enlightens and challenges the complexity of the relationships between speech variables and perceived affect, especially the significant correlations between speech and emotion ratings for each rater and tuner length and the relationship between pitch range at the end of a tune and net affect, without neglecting the gender and rater effects, and the relationship to machine recognition and psychological theory. Petri Laukka, Nicolas Audibert and Véronique Aubergé's work can be situated in continuity with the Cowies' proposal of integrating the various theories of cognitive psychology in their interpretation of natural emotional speech, since Laukka *et al.* use work on categorization in their research. They examine what determines typicality, namely graded structure, in vocal expressions of emotion. The tests conducted show that the typicality of vocal expressions is in most cases influenced by their similarity to ideal category members, and not by the frequency of instantiation or similarity to central tendency. The findings suggest that instead of classifying prototypical vocal expressions as common taxonomic categories, it would be more appropriate to characterize them as goal-derived categories. The cognitive model under examination could well be of interest to make useful comparisons between prototypical and spontaneous expressions of emotional speech.

The next two studies focus on advanced algorithms and statistical models with a view to enhancing emotion recognition by machines. In order to predict the relevant variations of prosodic parameters in relation to expressivity, defined as an information level of communication, Grégory Beller uses a Bayesian model, which can infer the variations corresponding to a new utterance, whose context is known. This statistical context-dependent method presents the advantage of inferring new cases, which are absent from the learning experience and are necessary for the transformation of new utterances, while maximising the likelihood of observed data. By taking into consideration recent results on acoustical transformations, this model turns out to be a good intermediary between data and rules, as it can be a useful tool for artistic creation, and it contributes to render human-machine interfaces more credible. Björn Schuller, Martin

Wöllmer, Florian Eyben, and Gerhard Rigoll center their research on how to identify the most adequate emotion-signalling features. They investigate feature effects on multiple, partly public databases, using layer-wise optimized Support-Vector-Tree constructions, together with an attribute evaluator based on Correlation-based Feature Subset-selection (CFS). The results show that spectral features display the best information about emotion within speech, whether it be in the recognition performance or in the results of correlation-based feature subset-selection. The findings can be used to design machines more efficiently due to lower extraction effort and more compact feature space representation

Carlos Busso, Murtaza Bulut, Sungbok Lee and Shrikanth Narayanan criticize the standard approach in current emotion recognition and analysis systems, which analyzes high-level information in terms of various statistics of prosodic and spectral features. Although powerful, such methods do not directly take into account the interactions between different parameters and therefore are not sufficient to represent the complex variations in acoustic parameters that occur during expression of emotions. Their chapter presents results of a detailed analysis on F_0 contour, energy and duration characteristics. The purpose is to identify how these parameters are manipulated in expressive natural speech and to show how they can be used in the implementation of emotion recognition and synthesis systems. The results present a useful guide for the design of human-machine interaction interfaces that better incorporate expressive content.

The last two contributions are concerned with the way synthesis systems can contribute to the improvement of human-machine interfaces. Olivier Piot's chapter studies the prosodic expression of two attitudinal parameters, one being ignorance of the speaker/hearer, the other being the desire to know/inform. Relying on Klatt-synthesized stimuli in standard French, the experiments make sure that speech rate, accent loudness and F_0-range are cross-variated. In both questions and assertions, the value of the F_0 has a highly positive influence on the two attitudinal evaluations tested. A higher speech rate iconically reflects a more intense desire to know; in the same way, a lower speech rate iconically shows greater hearer's ignorance. A higher loudness on a stressed syllable emphasizes both cognitive parameters in assertions but has no impact on questions. The results are also discussed in relation to the main theories of affective speech. Ioulia Grichkovtsova, Michel Morel and Anne Lacheret conduct three perception tests in French and in English with the speech synthesizer Kali, relying on the gating and transplantation paradigms, which help identify the role played by voice quality and prosodic pattern in the studied affective states. Their main goal is to develop prototypical constructions for vocal emotions in both languages with this synthesizer. The findings are discussed in relation to the methodological problems encountered and to the practical applications to be developed.

In conclusion, by thoroughly discussing the interaction of empirical data, methodological discussions and theoretical issues, this volume shows how fine-grained analyses of prosody in everyday emotion-coloured conversations can contribute to a better understanding of affective speech.

Last but not least, the author of this volume would like to thank the ERIAC research group from the university of Rouen for funding this project.

References

Benveniste, Emile 1966. *Problèmes de linguistique générale,* vol. 1. Paris: Gallimard.

Culioli, Antoine 1995. *Cognition and Representation in Linguistic Theory*. Amsterdam: Benjamins.

Lyons, John 1982. Deixis and Subjectivity: Loquor, ergo sum . In Jarvella, Robert J. / Klein, Wolfgang (eds) *Speech, Place, and Action.* New York: John Wiley and Sons, 101-124.

Sociolinguistic Variables

JOHN J. OHALA

The Ethological Basis of Certain Signals of Affect and Emotion[1]

1. Introduction

When someone speaks, several messages are transmitted. Acoustically the signal conveys information about the linguistic elements in the message (phonemes, syllables, words, phrases, and so on) – these are the elements that could be included in written transcript of the utterance (even if the full complexity of this component would require IPA transcription). But the signal also conveys information about the speaker's dialect (which may be a reflection of their geographical origin), their first language background or the degree of competence they have in the language they are speaking, their sex or sexual orientation, their approximate age, their state of health, possibly their level of education or 'social refinement', and their personal identity. In addition, the speech signal may convey something about the speaker's attitude or emotional state (i.e., ironic, sincere, confident, subservient, etc.). In face-to-face communication some of the same 'messages' are conveyed via the visual channel, via facial expressions and other bodily movements and postures – the latter commonly known as 'kinesics'. Recognizing and parsing these various 'messages' is of considerable interest currently in the domain of human-machine interaction via spoken language. There is particular interest in identifying those aspects of the signal conveying attitude and emotion. In automatic speech recognition (ASR) identifying these elements could assist in indicating where in the utterance the speaker is putting emphasis, whether the speaker is cooperative or not or, perhaps, the

1 This is a revision of Ohala (1996).

possibility that the speaker may be lying. For automatic synthesis of speech, including especially that form of synthesis that includes an image of a talking face, knowledge of how these so-called non-linguistic or extra-linguistic messages are conveyed could help to create more naturalistic synthesis incorporating some natural human emotions.

In this chapter I hope to demonstrate that ethology – broadly, the study of the factors that contribute to species-specific and cross-species behavior – can provide us with data, methods, and theories that can help us to understand how humans signal affect and emotion. The goal is to arrive at a theory of such signals that is as general as possible, encompassing both vocal and gestural signals in humans and non-humans.

Today most ethological explanations are expressed in evolutionary terms. Although all species exhibit a whole spectrum of behaviors, ethology focuses its energies on behaviors that are stereotyped – exhibited in more or less the same form given the same or similar circumstances – and behaviors which are species-specific or, even better, common to a variety of species – and, behaviors which are readily determined as contributing to the survival or 'fitness' of the species. An example is the 'broken-wing' feint exhibited by several birds when a predator gets too close to the nest of young. This is found in such diverse species as the Little Ringed Plover, the Common Gallinule, Kildeer, the White-Crowned Sparrow, and the Great Horned Owl. It is presumably designed to lead the predator away from the nest when a more easily obtainable prey presents itself. Obviously to the extent that this trick works (the nestlings remain safe and the adult bird perpetrating the feint flies away, avoiding attack) this behavior increases the survivability or 'fitness' of the species.

Not coincidentally, Charles Darwin (1872) was among the first to speculate in a systematic way about the genetic (inheritable) basis of certain behaviors, especially the expression of emotion in man and animals, e.g., he even pondered the possible relationship between characteristic mouth shapes exhibited in expressions of emotion and the nature of the sound produced – citing Helmholtz (1868). There were many other earlier, less rigorous, speculations on the evolution of behavior, including some by Darwin's grandfather, Erasmus

Darwin (1803). But the accumulated literature on comparative behavior is a precious resource for any speculations on the origin of the expression of emotion and affect – including those presented here. The fact is, there are remarkable similarities – in both macro- and micro-patterns – in the expression of affect or emotion in humans and certain non-human species, especially those non-human species anatomically and physiologically capable of using some of the same signaling modalities as humans, i.e., the vocal-auditory channel and modification of a plastic facial covering, i.e., 'facial expressions'. Specifically, when it comes to facial expressions, only certain mammalian species have a 'plastic' facial covering that can be modified for signaling purposes. This leaves out birds and most reptiles. But it includes other mammalian classes such as primates and canids. When it comes to vocal signals, even avian and amphibian classes may show patterns of behavior similar to humans and other mammalian species. As a result we humans believe we can 'understand' the facial and vocal aspects of dogs' and monkeys' displays because at some basic level they resemble or are essentially the same as ours.

2. Identifying the function of the displays of emotion and affect

An important theoretical and practical issue in the study of displays of emotion and affect is whether they arise directly from or at least mirror the inner physiological and psycho-physiological state of the signaler or whether they might constitute contrived or even deceitful signals whose purpose is not so much to reflect the state of the signaler bur rather to influence the behavior of the receiver of the signal. In this latter case, given the default Darwinian dictum that the result of evolution is something that increases the survivability or fitness of the individual, we would be asking if the stereotyped signaling behavior benefits the signaler. To begin to address this issue we have to acknowledge that certain vocal and non-vocal gestures are closely linked to the signaler's inner physiological state even in situations where it might not be to the signaler's benefit to allow this information to 'leak out', e.g., the slight tremolo evident in the fundamental frequency (F_0) in the voice of nervous or frightened individuals as well as the conceivably related tremor or shaking of hands and arms. Similarly, excessive perspiration in humans that is easily detected by others is commonly displayed by frightened individuals. Possibly in the same category of easily detectable signs of the inner psycho-physiological state of the individual is the reduced F_0 range of people who are depressed – often accompanied by lethargy and slow movements of limbs, head turning, etc. Even so, we can still entertain the hypothesis that some of the common emotional signals might better be viewed as designed to produce a response from those receiving the signal that is favorable to the signaler. Ethological studies suggest that this is, indeed, the case.

3. Voice F_0

An important breakthrough in this area originated with Morton (1977) who documented an impressive cross-species homology in the shape of the acoustic component of agonistic displays (those produced in face-to-face competitive encounters) by both mammals and birds (28 species in both orders): the confident aggressor emits a vocalization with a low F_0 (within the range that they are capable of) and which may be rough and aperiodic. A submissive vocalization, in contrast, has a high F_0 and is tone-like (i.e., without any aperiodicity). The dog's aggressive growl and submissive yelp are familiar examples of these patterns. As it happens, Morton showed that the same pattern, labeled the 'frequency code' by Ohala (1984), recurs in species ranging from the rhinoceros to the shrew. (It is also found in some species of toads (Davis/Halliday 1978).) As Morton argued, this pattern can be explained as a kind of bluff (deceit) by the animal and the animals' exploitation of physical principles. The relative size of the animal is a good predictor of the outcome of a competition if, after all posturing and 'persuasions' have been exhausted, actual combat ensues. Therefore, to appear as large as possible in order to intimidate its adversary and thus forestall such a fight, the animal erects its hair or feathers, elevates its tail or tail feathers, and, in general, manipulates all the plastic features under its control to convey the signal 'I am large and a threat to you'. Since the F_0 of the 'voice' of an animal is inversely related to its bodily dimensions, a low F_0 also enhances the gestalt impression of the vocalizer being large, mature, and potentially more threatening. The roughness or aperiodicity contributes to this impression, too, since larger vocal cords or syringeal membranes are likely to have secondary modes of vibrations which, when they interact with the primary vibration, create some aperiodicity. Conversely, an animal that submits to an aggressor in order to avoid a fight does the opposite to convey an impression that it is small and non-threatening. Some aspects of submissive displays quite clearly employ mimicry of infants and thus probably exploit the powerful genetically-dictated inhibitions against harming infants. Submissive dogs (or, indeed, most canids) that roll onto their back exposing their stomach are said to be imitating a routine common to puppies inviting maternal licking. Ohala (1984, 1994) presented evidence that the frequency code operates in human vocalizations, too: low F_0 to convey threat or self-confidence, high F_0 to convey non-threat or deference. He used natural utterances that were re-synthesized in a way to eliminate all spectral parameters of speech but retaining F_0 which had either the original F_0 or with an upshifted F_0. Listeners judged samples with the lower F_0 as 'more dominant, more self-confident'. In addition, in the case of two utterances similarly stripped of spectral details but with one having a falling F_0 at the end and the other a rising F_0, listeners judged the one with falling F_0 as 'more dominant'. He also invoked the frequency code to account for the near-universal pattern where statements are coded by a low or falling F_0 but questions (that are not otherwise coded by grammatical or syntactic means) have a high or rising F_0 (Bolinger 1978).

Some important principles are manifested in such ethological accounts of the correlation between signal shape and signal function.

- First there should be a predictable and recognized relation between some parameter, *P*, of the signals and a feature, *F*, of the signaler that has some functional import, i.e., *P P F*, e.g., the rate of vibration of the laryngeal (or syringeal) folds and overall size of the signaler (where size is a predictor of success in competition).
- Second, that within a specified range, the signaler can vary *P*.
- Third, that depending on what seems to yield the most favorable outcome from a competitive encounter, the signaler can vary *P* in order to convey the impression of *F'*, different from its intrinsic *F*.

Two important qualifications must be made: in addition to parameters that can be varied, one can also identify anatomically implastic features that serve a similar function in signaling: e.g., piloerection in canids is plastic but the large mane of hair around the head of male lions and some monkeys are implastic. Also, though verbs of volition may sometimes be used to describe the signaler's intent, e.g., "The aggressive bird makes itself look bigger by ruffling its feathers, extending its wings and elevating its tail feathers (in order that it will subtend a larger angle in the view of the receiver)", this is ethological 'shorthand' for "The bird reacts [in such a way] because that behavior provides it (and it has provided its ancestors) a selectional advantage; it is genetically predisposed to act thus". No conscious strategy of willful deceit is attributed to the signaler – even to human signalers.) The above principles probably apply to other vocal and kinesic displays as outlined in the following sections.

4. The smile and the 'o-face'

Ohala (1980, 1984, 1994) speculated that the smile, a non-threatening display, and what he calls the 'o-face' (because it seems not to have any other convenient label comparable to 'smile'), i.e., with lips constricted and somewhat protruded, which is exhibited in threats, may have originated as part of the acoustic component of submissive/aggressive displays: retracting the corners of the mouth (= 'smile') effectively shortens the vocal tract and thus raises the resonant frequencies; constricting and protruding the lips (= 'o-face') lengthens the vocal tract and thus lowers the resonant frequencies. These modifications of the resonant frequencies would contribute to the impression of the overall size of the signaler since normal resonant frequencies vary inversely with other linear bodily dimensions. Through ritualization the smile may have become to a large extent a visual (kinesic) signal but its origin is revealed in apes and monkeys where the same mouth shape invariably accompanies high-pitched submissive vocalizations (Bauer 1987). This scenario resolves the long-standing paradox of why the smile, an affinitive display, shows so many teeth, normally regarded as potential weapons and thus seemingly more appropriate for an aggressive display. It is often thought that in humans the smile, at least, is a reflection (somehow) of inner contentment and well-being. But Kraut and Johnson (1979: 1539) have demonstrated convincingly "a robust association of smiling with a social motivation and an erratic association with emotional experience".

5. Sexual dimorphism of the vocal anatomy

It was mentioned above that signals can be plastic and implastic. Clearly the use of F_0 variations and mouth shape to express aggression or submission fall into the category of plastic signals. But, just like the lion's mane, there are implastic anatomical features in humans which may also convey similar signals. It is well known that there is marked sexual dimorphism in the human[2] vocal anatomy: adult males' vocal tracts are some 15% to 20% longer than those of adult females. But there is an even greater disparity in the larynx: males' vocal cords are

2 But also in certain non-human species, as well, e.g., the howler monkey.

some 50% longer than those of females. The 50% greater length probably implies a 100% greater mass that is free to vibrate. Accordingly, the resonances of the male vocal tract are lower than those of females and the male F_0 is on average a full octave below that of the female. These dimorphic traits begin to appear at puberty at the same time as the growth of facial hair in the male, another implastic signal akin to the male lion's mane (and for that matter countless other cases of sexual dimorphism documented in many species). The implastic signals have the same function as the 'aggression'-related plastic signals.

It might be asked why it is the male's lot to have the implastic signals of aggression. The answer is that it is the male who has to compete for acceptance by the female (Puts/Gaulin/Verdolini 2006) and this is where manes, facial hair and low voices are advantages. Males have more of the hormone testosterone and this inclines them to be, in general, more aggressive. There may be an underlying biological rationale for this: males have the less valued gamete; the ovum of the female is many times larger (than sperm), takes more metabolic energy to produce, there are fewer orders of magnitude in the reproductive life-span, and they are metered out at regular intervals. Being aggressive has its risks; males take this risk because, sociobiologically the loss is less than in the case of females.

Another elaboration of the above account of why high acoustic frequency of vocalizations (of F_0 and resonances) is associated with non-threat (and a lead-in to the next topic): it is possible that the higher frequencies actively serve to inhibit any threat or aggression from the receivers of the signal because they approximate the kind of signals characteristic of the young. As mentioned earlier, for obvious reasons, every species must have an innate inhibition against aggression toward its young. Consider the case of human babies: given how much trouble and effort they require to be raised, if an innate inhibition against harming them did not exist, then neither would we (exist, that is). It is obvious that we find babies endearing, attractive, and worthy of our attention and sympathy.

I move on to an admittedly speculative account of facial expressions related to aggression and submission and involving eyes.

6. Eyes and eyebrows

It is well documented and it is part of common lore that raised eyebrows signal non-threat or a friendly greeting whereas lowered eyebrows convey threat (Eibl-Eibesfeldt 1975, Ekman 1969). Again, this is true not only with humans but with non-human primates and canids as well (van Hoof 1962). A functional account of this pattern is often given in terms of the needs of vision: raised eyebrows when a wide field of vision is required and lowered brows for narrow, focused, viewing (Andrew 1972). But this would predict that in a situation where the signaler is conveying non-threat, i.e., submission or capitulation, when confronted with a specific recognized threat, lowered brows would be expected in order to closely monitor the source of threat. But the opposite is found. An alternative, ethologically-based, account is possible (Ohala 1994) which is more in line with the explanations given above for voice F_0, voice resonance (and hence for mouth shape), viz., that eyebrows, like voice F_0 and resonances, can help to convey an impression of the size or maturity of the signaler. As is well known, the dimensions of eyes do not change as much as overall bodily dimensions during maturation. Babies are well known to have 'big eyes'. There are even metaphorical expressions testifying to this, such as the English phrase 'wide-eyed innocence'. In fact eyes do enlarge with progressive maturation but not as much as the head encasing the eyes. Babies at birth have an eye diameter that is about 75% to 85% the diameter that the eye will eventually achieve at maturity. Obviously other bodily dimensions, the head, spine, limbs, etc. grow much more in maturity. Thus the ratio of eye diameter to head diameter gradually gets smaller reaching an asymptote some time after sexual maturation. As a consequence, a visual estimation of this ratio (eye diameter/head diameter) is a rough indicator of age and size of signaler and thus the degree of potential threat posed. Subtle plastic variations in the portion of the eye externally visible accompany displays conveying threat and non-threat: threat involves a narrowing of this opening – what is commonly called in English, a 'squint' (German, *schielen*) whereas non-threat involves a widening of the eye opening. Now eyebrows are not actually the outer visible limits of the eye but I would speculate that they convey a visual impression of their boundaries.[3] This account also may help to explain the popularity (primarily in females) of cosmetics such as mascara, eyeliner, and eye shadow which, as cosmetologists will immediately confirm, make the wearer's eyes 'look bigger' (http://www.howcast.com/videos/441-How-To-Make-Your-Eyes-Look-Bigger). There may be some optical illusion at work here where providing more contrast between the necessarily white of the eye sclera and the surrounding flesh, gives an impression of larger eyes. This needs further investigation. Another possibility is that the contrasting colors draw attention to the eyes and this focusing of attention on them triggers a cognitive impression of larger eyes.

Another cosmetic modification made in the pursuit of beauty is enhancements to the eyelashes: either making them seem longer or more prominent with mascara or with eyelash curlers or even the use of artificial eyelashes (invariably longer than the wearer's own eyelashes). There is no obvious way that these practices would make the eyes themselves seem larger but, as it happens, this could still be a manifestation of the strategy to achieve appearances that mimic those of babies. In a quite remarkable (to me, at least) study, Pucci *et al.* (2005) measured eyelash length in a large group of subjects of varying age from infants to adults. The study was primarily devoted to the effects of the pathological condition known as vernal keratoconjunctivitis but it

---

3 It is an interesting question by itself as to why humans have eyebrows at all. Some have suggested that they help to keep rainwater or sweat out of the eyes, others that they augment the function of the bony projection in the skull above the eyes in shading the eye from strong sunlight. As a hiker who likes hills and other sweat-producing exercises, I can personally testify that eyebrows do not function well to keep rain or sweat out of eyes. As for shading eyes, it seems eyebrows are a meager addition to what the skull shape already provides. It seems to me that all of these explanations ignore the fact that eyebrows can be elevated or depressed by voluntary contraction of an array of facial muscles (the frontalis, the corrugator supercilii, and the obicularis oculi). Such plasticity seems more congruent with the idea that eyebrows exist to serve a signaling function.

included a control group without that condition. They reported that "[i]n healthy subjects, a negative correlation was found between eyelash length and age" (2005: 86). It needs to be emphasized that the negative correlation was *not* to the *relative* length of the eyelashes, i.e., proportional to other anatomical dimensions, rather it was to the *absolute* length of the eyelashes. Babies, it seems, have longer eyelashes (on average) than do adolescents and adults. That babies do have long eyelashes is confirmed by an informal sample of mothers that I consulted. I refrain from speculating as to why eyelash length varies in this way but it seems credible that the enhancement of eyelashes in adults is another way to mimic this trait in infants and thus to evoke in viewers some of the same innate positive reactions.

Why do babies (of many species) have a relatively large ratio of eye diameter to head diameter? The probable answer is emmetropization (van Alphen 1990). Emmetropization is the feedback relationship between the retina and the processes which govern the growth of eyes. It has been shown that in order to preserve a well-focused image on the retina, the growth of the eye is inhibited.[4]

There is evidence, as a consequence, that, other things being equal, babyish faces (even those of adults – think of the silent movie stars 'Fatty' Arbuckle or W. C. Fields – are more closely interpreted by viewers as exhibiting fear than are angular mature faces (think of another silent movie star, William S. Hart)[5], which, in turn are interpreted by viewers as exhibiting anger (which is closely associated with threat) (Marsh/Adams/Kleck 2005).

4 Experiments with animals show that if one eye is covered or the eyelids sutured together, there is abnormal growth of the occluded eye. Nature sometimes implements the same experimental controls, even in humans, when one eye is affected by cataracts or other abnormal conditions which prevent normal focusing of images. In these cases, too, abnormal, excessive growth of the eye results.

5 If these names or their images are not familiar to the reader, see <http://www.goldensilents.com/>.

7. Conclusion

In the preceding discussion I have focused on cases where a given vocal and some non-vocal signals of what is called 'emotion' or 'affect' are designed to evoke from the viewer a response favorable to the signaler. These include signals involving plastic modulations of voice F_0 and vocal tract resonances (the latter primarily due to the shape of the mouth), as well as plastic modulations of the eyes and nearby structures. I have also brought into the same explanatory scheme implastic signals such as the growth of hair around the perimeter of the face as well as quasi-plastic cosmetic modifications of the eyes. This is not to deny that some aspects of emotional or affectual signals may in some way reflect the inner psychological or physiological state of the signaler, e.g., tremor or rapid eye-blinking of nervous or fearful individuals. And many other signals may be completely voluntary and possibly culturally-derived signals emerging from the conscious state of the signaler, e.g., tipping the hat, waving with hands, nodding the head, etc. There is, as we all know, a very rich 'vocabulary' of signals of emotion and affect and only a fraction of them have been adequately explained by theory or explored empirically. The message I would like to end with is: we can gain much in being able to differentiate these various types and origins of such signals from comparison of signals humans give with those given by animals in this same domain.

References

Van Alphen, Gerald W.H.M. 1990. Emmetropization in the primate eye. Ciba Foundation Symposium 155: Myopia and the control of eye growth. 115-125.

Andrew, Richard J. 1972. Information potentially available in mammal displays, in R. A. Hinde (ed.), *Non-verbal communication*. Cambridge University Press, Cambridge, 179-206, 1972.

Bauer, Harold R. 1987. The frequency code: oral-facial correlates of fundamental frequency. *Phonetica* 44.173-191.

Bolinger, Dwigh 1978. Intonation across languages. In Greenberg, Joseph H. (ed.). *Universals of human language*. Stanford University Press. 471-524.

Darwin, Charles 1872. *The expression of the emotions in man and animals*. John Murray, London. <http://www.darwinliterature.com/The_Expression_Of_The_Emotions_In_Man_And_Animals/index.html>.

Darwin, Erasmus 1803. *The temple of nature; or the origin of society: a poem with philosophical notes*. J. Johnson: London, <http://www.english.upenn.edu/Projects/knarf/Darwin/templetp.html>.

Davies, Nick B. / Halliday, Tim R. 1978. Deep croaks and fighting assessment in toads Bufo bufo. *Nature* 274.683-685.

Eibl-Eibesfeldt, Irenäus 1975. *Ethology. The biology of behavior*. 2nd ed. Holt, Rinehart, and Winston, New York.

Ekman, Paul 1969. Pan-cultural elements in facial displays of emotion. *Science* 164.86-88.

Helmholtz (von), Hermann 1868. *Théorie physiologique de la musique*. Victor Masson et Fils, Paris.

van Hooff, Jan A. R. A. M. 1962. *Facial expressions in higher primates,. Symposium of the Zoological Soc. of London, No. 8: Evolutionary aspects of animal communication.* 97- 125.

Kraut, Robert E. / Johnston, R. E. 1979. Social and emotional messages of smiling: An ethological approach. *J. Personality & Social Psych*. 37.1539-1553.

Marsh, Abigail A. / Adams, Jr. / Reginald B. / Kleck, Robert E. 2005. Why do fear and anger look the way they do? Form and social function in facial expressions. *Personality Social Psychology Bulletin*. 31.73-86.

Morton, Eugene W. 1977. On the occurrence and significance of motivation-structural rules in some bird and mammal sounds. *American Naturalist* 111.855-869.

Ohala, John J. 1980. The acoustic origin of the smile [Abstract]. *Journal of the Acoustical. Society of America* 68.S33.

Ohala, John J. 1984. An ethological perspective on common cross-language utilization of F_0 of voice. *Phonetica* 41.1–16.

Ohala, John J. 1994 The frequency codes underlies the sound symbolic use of voice pitch,. In Hinton, Leanne / Nichols , Johanna / John J. Ohala (eds), *Sound symbolism*. Cambridge: Cambridge University Press. 325-347.

Ohala, John J. 1996. Ethological theory and the expression of emotion in the voice. In *Proceedings ICSLP-1996*, 1812-1815.

Pucci, Neri / Novembre, Elio / Lombardi, Enrico / Massai, Cristina / Bernardini, Roberto / Caputo, Roberto / Campa, Luciana / de Libero, Cinzia / Vierucci, Alberto 2005. Long eyelashes in a case series of 93 children with vernal keratoconjunctivities. *Pediatrics* 115.e86-e91.

Puts, David A. / Gaulin, Steven J. C. / Verdolini, Katherine 2006. Dominance and the evolution of sexual dimorphism in human voice pitch. Evolution and Human Behavior. 27:283-296.

TAKAAKI SHOCHI / ALBERT RILLIARD / VÉRONIQUE AUBERGÉ / DONNA ERICKSON

Intercultural Perception of English, French and Japanese Social Affective Prosody

1. Introduction

In the speech communication between humans or between humans and machines, the expression of mental states, emotional states, moods, feelings, intentions, or the attitudes of the speaker are a source of information that both the speaker and listener use, often as a main channel of information, depending on the situation. Psychological and affective computing studies (i.e. affective sciences) offer more and more evidence of the fundamental role of affects in human communication encoding, decoding and understanding. Affects in speech are expressed following different cognitive processing levels, from involuntarily controlled expressions – the so called basic emotions - to the intentional control of social affects that express the speaker's intentions, attitudes and linguistic message (choice of lexicon and grammatical paraphrases). Basic emotions are expressed when the arousal vs. the inhibition ratio is such that arousal is greater than inhibition. They are rarely expressed in everyday life situations (Campbell 2000), even though they constitute decisive information when happening.

Similarities in the perception of affect perception (and notably the facial expression of emotion) have drawn the attention of scientists (e.g. Darwin 1872; Ekman 1972; Kramer 1964; Izard 1971). However, cultural specificity was not their main point of interest, as they mainly tried to determine the universal emotional expressions, not the divergences between languages and cultures (Matsumoto/Assar 1992). Due to research about universal affective expressions, we are now aware of the discrepancies of perceptive behaviour existing across cultural contexts. For example, Izard (1971) shows that both Americans and Europeans have higher identification scores than Japanese or Africans subjects in recognizing facial affects. Such work clearly indicates the importance of the cultural parameter in the expression of affects. More recently, Fónagy (1991: 138), in a descriptive passage on the confusions between 'joy' and 'anger', pointed out that six out of 30 Japanese subjects interpreted the Hungarian 'quarrel' as 'jubilation'. Thus, besides the problem of possible erroneous interpretations of emotional expressions in cross-cultural contexts, the question is raised of the erroneous interpretations of affective values in a foreign language due to specific features that belong to that native language.

Social affective expressions (like authority, doubt, surprise, politeness etc.) are a main part of the language interaction built by face-to-face human contact, always present during any interaction. Even if the speaker chooses to produce a speech act without any attitude, he/she is expressing the attitude that he/she has no attitude (Aubergé *et al.* 2004). This kind of affect deeply relies on the social situation and is sophistically anchored in the culture. From these social affects, it can be expected that, among the universal attitudes shared by each culture, some specific attitudes have been developed to express specific situations made explicit by the culture. These specific social affects are part of the cultural identity, and as such must be learned by both children as part of their native language (Roseberry-Mckibbin/Brice 1999) and foreign learners as part of the new language (Abelin/Allwood 2000, 2002).

Following a methodology well-tried in several studies for attitudes in French (Aubergé *et al.* 1997) and in English (Diaferia 2002), we examine here the cross-cultural perception of attitudes in three languages in order to compare oriental vs. occidental cues: Japanese, French and British English. A large set of social affective expressions was compared among these three languages, including variable social values such as politeness or dominance. This work aims at investigating the perceptual recognition performances of French, English and Japanese listeners of the three languages in order to identify similarities and differences of the languages' social affective expressions.

2. Cross-listening of multicultural social affects

i) Selection of social affective expressions

Based on literature reviews and language teaching methods for each of the three languages (British English, French and Japanese), three sets of social affective expressions were selected and recorded by trained professional speakers in a soundproof room.

For British English expressions, a set of eleven British English attitudes, perceptually validated in Diaferia (2002), were used as the British English corpus. A British English teacher recorded these attitudes: doubt-incredulity (DO), evidence (EV), surprise (SU), command-authority (CO), irritation (IR), scorn-aloofness (SC), sarcastic irony (SI), seduction (SE), politeness (PO), declaration (DC) and interrogation (IN) The definitions given by Diaferia (2002) are the following. The exemplar sentences are furnished by the authors to better illustrate the attitudes:

- Declaration: neutral declarative sentence (ex: 'He's a vegetarian.')
- Interrogation: neutral interrogative sentence (ex: 'He's a vegetarian?')
- Doubt-incredulity: The speaker expresses a feeling of being uncertain about something or of not believing something; he expresses a suspicion about what has previously been expressed (ex: 'I'm not really sure he's a vegetarian')
- Evidence: The speaker says something he feels is self-evident. (ex: 'He's a vegetarian, for sure')
- Surprise: The speaker expresses his surprise at the moment he speaks. (ex: 'Oh! He's a vegetarian!')
- Command-authority: The speaker expresses himself in order to influence other people or to impose his view or wish. He acts with authority and gives orders that must be obeyed. (ex: 'You must absolutely be a vegetarian!!!')
- Irritation: The speaker expresses his irritation towards what has been said; he protests because of this irritation. (ex: 'He's a vegetarian, and it really irritates me!!')

- Sarcastic irony: The speaker calls into question (and even contradicts) a statement his interlocutor has said. He wants to show he doesn't agree and even that he's annoyed with what he's hearing, he condemns what is said or what happened, by using an intonation contour which could mean: 'Yeah, sure! I believe you ... (meaning, I don't)'. (ex: 'Yeah, sure! He's a vegetarian...')
- Scorn-aloofness: The speaker says something in an arrogant, aloof way, showing he gives no credit to what has been said. (ex: 'Poor stupid guy! He is a vegetarian. How pathetic!')
- Seduction: The speaker says something to seduce his interlocutor. (seduction relationship – ex: 'I am a vegetarian, (I know you find vegetarians very 'sexy', and I would like you to know that I am interested in having a closer relationship with you))
- Politeness: The speaker says something in a polite way. (ex: 'I hope you don't mind. I am a vegetarian')

Some social affective expressions among these twelve are specific to the British culture, in particular the seduction expressed by a male speaker that might be difficult to elicit in the Japanese society. In addition, sarcastic irony and scorn-aloofness may also carry strong cultural specificities.

For French language expressions, we start from the six French attitudes studied by Morlec (1997) and Aubergé *et al.* (1997): suspicious irony, doubt-incredulity, evidence, exclamation of surprise, declaration and interrogation, correctly recognized by native speakers, in order to construct a more complete set of twelve social affects for French: declaration, simple question, surprise exclamation, evidence, doubt-incredulity, authority, irritation, sarcastic irony, scorn, politeness, seduction, admiration. These twelve social affects are defined as follows. They are similar to the British attitudes described above, and the exemplar sentences for the British attitudes can also be applied for the French ones. In addition, note for French, there is also admiration.

- Declaration: the speaker gives information, without any personal perspective
- Simple question: the speaker requests information, without any personal perspective, awaiting a simple answer.
- Surprise exclamation: the speaker expresses his surprise.
- Evidence: the speaker talks about something he considers completely certain.
- Doubt-incredulity: the speaker expresses his uncertainty or his lack of conviction about some information given by his interlocutor; he expresses his suspicion while repeating the same information in his speech.
- Authority: the speaker means to influence or impose his opinion or his desire on his interlocutor.
- Irritation: the speaker is strongly displeased by something that has just been said, and expresses this discontentment.
- Sarcastic irony: the speaker calls into question or even opposes his interlocutor's assertion. He shows disagreement or vexation from what has been expressed by the use of a specific intonation pattern to indicate that the interlocutor is 'going against his words'.
- Scorn: the speaker talks in an uppity and scornful way, showing his opinion on what has been said.
- Politeness: whatever the social status of the speaker in respect to his interlocutor, he expresses politeness and courtesy
- Seduction: the speaker tries to draw his interlocutor's attention, usually in a sexually provocative way.
- Admiration: the speaker expresses his delight, amazement and approval. (ex: 'Wow That's wonderful! You're a vegetarian...')

For Japanese language expressions, a set of twelve attitudes were selected on the basis of the previous work in this field (Maekawa 1998; Ofuka *et al.* 2000; Sadanobu 2004; Ito 2003) and Japanese teaching system (Mizutani/Mizutani 1979). The perceptive pertinence of these twelve social affective expressions was validated in Shochi *et al.* (2006) by native Japanese listeners. These social affective expressions are: doubt-incredulity (DO), evidence (EV), exclamation of surprise (SU), authority (AU), irritation (IR), arrogance (AR), sincerity-politeness (SIN), admiration (AD), kyoshuku (KYO), simple-politeness (PO), declaration (DC) and interrogation (IN) (see Shochi *et al.* 2006 for definitions). Some of these attitudes are specific or specifically important for the Japanese culture, especially those linked to the politeness strategy: simple-politeness, sincerity-politeness and kyoshuku vs. arrogance. The sincerity-politeness attitude appears when a socially inferior speaker is talking to someone superior to him in the Japanese society: the speaker expresses a serious and sincere intention by using this prosodic attitude. The kyoshuku attitude (there is no lexical entry to translate this in English) is a typically Japanese cultural attitude. Even if such situations occur in all cultures, the Japanese language has chosen to encode this situation as a prosodic attitude ('attitudineme'). A speaker uses kyoshuku when he wants to express a conflicting opinion to an interlocutor considered socially superior, aiming not to disturb him but to help him, or when the speaker desires to get a favour from his superior. It is described by Sadanobu as "a mixture of suffering ashamedness and embarrassment, (which) comes from the speaker's consciousness of the fact that his/her utterance of request imposes a burden to the hearer" (2004: 34).

The definition of attitudes we used for French and American subjects is essentially the same, but it was presented in the listeners' native language. Because French and American culture have no lexical entry for the attitude of kyoshuku, this attitude was named as 'kyoshuku' in the list of presented attitudes, with an additional explanation for French, British and American subjects to understand the concept and the context in which this attitude is used.

ii) Corpus recordings

Corpus recordings took place in a sound proof room at GIPSA-Lab. For each language, a trained speaker recorded all sentences in each of the selected social affective expressions. For each language corpus, several sentences were constructed so that they carried no specific attitudinal meaning, and were systematically varied in their syntactic structure. Details about the sentences are given in Tables 1-3 for each language.

No. of syllables	Utterance	Nb of syllables	Utterance
2	Ma*ry	5	Interroga*tion
2	Beware*	5	Man* commu*nicates
2	Men* work*	5	A man* ma*nages
2	Man* counts*	5	A new* man* ar*gued
5	Li*beralizes	5	A new* hu*man counts*
5	Unpre*cedented	5	Tele*phony works*

Table 1. English corpus: 12 sentences of 2 or 5 syllables, with the lexical stress position marked by a star.

No. of syllable	Utterance	Translation
1	L'eau	The water.
2	L'eau bout	The water boils
5	L'auto dérapait	The car was skidding.
7	Les gars coupaient des rondins	The boys were cutting logs.

Table 2. French corpus: 4 sentences of varying length.

No. of mora	Utterance	Translation
1	Me	The eye
2	Na*ra	Nara
5	Na*rade neru	He sleeps in Nara
8	Na*goyade nomimas [u]	He drinks at Nagoya
8	Nara*shide nomimas [u]	He drinks in Nara town
8	Matsuri*de nomimas [u]	He drinks at the festival
8	Naniwade nomimas [u]	He drinks at Naniwa

Table 3. Japanese corpus: 7 sentences of varying length, with different lexical stress positions marked by a star.

For British English, twelve sentences of two or five syllables, with either a single isolated word or a verb-object structure as the syntactic structure, were used. The position of the lexical stress is also systematically distributed in different positions in order to neutralize a possible stress effect. A male speaker, professional English teacher, recorded each sentence with all attitudes. A total of 148 stimuli (twelve sentences x twelve different attitudes) were digitally recorded at 44.1 kHz sampling rate stereo with a Sony DATTCD-D7 recorder and a AKG.C.1000S microphone.

The French corpus is based on seven sentences of one, two, five or seven syllables, with either a single isolated word or a verb-object syntactic structure. All sentences were used in previous research (Morlec 1997; Aubergé et al. 1997). Each sentence was recorded with all attitudes by a female French native language phonetician. A total of 48 stimuli were digitally recorded at 44.1 kHz sampling rate stereo with a Sony DATTCD-D7 recorder and a SHURE WBH53 headset microphone.

The Japanese corpus consists of seven sentences of 1, 2, 5 or 8 moras (a mora being a rhythm unit in Japanese consisting of a (C)V, syllabic nasal, or geminate consonant), with either a single word or a verb-object structure as the syntactic structure. For the eight mora utterances, the lexical stress position may be on the first, second, and third mora, or absent. In order to express some attitudes like doubt or surprise, the vowel [u] may be inserted at phrase final position, and the lexical stress will be realized at the seventh mora, also. Each sentence was recorded with all attitudes by a male native Japanese language teacher. A total of 84 stimuli were digitally recorded at 44.1 kHz sampling rate stereo with a Sony DATTCD-D7 recorder and a SHURE WBH53 headset microphone.

iii) Experimental methodology

In order to cross-linguistically evaluate the recorded attitudes, a computer-displayed interface was developed and used amongst several groups of listeners (one group of listeners being composed from a set of male and female listeners with the same native language – listening to the social affective expression of only one language) with either a native ability in the language listened to, or no ability in this language. The test interface proposes the definitions of each label in the listener's native language, and was introduced by a detailed explanation of the meaning of each social affective expression, including examples of relevant situations. No listener expressed problems in understanding the concepts referred to by the labels.

Each subject listened to each stimulus only once. For each stimulus, they were asked to indicate the perceived attitude amongst the eleven (for English) or twelve (for French and Japanese) possible ones. The presentation order of stimuli was randomized for each subject. No listeners participating in this experiment reported any listening disorder.

There were four groups of language listeners, a total of 94 subjects, who participated in the evaluation of the British English corpus. The first group was composed of 10 native British English listeners (4 females and 6 males, mean age = 31), the second group of 20 mid-western Americans (11 females and 9 males, mean age = 25.1), the third group of 30 French (16 females and 14 males, mean age = 22.5) and the fourth group of 34 Japanese (20 females and 14 males, from the central region of Japan, mean age = 22.5). The English skill of the French and Japanese listeners was not at the level of that of a native speaker, but they had a basic knowledge of the English language. American subjects had never been in Britain.

There were three groups of language listeners, a total of 89 subjects, who participated in the evaluation of the French corpus. The first group was composed of 30 native French listeners (16 females and 14 males, mean age = 22.5), the second group of 21 mid-western Americans (12 females and 9 males, 28.8) and the third group of 38 Japanese (23 females and 15 males, from the central region of Japan, mean age = 20.3). No American and Japanese participant was competent in either the French language or culture.

There were three groups of language listeners, a total of 50 subjects, who participated in the evaluation of the Japanese corpus. The first group was composed of 15 Japanese (11 females and 4 males, Tokyo dialect, mean age = 29.5), the second group of 15 French (10 females and 5 males, level 0 in Japanese, mean age = 25.4), and the third one of 20 mid-western American listeners from South Dakota (12 females and 8 males, level 0 in Japanese, mean age = 24.9). No American or French participants had specific knowledge of the Japanese culture and language.

iv) Results analysis

Results of these perception experiments will be described based on a set of statistical analyses. Results are presented inside distribution matrices, each with 11 or 12 presented attitudes in the rows, and the percentage of recognition scores in the columns. Confusion matrices were analysed for each language, and for each group of subjects, first with a chi-square analysis, and then with a clustering analysis. The chi-square analysis allows testing for possible effects of the stimuli's length and to test whether the listener's answers had a chance distribution. The clustering analysis, by computing the distances between the rows (i.e. the attitudinal expressions) of the matrices, allows graphic representation of the similarities and dissimilarities of perception by listeners across the various social affective expressions. A detailed examination of the confusion matrices affords an understanding of the recognition and the confusions of attitudinal expressions.

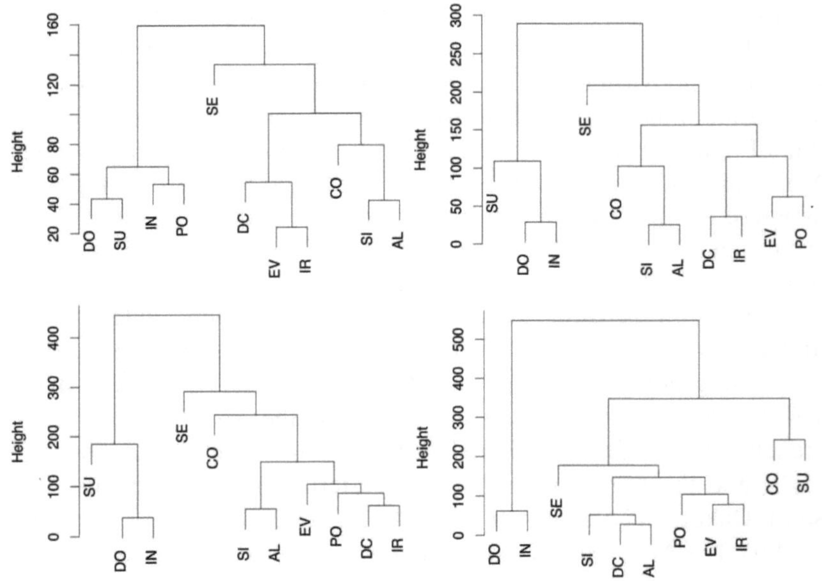

Figure 1. Clustering analysis for British English attitudes. The first figure indicates British English listeners' perceptual behaviour, the second figure indicates American listeners' perceptual behaviour, third figure indicates French listeners' perceptual behaviour and fourth figure indicates Japanese listeners' perceptual behaviour.

Recognition of British English attitudes:

Chi-square analysis: Several chi-square tests were computed from the obtained results. The results show that the distribution of all attitudes is significantly above chance level, and that the length effect for the distribution of chosen attitudes (chi-squared difference between the mean distribution of answers obtained for each attitude, by each length of stimuli) is observed only for French and Japanese subjects. Both French and Japanese subjects show a significant influence of the length only between 2 and 5 syllable utterances (df=10, χ^2=73.42, p<.01 for French listeners, df=10, χ^2=80.67, p<.01 for Japanese listeners) for their perceptual behaviour.
Clustering analysis: According to the results of British English attitudes by clustering analysis, attitudinal expressions can be classified into three perceptual categories.

- Doubt, surprise and interrogation
- Sarcastic irony and scorn-aloofness
- Evidence, politeness, declaration and irritation

The first category expresses the query of a speaker to the partner, the second, the imposition of the speaker's opinion on the partner, and the third contains the other attitudinal expressions. The expression of irritation is located inside the third category, probably because listeners recognized this expression only weakly.

In addition to the above categories, seduction is particularly well discriminated by each of the four groups of language listeners, as are also command-authority and exclamation of surprise, even though there was some variation of identification rate among the listeners.
Similarities and differences in recognition of British English attitudes:

- British English listeners recognized all attitudes above chance level, that is, all attitudes are correctly validated by native speakers (Diaferia 2002). Comparing the accuracy rate among the four groups of listeners, the results showed that the native listeners are more accurate than non-native listeners. This result confirms the hypothesis of 'native language effect' which was reported in previous work (Erickson et al. 2003; Scherer et al. 2001; Shigeno, 1998).

- Four attitudes (exclamation of surprise, command-authority, declaration and interrogation) are recognized well by the four different groups. That means that both the concept of these attitudes and the way of expressing these attitudes was shared by the four groups.
- Generally, all participants (including British English listeners) did not recognize well three attitudes: irritation, sarcastic irony and politeness.
- Three attitudes (seduction, doubt-incredulity and evidence) showed perceptual behavioural differences among the four groups of listeners.

British seduction: No group showed any particular confusion for this attitude, but Japanese subjects did not identify this attitude well (27%), unlike the Western subjects who recognized it much better (72.2% for English subjects, 56.7% for American subjects and 58.1% for French subjects).

Perceived	*Presented attitudes (recognition scores in percentages)*										
attitudes	*CO*	*DC*	*DO*	*EV*	*IN*	*IR*	*PO*	*SI*	*AL*	*SE*	*SU*
Com. Authority	**53**	3	0	3	0	8	2	12	1	3	2
Declaration	15	**57**	0	***30***	3	***31***	16	15	7	5	0
Doubt	0	0	**43**	2	***20***	2	16	2	1	2	***27***
Evidence	12	13	2	**42**	1	***33***	9	15	7	2	5
Interrogation	0	0	***20***	1	**48**	0	13	1	0	1	7
Irritation	14	5	0	7	2	**17**	8	***19***	10	1	1
Politeness	0	16	2	13	6	2	**24**	3	3	3	3
Sarcastic Irony	2	3	12	0	4	8	7	**16**	***25***	8	5
Scorn Aloof.	4	1	3	1	1	2	3	15	**43**	3	3
Seduction	0	3	0	0	2	0	0	3	3	**73**	0
Surprise	0	0	19	2	14	0	3	0	1	0	**48**

Table 4. Confusion matrix for 10 English listeners. Recognition values above chance are in bold, important confusions are in bold italic. Meaning of abbreviations: DC(declaration), IN(interrogation), SU(surprise), DO(doubt-incredulity), EV(evidence), CO(command-authority), IR(irritation), PO(politeness), AL(scorn-aloofness), SE(seduction) and SI(sarcastic irony).

Perceived attitudes	*Presented attitudes (recognition scores in percentages)*										
	CO	*DC*	*DO*	*EV*	*IN*	*IR*	*PO*	*SI*	*AL*	*SE*	*SU*
Com. Authority	**38**	2	2	6	1	8	3	10	7	3	2
Declaration	***18***	**54**	3	***24***	12	***47***	***23***	***23***	***18***	10	2
Doubt	3	8	**11**	6	8	2	8	4	3	4	12
Evidence	8	11	7	**26**	7	16	12	13	13	4	2
Interrogation	0	1	***40***	0	**41**	2	***20***	3	2	1	***19***
Irritation	***20***	4	1	3	1	7	3	14	12	2	3
Politeness	3	12	10	***21***	12	6	**18**	4	3	5	6
Sarcastic Irony	3	2	8	2	5	5	7	**11**	17	8	11
Scorn Aloof.	7	2	3	3	2	5	3	15	**20**	6	3
Seduction	1	4	0	0	1	0	2	3	5	**57**	0
Surprise	1	1	14	9	9	2	2	0	0	1	**39**

Table 5. Confusion matrix for 20 American listeners.

Doubt-incredulity: All four groups confused this attitude with simple interrogation which is supposed to affirm the intention of the speaker (Aubergé *et al.* 2004). Only British subjects, however, recognized this attitude well (41.7%), while non-native speakers had some difficulty identifying it (11.3% for American subjects, 10.8% for French and 18.9% for Japanese).

Perceived attitudes	*Presented attitudes (recognition scores in percentages)*										
	CO	*DC*	*DO*	*EV*	*IN*	*IR*	*PO*	*SI*	*AL*	*SE*	*SU*
Com. Authority	**44**	3	0	6	1	4	2	7	2	1	5
Declaration	15	**43**	11	***31***	10	***48***	***33***	***27***	***24***	12	5
Doubt	0	3	**11**	1	12	1	8	2	2	2	5
Evidence	12	11	7	**35**	8	***24***	15	16	15	9	13
Interrogation	0	0	***38***	2	**46**	0	13	0	0	0	12
Irritation	***18***	10	1	6	1	4	7	10	2	1	6
Politeness	1	6	8	10	5	5	8	5	8	6	2
Sarcastic Irony	2	3	6	2	4	4	2	5	6	6	11
Scorn Aloof.	7	11	1	1	2	6	7	13	**18**	4	5
Seduction	1	9	2	0	3	3	1	14	***23***	**58**	1
Surprise	0	0	15	4	9	1	4	1	1	1	**35**

Table 6. Confusion matrix for 30 French listeners.

Perceived	*Presented attitudes (recognition scores in percentages)*										
attitudes	*CO*	*DC*	*DO*	*EV*	*IN*	*IR*	*PO*	*SA*	*AL*	*SE*	*SU*
Com. Authority	**34**	2	2	5	1	7	1	9	3	4	7
Declaration	16	**36**	6	***37***	2	***48***	***31***	***30***	***32***	15	2
Doubt	0	3	**19**	2	15	3	8	3	4	4	12
Evidence	7	6	7	**16**	3	7	10	8	6	6	3
Interrogation	0	1	***43***	2	**56**	1	***18***	0	0	0	4
Irritation	***26***	8	1	5	0	5	3	14	8	5	12
Politeness	7	12	8	12	9	16	**16**	9	12	17	2
Sarcastic Irony	4	8	5	5	2	5	7	8	12	11	7
Scorn Aloof.	4	16	1	2	3	4	4	13	**13**	10	1
Seduction	0	7	2	1	4	2	0	6	10	**27**	0
Surprise	2	1	7	12	5	1	1	0	0	1	**49**

Table 7. Confusion matrix for 34 Japanese listeners.

Evidence: All four groups confused this attitude with simple declaration, except American subjects who confused it with politeness. European listeners (i.e. English and French listeners) were generally more accurate than non-European listeners (45.8% for English subjects, 35.3% for French vs. 25.8% for American and 16.2% for Japanese subjects). Japanese subjects showed the lowest score among the four groups.

As for the three attitudes listed above, English seduction may be linked to some other attitudes, which are not in the list of 12 choices for Japanese subjects, contrary to the Western listeners who recognized this attitude correctly. The cause of the low identification rate of the attitude by Japanese listeners is perhaps the lack of an appropriate translation of the word 'seduction' (for example, the term 'seduction' is synonymous with 'temptation' or 'incitation' according to the Progressive English-Japanese Dictionary (2006). With regard to English doubt-incredulity, this may be a potential case of a 'false friend' that is, "an expression whose similar acoustic characteristics lead non-native listeners to understand it according to their own language, but actually it is different from what was intended by the native speaker" (Shochi et al. 2006: 696). With regard to English evidence, the reason this attitude was identified least well by Japanese listeners may be because Japanese share neither the language nor the

European culture, whereas British, American and French listeners do, which allowed them to recognize this concept.

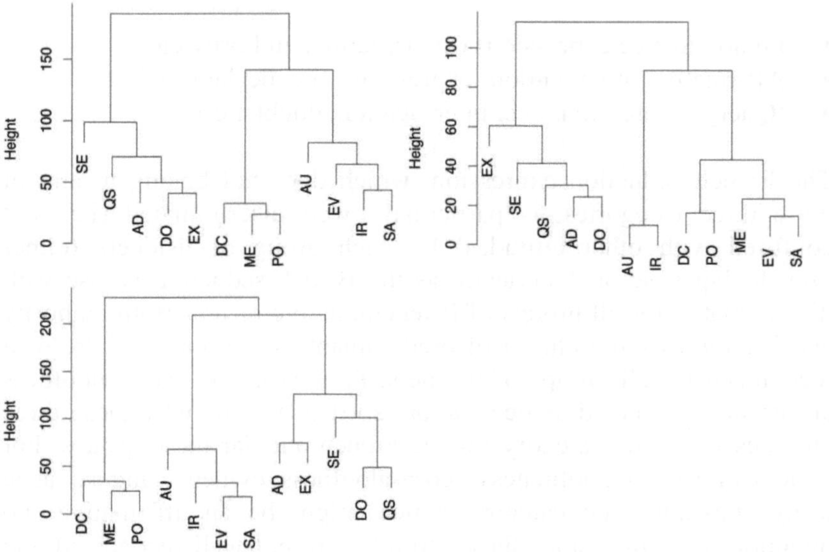

Figure 2. Clustering analysis for French attitudes. The first figure indicates French listeners' perceptual behaviour, the second figure indicates American listeners' perceptual behaviour and the third figure indicates Japanese listeners' perceptual behaviour.

Recognition of French attitudes:

Chi-square analysis: The results of the chi-square test showed that the distribution of all attitudes was significantly above chance level, and that the length effect for the distribution of chosen attitudes is observed only for French and Japanese subjects. Both French and Japanese subjects show a significant influence of the length only between 2 and 5 syllables utterances (df=11, χ^2=36.70, p<.01 for French listeners, df=11, χ^2=46.29, p<.01 for Japanese listeners) for their perceptual behaviour.

Clustering analysis: According to the results of French attitudes from clustering analysis, attitudinal expressions can be classified into three perceptual categories.

- Predominance expressions (i.e. irritation, authority etc.)
- Affirmative 'no intention' expressions (i.e. declaration)
- 'Query' expressions (i.e. interrogation, doubt etc.)

The French seduction expression, which does not belong to any of these three categories, is particularly well discriminated (i.e., not confused with other attitudes) by each group of listeners (either French, Japanese or American), as the British seduction is also well discriminated for all groups of listeners, native or not. Both authority and irritation form a cluster of predominant expressions and are well recognized for all groups of listeners. Politeness and scorn-aloofness are usually perceived as declaration, so that may be why these three attitudes form one category for the French and Japanese groups. For American listeners, politeness, scorn-aloofness, evidence and sarcastic irony constitute one category which might be an affirmative 'no intention' category, since these attitudes are not well recognized and in most of the cases, are perceived as declaration.

Similarities and differences in the recognition of French attitudes:

- French listeners recognized all attitudes above chance level, that is, all attitudes are correctly validated by native speakers. Comparing the accuracy rate among the three groups of listeners, the results show that the native listeners were generally more accurate in perceiving the attitudes than the non-native listeners. This result confirms our 'native-listener' hypothesis, mentioned above.
- Five attitudes (exclamation of surprise, irritation, seduction, declaration and interrogation) were recognized well by the three different language groups. That means that both the concept of these attitudes and the way of expressing these attitudes was shared by the three groups.
- Generally, all participants (including French listeners) did not recognize three attitudes well: scorn-aloofness, politeness and sarcastic irony. A probable reason for this weak recognition may

be that the French speaker who uttered these utterances produced them with less clarity than might have been desired.

- One attitude (evidence) showed different perceptual behaviour among the three groups.

Perceived	*Presented attitudes (recognition scores in percentages)*											
attitudes	*AD*	*AU*	*DC*	*DO*	*EV*	*EX*	*IR*	*ME*	*PO*	*QS*	*SA*	*SE*
Admiration	**25**	0	0	1	1	3	0	2	5	1	1	1
Authority	1	**53**	3	0	13	1	13	3	0	2	12	0
Declaration	4	2	**65**	3	14	0	12	***41***	***51***	***18***	15	8
Doubt-Incredulity	10	1	3	**23**	3	13	0	0	3	9	3	13
Evidence	8	2	8	0	**53**	0	7	16	17	4	***23***	5
Surprise	***26***	0	0	***32***	0	**59**	0	2	2	3	2	1
Irritation	1	***40***	5	0	7	0	**43**	4	1	5	11	1
Scorn Aloofness	0	3	11	0	4	1	***19***	**15**	3	4	***23***	2
Politeness	1	0	4	1	0	0	1	8	**16**	0	1	11
Question	14	0	0	***37***	3	***19***	1	0	0	**48**	0	4
Sarcastic Irony	3	0	1	3	2	3	6	7	2	7	**10**	4
Seduction	8	0	1	1	0	1	0	4	3	0	1	**50**

Table 8. Confusion matrix for 30 French listeners. Recognition values above chance are in bold, important confusions are in bold italic. Meaning of abbreviations: DC (declaration), QS (interrogation), EV (evidence), IR (irritation), AU (command-authority), ME (scorn-aloofness), SA (sarcastic irony), DO (doubt-incredulity), EX (surprise), SE (seduction), PO (politeness) and AD (admiration)

Perceived	*Presented attitudes (recognition scores in percentages)*											
attitudes	*AD*	*AU*	*DC*	*DO*	*EV*	*EX*	*IR*	*ME*	*PO*	*QS*	*SA*	*SE*
Admiration	**12**	0	2	2	1	2	1	1	10	0	5	4
Authority	2	**32**	4	0	***26***	1	***25***	8	2	5	***19***	1
Declaration	1	1	**48**	1	14	0	7	***19***	***35***	15	***20***	7
Doubt-Incredulity	8	1	6	**12**	12	5	1	6	5	2	2	10
Evidence	6	5	7	0	**11**	1	7	14	14	5	11	7
Surprise	***20***	2	2	***24***	7	**62**	2	2	2	0	1	2
Irritation	4	***45***	8	1	7	2	**39**	1	1	4	8	0
Scorn Aloofness	1	7	6	0	10	1	7	**11**	7	4	12	2
Politeness	13	0	13	4	1	4	1	***19***	**19**	8	5	14
Question	***25***	1	4	***49***	7	15	4	4	2	**49**	6	17
Sarcastic Irony	4	5	0	7	4	5	4	8	0	4	**11**	5
Seduction	4	0	0	0	0	1	1	6	2	5	0	**31**

Table 9. Confusion matrix for 21 American listeners.

Evidence: The French evidence was very clearly identified among native listeners with a rate of 53.3%. But non-native listeners did not recognize this attitude well (10.7% for American and 12.5% for Japanese subjects); Americans showed confusion with authority, and Japanese with irritation.

Perceived	*Presented attitudes (recognition scores in percentages)*											
attitudes	*AD*	*AU*	*DC*	*DO*	*EV*	*EX*	*IR*	*ME*	*PO*	*QS*	*SA*	*SE*
Admiration	**19**	2	0	1	3	3	2	5	3	0	5	1
Authority	1	**45**	1	1	12	3	***19***	2	1	1	***20***	0
Declaration	9	0	**57**	1	14	0	6	***45***	***42***	7	8	8
Doubt-Incredulity	15	0	1	**33**	3	13	0	3	6	12	4	11
Evidence	6	1	6	1	**13**	0	11	14	4	5	9	1
Surprise	***18***	7	0	11	10	**62**	3	3	1	1	11	0
Irritation	7	***40***	3	3	***23***	9	**38**	2	3	5	***25***	0
Scorn Aloofness	5	3	9	2	9	1	14	4	7	2	10	2
Politeness	3	0	5	1	3	0	0	14	**18**	2	1	9
Question	10	0	3	***41***	3	9	1	2	0	**61**	2	***22***
Sarcastic Irony	4	3	9	4	8	1	5	4	5	2	7	1
Seduction	5	0	6	0	1	0	0	1	10	4	0	**46**

Table 10. Confusion matrix for 38 Japanese listeners.

The perceptual behaviour of non-native subjects for the expression of evidence in French indicated a possibility that non-native subjects tended to perceive this attitude as an attitude of predominance, in contrast with the native listeners who correctly identified it. It is possible that this attitude is also a case of a prosodic 'false friend'.

Recognition of Japanese attitudes:

Chi-square analysis: The results of the chi-square test showed that the distribution of attitudes is significantly above chance level, and that the length effect for the distribution of the selected attitudes was observed among the subjects of the three different languages. Japanese subjects showed a significant influence of the length only between 5 and 8 mora utterances (df=11, χ^2=34.5, p<.01) for their perceptual behaviour; French subjects showed a significant influence of the length between 1 and 2 moras, (df=11, χ^2=32.2, p<.01) and between 5 and 8 mora utterances (df=11, χ^2=34.5, p<.01) for their perceptual behav-iour; American subjects showed a significant influence of the length only between 2 and 5 mora utterances (df=11, χ^2=35.88, p<.001) for their perceptual behaviour. However, the significant effect of Japanese lexical accent is not identified for the three groups (df=10 except admiration, χ^2=16.5, p>.01 for Japanese subjects, df=33, χ^2=28.8, p>.01 for French subjects and df=33, χ^2=40.75, p>.01 for American listeners).

Clustering analysis: According to the results of Japanese attitudes from the clustering analysis, three perceptual categories of attitudinal expressions can be seen.

- Predominance expressions (i.e. arrogance, authority etc.)
- Politeness expressions (i.e. sincerity-politeness, simple-politeness etc.)
- 'Query' attitudes (i.e. interrogation, doubt etc.)

For Western listeners, another category was observed: affirmative 'non intention' (i.e. declaration).

For Japanese listeners' results, almost all attitudinal expressions are discriminated very well, in particular, irritation and interrogation. They showed confusion between two politeness attitudes (i.e. kyoshuku and sincerity-politeness). In contrast, French and American listeners showed quite different perceptual behaviour for kyoshuku which is not located inside the category of politeness expressions, but inside that of predominance expressions, showing confusion with irritation.

Arrogance is located in the predominance cluster for Japanese listeners; however this attitude is located in the affirmative non-intention cluster for non-native listeners.

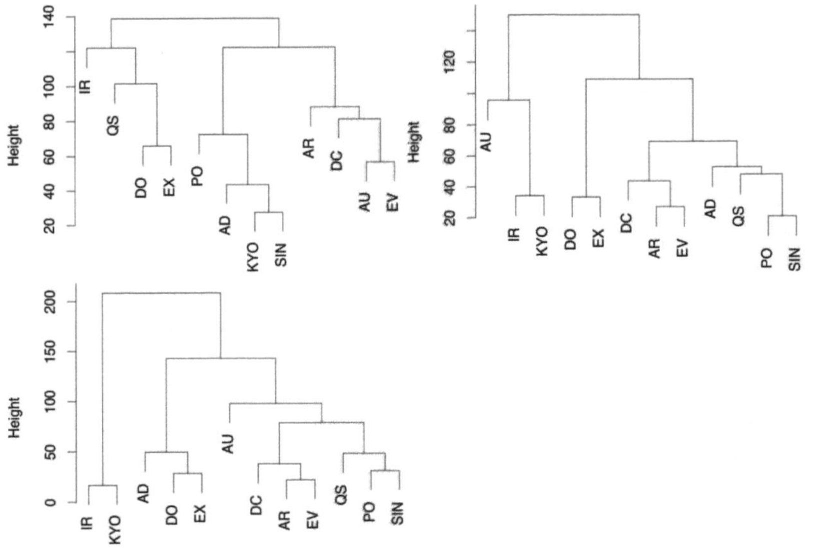

Figure 3. Clustering analysis for Japanese attitudes. The first figure indicates Japanese listeners' perceptual behaviour, the second figure indicates French listeners' perceptual behaviour and the third figure indicates American listeners' perceptual behaviour.

Similarities and differences in the recognition of Japanese attitudes.

- Japanese listeners recognized all attitudes above chance level, that is, all attitudes are correctly validated by native speakers. Comparing the accuracy rate among the three language groups of listeners, the results showed that the native listeners generally were the most accurate among the three groups. This result confirms our native-listener hypothesis.
- Four attitudes (exclamation of surprise, irritation, authority and declaration) are recognized well by the three different language groups. That means that both the concept of these attitudes and the way of expressing these attitudes was shared by the three language groups.

- Two attitudes (kyoshuku, sincerity-politeness, arrogance and interrogation) show different perceptual behaviour among the three language groups.

Kyoshuku: Japanese listeners showed confusion between kyoshuku and sincerity-politeness. Occidental listeners did not recognize this attitude at all: French subjects perceived this attitude as arrogance or authority, and American subjects, as arrogance or irritation.
Sincerity-politeness: Japanese and French listeners showed confusion for this attitude with kyoshuku and simple politeness. This result implies that Japanese and French recognized this attitude as a *politeness expression:* American subjects, however, did not recognize this attitude; but, since there is no matching attitude for American English, this attitude was classified as 'unknown'.
Arrogance: Japanese subjects recognized well this attitude without showing any particular confusion. French listeners showed a confusion with declaration and authority. This indicates that the French perceived more or less the concept of imposition of the speaker's opinion. However, American listeners showed confusion only between this attitude and declaration.
Interrogation: Japanese subjects recognized well this attitude without showing any particular confusion. American subjects showed confusion between this attitude and simple-politeness. This confusion is probably due to their perception of the 'degree' of politeness, ranging between a 'neutral' level and a 'polite' level as expressed in a formal situation. French subjects, however, showed an important confusion with declaration. This type of confusion is not brought about by their perception of the degree of politeness, but rather by that of affirmative vs. interrogative. Acoustical analyses revealed that Japanese interrogation is characterized by a final rising F_0, similar to that for French interrogation, but the difference between this attitude in the two languages is the degree of intensity at the end of the utterances. Interrogation in Japanese showed a progressive decrescendo of intensity towards the end of the utterance, but interrogation in French maintained the intensity until the end of the utterance.

Perceived attitudes	Presented attitudes (recognition scores in percentages)											
	AD	*AR*	*AU*	*DC*	*DO*	*EV*	*SU*	*IR*	*KYO*	*PO*	*QS*	*SIN*
Admiration	**22**	0	0	0	2	0	1	0	2	5	0	4
Arrogance	2	**72**	6	10	6	***21***	0	3	2	0	1	0
Authority	0	10	**51**	3	1	10	1	11	15	0	2	1
Declaration	5	6	10	**66**	0	12	0	0	3	9	2	10
Doubt-Incredulity	0	0	0	0	**56**	0	14	0	0	1	4	0
Evidence	9	6	17	8	0	**46**	6	0	10	2	1	4
Surprise	10	0	0	0	14	5	**59**	0	1	2	1	2
Irritation	1	6	5	1	13	3	5	**86**	12	0	1	1
Kyoshuku	11	0	0	0	0	0	0	0	**25**	10	1	***28***
Politeness	***27***	1	5	11	0	1	0	0	3	**65**	9	***17***
Question	0	0	0	0	8	3	14	0	0	1	**77**	2
Sincerity-Polite.	14	0	6	1	0	0	0	0	***27***	7	2	**32**

Table 11. Confusion Matrices for 15 Japanese listeners. Recognition values above chance are in bold, important confusions are in bold italic. Meaning of abbreviations: AD(admiration), PO(simple-politeness), KYO (kyoshuku), SIN(sincerity-politeness), AR(arrogance-impoliteness), AU (authority), IR (irritation), DO(doubt-incredulity), EX (exclamation of surprise), QS(interrogation), EV (evidence) and DC (declaration).

Among the above four attitudes which the three language groups perceived differently, kyoshuku can be considered to be one of the typical cases of prosodic 'false friends'. Sincerity-politeness for American listeners can be an unknown attitude because of the lack of a corresponding attitude. A breathy voice was involved in the expression of this attitude; according to Pavlenko (2005), in English a breathy voice is used to convey a confession of the speaker's personal secret. Moreover, arrogance also must be one of the cases of 'false friends' for American listeners because in contrast to the intention of expressing arrogance by the Japanese speaker, Americans perceived this attitude as a simple declaration which is a 'neutral' politeness level (i.e. neither polite nor impolite). French listeners perceived the intention of speaker (i.e. imposition of the speaker's opinion) even if they could not identify correctly the intention of arrogance.

Perceived attitudes	*Presented attitudes (recognition scores in percentages)*											
	AD	*AR*	*AU*	*DC*	*DO*	*EV*	*SU*	*IR*	*KYO*	*PO*	*QS*	*SIN*
Admiration	**32**	0	0	0	10	0	1	2	0	4	1	2
Arrogance	1	**19**	14	0	10	11	0	10	***29***	0	0	6
Authority	0	***24***	**70**	3	0	8	0	10	***20***	0	0	9
Declaration	0	***22***	8	**50**	2	***22***	2	0	1	15	***22***	14
Doubt-Incredulity	7	3	1	1	**26**	3	***22***	5	5	1	4	8
Evidence	10	16	2	19	2	**29**	0	2	3	8	15	6
Surprise	16	0	0	3	***27***	3	**52**	2	0	6	1	2
Irritation	0	8	4	0	0	0	0	**66**	***42***	0	0	1
Kyoshuku	8	2	1	2	8	4	0	0	0	12	4	***17***
Politeness	11	4	0	6	1	5	1	2	0	**32**	12	***19***
Question	3	0	0	3	12	3	***22***	0	0	3	**32**	2
Sincerity-Polite.	11	3	0	13	4	13	0	3	1	***19***	9	**15**

Table 12. Confusion matrices for 15 French listeners.

Perceived attitudes	*Presented attitudes (recognition scores in percentages)*											
	AD	*AR*	*AU*	*DC*	*DO*	*EV*	*SU*	*IR*	*KYO*	*PO*	*QS*	*SIN*
Admiration	**11**	0	0	1	4	3	4	2	0	7	2	7
Arrogance	1	**15**	***19***	6	7	6	1	11	***18***	4	2	6
Authority	3	14	**50**	6	1	***17***	1	11	8	4	1	9
Declaration	2	***26***	9	**36**	1	***29***	1	3	3	9	14	6
Doubt-Incredulity	9	6	1	3	**20**	3	12	7	1	5	4	11
Evidence	4	15	6	9	1	**11**	2	0	4	7	6	7
Surprise	***25***	2	1	2	***21***	2	**38**	6	2	2	1	1
Irritation	1	6	12	1	2	3	0	**59**	***59***	2	1	15
Kyoshuku	10	2	0	4	5	1	2	0	1	9	6	12
Politeness	9	4	1	***26***	3	14	4	0	1	**26**	***23***	14
Question	8	6	1	1	***29***	6	***32***	0	4	9	**32**	4
Sincerity-Polite.	***18***	1	1	5	6	4	3	1	0	15	6	8

Table 13. Confusion matrices for 20 American listeners.

6. Conclusion and perspective

In our current work, in order to identify the similarities and differences in perception of social affective expressions by listeners with different language/culture backgrounds, we investigated the perceptual patterns of French, English and Japanese speakers as they listened to each of the three languages. Results showed the following:

First, according to chi-square tests, the distribution of the selected attitudes of all groups of subjects was above chance. For the Japanese attitudes, influence of lexical accent was not identified in the distribution of the selected attitudes in the three language groups. However, a sentence length effect was observed. For British English and French attitudes, American subjects did not show an influence on their perceptual behaviour from the length of the utterances, nor did British English subjects show an influence from length for British English utterances. However, French and Japanese subjects showed different perceptual behaviour for the British and French attitudes according to the length of the utterances.

Second, clustering analysis and confusion analysis showed that the native listeners correctly recognized all attitudes above chance level. Moreover, two attitudes (exclamation of surprise and declaration) in all three languages were recognized by Americans, French and Japanese, suggesting that these attitudes might be universal. In addition, seduction, doubt-incredulity, evidence in British English, evidence in French and Japanese politeness expressions may be a potential case of a 'false friend' that is, "an expression whose similar acoustic characteristics lead non-native listeners to understand it according to their own language, but actually it is different from what was intended by the native speaker" (Shochi *et al.* 2006: 696). Moreover, one of the Japanese politeness expressions (i.e. sincerity-politeness) is an unknown attitude for American listeners.

When we analyzed the perceptual behaviour, we found that some attitudes that were expressed in each of the three languages, such as surprise and declaration, were recognized by listeners in the three language groups; however, some attitudes expressed in each of the languages, such as irritation, were recognized by listeners in the three language groups only for the Japanese and French expressions of irritation, not the British English ones.

Acknowledgements

We are deeply grateful to T. Sadanobu from Kobe University for his helpful advice and contribution on Japanese attitudes. We also thank students at Gifu City Women's College and at Black Hills State University, Spearfish, S.D. for their participation in the perception tests. This work was performed as a collaboration between the Graduate School of Cultural Studies and Humane Science of Kobe University and the GIPSA-Lab of Grenoble under the auspices of the College Doctoral Franco-Japonais. It was supported in part by the Japanese Ministry of Education, Science, Sport, and Culture, Grant-in-Aid for Scientific Research, (2007-2010): 19202013 (A) directed by T. Sadanobu and (2007-2010): 19520371 by the fourth author, and by the French CNRS-SHS ATIP grant "Prosodie des affects" by the second author.

References

Abelin, Åsa / Allwood, Jens 2000. Cross linguistic interpretation of emotional prosody. *ISCA workshop on Speech and Emotion*. Newcastle, Northern Ireland, 110-113.

Abelin, Åsa / Allwood, Jens 2002. Cross linguistic interpretation of emotional prosody. *Gothenburg papers in theoretical linguistics*. Göteborg, Sweden.

Aubergé, Véronique / Grépillat, Tuulikki / Rilliard, Albert 1997. Can we perceive attitudes before the end of sentences? The gating paradigm for prosodic contours. *Proceedings of EuroSpeech'97*. Rhodos, Greece, 2, 871-877.

Aubergé, Véronique / Audibert, Nicolas / Rilliard, Albert 2004. Acoustic morphology of expressive speech: what about contours? *Proceedings of Speech Prosody 2004*. Nara, Japan, 201-204.

Beier, Ernst G. / Zautra, Alexander J. 1972. Identification of vocal communication of emotions across cultures. *Journal of Consulting and Clinical Psychology*. 39, 166.

Brown, Penelope / Levinson, Stephen 1986. *Politeness. Some universals in language use*. Cambridge: Cambridge University Press.

Calbris, Geneviève / Montredon, Jacques 1981. *Oh là là. Expression intonative et mimique*. Paris: CLE international.

Calbris, Geneviève / Porcher, Louis 1989. *Geste et communication*. Paris : Hatier-Crédif.

Calbris, Geneviève / Montredon, Jacques 1986. *Des gestes et des mots pour le dire*. Paris: CLE international.

Callamand, Monique 1973. *L'intonation expressive*. Collection le français dans le monde, B.E.L.C. Librairies Hachette et Larousse.

Callamand, Monique 1987. *Grammaire vivante du français : français langue étrangère*. Paris: Larousse, Diffusion CLE International.

Campbell, Nick 2000. Datebases of Emotional Speech. *Proc. ISCA workshop on emotion 2000*. Northern Ireland, 34-38.

Campbell, Nick / Mokhtari, Parham 2003. Voice Quality : the 4th Prosodic Dimension. *15th International Congress of Phonetic Sciences*. Barcelone, Spain, 2417-2420.

Campbell, Nick / Erickson, Donna 2004. What do people hear? A study of the perception of non-verbal affective information in conversational speech. *Journal of the Phonetic Society of Japan*. 8/1, 9-28.

Delattre, Pierre 1966. Les dix intonations de base du français. The French *Review*. 40/3, 1-14.

Diaferia, Marie-Laure 2002. *Les Attitudes de l'Anglais : Premiers Indices Prosodiques*. Master thesis in Cognitive Science, Institut National Polytechnique de Grenoble.

Dromey, Christopher / Silveira, Jose / Sandor, Paul 2005. Recognition of affective prosody by speakers of English as a first or foreign language. *Speech Communication*. 47/3, 351-359.

Ekman, Paul 1972. Universals and cultural differences in facial expression of emotion. In Cole, J.R. (ed.) *Nebraska Symposium on Motivation*. Lincoln: University of Nebraska Press, 207-283.

Ekman, Paul 1999. Facial Expressions. In Dalgleish, T. / Power T. (eds) *The Handbook of Cognition and Emotion*. Sussex: John Wiley & Sons, 301-320.

Elfenbein, Hillary Anger / Ambady, Nalini 2002. On the universality and cultural specificity of emotion recognition: a meta-analysis. *Psychological Bulletin*. 128/2, 203-235.

Erickson, Donna / Maekawa, Kikuo 2001. Perception of American English emotion by Japanese listeners. *Proc. Spring Meeting of Acoustical Society of Japan*. 333-334.

Erickson, Donna / Hayashi, Seiko / Hosoe, Yukiko / Suzuki, Mayuko / Ueno, Yuka / Maekawa, Kikuo 2002. Perception of American English sarcasm by Japanese listeners. *Proc. spring Meeting of the Acoustical Society of Japan*. Yokohama, Japan, 277-278.

Erickson, Donna / Ohashi, Seiko / Makita, Yuko / Kajimoto, Natsuki / Mokhtari, Parham 2003. Perception of naturally-spoken expressive speech by American English and Japanese listeners. *CREST International Workshop on Expressive Speech Processing*. 31-36.

Fonagy, Ivan 1991. *La Vive Voix*. Paris: Payot.

Greenberg, Yoko / Tsuzaki, Minoru / Kato, Hiroaki / Sagisaka, Yoshinori 2005. Communicative speech synthesis using constituent word attributes. *Proc. Inter Speech 2005*. Lisbon, Portugal, 517-520.

Ito, Mika 2003. The Contribution of Voice Quality to Politeness in Japanese. *VOQUAL'03*. Geneva: Switzerland, 157-162.

Izard, Carroll E. 1977. The Emotions and Emotion Concept in Personality and Culture Reseach. In Cattell, Raymond B. / Dreger, Ralph M. (eds) *Handbook of Modern Personality Theory*. Washington D.C.: Hemisphere.

Kramer, Ernest 1964. Elimination of verbal cues in judgments of emotion from voice. *Journal of Abnormal and Social Psychology*. 68, 390–396.

Loveday, Leo 1981. Pitch, politeness and sexual role: An exploratory investigation into the pitch correlates to English and Japanese politeness formulae. *Language and Speech*. 24/1, 71-89.

Maekawa, Kikuo 1998. Phonetic and phonological characteristics of paralinguistic information in spoken Japanese. *Proceedings of the 5th International Conference on Spoken Language Processing*. Sydney, Australia, 635-638.

Maekawa, Kikuo 2004. Production and Perception of 'Paralinguistic' Information. *Proc. of Speech Prosody*, Nara, Japan.

Matsumoto, David / Assar, Manish 1992. The effects of language on judgments of universal facial expressions of emotion. *Journal of Nonverbal behavior.* 16, 85-99.

Mejvaldova, Jana 2000. *Expressions prosodiques de certaines attitudes en tchèque et en français: étude comparative.* PhD University Paris 7, Paris, France.

Mizutani, Osamu / Mizutani Nobuko 1979. *Aural Comprehension Practice in Japanese.* Tokyo: The Japan Times.

Mokhtari, Parham / Campbell, Nick 2003. Automatic measurement of pressed/breathy phonation at acoustic centres of reliability in continuous speech. *Sp. Issue on Speech Information Proc. IEICE Transactions on Information and Systems*, (E-86-D), 574-582.

Morlec, Yann / Bailly, Gérard / Aubergé, Véronique 2001. Generating prosodic attitudes in French: Data, model and evaluation. *Speech Communication.* 33/4, 357-371.

Moroni, Véronique 1997. *Enquête sur les attitudes du français: définition et interprétation.* Master thesis, Univ. Grenoble 3, France.

Nakamichi, Ayako / Jogan, Aki / Usami, Michie / Erickson, Donna 2003. Perception by native and non-native listeners of vocal emotion in a bilingual movie. *Bulletin of Gifu City Women's College*, 52, 87-91.

Ofuka, Etsuko / McKeown, J. Denis / Waterman, Mitch G. / Roach, Peter J. 2000. Prosodic cue for rated politeness in Japanese speech. *Speech Communication.* 32, 199-217.

Ohala, John J. 1984. An ethlogical percpective on common cross-language utilization of F_0 of voice. *Phonetica.* 41, 1-16.

Ohala, John J. 1996. Ethological Theory and the Expression of Emotion in the Voice. *Proc. International Conference on Spoken Language Processing.* Philadelphia, 1812-1815.

Pavlenko, Aneta 2005. *Emotions and Multilingualism.* Cambridge: Cambridge University Press.

Progressive English-Japanese Dictionary (2006). Syogakkan, Tokyo, Japan.

Rilliard, Albert / Martin, Jean-Claude / Aubergé, Véronique / Shochi, Takaaki 2008. Perception of French Audio-Visual Prosodic attitudes. *Speech prosody 2008*. Campinas, Brazil, 685-688.

Rilliard, Albert / Shochi, Takaaki / Martin, Jean-Claude / Erickson, Donna / Aubergé, Véronique To appear. Multimodal indices to Japanese and French prosodically expressed social affects. *Language and Speech*.

Roseberry-Mckibbin, Celeste / Brice, Alejandro 1999. The perception of vocal cues of emotion by Spanish-speaking limited English proficient children. *Journal of Children's Communication Development*. 20/2, 19-24.

Sadanobu, Toshiyuki 2003. Expressive Speech and Grammar – with Special Reference to Pressed Voice in Japanese. *CREST International Workshop on Expressive Speech Processing*. 55-59.

Sadanobu, Toshiyuki 2004. A natural history of Japanese pressed voice. *Journal of the Phonetic Society of Japan*. 8/1, 29-44.

Sawamura, Kanae / Dang, Jianwu / Akagi, Masato / Erickson, Donna / Li, Aijun / Sakuraba, Kyoko / Minematsu, Nobuaki / Hirose, Keikichi 2007. Common factors in emotion perception among different cultures. *International Congress of Phonetic Sciences*, Saarbrucken, Germany, 2113-2116.

Scherer, Klaus R. 1986. Vocal affect expression : A review and a model for future research. *Psychological Bulletin*. 99/2, 143-165.

Scherer, Klaus R. / Banse, Rainer / Wallbott, Harald G. 2001. Emotion inferences from vocal expression correlate across languages and cultures. *Journal of Cross-Cultural Psychology*. 32/1, 76-92.

Scherer, Klaus R. / Ellgring, Heiner 2007. Multimodal Expression of Emotion: Affect Programs or Componential Appraisal Patterns? *Emotion*. 7/1, 158-171.

Shigeno, Sumi 1998. Cultural similarities and differences in the recognition of audio-visual speech stimuli. *International Conference on Spoken Language Processing*. Sydney, Australia.

Shochi, Takaaki / Aubergé, Véronique / Rilliard, Albert 2006. How prosodic attitudes can be false friends: Japanese vs. French social affects. *Speech Prosody*. Dresden, Germany, 692-696.

Shochi, Takaaki / Aubergé, Véronique / Rilliard, Albert 2007. Cross-listening of Japanese, English and French social affect: about universals, false friends and unknown attitude. *International*

Congress of Phonetic Sciences. Saarbrucken, Germany, 2097-2100.

Shochi, Takaaki / Erickson, Donna / Rilliard, Albert / Aubergé, Véronique / Martin, Jean-Claude 2008. Recognition of Japanese attitudes in Audio-Visual speech. *Speech prosody*. Campinas, Brazil, 689-692.

Swerts, Marc / Krahmer, Emiel 2005. Audiovisual prosody and feeling of knowing. *Journal of Memory and Language*. 53/1, 81-94.

Thorsen Nina 1980. A study of the perception of sentence intonation – Evidence from Danish. *Journal of the Acoustical Society of America*. 67/3, 1014-1030.

Van Bezooijen, Renée / Otto, Stanley A. / Heenan, Thomas A. 1983. Recognition of vocal expressions of emotion. *Journal of Cross-Cultural Psychology*. 14, 387-406.

Wilting, Janneke / Krahmer, Emiel / Swerts, Marc 2006. Real vs. acted emotional speech. *Proceedings of the 6th Interspeech*, Pittsburgh, USA.

SOPHIE DE ABREU / CATHERINE MATHON / ALESSANDRA MOSCA

Prosodic Cues of Anger in French: A Comparative Study with Two Other Romance Languages, Italian and Portuguese

1. Introduction

Studies about the role of prosody in the expression of emotions have increased along with those of speech engineering by developing new types of corpus and analysis tools. However, many phenomena and types of corpus are still to be explored in order to characterize finer emotions observed with variations in acoustic cues. We are interested in studying the way anger is expressed in French. It also seemed interesting to compare comments about anger in French with the ones on two other Romance languages: Italian and Portuguese. Despite belonging to the same language family, these languages show significant differences at the stress level. This purpose of comparative study is to measure the impact these stress differences may have on the expression of emotion.

Studies on the vocal aspect of emotions often consist of a statistical classification of emotions from the most salient values and variations of acoustic parameters. We consider here the expression of emotion in an interactive framework taking into account the relationship of acoustic parameters with the linguistic and discursive structure of language, thereby falling under phonostylistic analysis. The corpus was constructed to reflect the conversational framework in which the expression of emotion arises. Thus we recorded speakers who read a literary dialogue with expressive parts. Knowing that prosody has several functions (linguistic, expressive and discursive), we verified that the variations in acoustic parameters (generally described as constituting anger) can be attributed to other functions of prosody, forcing the speaker to use different strategies to express emotion as well as combining the prosodic setting.

2. Prosody and emotions: some generalities

In recent years, research on emotion has become more and more important in the international field. This is the consequence of progress made in different domains such as cognitive psychology, neurology, prosody and speech processing. Indeed, progress in speech processing has permitted the development of better recording conditions (Campbell 2000) and signal analysis. Furthermore, this phenomenon was strengthened by the emergence of commercial applications concerning the recognition and the synthesis of emotional speech.

In the psychological sciences there are descriptive models of emotional processing and definitions of emotions. Recent research has generally defined emotion as a relatively brief episode, which constitutes an answer of the organism to the evaluation of an external or internal event (Scherer 2000). The answer of the organism is partly physiological. Psycho-neurologists applied themselves to characterise the physiological answers of the organism depending on the emotions felt and drawn up a cartography of the brain areas activated by emotions. The emotional process partly consists of corporal answers.

Since the speech is produced by the vocal organ, it has been theorized that emotion could act upon vocal realisations. Indeed numerous studies showed that acoustic parameters may be modified by the emotional process and could vary depending on the emotion felt. Hence typologies of emotions have been established according to vocal characteristics (Banse/Scherer 1996; Bänzinger *et al.* 2001).

In these research projects, acoustic analyses consist in considering principally the variations of fundamental frequency (F_0), of intensity and phenomena of duration and tempo. From one study to another the parameters extracted and the statistical analyses conducted vary. Concerning the fundamental frequency expressed in Hertz (Hz), central tendencies i.e., mean and median, maximum and minimum values and the delta difference between them (F_0 range) are generally taken into account. Measuring intensity expressed in decibels (dB) raises more difficulties, since it is a matter of relative intensity not of an absolute one. Intensity mainly depends on recording conditions of the vocal expressions and on the voice of the speakers. Finally it is often difficult to compare different speakers. Likewise it is not possible to compare the intensity of relatively long periods of speech even from a same speaker. In the studies which take into account intensity parameters, central values and variations between maximum and minimum levels are also measured. Tempo is measured in terms of speech rate, i.e., the number of syllables per second. The number of pauses depending on the duration of the expression can also be calculated.

By reading these studies on the vocal expression of emotion, one realizes that the results differ from one methodology to another, and it is difficult to establish a vocal profile by emotion. However, we can classify emotions into two categories with different vocal characteristics. The first, characterized by a high average F_0, a wide variability of F_0, a high intensity and a fast tempo concerns the emotions that convey strong excitement. It includes joy, anger and fear. The second category relates to the emotions defined by low excitement. It is characterized by a low average F_0, low variability of F_0 and a slow tempo, and it includes indifference, contempt, boredom and sadness.

To provide a greater specification of acoustic parameters compared to the emotions expressed, current research has increased the acoustic parameters studied, including spectral measurements. Banse and Scherer (1996) have examined the energy on different frequency bands compared to the total energy. Measures concerning the quality of the voice have also been proposed, including the height of formants and their bandwidth (Juslin/Laukka 2001). The results of these studies suggest the following acoustic characteristics (Bänzinger 2004) related to anger:

- rising values of F_0 (average, maximum, range);
- an increase in the speech rate;
- rising energy in the high pitches;
- and an increase in the average intensity.

In addition to these parameters, some fairly rare studies included a description of the melodic contours (Fónagy 1987; Léon 1993). Thus anger, which particularly concerns us here, is distinguished by a switchback contour in the high register with sharp melodic variations and a steep fall at the end of the utterance.

Although most studies seem to agree on the relevance of numerous acoustic parameters for the study of emotions, none of these studies has yet actually proposed a stable vocal profile for each emotion. Indeed the variability of results does not allow definitive conclusions to be drawn. This is partly explained by the different methodologies used particularly at the source of emotional expressions. There are three main sources:

1. The speech used by actors, professional or not, is still today the most widely analysed because it has many advantages: optimal recording conditions, a set of emotional categories predefined by the investigator, lexical content which does not vary and is often chosen to be semantically neutral. However, one can question the authenticity of these types of emotional expressions as they do not correspond to physiological changes from a real emotion. These expressions can be viewed as communication prototypes, which lead to an exaggeration of emotional expression. Some studies are also conducted of emotional speech produced by professional actors extracted from films (Boulakia 2007) or plays. In this research the risk of exaggeration is perhaps even more present; however, this type of corpus does not permit a strict control of both the conditions of recordings and the linguistic content.
2. Emotional speech conducted in a laboratory consists of placing subjects under conditions that may elicit an emotional reaction. In most cases subjects perform a specific task which can limit the lexical content of the utterances produced. The scenarios

vary according to studies and may even be based on a video game (Johnstone/Scherer 1999) or a computer task.

3. Finally some studies focus on spontaneous emotional speech. The speech situations are as various as television broadcasts (Chung 2000; Mathon 2007) or communications recorded in call centres (Vidrascu/Devillers 2005). This methodology allows working on 'authentic' emotions. However, the spontaneous emotional speech still causes many problems because of a lack of overall control parameters of the experiment:
   - the signal is quite often of poor quality;
   - the situation cannot always cover a wide range of emotions;
   - lexical content of the statements is not controlled;
   - finally the emotional states present in the corpus are defined after the actual recording either by means of perceptual tests or on the basis of categories annotated by the investigators, but in all cases with a subjective component.

Spontaneous speech is being used more and more in the field of emotions, and significant progress in speech processing permits producing particularly sharp acoustic analyses. However, technological innovations cannot overcome some problems implied by the use of spontaneous speech corpora. Thus spontaneous speech would naturally prove to be quite difficult for comparative studies of the expressive phenomenon in different languages. Indeed it is difficult to find in spontaneous speech emotional expressions which correspond from one language to another. Furthermore the utterances to be compared are chosen according to the emotions expressed and perceived but do not take into account the syntactic or lexical constraints specific to each language.

Moreover the expressive function is not the only one assumed by prosody (Caelen-Haumont 2005, Fónagy/Bérard 2006). One of the most investigated functions of prosody is syntactic, i.e., the fact that prosody permits the delimiting and the identifying of the syntactic units of the utterance. Prosody also marks differences of meaning related to the modalities of the sentence or by a focus on a lexeme in the sentence.

Prosody also carries pragmatic information like the age of the speaker. In a natural speech situation all these functions of prosody are closely dependent and make the distinction of the parameters relevant and thus the various functions of the prosody more difficult.

3. Description of the corpus

The study on anger that we propose here has been undertaken from a comparative point of view between French and two other Romance languages: Portuguese and Italian. The comparative purpose of our study influenced the choice of the corpus. Thus we preferred an acted-out speech corpus to spontaneous speech since we would thus be able to control linguistic contents, and what corresponds best from one language to the other. As we wanted to show the relationship between expressiveness and discourse, we discarded the framework of the isolated sentence and chose another unit: turn taking.

3.1. Oral corpus description

The text required the staging of several characters interacting with each other and providing expressiveness. We chose an excerpt from Chapter 7 of *The Little Prince* by Saint-Exupéry (2001) which is a narration of an encounter between an aviator who crashed in the desert and a child who originated from another planet. The seventh chapter recounts the altercation that broke out between the Little Prince and the Aviator. The child is concerned about the fate of his flower (Will the sheep eat it?) and the Aviator about his own survival (Will there be enough water until he finishes repairing the plane?). The quarrel arises from the misunderstanding of each other's needs. In the final monologue, the Little Prince shows to the Aviator that his concern for his flower, which may seem trivial is actually more profound. Why have roses had thorns for millions of years and have not stopped sheep from eating them?

This excerpt seemed particularly relevant because it is not only the most expressive, but also because of its structure, which is one of the closest to oral dialogue (interruptions and extracts in reported speech). In addition, this text has been selected because it is part of collective imagination in all three languages. Speakers have some familiarity with the text prior to reading. The corpus includes conversational sequences. As it is made up of written speech, the expression of emotion here is less authentic than in a spontaneous corpus. However, it allows us on the one hand to overcome the difficulty of comparing speakers as mentioned above and on the other hand of comparing speech productions in several Romance languages. Indeed one of the problems in comparing oral speech is the difficulty in obtaining the same utterances with different speakers and even more so in different languages. This difficulty is overcome by reading a written text.

The speakers recorded are not professional actors so as to avoid theatrical speech whose prosodic execution is often overacted when they try to meet a theatrical standard on mimicry of emotions (Mouratidou 2007). We believe that the reading by non-professional native speakers reflects their perception of language and their representation of the prosody of emotion. In addition, it seemed interesting not to appeal to several people to 'act out' the different characters for two reasons: firstly the speaker-reader is compelled to voluntarily mark the difference between the enunciative voices, and secondly the speech produced for each enunciative voice remains comparable because it is the same reading voice. We recorded three female speakers in each language which corresponded to about 25 minutes of reading, 7.8 minutes in French, 8.2 minutes in Italian and 9.4 in Portuguese. The instructions were as follows: "Here is an excerpt from the *Little Prince*. Read it as expressively as possible."

3.2. Written corpus description

To determine the information given by the text to the speaker-reader we analysed the written corpus, according to Adam's (2001) textual analysis theory. This theory consists in analysing texts in different prototypical sequences (narrative, argumentative, conversational prototype, etc.), showing the internal structure of the extract. The sequence (Adam 2001) is defined as the intermediate unit between the text and the macro-proposal units. The macro-proposal is a combination of proposals based on the meaning (chronological landmark, cause and effect relationships, etc.). According to Adam, the sequence is "a relatively autonomous entity with an internal organization of its own, in a dependence/independence relationship with the wider set it is part of" (2008: 131, our translation). It is a structure made of parts linked together under a "hierarchical network of relationships" (2008: 131, our translation). The entry *séquence* of the *Dictionnaire d'Analyse du Discours* (Adam 2002) presents the longest synthesis of this theory of sequences. The excerpt studied here is only composed of narrative and conversational sequences. We call 'narrative sequence' any extract in which enunciation is supported by the narrator. This definition, though inexhaustive, is sufficient to identify a narrative sequence in a text, whether oral or written.

Relating to the conversational sequence we wish to note that conversation is directed towards an interlocutor (imaginary or not, present or not), and has a conversational structure (alternation of turn takings). In this way Kerbrat-Orecchioni considers that "To compose a conversation, it requires at least two people who speak alternately are physically present and testify by their non-verbal conduct to their 'commitment' in the conversation, but their respective statements also have to be mutually determined" (1990: 145, our translation). Adam gives the following definition on the sequential aspect of the conversation: "Dialogue and conversation are generally synonymous and one speaks about conversational analysis in general. We prefer to say that dialogue and conversation are two points of view about alternated speech. Conversation deserves to be regarded as a psycho-socio-discursive point-of-view or as a type of discourse as well as a debate, an interview, a telephone conversation, and so on. Dialogue is nothing other than a textual composition unit (oral or written)" (2001: 148, our translation).

The excerpt from the *Little Prince* has many conversational passages produced by alternating the voices of the two main characters, the Aviator and the Little Prince, and in the form of a narrative text-type. The selected excerpt is made up of 24 sequences: 11 narrative, 11 conversational and 2 reported-speech. The sequences and turn taking structure of this excerpt are based on the theme of the argument. The quarrel stems from the difficulty of the Aviator to understand what is important for the Little Prince, who thus becomes angry. The sequence structure was reconstituted from indices at various levels. First of all, the written text has oral features. By the graphic structure of the text, like cutting into paragraphs or the use of quotes, that indicate the transition between narration and dialogue much information is given to the speaker-reader. From a linguistic point of view, the verb tenses (past versus present) and the use of personal pronouns (1st and 3rd person versus 1st and 2nd) provide more information about the narrative or conversational nature of the sequence.

Our goal is to study the expression of anger in the reading of this excerpt. We chose to determine the passages as attitudinally marked relying on the information given by the text itself. The lexical content provides crucial information in relation to anger, as stage directions prescribe the reading of the turn taking they introduce. We notice :

1) « il me lança, avec une sorte de rancune :
   - Je ne te crois pas ! Les fleurs sont faibles. Elles sont naïves. Elles se rassurent comme elles peuvent. Elles se croient terribles avec leurs épines... »
2) « - Tu parles comme les grandes personnes !
   Ça me fit un peu honte. Mais, impitoyable, il ajouta :
   - Tu confonds tout... tu mélanges tout ! »
3) « Il était vraiment très irrité. Il secouait au vent des cheveux tout dorés :
   - Je connais une planète où il y a un Monsieur cramoisi. Il n'a jamais respiré une fleur. Il n'a jamais regardé une étoile. Il n'a jamais aimé personne. Il n'a jamais rien fait d'autre que des additions. Et toute la journée il répète comme toi: "Je suis un homme sérieux ! Je suis un homme sérieux !" et ça le fait gonfler d'orgueil. Mais ce n'est pas un homme, c'est un champignon !
   - Un quoi ?
   - Un champignon ! »

4) « Le petit prince était maintenant tout pâle de colère.
- Il y a des millions d'années que les fleurs fabriquent des épines. Il y a des millions d'années que les moutons mangent quand même les fleurs. Et ce n'est pas sérieux de chercher à comprendre pourquoi elles se donnent tant de mal pour se fabriquer des épines qui ne servent jamais à rien ? Ce n'est pas important la guerre des moutons et des fleurs ? Ce n'est pas plus sérieux et plus important que les additions d'un gros Monsieur rouge ? Et si je connais, moi, une fleur unique au monde, qui n'existe nulle part, sauf dans ma planète, et qu'un petit mouton peut anéantir d'un seul coup, comme ça, un matin, sans se rendre compte de ce qu'il fait, ce n'est pas important ça ! »

These stage directions show a gradation in the expression of anger by the Little Prince, described by the narrator ("stunned", "shame", "ruthless", "shaking", "pale with Anger"). Inside the Little Prince's speaking turns, the lexical items marking expressiveness are pejoratively connoted: "occupé" (occupied), "inquiet" (anxious), "peur" (fear), "irrité" (irritated), "Mais non! Mais non!" (No! No!), "rien" (nothing), "n'importe quoi" (anything). Punctuation also provides indications on the expressiveness of turn takings (Catach 1996). There are, for example, seven exclamation points after the Little Prince's speaking turns (five in the Aviator's). Even if the exclamation point is used to mark expressiveness, it does not define the kind of emotion it is intended to convey (Danon-Boileau/Morel 1995). However, this punctuation mark appears in the extract after the stage directions to indicate the Little Prince's anger.[1]

The text is supported by four enunciative voices: the Narrator (which corresponds to the Aviator, at another point in time), the

1 « Je ne te crois pas! »
« De choses sérieuses! »
« Tu parles comme les grandes personnes ! »
« tu mélanges tout ! »
« Mais ce n'est pas un homme, c'est un champignon ! »
« Un champignon ! »
« Et si je connais, moi, une fleur unique au monde, qui n'existe nulle part, sauf dans ma planète, et qu'un petit mouton peut anéantir d'un seul coup, comme ça, un matin, sans se rendre compte de ce qu'il fait, ce n'est pas important ça! »

Aviator, the Little Prince, and the Mushroom. We will call here narrative sequences (SqN) an intervention of the narrator alternating with a conversational sequence, and retort (R) an intervention of a character involved in the dialogue. Traverso (2002) points out in the *Dictionnaire d'Analyse du Discours* that, in theatrical dialogue, the term 'retort' is equivalent to turn taking in conversational analysis. We opted for this term in order to reserve the use of the term 'turn taking' to the field of strictly oral interaction but also to avoid introducing confusion. However, the retort satisfies the criterion of alternating turns used to define turn taking. The table below shows the text distribution of the enunciative voice, as opposed to narrative sequences, and number of words.

Enunciative Voice	Narrator	Aviator	Little Prince	Mushroom
Number of R/SqN	34	19	44	3
Number of words	35.5	12.5	50	2

Table 1 Distribution by number of occurrences and number of words quantification for each enunciative voice (%).

The proportion of occurrences of the narrative enunciative voice is provided here to give an idea of the weight of narrative sequences compared to conversational sequences. This will not be treated in the future, since this enunciative voice is not at the same level in the sequence structure as the voices in the dialogue. In addition, given the low proportion of speech pronounced by the Mushroom, we have not measured those utterances. We therefore propose to compare the speech productions of readers-speakers for the enunciative voices of the Aviator and the Little Prince.

3.3. Corpus processing

The corpus was transcribed and cut into smaller utterances for analysis by signal processing software. The oral productions of the speakers-readers were first transcribed by the software Transcriber 1.5 (http://trans.sourceforge.net/en/presentation.php). This software allows a fast alignment of the transcription with the signal. The signal severance was marked according to the internal structure of the text described above, i.e., by cutting the signal each time a change of enunciative voice was observed and by placing it on a different line. The transcript makes it possible to distinguish narrative sequences, labelled 'Narrator' at the outset, and inside conversational sequences to distinguish utterances allocated to the enunciative voice of the Aviator, the Little Prince or the Mushroom. The transition from one speaker to another is called 'turn taking' by users of Transcriber and designates what we called 'retort'. Pauses located at the border between two enunciative voices were transcribed outside those enunciative voices, in a specific 'turn taking' of Transcriber (TT-Trans). On the contrary, the internal pauses to a retort of an enunciative voice have been transcribed within these TT-Trans, on a different layer of actually occurring speech.

3.4. Prosody and enunciative voices

We assumed that the speaker-reader marked differences between enunciative voices by prosody, and noticed especially by varying the voice pitch and the functions of the enunciative sequence. We verified this hypothesis by measuring the voice pitch of the speaker's productions in French, Italian and Portuguese. Using the WinPitchPro software (Martin 2004) we extracted automatically every 20 milli-seconds, the F_0 values for each enunciative voice. Indeed WinPitchPro can produce outputs of the transcription software Transcriber, which takes into account the segmentation and transcripts stored in XML files. WinPitchPro recognizes speaker tags (the enunciative voices), established under Transcriber, and treats them separately in specific files. With these F_0 values we calculated the average, the minimum and maximum F_0 range for each speaker and for each enunciative voice. We worked particularly on voice alternation in the conversa-tional part, i.e., alternation between the Aviator enunciative voice (EVA) and that of the Little Prince (EVLP).

For each of the three French speakers, we compared the fundamental frequency of the oral productions for the Aviator's voice with those of the Little Prince's voice (Figure 1). This comparison showed that the EVLP is performed of a higher register than the EVA. This difference is not significant concerning the pitch average. However, increase in values between the two voices is relevant for pitch range and pitch maximum. The speaker-reader seems to use these prosodic parameters to distinguish the enunciative voice of the Aviator and of the Little Prince in the dialogue. We made the assumption that the speaker imitates a child's voice in his reading.

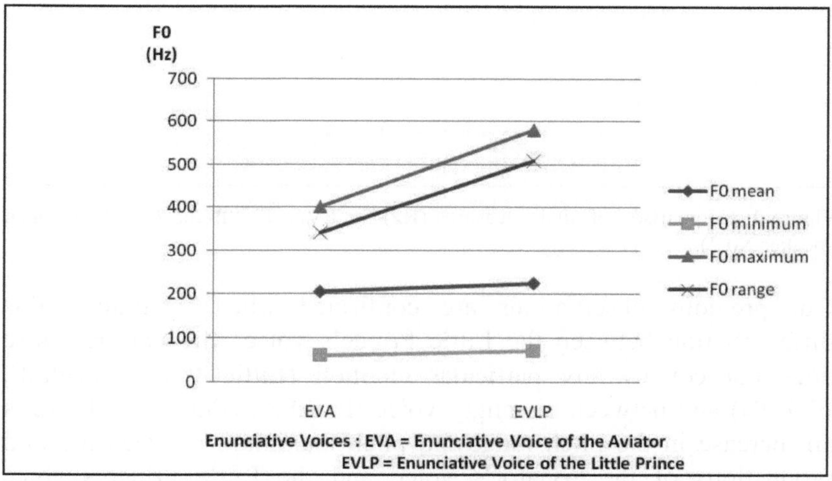

Figure 1: Comparison of pitch measures (Hz) for EVA and EVPP (French speaker No.1).

The problem lies in the fact that the increase in the pitch range and the pitch maximum is traditionally linked to the expression of anger. In this case, would the difference between the two enunciative voices be the consequence of the Little Prince's speech carrying more anger than the Aviator's? To verify this we introduced an additional differentiation by distinguishing the Little Prince's voices and the emotional state stage directions attributed to it.

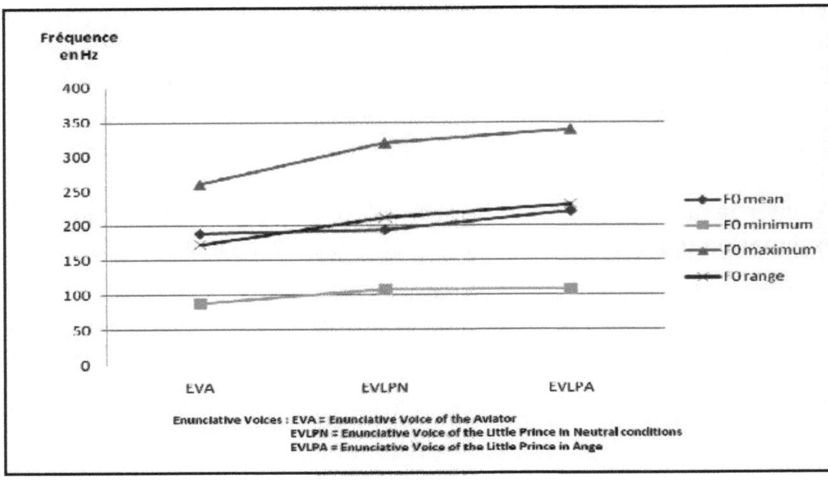

Figure 2: Comparison of pitch measures (Hz) for EVA, EVPP and EVPPA (French speaker No.2).

Our previous observations are confirmed when integrating this differentiation between the Little Prince's voice when his response does not convey any particular emotion (Little Prince 'neutral', EVLPN) and between his angry voice (EVLPA) (Figure 2). There is an increase in the pitch range and pitch maximum between the oral productions of the Aviator's voice and the Little Prince's voice regardless of the expressive factor. Indeed pitch range and pitch maximum increase between the voice of the Aviator and the Little Prince's 'neutral' voice. In addition, those parameters increase between the Little Prince's 'neutral' and his 'angry' voices. We can conclude that French speakers use pitch variations to mark both the difference between the voices of the characters and to express emotion.

Italian speakers behave like French speakers. They use the pitch range at its maximum to differentiate narrative voices. Figure 3 shows an example of one of the speakers:

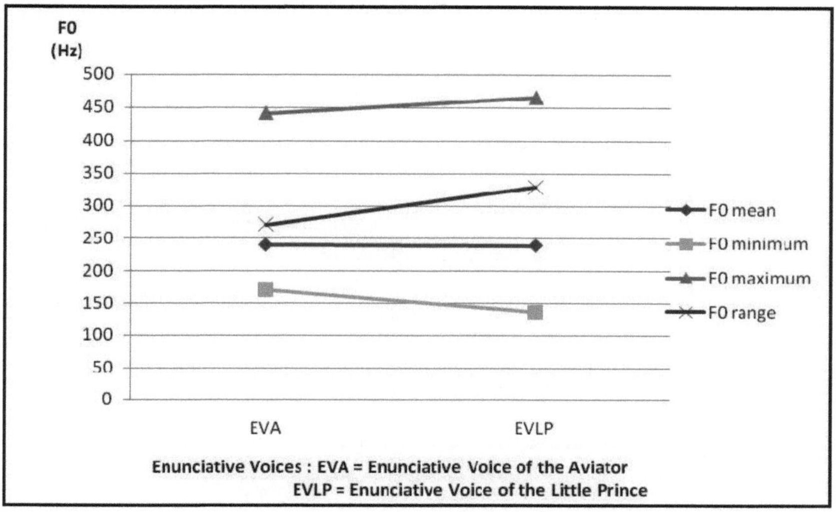

Figure 3: Comparison of pitch measures (Hz) for EVA and EVPP (Italian speaker No.2).

The speakers use the same pitch variations to express anger as shown in Figure 4. However, all speakers do not use pitch variation in the same way. The pitch maximum level and the pitch range may remain static or even decline. This may be related to the sentence moods characterizing sequences analyzed here. Among 'neutral' sequences, there are some questions and speakers increase the pitch maximum level to mark this mood.

Portuguese speakers also differentiate the enunciative voice of the Aviator with that of the Little Prince; EVLP is indeed wider than the EVA with a pitch minimum level slightly lower and a maximum level much higher (Figure 5).

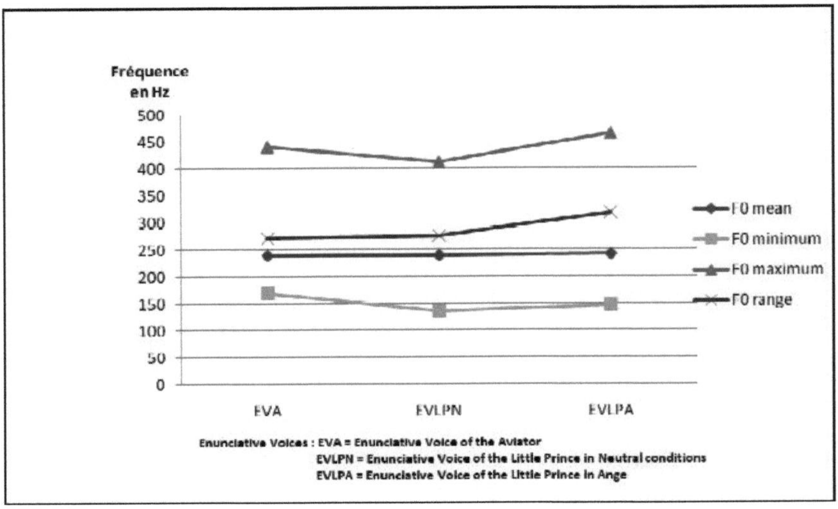

Figure 4: Comparison of pitch measures (Hz) for EVA, EVPPN and EVPPA (Italian speaker No.2).

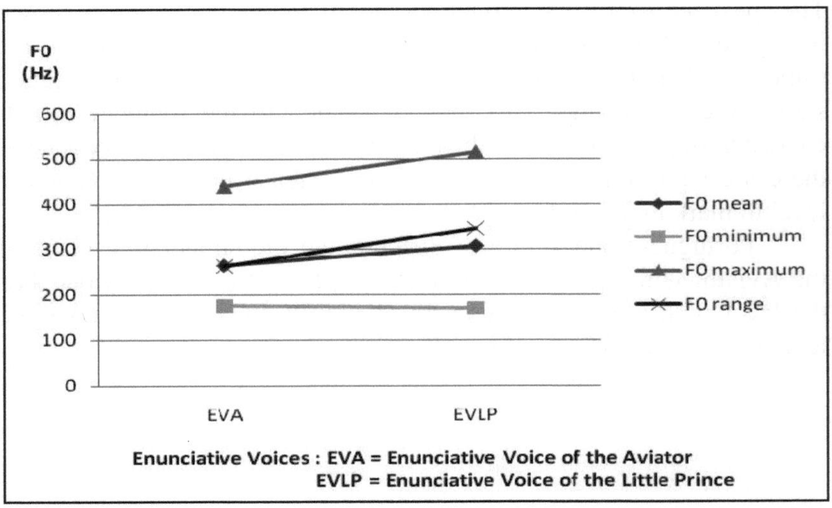

Figure 5: Comparison of pitch measures (Hz) for EVA and EVLP (Portuguese speaker No.1).

Considering the distinction between EVLPN and EVLPA, we noticed that pitch average is higher when speakers read EVLP extracts (whether the expressive value be neutral or angry) compared to EVA ones. Speakers therefore differentiate enunciative voices with prosody. For extreme measures (minimum, maximum and pitch range) values are lower for EVLPN than for EVA and EVA is lower than EVLPA. This gradation is a consequence of EVA utterances not being necessarily neutral. EVLPN differs from the two other enunciative voices by higher pitch range and pitch maximum. We can conclude that Portuguese speakers use average pitch to distinguish enunciative voices and maximum pitch to mark expressiveness and especially anger.

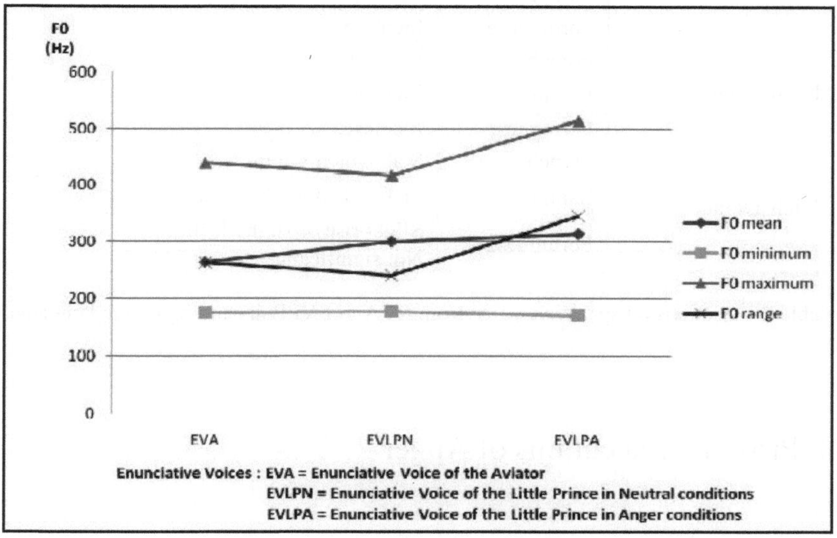

Figure 6: Comparison of pitch measures (Hz) for EVA, EVLPN and EVLPA (Portuguese speaker No.1).

We also measured the fundamental frequency for Italian and Portuguese speakers to determine whether speakers use pitch variations in the same way. Table 2 presents a comparative synthesis. Fundamental frequency is a key parameter used to express anger as is shown by the distinct enunciative voices in this corpus. In addition, we make the assumption that some speakers raise their voices to their highest frequencies to imitate the childish voice of the Little Prince, a characteristic of the vocal expression of anger. It seems that the prosodic parameters traditionally described as typical of anger also result here in the discursive function of prosody since they are used to mark enunciative voice alternation.

Prosodic parameters	Language	Variation from EVA to EVPP
Pitch minimum	French	Stable
	Italian	Stable or declining
	Portuguese	Slight fall
Pitch maximum	French	Increase
	Italian	Increase
	Portuguese	Increase
Pitch range	French	Increase
	Italian	Increase
	Portuguese	Increase
Pitch average	French	Stable or slight increase
	Italian	Stable or slight increase
	Portuguese	Slight rise or slight decline Not significant

Table 2 Variations on speaker's voice from EVA to EVPP depending on the language.

4. Prosodic Executions of Anger

We reported the characteristics of our corpus and pointed out one of its particularities and difficulties. The different enunciative voices of the text are read loudly by only one speaker-reader. That is why the speaker has to use prosodic marks in order to alternate the roles, the enunciative voices, especially in the conversational parts of the text. However, one of the most relevant cues for anger expression and detection, i.e., F_0 mean and F_0 variations, is also used in our corpus to indicate the changes of enunciative voices. The F_0 range and F_0

maximum level have two functions in our corpus: expressive and discursive. So we can suppose that the other cues have distinguishing expressive parts compared to 'neutral' ones. Since F_0 values are not only assigned to the expressive function, we took into account other parameters like tempo, and more particularly speech rate. Furthermore, we drew up a typology of the melodic patterns of anger productions.

4.1. Speech and Elocution Rate

In this literature, speech and elocution rate are distinguished. Speech rate is calculated by timing the speech units (syllables, words, etc.) in seconds or minutes. Speech rate includes pauses since the elocution rate takes into account only utterances pronounced in a certain time unit. Speech and elocution rates have been calculated (syllables/second) for the three French speakers in the EVPPN and EVPPA conditions.

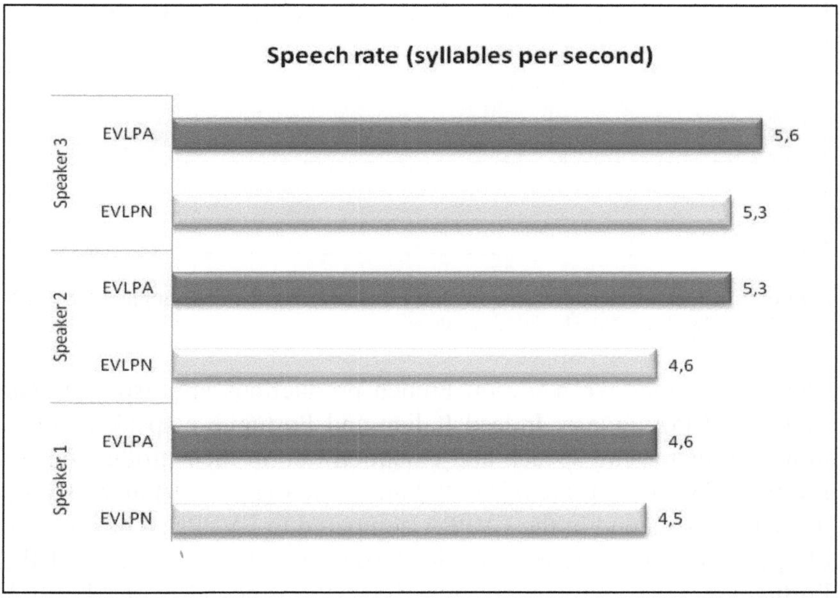

Figure 7: Values of speech rate (syllables/second) for the realisations of EVPPN and EVPPA by three French native speakers.

Both figures show that tempo accelerates in the realisations of EVPPA compared to EVPPN ones. Indeed speech and elocution rates increase when expressing anger. This increase is observed for all the three French speakers but it is more significant for the values of the elocution rate. These results correspond to those obtained in previous studies. The results also show that tempo is a parameter as relevant as fundamental frequency for the expression of anger. Rhythm can also act as an alternative to F_0 in case F_0 assumes another function than the expressive one.

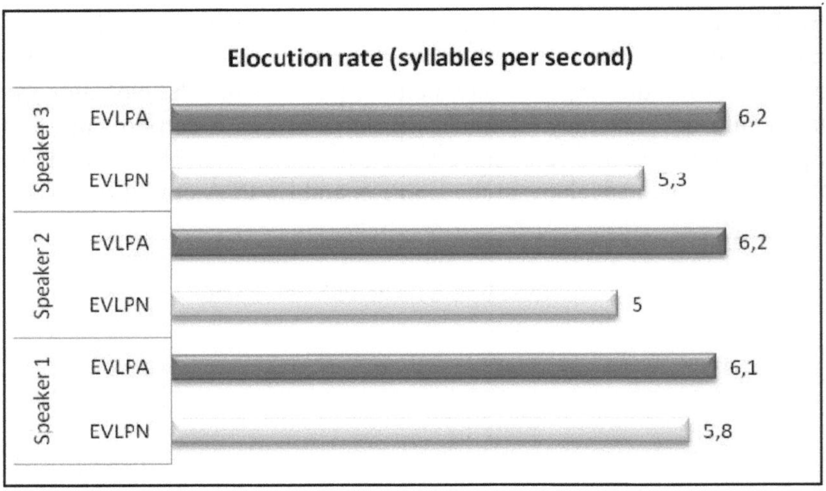

Figure 8: Values of elocution rate (syllables/second) for the realisations of EVPPN and EVPPA by three French native speakers.

The observations we made on French productions are also valid for Italian and Portuguese. Indeed Italian and Portuguese speakers seem to use an increasing speech and elocution rate in their productions of EVPPA. The speech rate of the Italian speaker (Figure 9) increases by 0.3 syllables/second in the EVPPA compared to EVPPN. The increase of speech rate is more relevant in Portuguese: the speech rate of the Portuguese speaker increases by 1.1 syllables/second in the EVPPA compared to EVPPN, and the elocution rate increases by 1.2 syllables/second. In contrast to the French Productions, the difference between speech and elocution rates is not significant (0.1 syllables/second for both enunciative voices in Italian; 0.4 syllables/second for the EVPPA and 0.3 syllables/second for the EVPPN in Portuguese). These results suggest that Portuguese and Italian speakers do not use pauses for both EVPPA and EVPPN. But for these three languages (Italian, Portuguese and French) tempo is one of the prosodic cues relevant for the expression of anger.

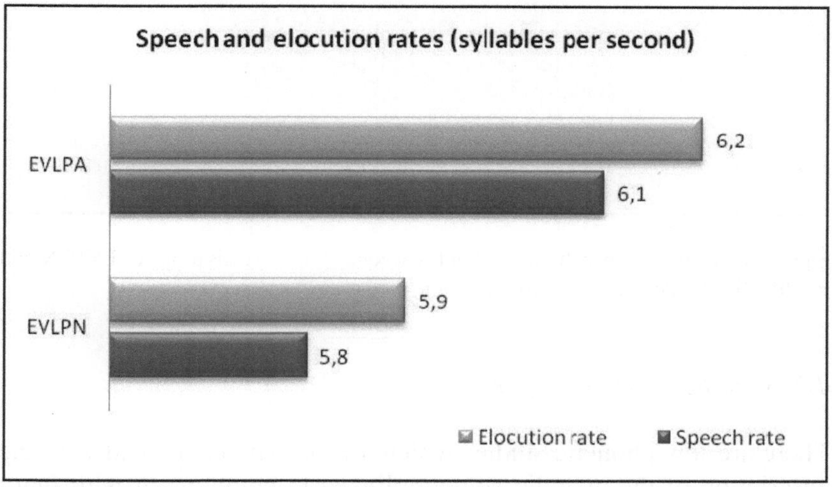

Figure 9: Values of speech rate (syllables/second) for the realisations of EVPPN and EVPPA (Italian speaker No.3).

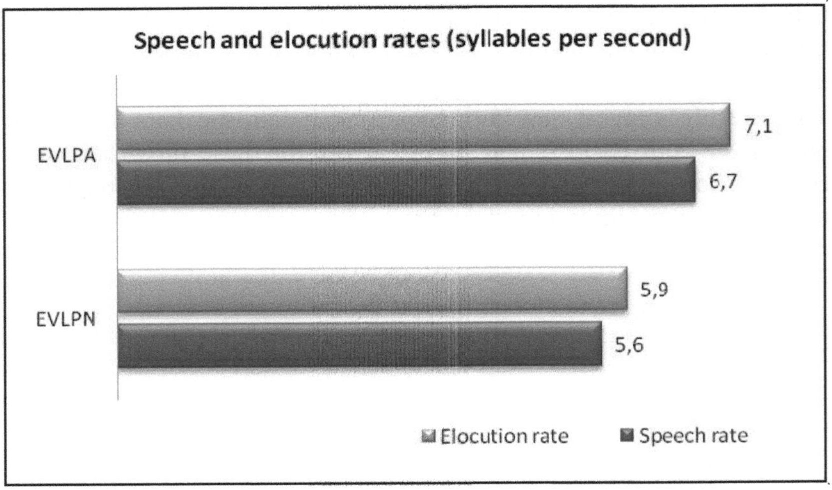

Figure 10: Values of speech rate (syllables/second) for the realisations of EVPPN and EVPPA (Portuguese speaker No.2).

4.2. Melodic curves of anger

There are few phonetic studies which are actually concerned with the description of the melodic contours linked to emotions. It is difficult to isolate the various factors of the prosodic variations and attribute them to the different functions of intonation. Fónagy (1983) is one of the few besides Léon (1971), van Bezooyen (1984), Anolli/Ciceri (1992), Ohala (1996). Fónagy offers a description of the melodic contour of anger as follows:

> A straight melodic line is interrupted at quite regular intervals on strong prominent syllables by sudden pitch which rises up to a fourth or a fifth. (1983: 909-912, our translation)

Abadjieva *et al.* (1983) notices that anger is also characterized by a strongly descending pitch which falls at the end of the utterance.

4.3. Some Examples of Melodic Curves in French

We were interested in the productions of anger by French speakers in order to see whether they corresponded to the descriptions from previous studies. Figure 11 below represents the melodic curve for the sentence 'Ce n'est pas important, ça!' ("It is not important, that!") which is the Little Prince's utterance in our corpus.

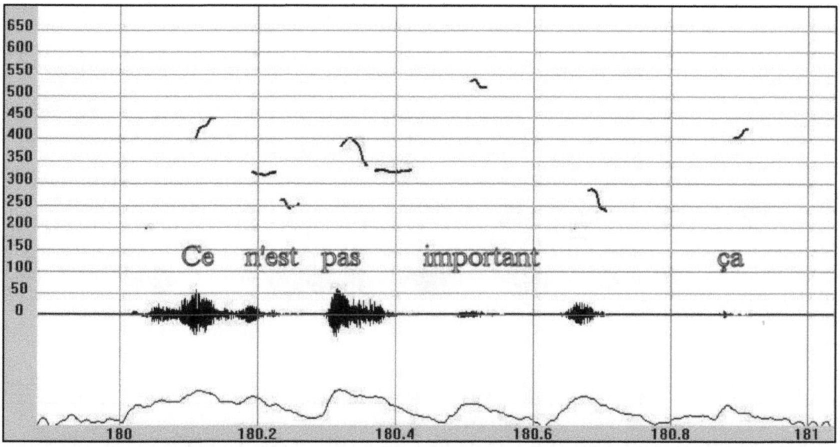

Figure 11 *:* Representation of the Melodic Curve (WinPitch Pro) of the sentence "It is not important, that!" (French speaker No.1).

The pitch rise on the last syllable "that" is due to the interrogative meaning of the sentence. However, we can attribute the high register of this final rising contour to the exclamation mark that ends the written sentence. This mark conveys expressiveness and has been acted out by the speaker-reader as an angry contour. The exclamation mark is present in the two other languages too. In addition, one finds that pitch rises as described by Fónagy in particular on the penultimate syllable of "important". The voice rises almost 200Hz up to 550Hz, which is a very high frequency value even for a woman's voice. In general the sentence is produced at a rather high register since the F_0 values do not decrease to a lower value than 250Hz. The pitch rise is not necessarily congruent with the last stressed syllable of the syntactic group.

The example below (Figure 12) presents a flat melodic contour, at least at the beginning of the sentence, with a very sharp pitch fall on the last syllable (Abadjieva & al. 1993). It is also produced at a relatively high register (above 300Hz).

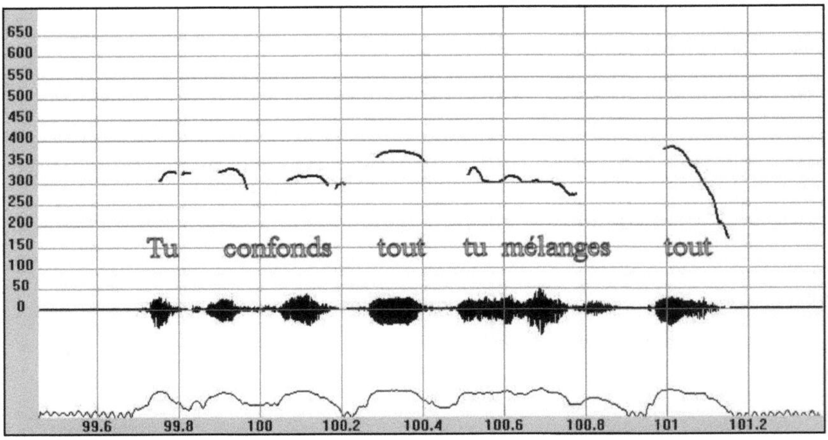

Figure 12 : Representation of the Melodic Curve (WinPitch Pro) of the sentence "You confuse everything, you mix everything !" (French speaker No.2).

The utterance is divided into two parts each one beginning on a flat F_0 line and ending with a higher value on the last syllable (the final syllable having a sharp dive). Moreover these two syllables are lengthened, compared to the other ones, which accentuates their prominence. As a whole it gives the impression of a Weak-Strong-W-S (iambic) rhythm. The second part is at a faster tempo. The high melodicity of the first example is replaced here by variations at the temporal level.

This example does not indicate that melodic rises are as important as in the example above. However, there is a final contour which dives sharply at the end of the utterance. On the last syllable of the sentence the melodic contour drops abruptly, a fall of more than 200Hz.

In this example, we have an illustration of the relation between syntactic and prosodic structures. The utterance is divided into two parts with a falling final contour: the first part does not end on a rise but rather on a flat high contour which indicates that it is not the end and that there is no dependent relation which follows. It is like an enumeration of exclamatory phrases. Within each sentence there is a 'slope contrast'. We can say that in spite of the obvious expressive function of intonation, the phonosyntactic organization of the utterance is respected (Martin 2006). The melodic patterns conveying the expression of anger in French fairly well match descriptions found in previous studies.

4.4. Stress and prosodic features in Italian and Portuguese

Before describing intonation curves in our Italian and Portuguese corpora, we think that it is important to remember some facts concerning prosody and stress patterns of these two languages when comparing them to French. Despite some common characteristics in prosodic structure such as declination and concentration at the end of the phrase (sentence or clause) of the enunciation modality marks (Bertinetto/Magno Caldognetto 1993; Mateus 1982), the location of stress is different in French, Italian and Portuguese. It has an impact on prosody. French has syntagmatic stress while Italian and Portuguese have lexical ones (Mateus/Falé/Freitas 2005, Léon 1992). Therefore, stress can play a demarcative role. It can be a cue for syntagm boundaries in French and a cue for each word in the other two languages. Stress is not fixed in Italian and Portuguese. It may fall on one of the last three syllables. It may be predicted according to phonological rules but it bears more frequently on the penultimate (for Italian, see Rossi 1998, and for Portuguese, Mateus/Andrade 2000). In these two languages the final intonation contour indicating modality occurs on the last stressed syllable and stretches on the following unstressed syllables (Martin 2005).

In French the final prosodic contour and the last stress of the syntagm coincide on the final syllable. Hence, the distinctive pitch variation occurs only on the last syllable. In Italian and Portuguese, prosodic feature variation (F_0, intensity, duration) is used jointly to express word stress and intonation pitch. In P. Martin's model, the use of variation on prosodic features is strictly connected to stress. A 'prosodic word' is defined by the fact that it contains one stressed word and perhaps several un- or de-stressed words. In French a pitch change occurring somewhere other than the final syllable of a group implies emphasis, while in the other two languages this same variation depends on the variable stress position. Whatever its expressive effect may be, this new prominence is superimposed to the stress pattern of the sentence. The emphasis, whether a focus or an expressive effect, adds to lexical stress.

Regarding intonation patterns the final intonation contour indicating modality, as in French, rises for a yes-no question and falls for statements (Martin 1998). Preceding contours are organised according to Martin's 'slope contrast' principle: the contours contrast if there is a syntactic dependency between two phrases. In Italian the contour of the previous group does not necessarily depend on the final contour. Two contours are possible: a 'simple' contour rising on the stressed syllable and falling on the following syllable(s), or a "complex" falling-rising one. The initial contour of the sentence seems to be always rising (Bertinetto/Magno Caldognetto 1993). In Portuguese, taking into consideration a SN-SV structure, there is a contrast between the slope of the final contour and the previous major contour (Martin 1999). Within the first syntagm the first contour is always rising and the second one falling, while the contour on the stressed syllables located between the second and the last contour is neutralized (it can be considered as a 'floating contour'). It seems essential to take into account these differences on stress and intonation structure when analyzing the utterances of anger in our corpus.

4.5. Examples of Melodic Contours in Italian and Portuguese

Looking at the Italian sentence 'Tu confondi tutto, tu mescoli tutto' (Fig. 13), which corresponds to the first French sentence analysed above (Fig. 12), we notice that it matches the characteristics described by phoneticians: an initial rising contour, a slight continuation of the rise on the last unstressed syllable of the first "tutto" and a final falling contour (Fig. 13).

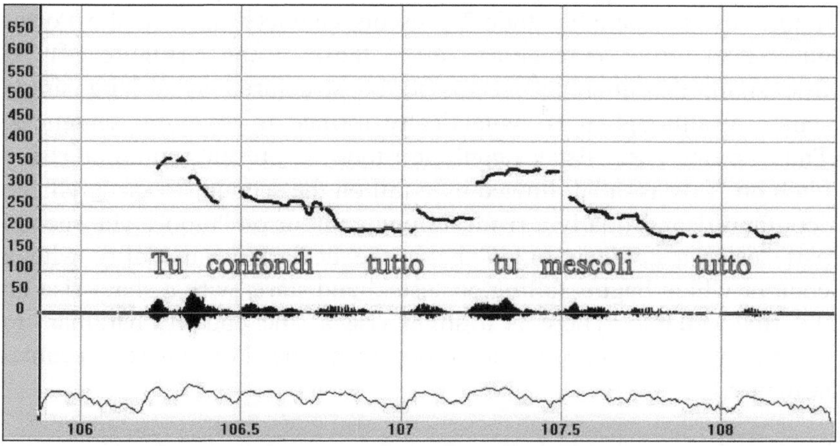

Figure 13 : Melodic curve (WinPitch Pro) of the statement "Tu confondi tutto, tu mescoli tutto", extracted from a Little Prince's sentence (Italian speaker No. 1).

If the phonosyntactic structure is not changed by the expression of anger, variations in pitch on the contrary are exaggerated in order to express the emotional state, as shown by Poggi and Magno Caldognetto (2004). The first syllable rises by 150 Hz compared to the last syllable of the previous sentence reaches a high register then falls sharply by 100 Hz in 200 ms a lower register (200 Hz) at the end of the first sentence. The same curve is repeated in the following sentence which gives the sentence a regular tempo. Lexical repetitions are emphasized. It is interesting to note that there is a mirror image of the French corresponding sentence in Italian: it is S-W / S-W, the same stress pattern and increase in anger. The speech rate used by the speaker for the utterances of anger is not fast (5.5 syllables per second on an average of 6.2). There is a notable shortening of the duration of the last stressed syllables, which are normally significantly longer than the final unstressed syllables. This variation in local tempo enhances the prominence of the preceding 'tu', thus giving the impression of a faster end which could be attributed to the fluctuation in emotion conveyed by stage directions.

The corresponding Portuguese sentence "Estás a confundir tudo... estás a baralhar tudo!" presents characteristics of the Portuguese declarative sentence as well as those of anger (Figure 14). At first sight, the utterance seems to be structured as a long single sentence, although it is syntactically formed by two full sentences. Thus the first part, "Estás a confundir tudo..." presents an initial rising pitch on "(e)stas+a " followed by a fall on the second stressed syllable "confundir" and finally a rising-falling contour on "tudo". The second part "estás a baralhar tudo!" bears the declarative modality with a contour which begins falling on 'estas' and starts with a sharp rise on the first syllable. There is a slight rise at the end of 'baralhar' to contrast with the final fall according to normal Portuguese accentual structure.

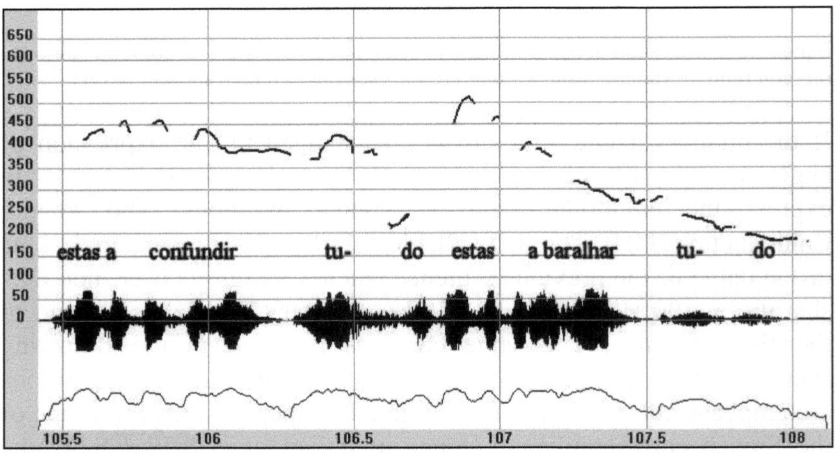

Figure 14 : Melodic curve (WinPitch Pro) of the statement "Estás a confundir tudo... estás a baralhar tudo!" (Portuguese speaker No. 1).

Cruz-Ferreira (Cruz-Ferreira 1998) describes the expression of aggressiveness in Portuguese as a succession of several abrupt falls on stressed syllables. Their starting point is higher and higher. This series of falls often ends by a creaky voice on the last syllables which is not really the case in our example. Anger in this example is marked by a high pitch at the beginning of each part. The first part 'estas a confondir tu-' lies between 458 and 385 Hz, contrasting strongly with the unstressed syllable '-do', falling to 217Hz. This abrupt fall of F_0 (more than 200 Hz, from 420 to 220 Hz) between the two syllables of "tudo" following the initial long prominence at 450 Hz, contributes to characterize anger.

In the second part, F_0 falls gradually from 514 to 180Hz on the final 'do' with a strong lowering in intensity. Here again it can be associated with 'desperate anger'. The resetting, from 220 Hz to 514 Hz at the beginning of the second part contributes to the realisation of successive falls. As a whole we find, like in Italian, a Strong-Weak-S-W // S-W rhythm.

Speech rate is also an important element to mark anger. While the whole sentence is uttered with a fast speech rate, the speaker varies the local tempo on the two 'tudo' and within each of them. This also contributes to the expression of anger.

5. Discussion and Conclusion

The aim of our study is to propose a prosodic analysis of anger in French compared to two other Romance languages: Italian and Portuguese. With this intention we chose to analyse a corpus of read speech and a corpus of acted out emotional expressions. Contrary to numerous studies based on a corpus of acted out speech, the emotional expressions were induced by the situation of text enunciation. We based our analysis on a corpus of emotional expressions whose semantic content was not neutralized. This characteristic led us to question the relevance of an analysis of anger based only on values and statistical calculations of prosodic parameters.

We showed that the expression of anger in French was characterized not only by a general increase of F_0 values but also that these same values could represent other aspects of communication:

they were not just useful for the expressive function. We also showed in this situation of enunciation the necessity of including melodic contours in the study of emotional expressions in order to distinguish the really relevant variations for the description of anger more clearly. From one Romance language to another, similarities were highlighted, such as melodic contours and the high register of anger in spite of intonation differences in these three languages.

While enabling us to establish the bases for a comparative analysis of an emotional expression in three Romance languages, this study opens up interesting perspectives on: i) a methodology that can lead to comparative analyses of several emotional expressions in different languages; ii) research relating to the same emotion which at the same time maintains multilingual aspects and uses as its basis a spontaneous speech corpus.

References

Abadjieva, Elissaveta / Murray, Iain R. / Arnott, John L. 1993. Applying analysis of human emotional speech to enhance syn-thetic speech. in *Eurospeech 93 Proceedings*, Berlin, 909-912.

Adam, Jean-Michel 2002. Séquence. In Charaudeau, Patrick / Maingeneau, Dominique (eds), *Dictionnaire d'analyse du discours*. Paris, Seuil, 525-528.

Adam, Jean-Michel 2001. *Les textes: types et prototypes*, Paris, Nathan.

Adam, Jean-Michel 2008. *La linguistique textuelle. Introduction à l'analyse textuelle des discours*, Paris, Armand Colin.

Anolli, Luigi / Ciceri, Rita 1992. *La voce delle emozioni*, Milano, Franco Angeli.

Banse, Rainer / Scherer, Klaus R. 1996. Acoustic profiles in vocal emotion expression. In *Journal of Personality and Social Psychology*, 70 (3), 614-636.

Bänziger Tanja 2004. *Communication vocale des émotions. Perception de l'expression vocale et attributions émotionnelles*, thèse, sous la direction de K.R. Scherer, Université de Genève, section de Psychologie.

Bänzinger, Tanja / Grandjean, Didier / Bernard, Pierre-Jean / Klasmeyer, Gudrun / Scherer, Klaus. R. 2001. Prosodie de l'émotion: Étude de l'encodage et du décodage. In *Cahiers de linguistique française*, 23, 11-37.

Van Bezooyen, Renée 1984. *Characteristics and recognizability of vocal expressions of emotions*, Foris, Dordrecht.

Bertinetto, Pier Marco / Magno Caldognetto, Emanuela 1993. Ritmo e intonazione. In Alberto A. Sobrero (ed.) *Introduzione all'italiano contemporaneo. Le strutture*, Bari, Laterza, 141-192.

Boulakia, Georges 2007. Voce e attitudini: recitazione d'Attore. Studio di fonetica sperimentale. In Proceedings of the international conference *Les langages de la voix. Hommage à Ivan Fonagy*, 12 Octobre 2007, Université Roma 3 (in press).

Caelen-Haumont, Geneviève 2005. Les états émotionnels et la Prosodie : paradigmes, modèles, paramètres. In *Phonologie et phonétique: forme et substance*, 397-424, Paris, Hermès.

Campbell, Nick 2000. Databases of emotional speech. In *Proceedings ISCA ITRW on Speech and Emotion: Developing a Conceptual Framework*, Newcastle, North Ireland, 5-7 September 2000, Belfast, 34-39.

Catach, Nina 1996. *La ponctuation*, coll. « Que sais-je ? », P.U.F, 63.

Chung, Soo-Jin 2000. *L'expression et la perception de l'émotion extraite de la parole spontanée : évidences du coréen et de l'anglais*, Thèse de l'Université Paris 3 (Sorbonne Nouvelle).

Cruz-Ferreira Madalena 1998. Intonation in European Portuguese. In Hirst/Di Cristo (eds), *Intonation Systems. A Survey of Twenty Languages*, Cambridge, Cambridge University Press.167-178.

Danon-Boileau Laurent / Morel Marie-Annick 1995. Présentation générale. In Faits de langues 6, 5-12.

Fónagy, Ivan 1983. *La vive voix: Essais de psycho-phonétique*, Bibliothèque scientifique, Paris, Payot.

Fónagy, Ivan 1987. Vocal expression of Emotions and Attitudes. Dynamic distinctive features. In *Affettività e sistemi semiotici. Le passioni nel discorso*, VS 47/48, Bompiani, 65-85.

Fónagy, Ivan / Bérard Eva 2006. Functions of intonation. In Kawagushi, Yuji / Fónagy, Ivan / Morigushi, Tsunekazu (eds) *Prosody and Syntax*, John Benjamins, 19-46.

Johnstone, Tom / Scherer, Klaus R. 1999. The effects of emotions on voice quality. In *Proceedings of the 14th ICPhS*, San-Francisco, 2029-2032.

Juslin, Patrik N. / Laukka, Petri 2001. Impact of intended emotion intensity on cue utilization and decoding accuracy in vocal expression of emotion. In *Emotion*, 1(4), 381-412.

Kerbrat-Orecchioni, Catherine 1990. *Les interactions verbales*, tome 1, Paris, Colin.

Léon, Pierre 1971. *Essais de phonostylistique*, Studia Phonetica 4, Paris, Didier.

Léon, Pierre 1992. *Phonétique et prononciation du français*, Paris, Nathan.

Léon, Pierre 1993. Précis de Phonostylistique: Parole et expressivité, Paris, Nathan.

Martin, Philippe. 2004. WinPitchPro A Tool for Text to Speech Alignment and Prosodic Analysis. In *Speech Prosody 2004 Proceedings*, 23-24 March 2004, Nara, Japon, 545-548.

Martin, Philippe 1998. *Prosodie des langues romanes: Analyse phonétique et phonologie*, University of Toronto.

Martin, Philippe 1999. L'intonation du français et du portugais: phonétique et phonologie. In *Revista de l'AMPOLL Sao Paulo*, vo. 5/7, 255-295.

Martin, Philippe 2005. Models of analysis and prosodic labeling systems. In *Atti del II Convegno Nazionale dell'Associazione Italiana di Scienze della Voce. Analisi Prosodica: teorie, modelli e sistemi di annotazione*, Fisciano, 30 novembre – 2 dicembre 2005, 43-56.

Martin, Philippe 2006. Intonation du Français : Parole spontanée et parole lue. In *Estudios de Fonética Experimental*, 15, 133-162.

Mateus Maria Helena et al 1982. *Gramatica da lingua portuguesa*, Almedina.

Mateus, Maria Helena / Andrade, Ernesto d' 2000. *The Phonology of Portuguese*. Oxford, University Press.

Mateus, Maria Helena / Falé, Isabel / Freitas, Maria-João 2005. *Fonética e Fonologia do Português*, Lisboa, Universidade Aberta.

Mathon, Catherine 2007. Multimodal Analysis of Anger in Natural Speech Data. In *Proceedings of 16th ICPhS*, Saarbrücken, 6-10 August 2007, 2117-2120.

Mouratidou Eleni 2007. Texte dramatique et indices intonatifs : la voix au théâtre. I*n Sémio 2007 : Rencontres sémiotiques. Les interfaces disciplinaires. Des théories aux pratiques professionnelles, Actes du colloque organisé par l'Association Française de Sémiotique et le laboratoire DynaLang-SEM*, Paris, Sorbonne, 15-17 novembre 2007 (in press).

Ohala, John 1996. Ethological theory and the expression of emotion in the voice. In *Proc. ICSLP 96, October 3-6, 1996. [4th International Conference on Spoken Language Processing,* Philadelphia]. Wilmington: University of Delaware. Vol. 3, 1812-1815.

Poggi, Isabella / Magno Caldognetto, Emanuela 2004. Il parlato emotivo. Aspetti cognitivi, linguistici e fonetici. In *Atti del convegno Il parlato italiano*, Napoli. 12-15 febbraio 2003, Napoli, D'Auria, CD-Rom.

Rossi, Mario 1998. Intonation in Italian. In Hirst/Di Cristo (eds), *Intonation Systems. A Survey of Twenty Languages*, Cambridge, Cambridge University Press 228-247.

Saint-Exupéry, Antoine, de 1997 [1946]. *Le Petit Prince*. Paris, Gallimard, 27-30.

Scherer, Klaus R. 2000. Psychological models of emotion. In J. Borod (ed.). *The neuropsychology of emotion*, Oxford/New-York, Oxford University Press, 137-162.

Traverso, Véronique 2002. Réplique. In Charaudeau, Patrick / Maingeneau, Dominique (eds), *Dictionnaire d'analyse du discours*. Paris, Seuil, 502.

Vidrascu, Laurence / Devillers, Laurence 2005. Detection of real-life emotions in dialogs recorded in a call center. In *Interspeech 2005 Proceedings*, Lisboa, September 4-8 2005, 1841-1844.

GENEVIÈVE CAELEN-HAUMONT

Emotion, Emotions and Prosodic Structure: an Analysis of Melisms Patterns and Statistical Results in the Spontaneous Discourse of Four Female Speakers over Four Generations

1. Introduction

As Cowie (2000) aptly notes, it is necessary first to identify two uses of the word 'emotion', uses that coincide with the singular and plural word forms. Thus in the plural, the term refers to pure emotions such as fear, joy, anger and so on, with their own characteristics, features and boundaries. In the singular, the term refers to the attributes of certain psychological states: for example, we often hear it said that such a person spoke with emotion. It therefore means an emotional state. Finally, to reflect other recent developments in research, the expression *emotional systems* should also be added for biological applications.

Since Descartes, it has also been customary to distinguish other basic emotions, usually listed as six, i.e. *fear, anger, joy, sadness, surprise, disgust,* plus sometimes *love* and *contempt,* and two declinations of *anger*: '*hot*' and '*cold*'. Emotional states, apart from these primary emotions are very diverse and Plutchik (1980), for example, has identified up to 142. These emotional states are sometimes referred to as secondary emotions. These emotional states are complex, insofar as they often combine several characteristics of the basic emotions.

In the field of affectivity, a related concept to that of emotion, and one frequently used in prosodic studies, is that of *attitude*. It is very difficult to distinguish/identify these two concepts by specific or defining traits. These attitudes still outnumber emotional states: O'Connor and Arnold (1973), for example, refer to almost 300, including: *abrupt, accusatory, affable, affected, approving, arrogant*, and so on. For an extensive review of work in the different domains of emotions, cf. Caelen-Haumont (2005), and Caelen-Haumont and Zei (2007).

The aim of this chapter is mainly to analyse more deeply an emotional state which corresponds to common personal involvement in speech. We will focus in particular on the structure of pitch prominences, termed *melisms* (see the definition below, §2.3). Founded on the one hand on a database containing 400 melisms (100 melisms x 4 speakers) with their context, including F_0 and timing features, and on the other hand on a method of description providing a high degree of precision, the study provides new results 1) on the pitch patterns of these so-called melisms, their specific motives, statistical results, also taking into account the problems of duration and speech flow rates, 2) a comparative study between melisms and sequences of joy using a different database.

2. Prosody and emotion(s)

2.1. Valence, power, activation

Concerning the domain of emotions, some methods and key concepts cut across the whole domain. In order to more objectively analyze the emotions perceived, psychologists work with a gradient definition of features, i.e. on dimensions, which requires the development of specialized tools. For example with FEELTRACE, Cowie et al. (2000) offer a representation in the form of a circular space where the dimensions of *activation* and *evaluation* are represented on two orthogonal axes, splitting up the disc into four sectors where users can place their observations on emotions. This device is supplemented by a study of parameter changes over time, "allowing the emotional dynamics of speech episodes to be examined" (ibid.). Activation measures the dynamics of the emotional state, i.e. the degree of *excitation*. *Evaluation* measures *valence*, a concept introduced into psychology by Kurt Lewin (1936) in the thirties. The *valence* is the positive or negative feeling associated with an emotional state vis-à-vis people, events or things. Thus, the emotions popularly referred to as negative, such as anger and fear, have a *negative valence*, whereas joy has a *positive valence*.

At the centre of this circular space is the point which corresponds to emotional neutrality, and on the outskirts, the degree of the most intense emotions.

The degree of *activation* is used to evaluate the strength according to which a person is willing to undertake some action rather than another. This dimension is to be associated in particular with Frijda's (1986) research in which emotional states are seen as trends to action. Correlates are also, of course, found in the field of speech, and studies have been conducted in this area to determine whether the voice parameters can account for the arousal states of emotions.

In the domain of speech, a *positive activation* such as joy, fear, anger (and to a certain extent, surprise, excitement, bewilderment) is considered in the literature as contributing to a raising of the *mean and range of* F_0, and to the tension of the voice, while a *negative activation*, such as sadness, grief, boredom is conversely associated with their *lowering*.

2.2. Semantics, Pragmatics and F_0 *range*

The problem of relations between, on the one hand, semantics, pragmatics and, on the other hand, the range of F_0 (ΔF_0), or the highest F_0 values (F_0max) in words, has been carefully studied in previous works. That study was carried out first in the context of three readings (Caelen-Haumont 1991; 1993; forthcoming) of the same text (12 speakers x 3 readings), presenting a panel of given/new information, expected and unexpected ones, and of words with a more or less complex meaning as well, and under three levels of intelligibility constraints (no constraint, intelligible reading, and very intelligible for a computer to understand). This work based on different quantitative models assessing different levels of complexity in semantics and of unexpectedness in pragmatics (and also complexity of the syntactic relation in the structure) showed, among other things, that the greatest ΔF_0, and the highest F_0max were related to the most complex words and unexpected ones. Moreover, Meiyé et al. (1998) and Meiyé (1999) in the psycholinguistic domain brought a confirmation of this work with a new corpus and specific methods attached to this field.

For spontaneous speech, different studies have been carried out in dialogue interactions (Caelen-Haumont 2004), in French conversations (Morange 2005) as well as in a tonal Bantu language, i.e. in Bàsàa (Makasso 2008), and in the context of interactions in a French nursery school between the teacher and pupils (Vuillet 2005). All these studies using the same semantic perspective of lexical networks (isotopy), converged on the conclusions that 1) there exist strong relations between the most important or unexpected information, which corresponds to the greatest speaker involvement in his/her speech, and ΔF_0 and F_0max; 2) the greatest ΔF_0 or the highest F_0 values (all in the melisms) concerned the lexical items within isotopy networks.

This new study, based on new corpora of spontaneous dialogues, aims to provide a complementary perspective, trying to structure the very unstable and variable stuff of the melodic prominences.

2.3. Intonation and melism spaces

Following earlier studies (Caelen-Haumont 1991, 2000, forthcoming), we can distinguish two melodic spaces: the space of intonation, and the space of melody and lexical prosody. The intonation space is the expression of the language structure as a social inheritance suitable for the community which implements it, and the place of a bequeathed, learned and shared practice. This practice is stable insofar as it is regulated by the social convention which endows it with a normative frame (standardization), exercising an action of coercive type. In these conditions, this practice leads to an invariant prosody, or rather, to a prosody which remains quite stable over decades.

This prosodic structure engendered in that ground is general, performing an external point of view, out of time, out of context (semantic and pragmatic), since it is syntagmatic or syntactic. As a result, it is usually inclined towards an outside authority, giving the speech a connotation of general, non-contingent truth. It puts the individual in an objectivized and rational relation to the world of people, objects and ideas. Intonation thus plays a function of morpho-syntactic, syntactic nature or simply syntagmatic. This is the domain of the make-known, make-heard and make-understood (Caelen-Haumont, forthcoming).

But this type of speech, based exclusively on intonation, quickly becomes boring and ultimately unpleasant. This effect of monotony comes not only because of the repetition of syntactic patterns of prosody. It also stems from the fact that the speaker is perceived as absent from his/her statement. Indeed, the subjective element at the root of the expression of words – the essential component of motivated speech, and especially spontaneous speech – is not then invested by the speaker: it is in fact relegated to an outside, absent authority. The basic pragmatic conditions (at least the *nunc* and *ego*) are not fulfilled, and interest is not aroused any more in the listener, who does not feel concerned, and nor does the speaker. But consequently, the space devoted to the structure, the place of the social practice (and hence power) in itself leaves little room for personal expression. Now for the message to be received in an optimal manner by a person or group, it should be perceived (and therefore produced) as the expression of a belief. To arouse this belief, then the support (but also, its corollary, the rejection), and even action, the message has to contain a subjective dimension, which is the space of the individual meeting and interaction.

This subjective dimension, to be perceived, is necessarily embodied in physical parameters and in a space, by nature and by necessity, distinct from the former. In oral production, the elements of personal expression repose naturally on subjectivity and its components. The practice of speech supposes then the existence of a dynamic spring of emotional type: in our view, this spring is belief. When we speak freely in a spontaneous way, our words usually express our conviction, i.e., what we perceive as our truth at that moment.

So a type of particular emotion is given way here, which can be qualified as *common emotion*, denoting in fact the *mechanism at the root of the subjective being, and of his/her commitment in the utterances*. It is this common emotion which supplies the reservoir common to all the actors of a situation of communication, which is the place of the actual meeting, sometimes even in the absence of a common language.

This common emotion, usually bound to the beliefs and the profound or more superficial values of the person, is thus always at work in speech. While this common emotion puts specific marks in the speech signal, and hence in the prosody contours, it differs from emotions referenced as joy, surprise, anger etc, but at any time, it may incline towards such emotions. The *common emotion is simply the expression of an attachment to a value, a person, an idea, an object* expressed most of the time by a single word in speech.

That common emotion, a fortiori the strong emotions, and the beliefs that underly them, determines in the speaker a mobilization of energy in terms of personal involvement. In fact, it seems that the more a person is convinced of this belief, because it belongs to his/her essential values, and/or because he/she is threatened by confrontation with other beliefs in the interaction, the greater his/her personal involvement. In this area, undoubtedly, this involvement is associated with a *hyperactivity of prosodic means*. As we shall see below with melisms, this hyperactivity is defined in terms of greater frequency contrasts, the F_0 values of which can be very high, with steeper rising or falling pitch slopes, more frequent tonal and temporal breaks, more contrastive speech flow rates, stronger intensity peaks, all of which corresponds ultimately to a more sustained effort on the part of the individual.

The more the speaker involves his faith in speech, the more he tries to be convincing, the greater the quantitative values of the prosodic cues, in particular of pitch, and the more the pitch and prosodic patterns depart from the regular syntax and intonation frames.

By these prosodic and melodic means that place words in the foreground or background, the speaker establishes a subjective scaling of the significant value of lexical units. This scaling enables him/her to report to his listeners that he/she is appropriating a sense, and so, to share his beliefs, whether involuntary, unconscious, conscious or even manipulative (to his/her knowledge or not).

2.4. F_0 range, prominence, pattern, focus and melism

In the last decades, a great number of studies have been devoted to characterizing F_0 changes in affective conditions of speaking. More precisely, concerning the matter of F_0 range, different terms are used in the literature. In fact none of these seems convenient. For instance, the term *prominence* (or *salience)* is very imprecise and refers to an impressive meaning. The term *range* refers to F_0 amplitude but delivers no information about the shape of the range. The term *pattern* is generic, it can be applied to local or global shape, and does not incorporate a phonological perspective. As for the term *focus*, it is probably one of the most common words used in this domain, but its meaning is still inadequate: indeed 'focus' refers to a binary process (focussed/unfocussed) whereas the process is actually scalar, as has been often noted. Moreover, it is rather fuzzy since it induces confusion between acoustic, semantic and pragmatic domains.

In these conditions, it was necessary to find a word 1) related to the acoustic and melodic *form*, 2) expressing the notion of a structured shape with a fitted granularity, 3) in terms of phonological structure, i.e. of a tonal system. To convey such a definition, the term *melism* appeared to be appropriate (Caelen-Haumont/Bel 2000).

The word 'melism', taken from the domain of singing and referring to a pitch pattern spreading over the duration of a word, with a series of different notes, sometimes greater than the number of syllables in the word, is applied to speech, where it is related 1) to the acoustic and melodic *form* in a scalar (and not binary) perspective, and 2) to the *subjective melodic expression*. A melism is characterised by an *raised pitch register and most of the time, by a large F_0 contrast between two successive values.*

3. Prosodic tools to explore the area of emotion(s)

3.1. PRAAT, MOMEL and MELISM tool

The procedure of the automatic MELISM tool, previously named INTSMEL, was exhaustively described in Caelen-Haumont/Auran (2004). In a few words, MELISM provides an automatic Praat TextGrid labelling (Boersma/Weenink 2008). In the overall procedure, MELISM is applied to the output of the MOMEL algorithm (Hirst/Espesser 1993, Hirst et al 2000, Hirst 2005), which computes targets and models F_0 contours. Based on perceptual grounds, the resulting MOMEL curve is thus similar to that found on a sequence of entirely sonorant segments.

The MOMEL procedure allows the automatic coding of the relevant variations of F_0, in the form of a sequence of targets which are, roughly, the turning points of the modelled F_0 curve (more precisely the points on the curve where the first derivative is zero). In this perspective, the F_0 curve is punctuated with labelled tones, regardless of the linguistic expression. The MELISM algorithm is then applied to automatically code the sequence of MOMEL target points, and this coding constitutes a surface phonological representation of tonal sequences.

Our particular purpose is to use the MELISM procedure in relation with the lexical items, which can be analysed as either isolated or integrated into the phrasal structure. Using a Praat Textgrid, the context of melisms is thus manually segmented into words.

3.2. Segmentation, automatic annotation, labelling and melisms

The target points automatically calculated by the MELISM procedure in the frame of each segmented word, are then grouped into a more or less complex sequence of phonological labels (for instance in figure 6 below, the word *sentimentales (= sentimental)*: /bb bb bb bS SH Hc cm/ ...) where the capitals correspond to the highest level targets (A,

S, or H), key points of the definition of melism. As seen in this figure, the phonological labels between two tonal targets denote the melism tones. These melism tones which occur within the limits of a word, by analogy to lexical syllables, are called *tonal syllables*.

More particularly, a set of 9 symbols (or 9 levels or thresholds): acute (= 9), supra (= 8), high (= 7), elevated (= 6), middle (= 5), centred (= 4), bottom (= 3), infra (= 2), grave (= 1) is used to automatically code absolute levels corresponding to fractions (on a logarithmic scale) of the whole speaker's pitch range.

The objectives of this phonological annotation using MELISM are:

- to give a quantitative information (F_0 value) on the speaker's targets,
- to propose on these grounds an annotation system and a stylisation independent from the phrase, sentence, corpus, speaker, gender or age parameters,
- to relate such a coding to absolute F_0 levels according to the syntagmatic axis of the utterance, but to relative levels according to the maximal speaker's pitch register,
- to phonologically describe in detail the internal structure of melismed words,
- to compare their different patterns in function of their syntactic status, their semantic, pragmatic, phonologic or prosodic values,
- to compare the different melodic systems existing in different languages, including accented ones and tonal ones,
- to objectively test theoretical hypotheses about the experimental procedures.

The present study is concerned first with the target points of the melism words, secondly with the tonal syllables, and the relations which occur between them in the frame of each melismed word.

3.3. Database

For the needs of the analysis, a database was constructed in the framework of the PFC working group (Phonologie du Français Contemporain, Projet PFC, <http://www.projet-pfc.net/>), whose objectives are to study samples of French in geographic space (all around France and in other countries in the world) and time (several generations), according to the same protocol. In such conditions, we gathered recordings from four generations of viticulturists in the same family, living for four generations in the same village and the same house in the South of France, namely Cussac-Fort-Médoc, not far from Bordeaux. From several hours of recordings, contexts where melisms occurred were manually segmented, then the MELISM procedure was applied and finally 100 melisms x 4 female speakers (thus 400 melisms on the whole) were extracted. In a second and very long task, all the data from the speakers were very carefully checked, for instance speakers F_0 extrema (F_0 minima/maxima) through their different wave files and Textgrids, or the thresholds of the procedures, etc., and hand corrected where necessary.

All the information about the four speakers' melisms were then integrated into an Excel spreadsheet, including the context and pauses, time (beginning, end, duration), the kind of melisms: *M, non-final melism* (i.e. occurring inside a prosodic group), *MP, final melism ending a group with a pause, MF, the same but without pause, MC, melism by contact* (before/after M, MP or MF), the *kind of slope* of each melism tone *(ascending, descending, plateau),* and the value in semi-tones corresponding to each target composing the melism tone.

Since true plateaux were very rare for the four speakers, they have been reported on the rising and falling melisms, in function of the details of their structure. Thus the population of the rising melisms is the biggest one, with 329 out of 400, since the number of falling melisms is only 71.

Since both rising and falling melisms do occur in speech, even though their population is not the same, this means that melisms are not directly concerned with the direction of the slope: in our opinion, the slope direction within the melisms is a matter of intonational space, not of melism, the two spaces running nevertheless as two embedded layers.

4. The structure of melisms

4.1. The extent of melism F_0 variability

The 400 melisms included 87 grammatical words, including coordinating and subordinating conjunctions, prepositions, pronominal pronouns, articles, determiners, presentatives, and consequently 313 lexical items. Since these rarely contain falling slopes (11% of them), the grammatical ones are most often decreasing (49% of them), as a consequence of their position after the melism.

The following four figures illustrate the basic descriptions of the melisms of our corpus. Figure 1 below shows the number of melisms in function of the number of tonal syllables in the 400 melisms. The most numerous melisms occur with two to five tonal syllables, and mainly with three or four syllable ones (71% of the overall melisms).

Figure 2 below presents the population of the nine tonal targets in melisms. For the highest range, the target H is the most numerous, while for the lowest ones, the targets b and c have the best rates. These two facts put together show that the most numerous melisms are focussed on the most central targets.

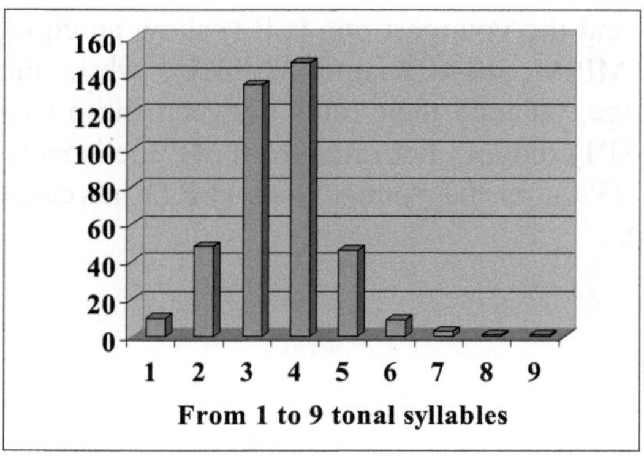

Figure 1: Number of melisms by the number of tonal syllables (over 400 melisms).

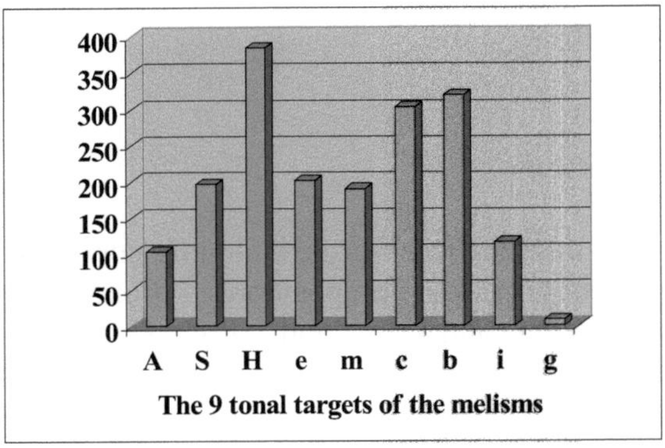

Figure 2: Number of the nine tonal targets (over 400 melisms).

Figure 3 below presents a distribution of the 400 melisms over the four melism contextual categories. The MP melisms (before a pause) is the main category (42% of all of them), but this global result hides some disparity among speakers (from 33 to 59%), the younger speakers producing less melisms before a pause than the older ones. Concerning the M melisms (which occur within a group), they represent on average 37% of the total.

These two categories being the most frequent, we now analyse in more details the contribution of each speaker. We observe that the four speakers achieve a sort of balance in the distribution of melisms. The oldest speaker (HV1) and the youngest one (LR2) show an equal distribution (respectively MP-M, 40-40% and 33-33%), while the other two, in the middle age, balance their rates between these two categories: the older one (SP1) reduces her rates from MP melisms to M ones (MP: 59% to M: 23%), as the younger one (LR1) increases hers (MP: 35% to M: 51%).

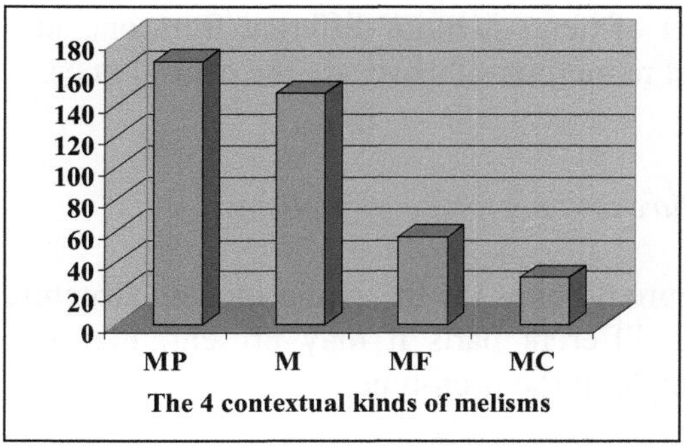

Figure 3: Number of melisms in each kind of melism structure.

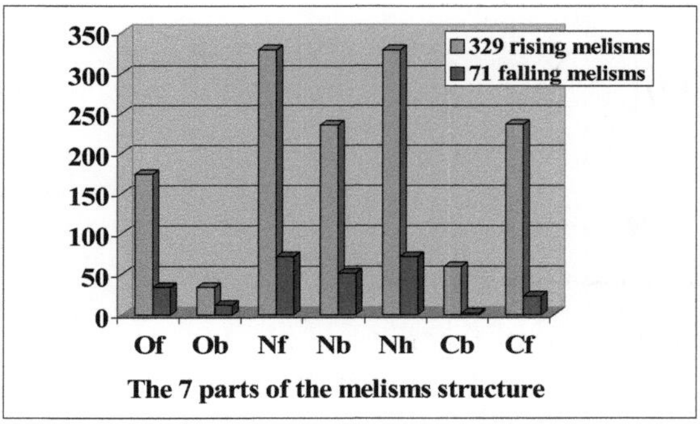

Figure 4: Number of melisms in each of their seven subparts.

Moreover the balance is completed with the MF melisms, denoting the melisms ending a group without a pause, which represent only 14% of all the melisms. As a matter of fact, for the three oldest speakers (HV1, SP1, LR1), the rates for the MP, M, and MF melisms are exactly equal (94%), the MC melisms as such being also equal (6%). On the other hand, the youngest one (LR2) presents the smallest dispersion of her items (MP: 33%, M: 33%, MF: 22%, MC: 12%).

Figure 4 above shows a distribution of the 400 rising and falling melisms over each part and subpart of the melism structure. This structure is presented and commented in the next section, but we can already observe 1) that the distribution of the two kinds of melisms according to the rising vs. falling direction of their slopes follow the same pattern, 2) the number of items is quite different from one subpart to the other, 3) the most numerous subparts are the central ones.

4.2. Internal melodic structure and prototype of Melisms

Here (see Figure 5 and Figure 6 below) is the rising melism structure prototype, showing all the different parts it may present. Figure 5 below shows an actual example of the prototype.

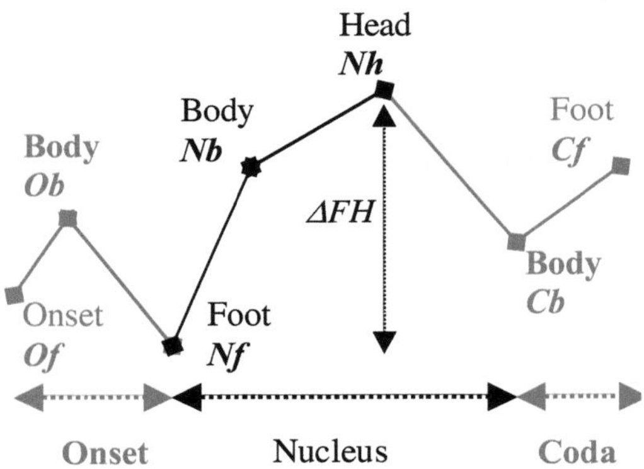

Figure 5: The rising melism structure prototype

Just like physiological units (phonetic or syllabic ones), we assume that this structure can be divided into three main parts: in chronological order, the *onset* or *O* (pale grey drawing), the *nucleus* or *N* (black drawing), and the *coda* or *C* (pale grey drawing). Of these three parts, *only the nucleus, including the F_0 minimum and maximum, is compulsory:* it is indeed the *heart of the melism* in terms of range and slope direction. Nevertheless, in many cases, the onset and the coda are present.

More precisely, each of these three parts can be made up of several subparts, and each subpart, of one or several targets. The subparts assuming the same function are denoted by the same terms, which are for instance for the rising melisms:

1- *foot*, in the sense of any *context anchorage*, is used for the beginning *(Of)* and the end *(Cf)* of the linguistic (i.e. lexical and more rarely grammatical) unit, and for the beginning of the nucleus part *(Nf)* which can also be the melism beginning. With the nucleus head *(Nh)* which is the melism highest F_0 value, *these four targets (Of, Nf, Nh, Cf) are the most important ones in the frame of the melism,*

2 *body* is used for the others that may occur between these main targets.

Table 1 below presents the properties of the melism com-ponents, the number and percentages of these items. The population and per-centages are computed on all the rising and falling melisms, as they occur in the data. In this kind of structure, there is a clear opposition between the 'body subparts' and the other subparts: the three feet (onset, nucleus, coda) and head (nucleus) targets are indeed only grounded on one value, whereas the body ones may correspond to several. Moreover the body onset and body coda are often absent from our data (respectively 12% and 15% of the 400 melisms). When they are present, they assume for better expressiveness a contrastive function vis-à-vis respectively the foot and the head nucleus.

Melism parts	Population and percentages	Melisms subparts
208 Onset *(O)*	208 (52%)	*Of:* Onset foot Only one target optional
	46 (12%)	*Ob:* Onset body One or more targets Optional and often absent
400 Nucleus *(N)*	400 (100%)	*Nf:* Nucleus foot One target Compulsory
	286 (72%)	*Nb:* Nucleus body One or more targets Optional and often present
	400 (100%)	*Nh:* Nucleus head One target Compulsory
259 Coda*(C)*	61 (15%)	*Cb:* Coda body One or more targets Optional and often absent
	259 (65%)	*Cf:* Coda foot One target optional

Table 1: Parts and subparts of the melisms, properties, number and percentages (over 400 rising and inverted falling melisms).

Perhaps for the same reason but due also to the fact that the nucleus heart is the most important part for perception, the body nucleus *(Nb)* is on the contrary much more common in the data, since it concerns 72% of the 400 melisms, with one or several successive F_0 values. In any case, the different *bodies* seem to be working as an aesthetic, substantial and constrastive material highlighting the nucleus edges using at least melody and time.

Concerning the task of decomposing the melism structure into chunks, the first step is to detect the nucleus edges, supporting the melism range, i.e. the lowest *(Nf)* and the highest *(Nh)* F_0 targets. Once done, it can be observed that between them, there can occur one or several other targets *(Nb),* the level of which being compulsorily equal to or higher than *Nf* and equal to or lower than *Nh.*

The next steps for decomposing the structure are the following: if a previous target *Of* stands before *Nf*, it cannot be lower than *Nf* or higher than *Nh.* If one or more targets *Ob* is/are produced between *Of* and *Nf*, in the same way as previously, its/their value can be anything except being lower than *Nf* or higher than *Nh.*

If a last target *Cf* occurs after *Nh*, it cannot be higher than *Nh,* or lower than *Nf.* If one or more targets *Cb* is/are produced between *Nh* and *Cf*, in the same way as previously, its/their value can be anything except being higher than *Nh* or lower than *Nf.*

Sometimes two or more targets, successive or not, may be equal in the melisms. So the analysis has to cope with two solutions: on the one hand, decomposing the melism structure in the order in which they occur; on the other hand, taking into account the actual minimum or maximum. The second solution was preferred, not because it could be perceptively relevant, but because of the relevance of using only one criterion for the overall analysis.

Comparing (Table 1 above) the percentages of the feet (onset and coda, respectively 52% and 65%), and then of the bodies (onset and coda, respectively 12% and 15%), one can note that the second part of the melism structure gets more targets than the first. A possible explanation could be that during the planning and production stages, more attention paid to the first part of the melism could require fewer targets in order to reduce the task complexity.

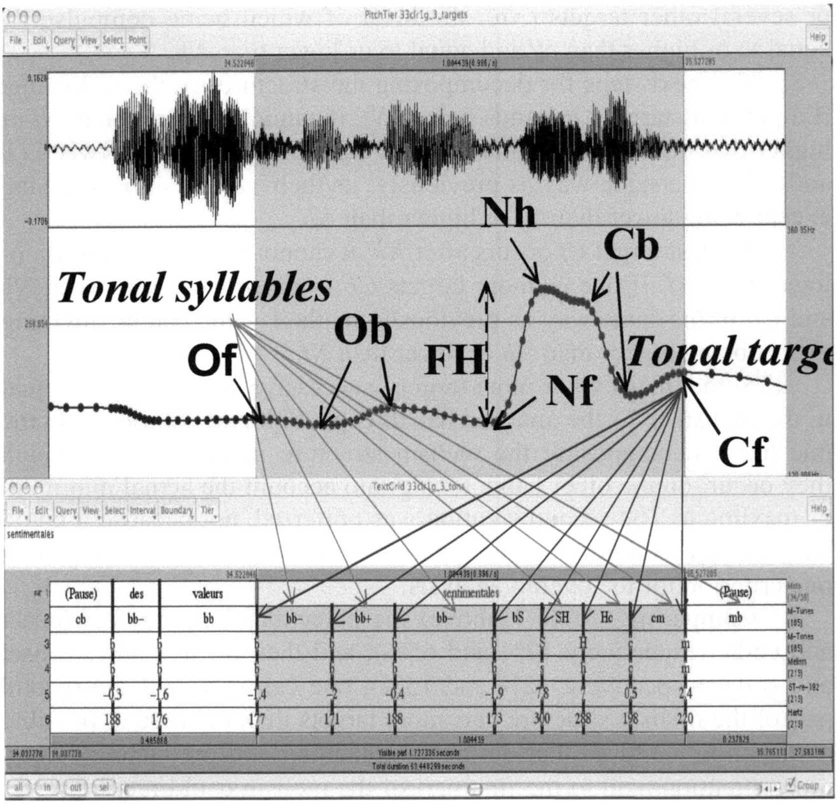

Figure 6: An example of a MP melism (French /sentimentales/, English /sentimental/) under Praat Procedure (Boersma/Weenink 2008). From bottom to top: F_0 values in Hz, then in semi-tones, the MELISM tonal codings, the tonal 'syllables' with, in capitals, the detection of the most acute values in the melism, the manual words segmentation, and finally the F_0 curve and the signal. The arrows indicating the tonal syllables and the tonal targets, and the subparts (Of, Ob, etc.) were manually added afterwards to the image.

One can note also that the onset and the coda parts are symmetrical, each composed of a foot (composed of one target) which is the junction between the melism and its lexical/intonational context, and a body (composed of one or more targets), the inner part of the onset or the coda.

This fact induces also another kind of symmetry, which occurs between rising vs. falling melisms. The structure is just the same but put in inverted order. In order to make the most accurate comparisons between them, i.e. the hardest conditions for matching them, a few targets (from 5% on the whole) were set aside. In these conditions, Figure 7 below shows the comparative range of the overall rising melisms (pale grey cases), and of the falling melisms (dark grey cases) put in inverted order to provide them with an appropriate shape for comparison. When the two shapes coincide at the best, the pale grey case is covered by the dark one. One can note that in any case, the range of the falling inverted melisms is totally embedded in that of the rising melisms.

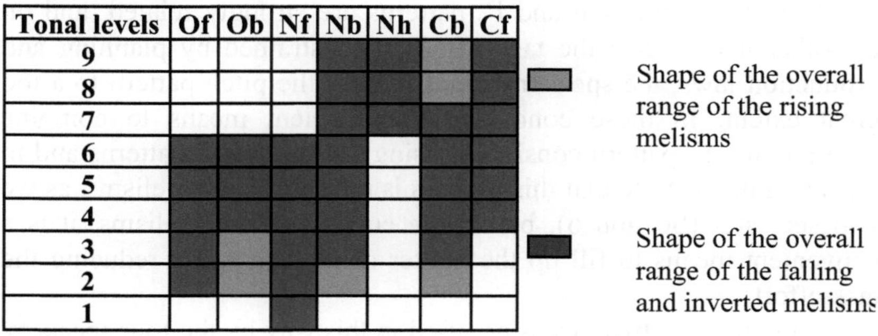

Figure 7: F_0 range comparison between the overall tonal patterns of the 95% rising and falling melisms.

From this, we can draw the conclusion that merging rising and falling melism data is not a problem. In these conditions, the statistics were applied to several kinds of data: rising melisms, falling melisms, then both merged (that is to say, 400 melisms, with falling structures put in inverted order to be consistent, i.e. as rising structures), and for every sort of melism: all the melisms (400), the melisms occurring inside a group (M), at the end of the group before a pause (MP), and then the same without pause (MF). The number of the contextual melisms (MC) remaining too small even through four speakers, the MC correlations are just reported but not taken into account.

4.3. Subjective melism motives

As is well known, the general melism function consists in focussing the listener's attention on a specific word content considered, consciously or not by the speaker, of great interest. To this function, as we saw in the previous section, the speaker uses the highest F_0 values (*A, S, H*), combined most of the time with a wide range. For a long time, many studies have reported this phenomenon.

We would now like to draw attention to a particular process which, to our knowledge, is not totally taken into account in the literature. Indeed, another means to get the listener's attention on specific words consists also in increasing the word duration. On the one hand since duration and F_0 patterns are strongly related, and on the other hand, since the task effort is constrained by planning and production laws, the speaker cannot modify the pitch pattern to a too great extent. In these conditions, an efficient means to combine duration and F_0 pattern consists in using specific pitch patterns and in repeating them. Note that this process is not specific to melisms, as we will see later (Section 6), but in the context of the melisms, it is a convenient means to fill up the matter of melism while reducing the task effort.

In our data, two means are used in this way by the four speakers, which are *symmetry* and *duplication*. This phenomenon is very frequent and used by the four speakers, and was brought to light thanks to the thin granularity of the F_0 range partition in nine levels. For instance, 69% of the 400 melisms are produced with these kinds of repetition, and among the four speakers, the rates spread from 62% to 79%.

More precisely, these 276 (69%) melisms can combine one (45%), two (21%) or three (3%) repetitions: on the whole these 276 melisms present 397 such repetitions. This process concerns all the melisms, short or long, with a single tonal syllable (example: *HH*) or many syllables. Of course the two or three repetitions of this process in the word need several syllables to take place, and so are the examples chosen here.

The first example corresponds to this sequence of six tonal syllables in the French male first name /Junior/: */mc cm mm mH Hm mm/*, speaker HV1. In such a sequence, every syllable is a part of this process:

- */mc cm/* is a symmetrical structure,
- */mm/* is a duplication of the same tonal target,
- */mH Hm/* is once more a symmetrical structure,
- */mm/* is once more a duplication of the same tonal target, and moreover the same as previously,
- but more generally, */mm mH Hm mm/* can be also regarded as a double layer symmetry.

So the seven successive tonal targets are based on only three different ones */m, c, H/*).

The second example shows this pattern of nine tonal syllables in the French word draconien (= drastic): /ib bg gb bi im mm mH Hm mm/, speaker LR1. In this structure,

- */bg gb/, /mH Hm/* are symmetrical,
- moreover */bg gb/* is embedded in another symmetry: */ib bg gb bi/,*
- and also is */mH Hm/* in */mm mH Hm mm/,* where */mm/* corresponds now to the same tonal target (and also the same symmetry as above for /Junior/).

So for this nine tonal syllable melism, with ten tonal targets, six different tonal targets are used.

These two examples illustrate how the speakers can highlight the words within the melisms, varying their tonal targets in time, increasing the time duration, by reducing at the same time, the planning and production tasks effort.

Now let us give a deeper insight into the structure of such melisms. Examining the melism structures, we observed three places where the target duplication occurs:

- at the beginning: it is given the name of *appeal* (or A), for instance, speaker HV1, word *midi (= noon)*, melism */**bb** bH/,*
- at the end: it receives the name of *echo* (or E), for instance, speaker SP1, word *beau (= beautiful)*, melism */bi iS **SS**/,*
- in between the beginning and the end: it is given the name of *murmur* (or M), for instance, speaker LR1, word *vrai (= true)*, melism */bc cH HS **SS** Sm/.*

Figures 8a and 8b below present the percentages of melisms per speaker. Figure 8a shows the general rates over the four kinds of motives (the so-called 'Appeal, Symmetry, Murmur and Echo'), summing up the melisms with one, two and three motives, and on the other hand, 8b presents the same but computed only with one motive.

From Figures 8a and 8b, we can observe that for the duplication series, the Appeal and Echo positions are a little bit more frequent than the Murmur one, and on the whole, also more frequent than the Symmetry one. The Echo position is indeed the most resistant one when the speakers produce only one motive in the melisms. In Figure 8a, we can also see that globally the rates follow the same proportions among the speakers from the first motive to the final one.

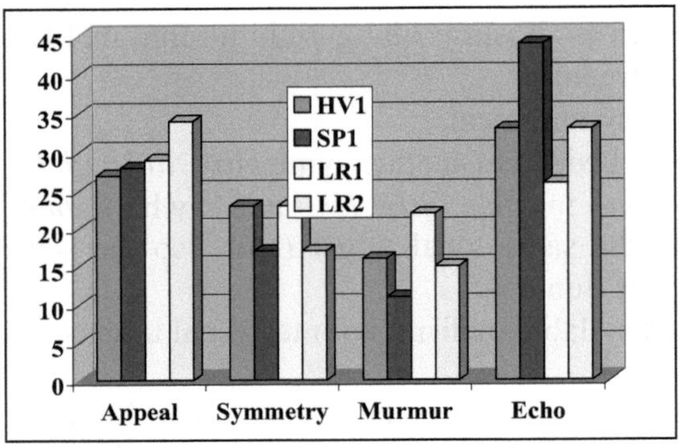

Figure 8a: Percentages of melisms by speaker over one, two and three kinds of motives..

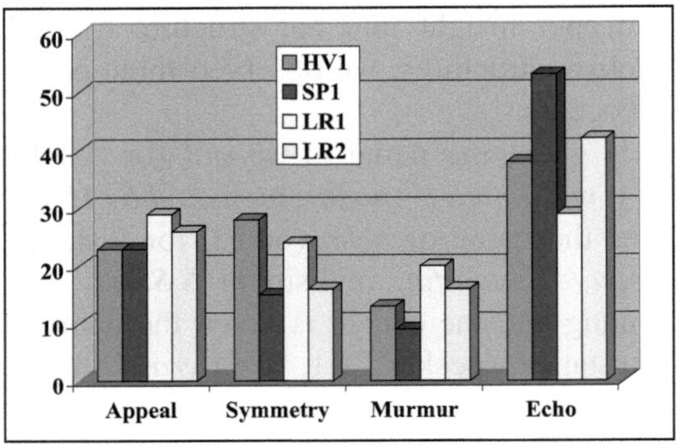

Figure 8b: Percentages of melisms by speaker over one motive only.

Figure 9 below presents the percentages of melisms by speaker over each combination of two motives. Three speakers out of four more frequently use the combination A + E, which is Appeal + Echo. Since 95% of the 276 melisms with motives have from one to five tonal syllables, this great proportion of A+E structures is surely the effect of the smallest structures, where at least the first and last position are always present or if not, merged. The second combination, the most consistent among the speakers is A + S, combining the Appeal with Symmetry, the others showing a greater variability among the speakers.

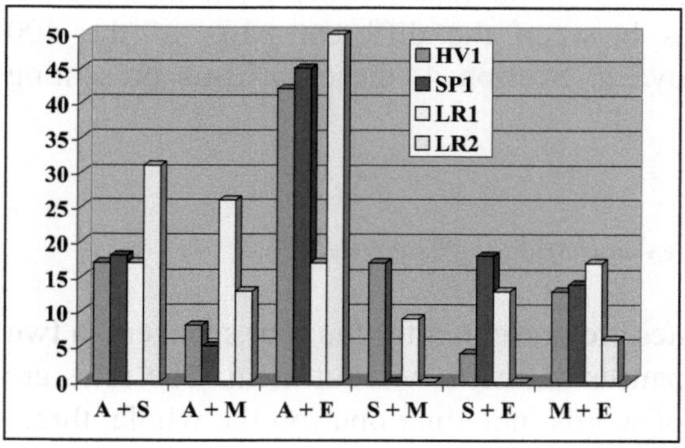

Figure 9: Percentages of melisms by speaker over each combination of 2 motives.

Table 2 below shows the number of melisms per speaker over each combination of three motives.

3 motives	A+M+E	A+S+E	A+S+M	S+M+E	TOTAL
HV1	0	0	0	1	1
SP1	1	1	1	1	4
LR1	0	1	1	1	3
LR2	1	0	2	0	3
TOTAL	2	2	4	3	11

Table 2: Number of melisms by speaker over each combination of the three motives.

Of course, this phenomenon is much less frequent, but all the speakers are concerned by it. Only 4% of the melisms with motives use three combinations, but we have to take into account that it is an effect of a greater number of syllables and indeed, five melisms out of the eleven concerned with this process have from five to nine syllables. Moreover this phenomenon is rare, as rare as the words of many syllables (13 out of 276 melisms with motives have six to nine tonal syllables).

In these conditions, the main interest is to make an inventory of this process, and understand it as a confirmation and an extension of the combination of two motives. The A+S+M (Appeal + Symmetry + Murmur) combination seems to be the most frequent. The next section considers the correlations between the different parts of the 400 melisms, as analysed above in Section 4, these melisms presenting motives or not.

4.4. Group duration, pauses and speech flow rates

In Figure 10 below, the rates are presented for the four speakers in two conditions, namely with pauses and with/without them. The rates are calculated on the groups of words including one (on the whole, three-quarter of the cases) or several melisms.

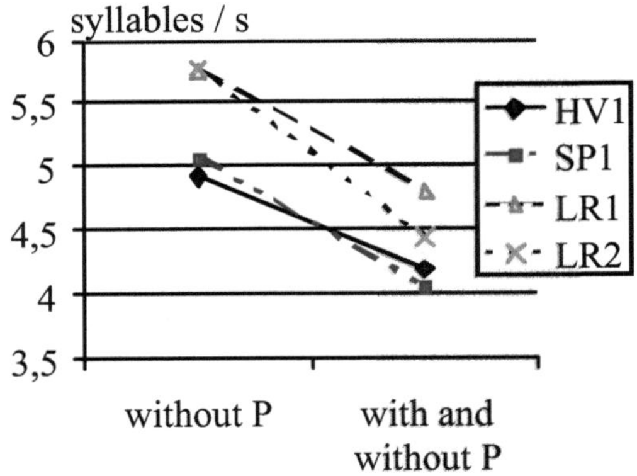

Figure 10: Four speakers' (HV1, SP1, LR1, LR2) speech flow (syllables per second), rates without pauses, and rates with and without pauses.

The first remark concerns the rates without pauses. These rates seem to be in tune with the age of the speakers, the youngest speakers (LR1, LR2) showing no difference between their rates. With a rate between 5.5 and 6 syllables per second, the youngest speakers' rates (LR1, LR2) can be considered as fast ones.

Concerning the rates with/without pauses as the speech arises naturally, they vary to a larger extent for the grand-mother (SP1) and the great-grand-daughter (LR2) than for the others speakers for whom the flow slows down more. This means that the pauses for SP1 and LR2 are longer on average (or more frequent) than for the other speakers.

This has the effect of modifying the order of the rates in such a way that they are not totally tuned to the speakers' ages.

Table 3 below shows the statistical correlations between the number of syllables per group and the group duration (cs). We expect the rates corresponding to the groups with (and without) pauses to be less good, and as we can see in Table 3 below, this expectation is verified.

Number of syllables and cs	HV1	SP1	LR1	LR2
Without a pause	0.93	0.87	0.8	0.94
With and without a pause	0.87	0.83	0.69	0.83

Table 3: Statistical correlation rates between the number of the syllables in the groups and the group durations.

On the whole, for the groups without pauses, there is a strong correlation between the number of syllables in the groups and the duration. According to their lower rates, the duration and the number of syllables of the speakers of the middle age seem to correlate less strictly, which may give rise to the expression of speech effects such as contrasts, but not exclusively in the time domain, but also in that of fundamental frequency (intonation and melisms).

Concerning the number of pauses, the analysis of the group durations led to taking into consideration a greater number of pauses than for the analysis of melisms.

Number of pauses	HV1	SP1	LR1	LR2
Melisms MP	40	59	35	33
Standard words with P	6	2	16	19
Total	46	61	51	52

Table 4: Number of pauses by speaker, according to the MP melisms, and in other contexts (end of a group without a melism).

From Table 4 above, one can draw the conclusions that 1) the number of pauses is not related to older age, 2) the more the MP melisms in the speech, the less the pauses in the standard words (i.e. no prominent ones) and vice versa. These results led us finally to compute the number of syllables by pause. We could expect the oldest people to get a lower number of syllables by pause.

Speakers	HV1	SP1	LR1	LR2
Number of syllables	582	779	762	627
Number of pauses	46	61	51	52
Ratio	12.65	12.77	14.94	12.06

Table 5: Ratio of the number of syllables by the number of pauses (four speakers).

Against our expectation, Table 5 above shows that the lowest ratio corresponds to the youngest speaker LR2, the highest one to her mother LR1. These results can be explained by several causes, where not only the factors due to age can be taken into account, but also other factors such as the shyness of the youngest one (who was 15 years old at the time of the recording), and the difficulty to impose her own point of view in a family context of three older women who could make decisions in her place (mother, grandmother, great-grandmother). Taking into consideration the facts that LR2 presents the fastest speech flow (5.81 syllables per second), and that she got the lowest ratio (12.06) of the number of syllables by the number of pauses, we can draw the conclusion that her pauses are more frequent/ longer than the other speakers, and assert that probably this time is left to find, improve, justify her arguments during the planning task.

On the other hand, her great-grandmother presents the lowest speech flow (4.92 syllables by second). Her ratio in Table 5 is not the lowest, but at the same time, the need to make breaks is all the less strong as the speech flow is slower.

5. Statistical results

This section undertakes a new perspective of research in the context of international studies, and thus new results will be reported.

For all the conditions, the analysis will consider in any case the same correlations: between respectively the Nucleus foot and Nucleus head *(Nf / Nh),* the Onset foot and the Coda foot *(Of / Cf),* and each one with respectively the Nucleus foot *(Of-Cf / Nf),* the Nucleus head *(Of-Cf / Nh),* and finally with the range between the Nucleus foot and the Nucleus head *FH (Of-Cf / FH).*

First of all we have to explain the respective distribution of the melisms in Table 6 below. On the left, the number indicates the overall quantity of the kind of melisms (for instance 329 rising melisms), and on the right, the number in brackets (for instance: 0.73 (172)), indicates that 172 out of 329 melisms display an *Of* with a *Of/Nf* correlation rate of 0.73.

Before any comment on the results, let us note that we don't expect any interesting correlation between *Of / Cf*, as they both establish the junction with left and right intonative contexts. In the same way, we don't expect any correlation either between *Nf / Nh* for the rising melisms, but for other arguments: if *Nf* and *Nh* were correlated, this would mean that this pitch range would be much more repetitive and less variable than it obviously is on the pitch and time domain, and moreover, that the speaker's expressiveness would be drastically reduced.

Besides, we don't expect either correlations between *Of* and *Nh, Nf* and *Cf* for rising melisms (and symmetrically, no correlations between *Of* and *Nf, Nh* and *Cf* for the falling melisms). As one can see in Table 6 below, for *Of / Cf*, and *Nf / Nh*, as expected, there are no correlations observed above 0.50, except *Of / Nf* for the falling melisms.

The first comment concerns the scores: the first part of the melism *(Of* target, in white cells) always seems to present better results than the second one *(Cf* target, in grey).

More precisely, comparing the symmetrical position, *Of / Nf* with *Cf / Nh,* respectively the first scores range from 0.63 to 0.78, as the second ones span from 0.53 to 0.59, and moreover with fewer correlations.

Secondly, comparing now *Of* and *Cf* with the F_0 minimum-maximum range (*FH* or ΔF_0), we observe that no anti-correlation exists between *Cf* and *FH,* as they exist in a small extent between *Of* and *FH* (-0.52 to -0.58). That means that there exists a slight tendency that the lower *Of* is, the greater the range of *FH*, and vice versa. This statement is not surprising as on the one hand *Of* and *Nf* are correlated, and on the other hand, *Nh* varies to a lesser extent (only acute levels); when *Of* and *Nf* increase their height, the range tends naturally to be smaller.

This general behaviour seems to be resistant to the kind of melisms, except for MP which seems to be more speaker dependent: in this case, one of the four speakers shows a strong absence of correlation, lowering the global scores.

On the other hand, this symmetrical behaviour ultimately justifies the legitimacy of our method consisting in merging the data of falling and rising melisms.

Concerning now the 71 falling melisms and the correlations between *Of (0.66)-Cf (0.81) / Nf,* it is interesting to note that:

1) for *Nf,* there exist correlations with both *Of* and *Cf,* which is an exception, as no *Cf / Nf* is observed besides for all the other kinds of melisms.

2) *Of-Cf / Nf,* due to their different slope direction, behave symmetrically: the best correlations are observed between *Nf* and *Cf,* in the same way as between *Nf* and *Of* with the rising melisms.

Correlations over:	*Nf and Nh*	*Of and Nf*	*Of and FH*	*Of and Nh*	*Cf and Nf*	*Cf and FH*	*Cf and Nh*	*Of and Cf*
400 rising and reversed falling melisms	0.19 (400)	***0.74*** (195)	***-0.52*** (195)	0.24 (195)	0.12 (271)	0.22 (271)	***0.55*** (271)	0.14 (130)
329 rising melisms	0.19 (329)	***0.73*** (172)	***-0.53*** (172)	0.21 (172)	0.08 (238)	0.24 (238)	***0.53*** (238)	0.08 (120)
71 falling melisms	0.21 (71)	***0.66*** (34)	-0.43 (34)	0.08 (34)	***0.81*** (23)	-0.44 (23)	0.23 (23)	0.40 (12)
167 rising and reversed falling MP	0.14 (167)	***0.63*** (90)	0.03 (90)	0.20 (90)	-0.03 (103)	0.43 (103)	***0.59*** (103)	-0.04 (52)
147 rising and reversed falling M	0.39 (147)	***0.78*** (63)	***-0.58*** (63)	0.49 (63)	0.34 (117)	-0.09 (117)	0.49 (117)	0.35 (51)
56 rising and reversed falling MF	0.25 (56)	***0.78*** (34)	***-0.53*** (34)	0.40 (34)	0.25 (45)	-0.01 (45)	0.44 (45)	0.40 (28)

Table 6: Four speakers' correlations between the main targets of all the melism kinds in a contextual perspective, with in bold italics, the correlations above 0.50. The number in brackets corresponds to the population. As Of and Cf are optional, their population is smaller than Nf and Nh ones which are conversely compulsory.

In these conditions one can state that 1) the *Nf* target, being relevant in both cases, i.e. for the ascending vs. descending melism slopes, seems to be the object of a precise mental planning as well as a precise production in speech, and that 2) the *Of* target, being relevant as well for the ascending vs. descending melism slopes (as the falling melisms supply a good demonstration of the strength of this process), is also the result of a consistent mental planning in mind and speech production.

It is a fact that *Of-Nf* presents the best correlation results, even though *Of* and *Nf* may be separated by one or several *Ob* targets. Now when exploring in detail the four speakers' results about the *Of / Nf* correlations, we note that the scores often reach more than 0.80, and sometimes more than 0.90.

Speakers	HV1	SP1	LR1	LR2
Statistical correlations *Of / Nf* (rising and reversed falling melisms)	0.55	0.84	0.64	0.85
Average Number of lexical Syllables / number of pauses (ANS)	12.65	12.77	14.94	12.06
Speech flow with pauses	4.18	4.04	4.8	4.43

Table 7: Comparison between the rates of the statistical correlations Of / Nf, the average number of lexical syllables by the number of pauses (ANS), the speech flow including the pauses duration.

In Table 7 above, we note that even though the average correlation *Of / Nf* is well established for all the melisms (0.74 on the whole), the rates are even so rather dependent on the speakers. Considering that the speech flow could be an important parameter to explain these results, we note that indeed LR2 presents the best correlations (0.85) with the lowest (12.06) average number of syllables (ANS), while conversely her mother LR1 presents rather bad correlations (0.64), with the highest ANS (14.94). In the same way, the duration of pauses is also an important factor, because SP1 shows very good correlations (0.84) while her speech flow is the lowest (4.04). HV1, who is the eldest speaker, shows rates with the worst correlations (0.55), despite a low speech flow and an ANS also rather low. Perhaps we could invoke the speaker's age (87 years old when she was recorded) and a weaker ability to tune her melodic targets. It seems, however, that there is no other evidence for this hypothesis.

Anyway, these results mean that *Of plays the role of an important step in the* F_0 *prominence construction of the melism.* This means first that the melisms, if they are the expression of subjective freedom, are nevertheless connected to the intonational context (by *Of* and *Cf*): as mentioned above, they are the junction points between the embedded layers, the intonational and the melism ones.

Moreover *Of* seems to *supply a tonal springboard for tuning Nf and* ΔF_0. So a question arises: is *Of* just a convenient ground for the next targets in the planning task, or could *Of, Nf* and *FH* also be really acoustically tuned?

From these statistical observations, we can conclude that through the great variability of the melisms in our data,

- there exists an *underlying structure which encompasses all the apparent chaos* of the F_0 values,
- the melodic subjectivity is constrained by some laws: in most of the cases, *the F_0 target (Of)* which binds the boundary of the melism to the lexical left context in the rising melisms, and the *lowest F_0 target (Nf)* of the melism are *covariant targets*, and are carefully and precisely planned in the mental programming and production stages.

Besides, grounded on the few most acute F_0 values, *Nh presents no correlations* with the first part of the melism. This front open space suggests, and confirms as well, that *the highest F_0 value is left to the speaker's freedom of expression.*

6. Personal involvement, emotion, emotions, and attitude

Our corpus and data are based on a specific kind of emotion which can be termed as a personal involvement. Each speaker in her spontaneous production indeed gives free rein to her feelings, impressions, motivations, arguments, values, and in these conditions gets involved in her discourse and interaction. This involvement entails modifications of the F_0 curve such as the production of acute F_0 targets, great F_0 ranges and contrasts which are reflected by the melisms, and moreover variations of the speech flow, speech energy etc. This personal involvement did not encompass in our perspective such emotions as for instance happiness or anger.

In these conditions, besides the 400 melisms, we also build up some other databases specialized in emotions or attitudes. In this section we propose to make some comparisons between the personal involvement cues and the emotional ones. Nevertheless we will limit the analysis to the kind of emotions which share some common cues between all of them, and moreover in the frame of one speaker's productions (speaker LR1). Under these restrictions, we will consider the cases of the expression of happiness.

It is well known that happiness is considered as an emotion with a positive valence, and a high degree of arousal. For instance, within the FEELTRACE circle display (Cowie et al. 2000), described above, Section 2: "the main axes were drawn and labelled – one (activation) running from very active to very passive; the other one (evaluation) running from very positive to very negative" (ibid.). Within this circle, happiness is represented in the sector *very active / very positive.*

In her speech, LR1 presents three periods characterised by happiness, which on the whole correspond to 70 successive words. Two sequences, referenced as G7 and G8, are short (both merged 20 words on the whole), and the other one, referenced as LT3, is longer (50 words). The first ones G7+G8 present quick incursions to joy/happiness, based only on a few words, sometimes on two words, whereas the LT3 is based on a progressive increase of joy, from neutral expression to happiness, then to hilarity and finally back to neutral conditions.

Now, it is indeed often argued in the literature that happiness considered as very active and very positive, leads to an increase in the average F_0 and its range. A question is thus worth asking: can these words produced under happiness be differentiated from the melisms which also are characterised by acute F_0 values? In these conditions these two extracts (G7 + G8) and LT3, shaped differently will be used in two ways in order to explore this question.
For the study of each of the three joy sequences, we use the same quantitative criteria:

1- Tonal targets in use
This information allows to assess the F_0 range span, and the relative height of each chunk.

2- Average number of tonal syllables used by the lexical syllables
This rate provides information about the degree of the tonal complexity in the lexical syllables, but not about the degree of variability which will be presented below in (3).

3- Pattern Difference Index (PDI)
This new index supplies information about the tonal variability. It is calculated by the ratio of the number of the *different* tonal patterns over the number of successive tonal syllables. Theoretically, its range can spread from 0.1 to 1 (reached when the number of different tonal patterns equals the number of successive tonal syllables).

4- Pattern Renewal Index (PRI)
This index, also new, takes into account the number of tonal syllables which are on their own within the chunk. It is calculated by the ratio of the number of tonal syllables which are not duplicated over the number of all the tonal targets of the chunk. This index conveniently completes the PDI because among the different patterns of the tonal syllables, some can be used several times. When none of the different tonal syllables is duplicated, the rate is the same for PDI and PRI.

5- Tonal motives in the words
This feature develops the ideas presented about the PRI index and presents some examples about the pitch motives. As mentioned in Section 4.3., the process described above about the melism motives is also used for the standard words without any F_0 prominence. As seen above, these processes are based on *symmetry* and repetition *(appeal, murmur and echo).*

Thus Table 8 below displays the main characteristics of the tonal syllables of the words extracted from the corpus G7 and G8 (the neutral condition presents no melisms), as just described above, plus some other general features. We have to keep in mind that from the lowest tones to the highest ones, the nine levels which share each speaker range are: /g = grave, i = infra-grave, b = bottom, c = centred, m = middle, e = elevated, H = high, S = supra-high, A = acute/.

Neutral (N) / Happiness (H)	N	H
Number of words	5	15
Number of lexical syllables	10	22
Number of successive tonal syllables	19	40
Number of successive tonal targets	24	55
Tonal targets in use	i,b,c,m,e	b,c,m,e,H,S
Average number of the tonal syllables in use / lexical syllables	1.9	1.82
Number of different tonal syllables patterns	10	21
Pattern Difference Index (PDI)	0.53	0.53
Pattern Renewal Index (PRI)	0.32	0.25

Table 8: Speaker LR1, sequences G7 and G8. Tonal characteristics of the speech chunks under the neutral conditions (N, white cells) and happiness (H, grey cells).

1- Tonal targets in use
One can note about the tonal targets in use, that for the LR1 neutral way of speaking, the F_0 range is lower and has a smaller extent than for that of happiness. However, the lowest note (/i/) may be due to the position of the word at the end of the group. If we do not take into account this tonal target, the range is even narrower.

2- Average number of tonal syllables in use by lexical syllables
The two conditions present no significant differences (respectively, 1.9 ~ 1.82).

3- Pattern Difference Index (PDI)
The *PDI* presents exactly the same rate (0.53) for the two speech conditions, which unfortunately results in the impossibility to make a difference between the two expressions.

4- Pattern Renewal Index (PRI)
As for PRI, there is a slight difference between the two expressions (respectively neutral: 0.32; happiness: 0.25), but contrary to any expectation, it is the neutral way of speaking which renews its tonal targets a little more than happiness.

5- Tonal motives in the words

We now refer to the previous study on melisms, and their tonal characteristics as a basis for comparison with the words expressed with joy. Concerning first the F_0 height point of view, there is no difference between words expressed with happiness and melisms grounded on personal involvement. Moreover, some words with happiness do not present very high values: /*Hello Machin, comme si on avait été ... (= Hi Mr What's-his-name, as if we had ...)* : /-bm mc[1]-cc cc cH He-cm mS SH He-eS Sh-He-em me-ee eH He-/. Such tonal structures as for instance /-cm mS SH He-eS Sh-/ do not diverge from the melism ones.

As for the pitch motives such as symmetry, and the three types of duplications, as can be observed in this last sequence, the processes of *symmetry*, and *appeal* are used, and so are the *echo* and *murmur* ones, for instance: *très très (= very very)*: /-me em mS SS-SS Se eH HH He-/.

So on the whole, for each of the different points concerning the perspective of F_0, there is *absolutely no distinction between the words expressed in the happiness condition considered one by one, and the melism structures, and even sometimes with the neutral condition words!*

Let us now take a look at the other sequence of 50 words (LT3), same speaker, LR1.

Concerning this passage, LR1 tells an event she witnessed when she was a girl, namely the flood of the attic due to gutters and the rush of her mother and her grandfather everywhere through the house to find basins. This passage is very interesting because it is well shaped and well balanced. Let us point out that the joy emotion, with its acoustic cues, does not coincide every time with the grammatical groups. In these conditions, we prefer to use the term 'chunk', and specify how many words they contain.

In fact, it seems that we can distinguish two grades for joy, for instance *happiness* which preserves the speech structure, and *hilarity* when speech and laughter are merged. Of course the speaker can pass successively, and easily from one state of joy to another.

---

1 For better clarity, each tonal word is put between dashes (for instance: -bm mc-).

Its structure is thus composed of five different chunks, namely:

- an introduction (I) where LR1 informs about the emergence of her memory (I, 5 words): neutral mood, no happiness,
- the passage with the flood and rush account (A, 12 words): happiness,
- then the explanation of the flood (E, 6 words), no happiness,
- a flash back to her funny memory (M, 12 words): happiness first (M1), then hilarity (M2),
- and finally, the return to reality, which is the report of an actual gutter in the bottle cellar (R, 12 words): neutral mood, no happiness.

From the speech rate perspective, the modification from one passage to another is very clear in time and energy domain, as Table 9 shows. In this table, we can easily follow the speech flow rate decrease, and at the same time the mean energy increase, when passing from the neutral mood (I, no happiness or NH) to happiness (A, happiness, or H), and then its increase to E (no happiness, NH) occurring with an energy decrease, and then once more the flow rate decrease and the energy increase (M1, happiness, M2, hilarity), and finally, the flow rate increase and energy increase (R, no happiness).

Happiness (H) / Hilarity (HL) / Neutral mood (N)	N	H	N	H	HL	N
Chunks	I	A	E	M1	M2	R
Speech rate (syllables / s)	6.48	5.25	6.54	5.68	5.49	6.43
Energy (mean dB)	67	70	68	71	71	65

Table 9: Analysis of the speech flow and energy modifications (without pauses) in each speech chunk (speaker LR1).

As the pauses are absent for the neutral mood, we will only consider the duration and speech flow without pauses. It is worth noting that there is no melism in the neutral condition. Let us note also that the pauses being conversely much more frequent during the happiness expression, this fact entails a drastic speech flow decrease, which emphasizes the discrepancy between the two speech flow rates, the happiness one being much lower.

This process being the same for the other happiness extracts (namely G7 and G8), on the whole, the global speech flow rate for the joy mood is 5.30 syllables per second without the pauses, falling to 3.67 syllables per second with the pauses included, while the neutral mood embedded in these extracts is 5.86 syllables without pauses, and while on the other hand, in the overall LR1 data, it reaches 5.81 syllables without the pauses, and 4.43 syllables with the pauses.
On the other hand, the frequency domain also provides another point of interest. In this domain, new results seem to be put forward.
In the same speech data as previously, we get not only these two kinds of joy (happiness and hilarity), but we find the implementation and the progress of the happiness (M1) process from the very beginning until its conversion into hilarity (M2).

We focus now on the tonal syllables and comment on Table 10 below according to its layers of information:

1- Tonal targets in use
Concerning the F_0 range span and the relative height of each chunk, the first target of the whole sequence (six chunks) is /m = middle/ which regularly corresponds to the usual mean F_0 occurring for French in the first syllables of the utterances. In Table 10 below, the target /m/ has not been taken into account. In fact the actual beginning is given by the second target /i = infra-grave/, the lowest of the whole passage. Its function is to initialise the whole passage and this target works as a personal and also perceptual landmark.

From the first chunk to the others, we observe a general tendency for each chunk in the neutral conditions to narrow down its F_0 range height, resetting progressively the F_0 values downwards after each joy sequence, while the chunks in the joy conditions continue to increase the F_0 height without any break from the low and middle ranges of the neutral conditions.

2- Average number of tonal syllables in use by lexical syllables
Concerning the degree of tonal complexity, one can notice in Table 10 below that there is a tendency for the chunks corresponding to the joy conditions to present in average more complex tonal patterns. The last chunk (R) seems, however, to be an exception with a high rate of

complexity (1.5), but in fact the speaker does not completely return to reality, she makes a joke as the word *chai (= cellar)*, uttered in the middle of the group with a perceptible joy then laughter, can prove.

3- Pattern Difference Index (*PDI*)
Between the neutral and happiness conditions, the difference is not clear, but the index rate emerges obviously for the hilarity conditions (0.71).

Neutral (N) / Happiness (H) / Hilarity (HL)	N	H	N	H	HL	N
Chunks	I	A	E	M1	M2	R
Number of words	5	12	6	5	7	12
Number of lexical syllables	6	21	10	10	9	16
Nb of successive tonal syllables	4	29	11	12	14	24
Nb of successive tonal targets	8	41	17	19	20	32
Tonal targets in use	i,b	b,c,m	i,b,c	c,m,e	c,m,e,H,S,A	b,c,m,e
Average number of tonal syllables in use / lexical syllables	0.67	1.38	1.1	1.2	1.55	1.5
Nb of different tonal syllable patterns	2	9	5	7	10	10
Pattern Difference Index (*PDI*)	0.5	0.31	0.45	0.58	0.71	0.42
Pattern Renewal Index (PRI)	0.25	0.06	0.09	0.25	0.71	0.17

Table 10: Speaker LR1, sequence LT3. Tonal characteristics of speech chunks under neutral conditions (N, white cells), happiness (H, grey cells) and hilarity (HL, grey cells).

4- Pattern Renewal Index (PRI)
As none of the different tonal syllables is duplicated within the M2 chunk, the rate is the same for PDI and PRI.

On the whole, this index shows a big contrast between the A and E rates (respectively, 0.06 and 0.09) which present indeed very few tonal syllables not duplicated (respectively, 2/29 and 1/11), and M2 where 10 tonal syllables out of 14 are never duplicated (0.71).

5- Tonal motives in the words
As for the tonal height, the observation is the same as for the G7 and G8 sequences: for the happiness condition, the levels are not high at all, the range spreads from /b/ to /e/ at the most.

For the hilarity condition, the range is greater (from /c/ to /A/), but is not different from the melism one, for instance: *j'me rappelle le grenier (=I remember the attic)*: /-AS SS SH-Hm mc cH Hm-me-eH HH HH-/.

Concerning now the processes of *symmetry* and *repetition (appeal, murmur and echo):*

- The I chunk (PRI: 0.25) is characterised by a succession of a single tonal syllable per word, and after the first one *rappelle (= remember)*: /ib/, the three following words use only the tonal syllable /bb/ (repeated three times).
- The A chunk (PRI: 0.06) presents a very weak variation among the words and within each one. A consequence is that several words present the same pattern: *courait toujours (= ran always):* /-bc cb bc cb-bc cb bc cb bb-/; *grand-père (= grandfather):* /cb bc cb bb/; *cuvettes (= basins)*: /cm mb bm/; *bassines (= basins)*: /cb bm mm mc/, etc..
- The E chunk (PRI: 0.09) is also characterised by a very weak variation of the melodic patterns, using as much as previously the symmetry and repetition motives: *pasque (= because)*: /cb bc cc/; *gouttières (= gutters)*: /ic cb bb/; *plein (= full)*: /bc cc/, etc.
- The M1 chunk (PRI: 0.25) proposes more frequent variations than previously, but the same method of duplication is used, employing symmetry and repetition at the beginning, in the middle or at the end of the word: *maison (= house)*: /cc cm mc/; *petite (= small)*: /mc ce ee/, etc.
- The M2 chunk (PRI: 0.71) on the contrary uses great variability and reduces the number of the same patterns, which are both a consequence of a big tonal range increase (from /c/ to /A/). However the same procedures of duplication are used to fill up the words, such as *j'me rappelle (= I remember)*: /-AS SS SH-Hm mc cH Hm-/ ; *grenier (= attic):* /eH HH HH/.
- The R chunk (PRI: 0.17) returns back to the lack of variability. The restricted F_0 range leads to the extension of the repetition process, thus we find a lot of examples such as *en fait (= in fact)*: /mc cm mm/; *bouteilles (= bottles)*: /mm mm mb/.

On the whole from our data based on a single speaker, for this study of happiness and hilarity, we can assert that when happiness takes place *in short sequences,* it seems that no cues consistently differentiate happiness from the neutral condition of speaking (words without F_0 prominence as well as the melisms). A hypothesis to explain this assessment could be that *personal involvement and happiness share the same space (and therefore the same F_0 cues) in the sector 'very active / very positive' on the activation and evaluation axes.*

On the other hand in the context of successive word groups (i.e. *in a long enough sequence), happiness provides more specific features.* In comparison with a neutral mood, happiness is thus characterised by middle F_0 values, a slower speech rate and an increase of intensity, and in comparison with hilarity, happiness is concerned with the restriction of the F_0 range, the reduction of the number of the F_0 patterns, and the increase of the same tonal structures in the words. *The PDI and PRI index show a significant increase of their rates for the hilarity condition.*

Other contextual cues seem also to be consistent in order to make oppositions:

1) between happiness – hilarity on the one hand, and melisms on the other. As a matter of fact, the melisms can also be differentiated from happiness and hilarity spreading on more than three words, as the melism process is always restricted to a single and at the most, two successive words.
2) between happiness – hilarity on the one hand and neutral expression on the other one, even using melisms.

This contextual cue consists in constantly using the upper range within the successive words (from /e/ to /A/). In reference to our method consisting of analysing carefully and precisely the F_0 domain, *the /e/ level seems to mark the break between the two modes of expression (neutral and joy).* The conjunction of a *consistent increase of intensity and the reduction of the speech flow rate* can consolidate the opposition between the expression of joy and the neutral one.

7. Conclusion

This chapter focussed essentially on a specific kind of emotion, which corresponds to the basic state of personal involvement in one's speech, that we have called *common emotion*.

The main contribution of this study was to provide new results 1) supplying a very precise analysis of the prominent words, the so-called melisms, 2) within a single speaker as well as for the four speakers, coping with a great variability of the melism forms, concerning mainly their F_0 levels and ranges, the number of their parts and sub-parts, their pitch motives, 3) clearing out the melism structure, which led us to bring to light a prototype structure of the melisms, 4) presenting some tonal motives which are used to fill up the melism material as well as the non-prominent words, using several kinds of tonal syllable duplication, namely *symmetry*, *echo*, *murmur* and *echo*, 5) informing that these pitch motives can contribute to the improvement of speech synthesis naturalness, 6) supplying consistent statistical correlations between the most important melism subparts, i.e. the junctions between the left *(Of)* or right *(Cf)* melism boundaries each with one of the melism core targets (*Nf* and *Nh*): *Of / Nf* provides the best and the most resistant ones, in comparison with *Cf / Nh*, 7) providing also some results in the fields of duration and speech flow, and of energy, and their relations with the pitch domain, 8) undertaking a substantial comparison between melisms, happiness and hilarity prosodic features, allowing mainly to clearly distinguish hilarity from happiness.

Acknowledgements

My thanks go to Daniel Hirst for his help with the English version of this text.

References

Boersma, Paul / Weenink, David 2008. Praat: doing phonetics by computer (version 5.0.20) [Computer program], Retrieved April, 2008, from <http://www.praat.org/>.

Caelen-Haumont, Geneviève, forthcoming. *Prosodie et sens : une approche expérimentale*, Paris, l'Harmattan-Marges Linguistiques.

Caelen-Haumont, Geneviève / Zei-Pollerman, Branka 2007. Voice and affect in speech communication, in Izdebski, Krzysztof / Zei,-Pollerman Branka (eds) *Voice and Emotions*, Vol 1, Chapitre 16, Plural Publishing Inc. publications, San Diego, CA, USA, 215-232.

Caelen-Haumont, Geneviève 2005. Les états émotionnels et la Prosodie : paradigmes, modèles, paramètres. In ouvrage collectif, Phonologie et phonétique : forme et substance, Paris, Hermès, 397-424.

Caelen-Haumont, Geneviève 1978, 1981. *Structures prosodiques de la phrase énonciative simple et étendue*, Thèse de doctorat de 3ème cycle. Université du Mirail, Toulouse (1978) / Hamburger Phonetische Beiträge, Band 34. Hamburg: Buske.

Caelen-Haumont, Geneviève 1991. Stratégies des locuteurs en réponse à des consignes de lecture d'un texte : analyse des interactions entre modèles syntaxiques, sémantiques, pragmatique et paramètres prosodiques, Thèse de doctorat d'état, Aix-en-Provence.

Caelen-Haumont, Geneviève 1993. Cognitive Processes and Prosodic Encoding: Speakers' adaptation to discourse conditions, *Cognitiva,* vol. 5 (2), 133-151.

Caelen-Haumont, Geneviève / Auran, Cyril 2004. The Phonology of Melodic Prominence: the Structure of Melisms, *Proceedings of Speech Prosody 2004.* Nara, Japan, 143-146.

Caelen-Haumont, Geneviève / Bel, Bernard 2000. Le caractère spontané dans la parole et le chant improvisés : de la structure intonative au mélisme. *Revue Parole*, 251-302.

Cowie, Roddy 2000. Describing the emotional states expressed in speech, *proceedings of the ISCA Workshop on Speech and Emotion*, Belfast, Proceedings on line, <http://www.qbc.ac.uk/en/isca /proceedings>.

Cowie, R.oddy / Douglas-Cowie, Ellen / Savvidou, S.uzie / Mcmahon, Edelle / Sawey, Martin / Schröder, Marc 2000. FEELTRACE: an instrument for recording perceived emotion in real time, *Proceedings of the ISCA Workshop on Speech and Emotion*, Belfast, Proceedings on line, <http://www.qbc.ac.uk/en/isca/proceedings>.

Frijda, Nico H. 1986. *The emotions*. Cambridge: Cambridge University Press.

Hirst, Daniel J. / Espesser, Robert 1993. Automatic labelling of fundamental frequency using a quadratic spline function, *Travaux de l'Institut de Phonétique d'Aix, 15,* 71-85.

Hirst, Daniel. J. / Di Cristo, Albert / Espesser, Robert 2000. Levels of representation and levels of analysis for intonation. In Horne, Merle (ed) *Prosody: Theory and Experiment.* Kluwer Academic Publishers, Dordrecht. 51-87.

Hirst, Daniel .J. 2005. Form and function in the representation of speech prosody. in Hirose, Keikichi / Hirst, Daniel / Sagisaka, Yoshinori (eds), *Quantitative prosody modeling for natural speech description and generation, Speech Communication* 46 (3-4), 334-347.

Lewin, Kurt 1936. Principles of topological psychology 1st edition. New York and London: McGraw-Hill book company, inc.

Meiyé, Jean-Philippe / Caelen-Haumont, Geneviève / Dubois, Danièle 1998. ΔF_0 comme indicateur cognitif des processus de compréhension en lecture. *Actes du VIIème Colloque de l'ARC, Saint-Denis,* 390-396.

Meiyé, Jean-Philippe 1999. Effets discursifs et calculs lexicaux sur les indices mélodiques en lecture, thèse de doctorat en sciences cognitives, INPG, Grenoble.

Makasso, Emmanuel-Moselly 2008. Intonation et mélismes dans le discours oral spontané en bàsàa, thèse de doctorat en sciences du langage, Université de Provence Aix-Marseille.

Morange, Séverine 2005. Approches structurale, prosodique, psycho-cognitive de quelques propriétés linguistiques subjectives de la parole : l'exemple de trois Montmartrois âgés, thèse de doctorat en sciences du langage, Université de Paris 3.

O'Connor, John D. / Arnold, Gordon 1973. *Intonation of colloquial English*, London, Longman.

Plutchik Robert 1980. *Emotion: A psychoevolutionary synthesis*, New York, Harper and Row.

Projet Phonologie du Français Contemporain, < http://wwwprojet-pfc.net>.

Vuillet, Jacques 2005. *La part de l'expressivité vocale dans le réglage de l'interaction et dans l'émergence de conduites langagières lors d'un atelier de langage en début d'école maternelle*, thèse de doctorat en sciences de la communication, Université Stendhal-Grenoble III.

BRIGITTE ZELLNER-KELLER

Aging, Interactions and Affects: Motivations and Methodological Issues

1. Introduction

Demographic projections suggest that Europeans aged 65 or older will by 2030 represent 25% of the population (16% in 2004). In developed countries, the average life span will continue to grow past the age of 80 (Source: United Nations 2007). In Switzerland, more than 10% of the 2000 generation will become centenarians, against 4% in 1900. The current quality of life and further progress in medicine will probably ensure for many retired people in our developed countries a normal and serene aging up to at least 70-75 years of age. This tendency for a longer life in good health represents a social phenomenon that was completely unknown to our ancestors.

In face of such a social evolution, it is striking to notice the scarcity of studies dedicated to the field of 'normal aging' and speech. How do neurophysiological and cognitive changes affect the communicative system? The interdependencies between cognitive activities such as speaking and biological functioning are highly complex. Very little is known about the adaptations of speech communication through aging, or how these adaptations are related to changes in the 'hardware resources' and to modifications in communicative needs.

From birth to death, human beings are in constant evolution, reorganising their brains, developing new abilities and loosing some others (Snowdon 2001, Goldberg 2005). Speaking does not escape from this general trend. Aged people tend to develop various psychological adaptations depending on the evolution of their health and personality, their life experiences, their social network, etc. In this perspective, 'to communicate' has different meanings for aged people, as compared to younger people, depending on physiological, psychological, social and ethical changes. For example, aged people – mainly after 75[1], enter a 'normal' weakening and general slowing down; they often have to accept hearing aids or braces – concomitant with changes in the musculature and jaws, that both modify the ease of perceiving and production of speech. The representation of aged people's self, associated with the effects of attitudes and beliefs about aging that younger speakers have, are also tuned in an indirect and subtle fashion with their human interactions, such as their motivations to interact, to argue, or to express intimate feelings. These are influenced by the speaker's inner capacities, by his beliefs about the importance and relevance of expressing what he thinks, and by his social interplay.

In this chapter, I propose to illustrate the relevance of extending our understanding of the speech communication system towards the effects of the aging of speech, in particular in the area of prosody.

2. Specificity of aged speakers

The fact that scientific research puts efforts into a topic or another is strongly associated with the psychosocial representation that we have developed of this topic. In that sense, we should briefly consider the current representations of aging in our societies, and in parallel, how aging is investigated in human sciences.

Psychosocial beliefs about aging are given for example by numbers of advertisements that communicate on the one hand an idealistic view of getting old, through images of serene and dynamic aging. Wrinkles, general weakening and fragility are avoided in these representations, even though the physiological process of aging is universal and inescapable. On the other hand, health and social workers document more and more difficulties related to aging: solitude, depression, physical and cognitive troubles, dementias. The tension

1 Fragility with age increases and life expectancy is reduced with the onset of the social pension plan around the age of 65.

between the idealistic view and the dark side of aging is illustrated in current jokes such as: 'hum, how to say, (pause), what is this word, (pause), oh oh, I've got the Alzheimer disease', as if there was an unspeakable and fearful belief of the order of: 'I am getting old, and I might be becoming insane'.

The scientific approach towards aging reflects this psychosocial tension to some degree. For example, the word 'aging' in our community of speech and communication is often understood as and associated with the degenerative illnesses that emerge in the aging process. What we currently know about aging and communicating and most of our knowledge on verbal performances of aged speakers is inferred from comparative studies between aged patients and aged speakers, as if we had a clear understanding and knowledge of what a 'normal aged speaker' is. This inference is based upon two assumptions. First, we suppose that the aging process is one-dimensional as if it should affect individuals at the same rhythm in the same way. Second, we presume that neural resources show considerable stability throughout one's lifetime.

2.1. Heterogeneity of the aged population

The precise definition of entrance into old age is unclear, even in recent studies where old speakers might be recruited already from the age of 60 (Federmeier/Kutas 2005). In the cognitive and neurophysiological literature, it is nowadays well demonstrated that the aging process varies from one person to another, and that the factors contributing to this process are numerous (Craik/Salthouse 1992). Among other factors one can name social and economic conditions, personality traits, motivation, attention span, state of health, one's life style, as well as neurobiological and neurophysiological factors (Valdois/Joanette 1991). This variability explains that chronological age is not necessarily equivalent to the physiological or psychological age. Beyond this variability however, gerontologists and geriatricians currently distinguish three phases in aging. During the first period, the young healthy seniors have an active retired life. Around the years 72-75, the first signs of weakening appear and possibly some serious health problems. Later, around the years 85-90, the elderly need increasing levels of care and might have to leave their home to go into nursing homes. Consequently, the concept of 'aged speakers' is fuzzy and inefficient.

Also, it is important in studies on speech and language to take into account the cohort effects, as they may be intermingled with the effects of age. This effect is related to the social and individual experiences of the compared generations. For example, the types of education, social and cultural beliefs and habits for a person born in 1930 are quite different from those of a person born in 1980. These differences may influence results based on communication media such as language and speech. According to the cultural life style, familiarity with particular concepts and objects vary among generations. Since the speed of the access to the mental lexicon is sensitive to word frequency, naming an object or a concept does not raise the same difficulty according to the age of the person, although age in itself is not the explaining factor.

In consequence, what is designed as a 'normal aged speaker' represents in fact an abstract entity that is poorly defined for the aging process of the speech communicative system is still under study (at the various physiologic, cognitive and linguistic levels).

2.2. Language lateralization along the lifetime

Comparisons of patients with control speakers involve another assumption about our representation of normal aged speakers. It is expected that similar neural resources are activated for speech processing, whatever the age is. Indeed, since Broca, the traditional lesion-based model for speech production and processing has considered that the activated cortical speech areas are strongly lateralized to the left hemisphere (Pulvermüller 1999, 2002). However, in recent decades, this vision has been nuanced. Particularly, recent studies based on neuro-imaging (fMRI, ERP, etc.) have demonstrated the considerable contribution of the right hemisphere to lexical and pragmatic processing, as well as certain aspects of the prosodic treatment (Pulvermüller 1999, 2002; Dolcos et al. 2002).

Moreover, it has been established that the organization of speech lateralization evolves with age. For example, Szaflarski et al. (2006) have studied the effects of age on lateralization on 170 right-handed subjects aged from 5 to 67 in a fRMI study. The task consisted in producing verbs. The authors observed that language lateralization grows in the dominant hemisphere up to 20, but that subsequently it slowly declines. This result can be attributed to neural death and/or to a change in the brain organization.

2.3. Language activity in the old age

Language activity also evolves with the psychological attitude typical of older speakers. Age-related shifts in both written and spoken language have been observed. In a study of the language change over life, Pennebaker and Stone (2003) developed the 'Linguistic Inquiry and Word Count' software with which they compared 3,280 participants' language samples (ages 8–85). They found that with increasing age, speakers tend to use more positive and fewer negative emotion words. Also, aged people appear to be more anchored in the present and future with respect to their use of verb tense, a result which was unexpected in terms of our societies' stereotypes of aging. In the same study, a drop in the use of first-person singular was found, suggesting that aged speakers tend to be more detached from their ego. Finally, looking at the linguistic markers of cognitive complexity, aged speakers demonstrated a general pattern of increasing complexity.

The process of aging is multifactorial, affecting both neural functioning and behavior. Although the entanglement between cognitive activities, such as speaking, and biological functioning is highly complex, it seems well motivated to assume that neural organization evolves along one's lifetime. According to age and experience, speakers do not recruit exactly the same resources. The following section will briefly summarize what is known about the aging communicative system, considering that the mentioned studies are based upon the two questionable assumptions raised previously in Section 2.

3. Aging of the language system

Despite tremendous variations between subjects in the speed of the aging process due among others to genetics, developmental trajectories of skill development and its maintenance, and life conditions, it is important to briefly point out that several changes of aging may have important effects on speech communication (Caruso et al. 1994), even if it is true that the 'preservation in many important areas of language knowledge helps most elderly adults maintain a very high level of functioning in day-to-day discourse processing' (Wingfield 2000: 374).

3.1 Neurophysiological aging of the speech system

Structural noticeable tissues changes such as bone tissue demineralization is often accompanied by bone deformations and remodeling. Also, the facial bones have been reported to continue to grow slightly into old age (Linville, 2001). Some laryngeal cartilages ossify. Neurological tissues are also concerned throughout the aging process. By the age of 90, it is expected that brain weight has decreased by ca.10% in comparison to young adults (Xu et al. 2000 in Linville 2001, Snowdon 2001, Goldberg 2005, Raz et al. 2005). The brain is nowadays considered as a device merging information from different modalities (Pulvermüller 2002). The nervous tissue loss requires various adaptations and compensations that might have an impact on its multimodal functioning such as speaking. Another important aspect is that part of the neurological tissue modifications are intertwined with hormonal functioning which triggers modifications of the vocal folds (Linville 2001). Changes of the structure and the length of the vocal folds are documented, and muscles, in particular facial muscles and respiratory muscles, loose elasticity and strength (Linville 2001). The neuromuscular control of voice production, which depends in part on the balance of pulmonary, lanryngeal, and articulatory elements, is consequently affected (Martin 1997). One major effect of these changes is the slowing-down of the speech rate (Linville 2001; see below section 3.4).

The ability to process sensory information is also modified, in particular declines in visual and hearing acuity. The auditory system is often affected either at the peripheric level because of transmission loss in the middle ear and loss of hair cells in the basilar membrane, and/or a deficit in central auditory processing. In that case, older adults often experience hearing loss in high-frequency sounds and deficits in frequency and temporal resolution (Wingfield et al. 2005). The frequency deficits render the separation of speech from noise difficult. The deficit in temporal resolution causes troubles with discriminating silent gaps, blurring words together. Yet the perceptual process is still most often correctly achieved thanks to the expert language knowledge the speakers have developed. However, the resources engaged in the effortful perceptual process can thus not be dedicated to the comprehension and memory operations (Wingfield et al. 2005).

3.2. Cognitive aging

Aging is often characterized by a cognitive and a motoric slow-down as well as memory troubles, in particular with the short-term memory (Craik/Salthouse 1992, Mortensen et al. 2006, Wingfield et al. 2006). The decline of the working and episodic memory in normal aging is commonly reported (Craik/Salthouse 1992, Light/Burke, 1988). It is currently assumed that functional aging does not affect the two hemispheres symmetrically. According to Thuillard and Assal (1991), visual-spatial and visual-perceptual areas are more rapidly affected in aging than verbal functions and cognitive strategies. Crystallized abilities, which are based on general knowledge acquired with life experience, are relatively well-maintained, contrary to fluid intelligence, inductive reasoning, episodic and working memory and processing speed (Bäckman et al. 2000). The latter, that are grounded on cognitive processes (memory, attention, reaction-time), are concerned earlier (Park et al. 2002; Bialystock et al. 2004). In conclusion, aging is more often characterized by the decline of the efficiency of attentional control rather than in the ability to use common procedures and knowledge (Bialystok et al. 2004). Changes in physiology and cognition have various impacts on language and speech, as summarized in the following sections.

3.3 Aging and language functioning

Speech production involves the ability to access the lexicon 'on the fly' and to organize words into a coherent utterance. This ability can be experimentally controlled. For example, Kemper et al. (2004) asked young and old participants to memorize sentence stems that differed in syntactic complexity and to produce a complete sentence with this stem. When placed in this controlled situation, older speakers tended to produce less complex utterances than younger speakers (Kemper et al. 2003, 2004; Wingfield 2005). Kemper suggests that the competence for syntactic processing per se might not be concerned in aging, but rather that there are the working memory limitations on the ability to produce long and complex utterances. Moreover, the time pressure due to certain tasks such as in Kemper's and/or the motivation to perform well in such types of experience might be perceived as more stressful by old people since the slowdown process by aged people is well-established nowadays.

Aged people often report more word-finding failures than younger people, whereas the semantic processes seem to be well-maintained (Burke/Shafto, 2004, Gillioz/Zellner Keller, 2008). The decline in word-retrieval is manifested for example by reformulations, filled pauses, slips of the tongue and tips-of-the-tongue. Burke and Shafto (2004) have reviewed the relevant literature on this issue and they conclude for evidence that normal aging selectively impairs certain language functions more than others. Although old speakers maintain or even improve their knowledge of words and word meanings, those production language deficits might be explained by weaker connections with the phonological system.

Some disfluencies may serve as a function of interaction (for example to express a metacognitive state), and others may signal a transitory overload in the speech production system. Bortfled et al. (2001) examined disfluency rates in conversation from the angle of the effects of age, relationship, topic, role, and gender. Their results show that older adults, aged between 63 and 72, produce marginally more speech errors than younger speakers (hesitations, pauses, repetitions, false starts, reformulations), especially when the topic of the conversation is unfamiliar, between two turn-takings. Compared to younger adults, aged speakers need more time to perform the same linguistic task, produce fewer lexical words per time unit and more hesitations and repetitions inside an utterance. Their interactive stream is thus less fluent, and the verbal communication less efficient. The authors explain this loss of efficiency by a slower lexical access. Moreover, compared to younger speakers, older adults produce also more disfluencies between two utterances, suggesting that they might encounter planning difficulties.

Mortensen et al. (2006) report that in response to autobiographic questions or in conversation, older adults tend to be more verbose and more disfluent than young adults, especially when the task is difficult and when it places few constraints on the content of the utterance. Older talkative speakers are also those who produce more irrelevant utterances according to Arbuckle et al. (2000). The authors interpret this verbosity and those discourse excursions in terms of an inhibition deficit.

In summary, old speakers compared to younger speakers tend to be more verbose, they experience more word-finding failures, and they use less complex sentences from a linguistic point of view.

3.4. Age-related changes on speaking functioning

The slowdown process

The slowdown process has indeed various impacts on speech production. For example, Balota et al. (1988) placed young and old subjects in a delayed pronunciation task to trace the time course of lexical access and a semantic priming task to determine the time course of spreading activation. They found from the delayed pronunciation task that older adults benefited more than younger adults from a preview of the word to-be-pronounced; there was little evidence of age-related differences in the rate at which activation builds up in semantic memory; but the analyses of the production durations indicated that there was a large age-related difference in the duration from onset to offset to pronounce a visually presented word.

Articulation and tempo

Evidence of slower articulation has been found for laryngeal functioning, the oral muscles and lip activity (Linville 2001). Smith et al (1987) asked 10 normal, elderly adults and 10 young adults to produce a variety of words and sentences at both normal and fast speaking rates. Segment, syllable, and sentence durations of older adults were 20 to 25% longer than those of the young adults at both speech rates. Greater variability in speech rate for older speakers is also reported (Linville 2001). However, Brückl and Sendlmeier (2003) in a study of aged female voices found that although the tempo in reading speech is slower with increasing age, articulation rate cannot be considered as directly correlated with chronological age.

Fast speech is not easily perceived by aged subjects. As pointed out by Wingfield et al. (2005) and Vaughan et al. (2002), it is not likely that older speakers loose speech recognition because of a slowing in their processing speed. Instead, it is the loss of the consonant acoustic cues that affects recognition of rapid speech. In the same way, Schneider et al. (2000) have tested young and old adults in listening condition to conversations before answering various questions. Some questions required an answer with specific details and others required a more integrative answer. Conversations were presented in two sound conditions, one in a calm environment, and the second in a moderate noisy environment. Authors found that when the listening conditions were adjusted to individual differences, there was no difference in the answers in both conditions (calm and noisy). It is in moderate noisy conditions that younger subjects could remember more details than older subjects.

F_0 and intonation

Aging affects fundamental frequency in both women and men. In female aging voices, F_0 decreases by ca. 30 Hz with a strong drop around the menopause. Men show a slightly decreasing curve followed by a strong increase by ca. 30 Hz starting around the fiftieth year (Linville 2001; Martin 1997; Brückl/Sendlmeier 2003). A number of studies have investigated the perceived aged voice and its acoustic correlates. Brückl and Sendlmeier (2003) found that the correlations between the perceived or the chronological age and the average fundamental frequency are stronger in spontaneous speech than in read speech. In agreement with Linville (2001) and Baken (2000), their various measures of F_0 stability did not show any systematic strong correlations. F_0 stability seems to be more affected by physical health, which is quite variable among speakers of the same age.

Intensity

Maximum vowel intensity decreases with age in both men and women (Linville 2001). This is likely due to the changes that occur into the respiratory and phonatory systems. Yet this lowering is not discernible in normal conversational speech (Linville 2001). According to Brückl and Sendlmeier (2003), a raised frequency tremor intensity index on sustained vowels is the best predictor of increased chronological and perceived age. The authors also found that spectral noise is more related to fitness than to chronological age.

Voice quality

The speed of the changes in the vocal tract of elderly adults varies from one speaker to another. Linville (2001) reports from the literature a tendency for old men to centralize vowels because of a less accurate tongue command. In her own study based on an LTAS analysis, she retrieved this tendency of centralization which is more pronounced for men than for women.

In summary, studies show that aged people tend to produce utterances with less complex syntax structures, they tend to hypo-articulate at a slower speech rate, with a higher or lower F_0, and a quivering and rougher voice. Perception is also affected and triggers compensations such as a different use of prosody. It is still unclear how fast this aging process affects speaking and language functioning. For example, it is unclear what the normal abilities of young seniors (up to 72) are, compared to older speakers (75-90) and the elderly.

4. Prosody and aging

Speech processing requires fast cognitive processing for the building of meanings in speech interactions. It involves the extraction of relevant features from the rapid transitory acoustic signal. Since it has been found that older speakers perform slower at the cognitive level and encounter difficulties in the perception of speech, one may ask how prosodic features are used in speech processing.

4.1. Linguistic Prosody

To our knowledge, there is no study on the prosody produced by aged healthy speakers compared to the prosody produced by younger healthy speakers. For example, we do not know whether old speakers convey prosody of questions in the same way as younger speakers. There are only studies where prosody of aged healthy speakers is compared for example to speakers with Parkinson's disease or other pathology. In other words, it is yet unclear how prosody in speech produced by aged healthy people evolves along the aging process, and how diverse among speakers this process is.

On the other hand, some authors have investigated in speech processing how prosody is used throughout the aging process. The importance of linguistic prosody for older listeners was demonstrated by Wingfield et al. (1999). Older listeners performed better on speech recognition when silences were inserted in sentences at natural phrase boundaries than when silences were simply added at regular intervals. Relevant silences helped to build semantically coherent units. Wingfield et al. (2000) also found a greater role of contextual cues for older listeners. They tested listeners of different ages in a recognition task of spoken words in different conditions: word onsets, word onsets followed by white noise indicating the full duration of the target word, or word onsets followed by a low-pass-filtered signal that indicated the number of syllables and syllabic stress (word prosody) in the absence of segmental information. The authors found that older adults tend to use longer stimulus durations for word recognition and that this age-difference is related to age differences in hearing sensitivity. The authors also found that word recognition was facilitated by knowledge of word prosody, in particular word stress, similarly for both groups. The greater role of prosody could be explained by some sort of compensation of the age-related effects (presbycusis, general cognitive slowing and poorer working memory performance).

Baum (2003) tested the hypothesis that elderly listeners (mean age: 70) rely to a greater extent than young subjects (mean age: 24) on contextual cues to aid in phonetic identification. At a first step, she investigated the role of the metrical stress pattern on low-level phonetic identification. For example, two voiced-voiceless alveolar stop continua were created by manipulating VOT by steps of five ms in the initial stop consonants of the two words ' 'digress' and 'ti'gress' These continua were then appended to both original word endings. The stimuli were then presented to both groups of listeners. Baum found that compared to younger listeners, older listeners were more strongly affected by the stress pattern rather than the VOT values, showing that older listeners rely more on prosodic cues.

4.2. Emotional Prosody

It is commonly reported that the elderly are less skilled in the processing of speech prosody. In an extended study, Orbelo et al. (2003) have evaluated the ability to produce and grasp affective prosody through the aging process. They have used the Aprosodia Battery, which included an assessment of attitudinal comprehension, and have investigated the relationship between age-related hearing loss on one hand, and age-related cognitive decline on the other hand. In the attitudinal task, subjects were asked to distinguish between sincere and sarcastic tones of voice. Their results show that comprehension of affective prosody shows a negative correlation with age. Older participants manifest a decline in grasping those prosodic affects. This is in agreement with Thompson et al. (2001) who conducted a study based on the perception of videotaped scenes. Emotional nonverbal information was conveyed at the end of each scene at low, medium, and high intensities. Older adults' ability to differentiate levels of emotional intensity was not as strong as compared to younger adults. Paulmann et al. (2008) also report a lower level of emotion recognition for older listeners (38-50) compared to younger listeners (18-28). In Orbelo et al.'s study (2003), the decline in comprehending affective prosody is not explained by mild to moderate peripheral hearing loss and only marginally by cognitive performance. The authors interpret their results for elderly speakers as a specific aging effect that impairs right hemisphere function, at the level of the para-Sylvian cortices.

5. Conclusion

What is designed as a 'normal aged speaker' represents mostly an abstract entity that is poorly defined for the aging process of the speech communicative system and it is still being investigated. A number of studies on aging and communication suffer from questionable methodological issues related to fundamental assumptions about aging.

A reasonable hypothesis would state that instead of a uniform picture, heterogeneity is likely to characterize the population of normal aged speakers and that one might investigate to what extent the three 'stages in aging' as documented in gerontology and geriatrics are retrieved in the aging of the communicative system. Our representation of the speaking system through aging would become more detailed and accurate. This would be useful both for the fundamental research and the treatment of neurodegenerative pathologies, as well as for the improvement of the quality of our interactions with old people in caring structures.

Acknowledgments

Thanks to Eric Keller for his valuable suggestions and improvements.

References

Arbuckle, Tannis Y. / Nohara-LeClair, Michiko / Pushkar, Dolores 2000. Effect of Off-Target Verbosity on Communication Efficiency in a Referential Communication Task. *Psychology and Aging*, 151, 65-77.

Bäckman, Lars / Small, Brent J. / Larsson, Maria 2000. Cognitive Functioning in Very Old Age. In Fergus Craik / Timothy Salthouse (eds) *Handbook of aging and cognition*. Hillsdale, New Jersey: Erlbaum. 499-558.

Baken, Ron J / Orlikoff, Robert F. 2000. *Clinical measurement of speech and voice*. Singular Publishing Group, San Diego, California.

Balota, David A / Duchek, Janet M. 1988. Age-Related Differences in Lexical Access, Spreading Activation, and Simple Pronunciation. *Psychology and Aging*, 3, 84-93.

Baum, Shari R. 2003. Age Differences in the Influence of Metrical Structure on Phonetic Identification. *Speech Communication* 39, 231–242.

Bialystok, Ellen / Craik, Fergus I. / Klein, Raymond / Viswanathan, Mythili 2004. Bilingualism, Aging, and Cognitive Control: Evidence from the Simon task. *Psychology and Aging*, vol. 19/2, 290-303.

Bortfeld, Heather / Leon, Silvia D / Bloom, Jonathan E / Schober, Michael F / Brennan, Susan E. 2001. Disfluency Rates in Conversation: Effects of Age, Relationship, Topic, Role, and Gender. *Language and Speech*, n° 44/2, 123-147.

Brückl, Marcus / Sendlmeier, Walter 2003. Aging Female Voices: an Acoustic and Perceptive Analysis. *VOQUAL '03*, 163-168.

Burke, Deborah M / MacKay, Donald G / Worthley, Joanna S / Wade, Elizabeth 1991. On the Tip of the Tongue: What causes Word Finding Failures in Young and Older Adults? *Journal of Memory and Language*, 30, 552-579.

Burke, Deborah M / Shafto, Meredith A. 2004. Aging and Language Production. *Current Directions in Psychological Science*, 13/1, 21-24.

Caruso, Antony J / Mueller, Peter B / Xue, Steve A. 1994. Relative Contributions of Voice and Articulation to Listener Judgements of Age and Gender: Preliminary Data and Implications. *Voice*, 3/1, 1-9.

Craik, Fergus I / Salthouse, Timothy A. (eds) 1992. *Handbook of Aging and Cognition.* Hillsdale, N.J., Lawrence Erlbaum Associates.

Davis, Daniel H. 2004. Dementia: Sociological and Philosophical Constructions. *Soc Sci Med*, 58/2, 369-378.

Dolcos, Florin / Rice, Heather J. / Cabeza, Roberto 2002. Hemispheric Asymmetry and Aging: Right Hemisphere Decline or Asymmetry Reduction. *Neuroscience Biobehavioral Reviews*, 26, 819-825.

Gillioz, Christelle / Zellner Keller, Brigitte 2008. Analyse du Mot sur le Bout de la Langue de 19 à 79 ans. *XXVIIèmes Journées d'Etude sur la Parole* JEP'08. Paper 1573.

Goldberg, Elkhonon 2005. *The Wisdom Paradox: How Your Mind Can Grow Stronger as Your Brain Grows Older*. New York: Gotham Books, Penguin.

Kemper, Susan / Herman, Ruth / Lian, Cindy H.T. 2003. Age Differences in Sentence Production. Journals of Gerontology: *Psychological Science,* 58, 260-269.

Kemper, Susan / Herman, Ruth E. / Liu, Chiung-Ju 2004. Sentence Production by Young and Older Adults in Controlled Contexts. *Journals of Gerontology, Series B: Psychological Sciences and Social Sciences*, 59, 220-224.

Light, Leah / Burke, Deborah M. 1988. *Language, memory and aging*. Cambridge University Press.

Linville, Sue E. 2001. *Vocal Aging*. San Diego: Singular Publishing Group.

Martin, C. 1997. Voice and Aging: Aspects of the Speech Signal that are Perceived as Characteristic of the Older Voice. *Unpublished BS Dissertation*. London: The Central School of Speech and Drama.

Mortensen, Linda / Meyer, Antje / Humphreys, Glyn 2006. Age-Related Effects on Speech Production: A review. *Language and Cognitive Processes,* 21/1-3, 238-290.

Orbelo, Diana M / Testa, Julie A / Ross, Elliot D. 2003. Age-Related Impairments in Comprehending Affective Prosody With Comparison to Brain-Damaged Subjects. Journal of Geriatric Psychiatry and Neurology. 16/1.

Park, Denise C / Gutchess, Angela H. 2002. Aging, Cognition and Culture: A Neuroscientific Perspective. *Neuroscience and Biobehavioral Reviews,* 26, 859-867.

Paulmann, Silke / Pell, Marc D / Kotz, Sonja A. 2008. How aging affects the recognition of emotional speech. *Brain and Language*, 1043, 262-269.

Pennebaker, James / Stone, Lori D. 2003. Words of Wisdom: Language Use over the Lifespan. *Journal of Personality and Social Psychology*, 85, 291-301.

Pulvermüller, Friedemann 1999. Words in the Brain's Language. *The Behavioral and Brain Sciences*, 22, 253-279.

Pulvermüller, Friedemann 2002. A Brain Perspective on Language Mechanisms: from Discrete Neuronal Ensembles to Serial Order. *Progress in Neurobiology*, 67, 85-111.

Raz, Naftali / Lindenberger, Ulman / Rodrigue, Karen M / Kennedy, Kristen M / Head, Denise / Williamson, Adrienne / Dahle, Cheryl / Gerstorf, Denis / Acker, James D. 2005. Regional Brain Changes in Aging Healthy Adults: General Trends, Individual Differences and Modifiers. *Cerebral Cortex*; 15, 1676-1689.

Schneider, Bruce A. / Daneman, Meredith / Murphy, Dana / Kwong See, Sheree 2000. Listening to Discourse in Distracting settings: The Effects of Aging. *Psychology and Aging*, 15, 110-125.

Smith, Bruce L / Wasowicz Jan / Preston, Judy 1987. Temporal characteristics of the speech of normal elderly adults. J Speech *Hear Res,* 304, 522-529.

Snowdon, David 2001. *Aging with Grace*. London: Harper Collins Publishers. Fourth Estate.

Szaflarski, Jerzy P. / Holland, Scott K. / Schmithorst, Vincent J. / Byars, Anna W. 2006. An fMRI study of language lateralization in children and adults. *Human Brain Mapping*, n° 27, 202-212.

Thompson, Laura A. / Aidinejad, Mohammad R. / Ponte, Janisse. 2001. Aging and the Effects of Facial and Prosodic Cues on Emotional Intensity Ratings and Memory Reconstructions. *Journal of Nonverbal Behavior*, 25, 101-125.

Thuillard, Françoise / Assal, Gil 1991. Données neuropsychologiques chez le sujet âgé normal. In M. Habib, Y. Joanette / I. Pue (eds) *Démences et Syndromes Démentiels: Approche Clinique et Neuropsychologique.* Masson, Paris. 125-133.

Valdois, Sylviane / Joanette, Yves 1991. Aspects neuropsychologiques du vieillissement normal. In Michel Habib / Yves Joanette / Michèle Puel (eds) *Démences et Syndromes Démentiels: Approche Clinique et Neuropsychologique.* Masson, Paris, 137-144.

Vaughan, Nancy E / Furukawa, Izumi / Balasingam, Nirmala / Mortz, Margaret / Fausti, Stephen A. 2002. Time-expanded speech and speech recognition in older adults. *Journal of Rehabilitation Research and Development.* 39/5, 559–566.

Wingfield, Arthur / Tun, Patricia A / Koh, Christine K / Rosen, Merri J. 1999. Regaining Lost Time: Adult Aging and the Effect of Time Restoration on Recall of Time-Compressed Speech. *Psychology and Aging*. 143, 380-389.

Wingfield, Arthur / Stine-Morrow, Elizabeth A.L. 2000. Language and Speech. In Fergus Craik / Timothy Salthouse (eds), *Handbook of aging and cognition..* Hillsdale, New Jersey: Erlbaum, 359-416.

Wingfield, Arthur / Tun, Patricia A / Mc Coy, Sandra L. 2005. Hearing loss in older adulthood. What it is and how it interacts with cognitive performance. *Current Directions in Psychological Science*, 14/3, 144-148.

Wingfield, Arthur / Grossman, Murray 2006. Language and the aging brain. Patterns of neural compensation revealed by functional brain imaging. *J. Neurophysiol.*, 96, 2830-2832.

D. ERIK EVERHART / AMY J. SHIPLEY / HEATH A. DEMAREE

Perception of Emotional Prosody: Establishing a Link Between Sex-related Differences, Brain Development, and Sex Hormones

1. Introduction

Advances in the understanding of prosody and associated neuroanatomical systems have been made since the well known paper of Monrad-Krohn (1947), which describes the acquisition of a foreign accent in a 30 year-old woman who was struck by a shell fragment during an air raid at Oslo in 1941. Over the course of the last several decades, research concerning the processing of emotional or affective prosody has proliferated, in part due to the development of theories of lateralized processing of emotion. One hypothesis indicates that the right hemisphere is specialized for the perception and expression of emotion (Borod 1993). Numerous studies have documented the important role of the right hemisphere with regard to perception of emotional prosody (Everhart/Demaree/Shipley 2006; Ross 1981; Ross/Thompson/Yenkosky 1997). The notion that the right hemisphere is dominant or that the right hemisphere acts alone in the perception of emotional prosody has become clouded, as a literature base also documents a role for the left hemisphere in the perception of some auditory emotional stimuli (Pell 2006; Ross et al. 1997). In addition, research has implicated multiple brain regions (including subcortical) in the processing of emotional prosody (Adolphs 2002; Adolphs/Damasio/Tranel 2002; Pell 2006; Rymarczyk/Grabowska 2007). It is also well known that neuroanatomical differences and performance on behavioral tasks differ as a function of the sexes (Gur/Gunning-Dixon/Bilker/Gur 2002; Gur et al. 1999), and sex-related differences in brain activity during task performance have been documented (Everhart/Shucard/Quatrin/Shucard 2001, 2004; Rymarczyk/ Grabowska 2007; Wildgruber/Pihan/Ackermann/Erb/Grodd 2002b). Given these identified issues, the purpose of this chapter is to review relevant research concerning the right hemisphere hypothesis of emotion as it pertains to sex-related differences in the perception of emotional prosody. An additional emphasis is placed on the review of sex-related hormones that may impact perception of emotional prosody. The chapter concludes with a discussion of the relevance of social neurocognition to the study of emotional prosody and provides directions for future research.

2. Processing of emotion within the right hemisphere

Almost 100 years ago, Mills (1912a; 1912b) observed a link between emotion processing and the right hemisphere; this observation was also noted by others such as Babinski (1914) and (Denney-Brown/ Meyer/Horenstein 1952) who noted that patients with right hemisphere lesions were often inappropriately indifferent. These observations and others led to the right hemisphere hypothesis, which posits that the right hemisphere is specialized for the perception, expression, and experience of emotion, regardless of valence (Borod/Koff/White 1983; Heilman/Bowers 1990; Ross 1985; Tucker 1981). To date, much of the supporting literature has focused on two channels of emotion processing: facial affect and affective (emotional) prosody (Demaree/Everhart/Youngstrom/Harrison 2005; Everhart et al. 2006).

With regard to facial affect, tachistoscopic studies (Landis, Assal/Perret 1979; Ley/Bryden 1979; McKeever/Dixon 1981; Suberi/ McKeever 1977), lesion studies (Adolphs/Damasio/Tranel/Damasio 1996; Borod et al. 1998; Cicone/Wapner/Gardner 1980; Etcoff 1986), and electrophysiological recording and neuroimaging studies support the notion that the right hemisphere is specialized for the processing of facial emotion (Kestenbaum/Nelson 1992; Laurian/Bader/Lanares/ Oros 1991; Munte et al. 1998; Vanderploeg/Brown/Marsh 1987).

In considering emotional prosody, and more specific to this chapter, Ross (1981) described a group of communication disorders referred to as the 'aprosodias'; this term largely reflects disturbance of the ability to perceive (sensory aprosodias) or to express (motor aprosodias) the emotional components of speech. Aprosodias are typically observed following right hemisphere lesions (Ross et al. 1997). Early dichotic listening studies demonstrated a left ear advantage in the recognition of emotional aspects of speech (Carmon/Nachshon 1973; Haggard/ Parkinson 1971; King/Kimura 1972), as did studies that utilized monaural presentations. As with facial affect perception, the findings from electrophysiological recording studies (Bostanov/Kotchoubey 2004; Everhart/Carpenter/Carmona/Ethridge/Demaree 2003; Jordan/ Everhart/Demaree 2004; Pihan/Altenmuller/Ackermann 1997) and neuroimaging studies (Buchanan et al. 2000; George/Parekh/ Roskinsky et al. 1996; Imaizumi et al. 1997) implicate the role of the right hemisphere in the perception of affective prosody. In revisiting these hypotheses, using the Aprosodia Battery with stroke patients, Ross and Monnot (2008) draw several conclusions. As with previous studies, it is concluded that affective prosody is a dominant and lateralized function of the right hemisphere, the intrahemispheric organization of affective prosody is analogous to the organization of propositional language in the left hemisphere, and aprosodic syndromes are cortically based as part of evolutionary adaptations underlying human language and communication.

It is noted that alternate theories exist with regard to hemispheric processing of emotional stimuli. For example, known as the valence model, this hypothesis posits that the right hemisphere is specialized for negative emotion and that the left hemisphere is specialized for positive emotion (Ehrlichman 1987; Silberman/ Weingartner 1986). A variant of the valence hypothesis contends that differential specialization exists for the expression and the experience of emotion as a function of valence, while *perceptual* processing of both positive and negative affective stimuli is a right cerebral function (Bryden 1982; Davidson 1984). A third model, the 'approach-withdrawal' model of emotion processing, posits that emotions associated with approach- and withdrawal-behaviors are processed within the left- and right-anterior brain regions, respectively. The overlap between the valence and approach-withdrawal models is extensive, with most negative emotions (e.g., fear, disgust) eliciting withdrawal behavior and most positive emotions (e.g., happiness, amusement) eliciting approach behavior (Davidson 1995). Another model that readily incorporates emotion processing and brain function is referred to as the Behavioral Activation / Behavioral Inhibition Model (BIS/ BAS) (Gray 1982). Activation within BAS is responsible for both approach and active avoidance behaviors and the emotions associated with these behaviors are generally positive in nature ('hope' for reward or 'relief' from non-punishment), while BIS activation is associated with behavior consistent with passive avoidance and extinction and its activation is generally associated with negative hedonic experience (e.g., anxiety, fear). Persons with higher BAS scores have been found to have increased left-frontal activation (Coan/Allen 2003; Harmon-Jones/Allen 1997; Sutton/ Davidson 1997) whereas individuals with higher BIS scores were found to have greater right-frontal activation (Sutton/Davidson 1997). Finally, although relatively new within the literature, there is some preliminary data that suggests that dominance (in addition to valence and arousal) may facilitate understanding of regional brain processing of emotion; this third dimension may also be associated with patterns of left and right brain activity (Demaree/Everhart/Youngstrom/Harrison 2005). While these other models are acknowledged (i.e, valence model and approach – withdrawal models), the present review focuses primarily on the right hemisphere model, given that much of the development and current understanding of the perception of emotional prosody is based on this model (Ross 1981; Ross/Monnot 2008; Ross et al. 1997).

The strongest evidence with regard to the 'right-hemisphere' model of emotion processing as it pertains to affective prosody is described by Ross (1981). In this study, Ross examined a series of ten patients with focal right brain damage. Patterns of deficits in processing affective prosody that were analogous to the anatomic patterns of aphasic deficits observed after focal brain damage to the left hemisphere were documented. Relevant to the current article, Ross described patients with sensory aprosodia and transcortical aprosodia, in which patients with deficits in comprehension or reception of prosody had damage to the posterior-superior temporal lobe or adjacent regions; these regions are similar in location to Wernicke's area (or adjacent regions) in the left hemisphere in which Wernicke's aphasia or transcortical aphasia are produced, respectively. These ideas were expanded upon in more recent articles by the same author (Ross 1985; Ross/Monnot 2008; Ross et al. 1997).

In general, the studies that have utilized patients with identifiable lesions have found evidence that supports a strong role of the right hemisphere with regard to the perception of emotional prosody; this is consistent with other channels of emotion processing (Adolphs 2002; Adolphs et al. 2002; Baum/Pell 1999; Borod et al. 1998; Borod et al. 2000; Pell 2006; Rymarczyk/Grabowska 2007). It is also noted, however, that subcortical regions and other regions that fall outside of the right hemisphere have been identified as playing an important role in the processing of emotional prosody (Pell 2006; Rymarczyk/Grabowska 2007)

Earlier ERP studies and neuroimaging studies also support the right hemisphere hypothesis. For example, one electrophysiological study found predominant activation of right frontal regions during the perception of emotional prosody. Participants were asked to discriminate pairs of sentences with happy, sad, or neutral intonation during two experiments. In the first experiment, the participants were asked to denote the original emotional category of each sentence pair, and to decide which of the two items displayed stronger emotional expressiveness. The second experiment required participants to repeat the utterances using inner speech. While results from the first experiment were indicative of right hemisphere activation, the results from the second experiment were suggestive of a left-hemisphere shift in activity; this shift is possibly associated with the verbal nature (i.e., use of inner speech) of the task (Pihan/Altenmuller/Hertrich/Ackermann 2000).

Previous PET studies also support the role of the right hemisphere in emotion processing. One PET study asked a group of 13 healthy individuals to listen to three similar sets of spoken sentences. In one task, they were asked to respond to emotional propositional content. Another task required the participants to respond to the emotional prosody of the sentence, while a third task required the listener to repeat the second word in the sentence. It was found that the 'understanding' of propositional content activated the prefrontal cortex bilaterally (left more than right), while responding to the emotional prosody activated the right prefrontal cortex (George/Parekh/Rosinsky et al. 1996).

Regarding the use of fMRI, Buchanan et al. (2000) asked ten right-handed males to discriminate words based on either expressed emotional tone (angry, happy, sad, or neutral) or initial consonant sounds (phonemes). Bilateral activity was observed when participants were asked to detect emotional or verbal aspects of language when compared to baseline activity. However, when compared with verbal detection, the detection of emotion task yielded significant activity in the right inferior frontal lobe. In contrast, detection of verbal stimuli compared with the detection of emotion yielded activation within the left inferior frontal lobe. It is noted by the authors of this study that the results are in general consistent with the right hemisphere hypothesis. However, the authors also noted that bilateral activity was observed regardless of condition (emotional or verbal). In summary of this section, early and recent lesion studies, behavioral studies, and more recent studies that incorporate functional neuroimaging have yielded results that are somewhat supportive of the right hemisphere hypothesis for the perception of emotional prosody.

2.1 Other brain regions involved in the perception of emotional prosody.

Interestingly, within the right-hemisphere, some functional imaging studies indicate that the prefrontal cortex is disproportionately important in perceiving and recognizing emotional prosody (Buchanan et al. 2000; George/Parekh/Roskinsky et al. 1996). More recently, Rymarczyk and Grabowska (2007) suggested that prefrontal cortex, temporo-parietal cortical regions, and basal ganglia constitute the core structures of the network that process emotional prosody. It is also noted that some data indicate that the perception (or processing) of emotional prosody requires bilateral involvement (Baum/Pell 1999; Pell 2006; Pihan et al. 2000) as well as the utilization of subcortical structures such as the basal ganglia (Pell 2006; Schirmer/Kotz 2006b).

For example, Pell (2006) suggests that the basal ganglia are necessary for promoting the salience of long-term prosodic variations in speech, while the left hemisphere likely shares a role in "retrieving meaningful information from emotional cues in speech". These statements are now fairly well supported with findings from clinical groups (see for review Pell 2006).

Growing support for these premises is also found in studies that utilize nonclinical populations. For example, in one fMRI study, Kotz and colleagues (Kotz et al. 2003) asked participants to listen to semantically neutral sentences spoken with positive, negative, and neutral intonations. In one condition of the study, the speech stimuli were presented normally (normal condition), while in the other condition, speech stimuli were filtered so as to suppress segmental and lexical information (emotional prosody condition). The purpose of this method was to create a condition in which emotional prosody was easily accessible, but no semantic information was available (i.e., filtered or 'emotional prosody' condition). During the normal conditions, peri-sylvian areas, frontal (left lateralized), and subcortical regions (bilateral putamen, thalamus, and head of caudate) were activated. During the filtered condition, bilateral fronto-opercular regions were activated (although left accentuated). Subcortical structures were also activated, although less so than in the normal condition. The authors conclude that the data are not supportive of an 'exclusive' right-hemisphere lateralization of emotional prosody.

In another study, Mitchell and colleagues (Mitchell/Elliott/Barry/Cruttenden/Woodruff 2003) used fMRI to examine brain activity during six separate scanning studies with the same participants, within which two different conditions (i.e., active versus passive) were contrasted. Overall, it was found that passive listening to emotional prosody activated the lateral temporal lobe, consisting of the superior and/or middle temporal gyri. Of note, the temporal lobe activity was relatively right-lateralized regardless of the inclusion of semantic information. When participants were asked to attend to semantics, the neural response was left lateralized. Attention to emotional prosody induced right-lateralized activity, including the middle temporal gyrus. While the majority of the findings from this study implicate the right hemisphere during the processing of emotional prosody, it should also be noted that additional activity was noted in the left mid-frontal gyrus when participants listened to pure emotional prosody. Also using fMRI, Wildgruber and colleagues (Wildgruber et al. 2005) used an affect recognition paradigm, in which participants were asked to recognize prosodic expressions of five basic emotions including happiness, sadness, anger, fear, and disgust. Another portion of the experiment required phonetic monitoring of the same stimuli. Both tasks (affect recognition and phonetic monitoring) yielded bilateral response within frontal, temporal, parietal, thalamic, and cerebellar regions. A right-hemisphere pattern of activation including the posterior superior temporal sulcus, and dorsolateral and orbitobasal frontal regions for prosodic recognition was evidenced. In contrast, left-sided speech areas were activated for the phonetic monitoring task. An earlier study from the same group found activation within the right inferior parietal lobule, the bilateral mesiofrontal cortex and, with an asymmetry toward the right hemisphere there was evidence of activation at the level of bilateral dorsolateral frontal cortex (Wildgruber et al. 2002b).

One study that utilized transcranial doppler ultrasonography (Vingerhoets/Berckmoes/Stroobant 2003) found results that are similar to those reported above. Participants were instructed to identify the emotion conveyed by prosody or semantics contained within a number of sentences. Blood flow velocity was significantly increased over the left hemisphere when participants were asked to label emotional semantics. In contrast, lateralization disappeared when attention was shifted to affective prosody. Thus, the lateralization effect disappeared due to increase in right hemispheric blood flow velocity during the affective prosody task.

In summary, while the findings from many studies support the role of the right hemisphere in the perception of emotional prosody, the notion of the right-hemisphere acting alone has been questioned (Pell 2006; Schirmer/Kotz 2006a). Given the findings of more recent research, it is now recognized that the left hemisphere, as well as subcortical structures, play a role in the perception of emotional prosody. In addition, difference in tasks or stimuli may account for some of the differences observed across studies. One under-developed area of research entails the systematic examination of sex-related differences and relevant hormones in emotional prosody. The notion of sex-related differences in emotion processing (Everhart et al. 2006; Hamann/Canli 2004; Schirmer/Striano/Friederici 2005) is now receiving increased attention within the literature. This information is reviewed in the pages that follow.

3. Sex-related differences in neuroanatomy

It is well known that the structures associated with regulating emotion include the amygdala, hypothalamus, orbitofrontal cortex, temporal cortex, and parietal cortex (Adolphs et al. 1996; Damasio 1998). Sex-related differences within these regions have previously been identified. In one study, Gur and colleagues examined the volumes of temporo-limbic and prefrontal cortex in normal healthy adult men and women. Within this study, men and women had identical volumes of amygdala, hippocampus, and dorsal prefrontal cortex. However, women had significantly larger orbital frontal cortices than men. The authors of this study speculate that this may be related to behavioral sex-related differences in emotion, particularly with regard to differences in aggression (Gur et al. 2002). These speculations stem, in part, from findings in a previous study in which volume was associated with increased brain functional capacity (Gur et al. 1999). Interestingly, some studies have found sex-related anatomical differences that vary as a function of developmental stage. For example, MRI studies have found that the amygdala is smaller in girls than in boys aged 7 to 11 (Caviness/Kennedy/Richelme 1996) as well as in normal adults (Goldstein/Seidman/Horton 2001). In contrast, Murphy (1986) found no sex difference in postmortem brains.

It is also well accepted that other anatomical differences exist between the sexes. For example, the splenium of the corpus callosum, is reportedly more 'bulbous' in women compared to men (Allen/Richey/Chai/Gorski 1991). Likewise, women also have a larger cross-sectional area of the anterior commissure, which is another system that connects the right and left hemispheres. The massa intermedia, which connects the two sides of the thalamus, is absent more often in men than in women (Knickmeyer/Baron-Cohen 2006). Overall, these neuroanatomical differences suggest that women have greater inter-hemispheric connectivity than men. These differences may contribute to sex-related differences in the perception of emotional prosody.

4. Sex hormones and cognitive function

The relationship between hormonal fluctuations and performance on tasks of cognitive ability have been previously explored and debated (Hampson 1990; Heister Landis Regard/Schroeder-Heister 1989; Maki Rich/Rosenbaum 2002; Rosenburg/Park 2002; Silverman/Phillips 1993). The results from some of these studies support the existence of a relationship between hormones and cognitive performance. These neurocognitive differences noted in males and females are thought, in part, to be attributable to differences in hormone exposure both early in development and following puberty.

Experiments within comparative populations have demonstrated that gonadal hormones are important and essential to the sexual differentiation of the brain (Knickmeyer/Baron-Cohen 2006). The genetic sex of humans is determined at the moment of conception by the presence of an X (female) or Y(male) chromosome in the sperm cell. The normal female is 46, XX and the normal male is 46, XY. The hormones that are important for differentiation include (but are not limited to) androgens (testosterone, dihydrotestosterone), estrogens (estradiol, estone, estriol) and progestins (progesterone). Within animal models, it is thought that the critical period for sexual differentiation of the brain occurs when sex differences in serum testosterone are highest, occurring between 12 and 18 weeks (Abramovich 1974; Smith/Hines 1987). It is also well known that males are born with elevated levels of testosterone, in part as a result of a sudden drop of 'inhibitory' estrogen levels (Knickmeyer/Baron-Cohen 2006).

The presence of sex-related neurocognitive differences early in development suggests an important role of prenatal and perinatal exposure to hormones such as estrogen and testosterone (Shucard/Shucard/Clopper/Schachter 1992; Shucard/Shucard 1990; Shucard/Shucard/Cummings/Campos 1981). For example, early electrophysiological studies found that infant girls showed evidence of processing both verbal and nonverbal stimuli relatively more with the left hemisphere than right, while infant boys showed the opposite pattern (Shucard et al. 1981). This pattern of asymmetry may change in six-month-old infant girls, but remains the same in six-month-old boys as in three-month-old boys (Shucard/Shucard 1990). Specifically, in contrast to three-month-old infant girls, six-month-old infant girls showed a higher left-hemisphere response for the verbal condition and a higher right-hemisphere response for the nonverbal condition. Following puberty, menstrual cycle effects on spatial memory have been demonstrated, with women performing better on such tasks during the nonmenstrual phase (Postma/Izendoorn/De Haan 1998). In addition, estrogen replacement therapy has been effective in improving some aspects of neurocognitive function such as working memory, and testosterone supplements have been associated with improved performance on working memory tasks among men (Janowsky/Chavez/Orwoll 2000). Also, cross-sex hormone treatment among transexuals has resulted in reliable changes in cognitive function (Slabbekoorn/van Goozen/Megens/Gooren/Coehn-Kettenis 1999).

Genetic disorders involving alterations of (or additions to) the X chromosome further implicate the importance of sex-related hormones. Turner syndrome (TS) is a genetic disorder involving a missing X chromosome, which provides the opportunity to study the effect(s) of reduced perinatal/postnatal estrogen exposure on neurocognitive development. Because TS females are hypogonadal, they lack the ability to produce estrogen. A variety of physical anomalies and cognitive deficits exist among TS females. Of the cognitive deficits, lower performance versus verbal IQ, impaired spatial processing, spatial memory, and attention and executive function are common (Pennington et al. 1985; Rovet 1991; Shucard et al. 1992). As such, many TS girls display characteristics that are similar to those observed with nonverbal learning disability (Sybert/McCauley 2004).

In an attempt to examine the impact of TS on one aspect of spatial processing (face processing), two previous event-related potential studies explored processing among 12 TS girls, 20 prepubertal control girls, and 20 prepubertal control boys during a face recognition memory task. For the N2 component of the ERP (which has been previously associated with evaluation of stimulus information, categorization difficulty, and attention), control boys displayed greater right versus left hemisphere amplitude, control girls displayed greater left versus right hemisphere amplitude, and there was no amplitude asymmetry for TS girls (Everhart et al. 2001, 2004). The authors of these two studies conclude that boys utilize right hemisphere resources for this task, girls utilize more left hemisphere resources, and TS girls utilize bilateral processing strategies for the task. In addition, it is noteworthy that lower ERP amplitude was observed for TS girls in comparison to control boys and girls. Overall, control girls displayed greater ERP amplitude. These differences in ERP amplitude may point toward fewer available neuronal resources for face processing among TS girls.

One study examined the capabilities of Turner syndrome girls with regard to the perception of emotional prosody (J. L. Ross/ Stefanatos/Roeltgen/Cutler 1995). It was found that girls with Turner syndrome, in comparison to age and verbal IQ matched controls, performed worse on a test that requires perception of emotional prosody. Other studies have found deficits in perception of facial affect among Turner syndrome girls (Lawrence/Kuntsi/Coleman/ Campbell/Skuse 2003; McCauley/Kay/Ito/Treder 1987), which indicates that the emotion processing deficits are not isolated to one modality. Regardless, utilization of this population remains a promising area for advancing the understanding of emotional prosody processing, particularly as it related to the differing capabilities of the hemispheres.

Altered perception of emotion, and specifically emotional prosody, has been observed in other genetic disorders. Klinefelter syndrome is a genetic disorder that results when an extra X chromosome is present, creating the 47, XXY chromosomal pattern. Within these individuals, specific deficits in neurocognitive development are observed. Disabilities in reading, articulation, phonemic processing, spelling, language expression, verbal memory, language comprehension, understanding words, finding words, and verbally expressing thoughts all result in lower verbal versus performance IQ (Geschwind/Boone/Miller/Swerdloff 2000). It is thought that the presence of diminished language function among individuals with Klinefelter syndrome may be related to left hemisphere abnormalities (Itti et al. 2006). More recently, processing of emotional prosody has been examined among individuals with Klinefelter syndrome. Individuals with XXY, compared to normal controls, displayed difficulty discriminating emotions in the tone of voice as well as in the verbal content of speech. However, the difficulties were more pronounced during the condition in which they were asked to discriminate emotions (van Rijn et al. 2007). The authors suggest that the emotional prosodic aspects of language are affected among individuals with Klinefelter syndrome and that these findings may point toward additional disruption of right hemisphere processes. In common with Turner syndrome girls, Klinefelter syndrome is characterized by an X chromosome abnormality. While the precise role of the X chromosome in functional development of emotional processing is poorly understood, these two genetic disorders suggest that the X chromosome plays a very important role.

4.1 The menstrual cycle and cognitive function

The menstrual cycle contains two main phases, follicular and luteal. Low estradiol and progesterone levels are associated with the follicular phase. This phase lasts from day 1 until approximately day 14 of the menstrual cycle, with a peak of estradiol level just before ovulation. The follicular phase ends at ovulation, which typically occurs near day 14 of the menstrual cycle. The luteal phase lasts from day 14 until day 28 and is characterized by high concentrations of both estradiol and progesterone (Maki et al. 2002). During menstruation, estradiol and progesterone levels are at their lowest. Research suggests that 17 β-estradiol levels affect cognitive functioning across the menstrual cycle and may play a role in the recognition and identification of emotional stimuli. Maki and colleagues (Maki/Zonderman/

Resnick 2001) found that ovarian hormones facilitate implicit memory abilities in young women. High levels of 17 β-estradiol have also been associated with a decrease in spatial ability and an increase in articulation and motor skills (Hampson 1990; Kolb/Wishaw 1990) whereas lower levels of estrogen are associated with increased performance on tests of spatial skills. Silverman and Phillips (1997; 1993) found that female participants performed better on tasks of mental rotation during the estrogen phase of the menstrual cycle. Performance decreased when estrogen levels were high (midluteal phase) for the same test battery.

Other studies have examined the impact of phase-related menstrual cycle changes on other forms of cognition. For example, Chiarello, McMahon, and Schaefer (1989) used a lexical decision task to compare male and female participants as female participants were monitored for variation of hormone levels across the menstrual cycle via response criteria and reaction time scores. Female participants performed better when estrogen levels were higher during the late follicular phase, and had the lowest scores when estrogen levels were at the lowest peak (menstrual phase). Throughout menstrual cycle changes, female participants never outperformed males, but the difference was smallest during high estrogen phases. Bibawi and colleagues (Bibawi/Cherry/Hellige 1995) studied cerebral asymmetries to determine the existence of fluctuations across the menstrual cycle for a divided visual field task. Women displayed a right visual field advantage during the midluteal phase, while males showed no asymmetry during the tasks. Heister et al. (1989) used four testing phases, menstrual, follicular, luteal, and premenstrual, in order to examine the effect of hormonal changes on lexical and face decision tasks. No changes across the menstrual cycle were found for the lexical component; however, scrambled faces were identified faster during all phases except the menstrual phase. This finding suggests that low levels of estrogen may decrease ability to identify faces when scrambled.

In the past, some but not all electrophysiological studies have found a link between hormonal changes and differences in the ERP response (Fleck/Polich 1988). Fleck and Polich studied female participants across the menstrual cycle to examine changes in the

P300 response after exposure to auditory tone stimuli. One potential limitation with this study, however, was the inclusion of participants using hormone altering oral contraceptives. In contrast, Walpurger et al. (2004) found that changes in early and late event related potentials occur during changes in the menstrual cycle. Of note, during the luteal phase of the menstrual cycle, the orienting response was found to be significantly less than during menses, indicating that higher levels of sex hormones may diminish arousal responses. In another ERP study, Orozco (1998) revealed that the P450 (a late positive component of the event related potential) response occurred later for female versus male participants in a facial stimuli study. For the same ERP component, female participants also had significantly higher amplitudes during the perception of facial expressions than did male participants. The authors of this study did not find differences that were associated with the menstrual cycle.

Mixed results in the literature have been found with regard to hormone or estrogen replacement therapy (HRT). Amano and colleagues (2002) found that women with Alzheimer disease, mild cognitive decline and normal cognitive functioning did not differ significantly from women within these same categories who took part in estrogen replacement therapy. Nonsignificant findings could be the result of unknown duration and unknown type of estrogen used by participants. Barret-Conner and Kritz-Silverstein (1993) found no connection between hormone replacement therapies and improvement on cognitive tasks in a study that used 800 older white women. However, Matthews and colleagues (1999) found that estrogen users, whether currently or in the past, had less cognitive decline over time and performed better on a modified version of the mini mental status exam. In addition, estrogen replacement therapy increased verbal memory on selected tests in a study of surgically menopausal women (Verghese et al. 2000). Maki and colleagues also found that hormone replacement therapy increased learning and memory performance on some tasks. Of note, women who had received some form of hormone replacement therapy performed better on tasks of verbal memory, but showed no difference on tasks of short term memory, mental rotations, attention, and working memory (Maki et al. 2001). In a comparison between female participants with naturally occurring menstrual cycles and female participants with regulated menstrual cycles via oral contraceptives, the performance of females with naturally occurring menstrual cycles increased on verbal span tasks as estrogen levels increased along the menstrual cycle and decreased as estrogen levels decreased. This indicates that verbal span tasks could be modulated by estrogen (Rosenburg/Park 2002).

In summary of the preceding section, a variety of studies have demonstrated a relationship between estrogen and cognitive function; some aspects of cognitive function fluctuate as a function of the menstrual cycle or hormone replacement therapy.

4.2 Testosterone, brain development and emotion processing.

The discussion thus far has focused on estrogen. However, discussion would not be complete without comment on potential effects of testosterone on emotion processing. One more recent proposition of the potential effects of testosterone on cognitive function includes the 'extreme male brain theory' the potential etiology of autism; autism is more common among males than females. Autistic spectrum disorders include impairment in social interaction, impairment in verbal and nonverbal communication, lack of imaginative play, and repetitive stereotypical behaviors and interests. One form of the disorder, Asperger syndrome, is frequently characterized by nonverbal deficits or nonverbal learning disability (Brumback/Harper/Weinberg 1996) as well as deficits in the perception of emotional prosody (Harrison/ Demaree/Everhart/Shenal 1998). As described by Knickmeyer and Baron-Cohen (2006), with the 'extreme male brain theory of autism', it is held that the typical male brain is more adept at systemizing (ability to understand systems in terms of rules) and the female brain is more developed at 'emphathizing' (ability to model and predict emotions, mental states, and behavior using theory of mind and reading emotions in face, voice, and body language). Some individuals with high-functioning autism or Asperger's disorder go on to highly 'systemized' fields of study (i.e., engineering), with much less focus on emotions and social relations.

There are several lines of evidence implicating testosterone (i.e., elevated levels) as a potential mechanism in the etiology of autism. For example, a subset of individuals with autism demonstrate elevated androgen levels and precocious puberty (Tordjman/Ferrari/Sulmont 1997). In addition, the ratio of the second to fourth digit (2D:4D ratio) is lower among autistic individuals in comparison to males and females (females typically have the highest ratio) (Manning/Baron-Cohen/Wheelright/Sanders 2001). The 2D:4D ratio is an index of prenatal testosterone exposure.

As with the genetic disorders previously discussed (Turner syndrome and Klinefelter syndrome in relation to estrogen), congenital adrenal hyperplasia (CAH) provides an opportunity to evaluate the potential effects of elevated testosterone levels on cognitive function. As a result of specific enzyme deficiency that impairs cortisol production by the adrenal cortex, overproduction of androgen beginning in the third month of fetal life is observed (New 2003). As reviewed by Knickmeyer and Baron-Cohen (2006), girls but not boys with CAH have superior spatial reasoning and display an increase in stereotypical male behavior (i.e., aggression). Also, as reported by the same authors, results from the Cambridge Fetal Testosterone Project demonstrate a relationship between the amount of eye contact (an important feature of socialization) and amniotic testosterone among 12-month-old children.

Potentially relevant to the above discussion, significant androgen receptor binding is observed in the cerebral cortex, cerebellum, mediobasal hypothalamus, amygdala, corpus callosum, and cingulate cortex of both sexes. However, sex differences are observed in the distribution of androgen receptors. That is, androgen receptor binding is higher in the right frontal lobe and the left temporal lobe of males compared with the contralateral side; females demonstrate symmetry for these regions (Handa/Connolly/Resko 1988; Handa/Roselli/Resko 1988; Knickmeyer/Baron-Cohen 2006; Sholl/Goy/Kim 1989; Sholl/Kim 1990).

5. Sex-related differences in the perception of emotional prosody

Multiple studies have demonstrated that males perform better on certain tasks requiring spatial skills, whereas females perform better on certain measures of verbal skills (Kimura 1992; Maccoby/Jacklin 1974; McGee 1979; Shucard et al. 1992; Shucard/Shucard 1990; Shucard et al. 1981). Likewise, with regard to the processing of faces, a previous study has demonstrated that prosopagnosia (inability to recognize familiar faces) is more common in men than in women following cerebrovascular accident (Mazzucchi/Biber 1983). With regard to previous studies in facial affect processing, some studies have demonstrated that women perform better in speeded emotion recognition tasks (Natale/Gur/Gur 1983) and are more expressive (Asthana/Mandal 1998). It is of note, however, that some studies have found that men demonstrate faster reaction times than do women when emotional facial stimuli are presented to the right hemisphere (Crews/Harrison 1994; Harrison/Gorelczenko/Cook 1990a, 1990b). Regardless of differences in these studies (which may be in part attributable to task-related differences), it is the general consensus that women recognize facial, gestural, and vocal expressions more accurately than do men (Hall 1978; Schirmer/Kotz/Friederici 2005). It is also well known that women are more prone to clinical depression, but less prone to aggression, and that mood fluctuations associated with the menstrual cycle exist (Gur et al. 2002).

Several laboratories have examined sex-related differences in emotional prosody. Schirmer/Kotz/Friederici (2002) examined the influence of emotional prosody on visually presented positive and negative target words in a cross-modal priming experiment. The stimulus material consisted of sentences produced with happy and sad intonation, with emotionally congruent or incongruent target words presented following an emotional sentence. Overall, women responded faster to congruent target words, and women showed a smaller N400 amplitude for congruent versus incongruent conditions. It is concluded from the results of this study that women may make faster use of emotional prosody during language processing. Schirmer and colleagues (Annett Schirmer et al. 2005) expanded on these findings in a more recent study that utilized the same stimuli. In contrast to the previous study, however, participants were now asked to indicate whether the target word matched the prosodic emotion of the preceding sentence. It is interesting to note that, unlike the previous study, sex-differences in the N400 amplitudes to emotionally congruent compared to noncongruent words were not revealed. The authors speculate that sex-related differences in emotional-prosodic priming tasks may depend on whether or not participants are instructed to take emotional prosody into account. Additionally, it is posited that emotion recognition in women may be less dependent on the allocation of attention than in men.

An 'Emotional Stroop Task' has also been utilized to examine sex-related differences. Specifically, this task entailed listening to words with a positive, negative, or neutral valence that were spoken with happy, angry, or neutral prosody. Across the various conditions of the paradigm, women responded more quickly than did men. In addition, a smaller N400 was demonstrated in women for congruent as compared to emotionally incongruent stimuli when participants were asked to judge word valence. The authors conclude that "women seem to integrate emotional information from prosody more readily into ongoing semantic processing" (Schirmer/Kotz 2003, p. 1146).

While the studies reviewed above entail use of emotional words or sentences, some laboratories have examined the processing of emotional 'utterances' in order to avoid potential confounds with linguistic processing. For example, Everhart and colleagues (2003) utilized emotional syllables adapted from a previous study (Erhan/Borod/Tenke/Bruder 1998). In this classic 'oddball' ERP paradigm, happy and fear emotional utterances (using the consonant vowel combination *ga*) were presented across a total of 600 trials. In one block (300 trials), the participants were asked to keep a running total of the number of fear stimuli that were presented, while in the other block, participants were asked to keep track of how many happy stimuli were presented. Overall, it was found that P300 amplitude was greater over the right versus left hemisphere regardless of valence (i.e., happy or fear). Interestingly, when the same paradigm is employed using emotional words rather than utterances, the P300 amplitude asymmetry is no longer observed (Gerding/Everhart/Davis 2007). The authors suggest that the lack of asymmetry observed for words versus utterances is attributable to an increase in verbal load or infusion of the non-emotional language system, and thus the use of left hemisphere resources. In examining sex-related differences observed during the presentation of utterances, a significant main effect for sex emerged, in that the P300 occurred later for men in comparison to women regardless of valence. These findings are consistent with previous studies that purport greater right hemisphere involvement in the processing of emotional prosody. However, the significant sex-related main effect also suggests that women may process emotional prosody more quickly than do men.

To date there are few studies that have examined the influence of hormones or menstrual cycle changes on the perception of emotional prosody. In our previous work we examined the relationship between the menstrual cycle and the perception of facial affect and emotional prosody using a P300 oddball paradigm (Jordan et al. 2004). In this classic oddball paradigm, participants were tested on two occasions, once during the high estrogen phase of the menstrual cycle and once during the low estrogen phase of the menstrual cycle. On each occasion, participants were required to complete two tasks. The first task required participants to count emotional utterances that depicted happiness or fear, while the second task required participants to count faces that depicted happiness or fear. Half of the participants were initially tested during the high estrogen phase, while the remaining were tested during the low estrogen phase. Regarding emotional prosody, greater P300 amplitude was observed over the right versus left hemisphere scalp sites during the high estrogen phase (luteal) of the menstrual cycle regardless of valence. In contrast, symmetry was observed during the low estrogen, or follicular phase. In addition, P300 amplitude was greater for happiness versus fear regardless of menstrual cycle phase. With regard to facial affect, only one phase-related interaction was observed. During the high estrogen phase, the P300 response occurred sooner for happiness than fear facial affect; this relationship was not observed during the low estrogen phase. This preliminary study indicates that emotion perception (and in particular perception of emotional prosody), may fluctuate according to the menstrual cycle. It is of particular interest that the asymmetry between the hemispheres may fluctuate, as evidenced by the changes in P300 amplitude.

Other groups have examined the effects of emotionally spoken syllables. For example, in one recent study, a mismatch negativity paradigm (MMN; very similar to P300 oddball paradigms) that entailed production of the syllables *dada* with neutral, happy, or angry prosody was utilized (Schirmer et al. 2005). Overall, the MMN was larger in response to angry and happy deviants when compared to the neutral deviants, although this finding was lateralized to the right hemisphere (consistent with the right hemisphere hypothesis). More relevant to this review, however, was the finding that only women demonstrated an influence of emotional prosody on MMN amplitude. The authors conclude that this difference is reflective of women responding to the emotional arousal associated with happy and angry prosody.

One study from another group (Sander/Roth/Scheich 2003) also utilized emotional intonations and fMRI in order to examine whether different lateralization patterns are associated with individually different stress-related coping strategies among women. Within this study, women were separated into 'high' or 'low' repressive groups. Two of the four tasks presented to participants required the detection of sad or happy intonations within an adjective mixture. It was found that high repressive women showed larger left hemisphere activation during the identification of sad intonations, while low repressive women showed larger right hemisphere activation during the identification of sad intonations. In contrast, identification of happy intonations was associated with larger right hemisphere activation regardless of coping style (high versus low repression). These findings were isolated to the temporoparietal regions.

Other fMRI studies have also found significant sex-related differences. For example, one study that used emotional sentences found higher response amplitudes within the left hemisphere posterior middle temporal gyrus in female subjects compared to males, whereas a larger increase of activation within the right middle frontal gyrus was observed in males (Wildgruber/Pihan/Ackermann/Erb/Grodd

2002a). This finding is consistent with previous ERP studies (Everhart et al. 2001; Jordan et al. 2004) that describe patterns of laterality among males and females. It is noted that not all fMRI studies have observed this pattern. For instance, Mitchell (2007) found that working memory for emotional prosody appeared to be right-lateralized in the prefrontal cortex. Supplementary separate analyses of males and females suggested that these language functions were less bilateral in females, but their inclusion did not alter the direction of laterality.

A recent lesion study has also examined sex-related differences in the perception of emotional prosody. Within this study, patients with frontal damage were mostly impaired in comprehension of happy intonations, those with temporo-parietal damage in assessment of sad intonations, and subcortical lesions affected comprehension of angry intonations. With regard to sex-related differences, frontal lesions were more detrimental to women, whereas subcortical lesions led to stronger impairment in men (Rymarczyk/Grabowska 2007).

6. Conclusion

This review has examined the Right Hemisphere Hypothesis within the context of sex-related differences in the perception of emotional prosody. Included within the review is discussion of sex-related neuroanatomical differences and sex hormones that impact brain development and cognitive function. In addition, a previous section of this manuscript described results from electrophysiological studies, imaging studies and lesion studies that have specific focus on sex-related differences in the perception of emotional prosody. It is acknowledged that only simplified description of the neuroanatomical structures associated with the perception of emotional prosody has been provided; more in depth discussion is provided by Adolphs (2002). It is also acknowledged that other models of emotion processing (i.e., approach-withdrawal) as well as increased focus on valence may have much to offer with regard to the understanding of emotional prosody. Finally, it is recognized that perception of emotional prosody entails more than assignment of evaluative emotional "judgments" on the part of the participant. Rather, duration (speech timing) and fundamental frequency (F_0) are two primary acoustic parameters that also play a role in the understanding of emotional speech (Pell 1999); in depth analysis and discussion of these very important parameters is beyond the scope of this chapter.

Thus far, studies of emotional prosody have been completed primarily without regard to a particular context. For instance, the studies reviewed are performed primarily within the laboratory, and the presented stimuli typically do not test differing contexts such as the importance of social judgment, social relevance, and culture. In reality, perception of emotional prosody is tied to decision making and social judgment; this complexity points toward the utilization of a diverse neuroanatomical framework. For instance, it is plausible that an individual with focal brain damage will adequately process emotional prosodic stimuli. However, the same individual, given lesions within specific places, may fail to utilize the processed information correctly within certain contexts. The field of cognitive neuroscience holds promise in advancing the understanding of how impaired processing of emotional prosody may impact an individual within differing contexts. For example, as reviewed by Adolphs (2003) the orbitofrontal cortex has been implicated in social reasoning, and the ventromedial prefrontal cortex is associated with advantageous decision making in real life. As per the literature, such decisions are made via the reliance on somatic markers that appear in anticipation of making choices. It is now important to examine the perception of emotional prosody within these varying contexts. For instance, it is established that women may experience menstrual cycle phase-related fluctuations in social judgment (i.e., perceived attract-iveness of faces) (Penton-Voak 1999). Likewise, some studies have indicated an aging effect on the perception of emotion, whereby reduced accuracy is associated with advancing age (Grunwald 1999). Multiple studies have also documented the notion that women identify emotions more quickly than men do, and that these differences may be attributable to a combination of differences in neuroanatomy and associated sex hormones as well as social context (Everhart et al. 2006). For example, studies suggest that theory of mind develops earlier in girls and that women may be better at making inferences about people's mental states and adjusting their behavior accordingly (Baron-Cohen/Jolliffe/Mortimore/Robertson 1997). A small but growing literature base on the influence of ethnicity or culture on affect perception also exists; some data suggest that specific ethnic groups are more accurate in decoding emotional cues from stimulus-containing individuals within the same ethnic group (Weathers/ Frank/Spell 2002); these findings potentially point toward the importance of learned within-group behavior. Finally, the complex interaction between these important variables and sex-hormones has yet to be studied. Some groups (Everhart et al. 2003; Sander et al. 2003; Schirmer et al. 2002) have highlighted the importance of these differences, and are actively pursuing this line of research.

References

Abramovich, D. R. 1974. Human sexual differentiation: In utero influences. *Journal of Obstetrics and Gynaecology, 81*, 448-453.

Adolphs, Ralph 2002. Neural systems for recognizing emotion. *Current Opinions in Neurobiology, 12*, 169-177.

Adolphs, Ralph 2003. Cognitive neuroscience of human social behaviour. *Nature Reviews: Neuroscience, 4*, 165-178.

Adolphs, Ralph / Damasio, Hannah / Tranel, Daniel. 2002. Neural systems for recognition emotional prosody: A 3-D lesion study. *Emotion, 2*(1), 23-51.

Adolphs, Ralph / Damasio, Hanna / Tranel, Daniel. / Damasio, Antonio R. 1996. Cortical systems for the recognition of emotion in facial expression. *Journal of Neuroscience, 16*, 7678-7687.

Allen, Laura S. / Richey, Mark F. / Chai, Yee M. / Gorski, Roger A. 1991. Sex differences in the corpus callosum of the living human being. *Journal of Neuroscience, 11*, 933-942.

Asthana, Hari S. / Mandal, Manak K. 1998. Hemifacial asymmetry in emotion expressions. *Behavioral Modification, 22*, 177-183.

Babinski, Joseph. 1914. Contribution of cerebral hemispheric organization in the study of mental troubles. *Revue Neurologique, 27*, 845-848.

Baron-Cohen, Simon / Jolliffe, Therese / Mortimore, Catherine / Robertson, Mary 1997. Another advanced test of theory of mind: Evidence from very high functioning adults with autism or Asperger syndrome. *Journal of Child Psychology and Psychiatry, 38*, 813-822.

Barret-Conner, Elizabeth / Kritz-Silverstein, D. 1993. Estrogen replacement therapy and cognitiver function in older women. *Journal of the American Medical Association, 269*, 2637-2641.

Baum, Shari R. / Pell, Marc D. 1999. The neural bases of prosody: Insights from lesion studies and neuroimaging. *Aphasiology, 13*(8), 581-608.

Bibawi, Darlene / Cherry, Barbara / Hellige, Joseph B. 1995. Fluctuations of perceptual asymmetry across time in women and men: Effects related to the menstrual cycle. *Neuropsychologia, 33*, 131-138.

Borod, Joan C. 1993. Cerebral mechanisms underlying facial, prosodic, and lexical emotional expression: A review of neuropsychological studies and methodological issues. *Neuropsychology, 7*(4), 445-463.

Borod, Joan C. / Cicero, Barbara A. / Obler, Loraine K. Welkowitz, Joan, Erhan, Hulya M. / Santschi, Cornelia, et al. 1998. Right hemisphere emotional perception: evidence across multiple channels. *Neuropsychology, 12*(3), 446-558.

Borod, Joan C. / Koff, Elissa / White, Betsy 1983. Facial asymmetry in posed and spontaneous expressions of emotion. *Brain and Cognition, 2*(2), 165-175.

Borod, Joan C. / Pick, Lawrence H. / Hall, Susan / Sliwinski, Martin / Madigan, Nancy / Obler, Loraine K., et al. 2000. Relationships among facial, prosodic, and lexical channels of emotional perceptual processing. *Cognition & Emotion, 14*(2), 193-211.

Bostanov, Vladimir / Kotchoubey, Boris 2004. Recognition of affective prosody: Continuous wavelet measures of event-related brain potentials to emotional exclamations. *Psychophysiology, 41*(2), 259-268.

Brumback, Roger A. / Harper, Caryn R. / Weinberg, Warren A. 1996. Nonverbal learning disabilities, Asperger's disorder, Pervasive developmental disorder: Should we care? *Journal of Child Neurology, 11*, 427-429.

Bryden, Mark P. 1982. *Laterality*. San Diego: Academic Press.

Buchanan, Tony W. / Lutz. Kai / Mirzazade, Shahram / Specht, Karsten / Shah, N. Jon / Zilles, Karl, et al. 2000 . Recognition of emotional prosody and verbal components of spoken language: an fMRI study. *Cognitive Brain Research, 9*(3), 227-238.

Carmon, Amiram / Nachshon, Israel 1973. Ear asymmetry in perception of emotional nonverbal stimuli. *Acta Psychologica, 37*, 351-357.

Caviness, Verne. S. / Kennedy, David N. / Richelme, C. 1996. The human brain age 7-11 years: A volumetric analysis based on magnetic resonance images. *Cerebral Cortex, 6* (726-736).

Chiarello, Christine / McMahon, Monica A. / Schaefer, Kim 1989. Visual cerebral lateralization over phases of the menstrual cycle: A preliminary investigation. *Brain and Cognition, 11*, 18-36.

Cicone, Michael / Wapner, Wendy / Gardner, Howard 1980. Sensitivyt to emotional expressions and situations in organic patients. *Cortex, 16*, 145-168.

Coan, James A. / Allen, John J. B. 2003. Frontal EEG asymmetry and the behavioral activation and inhibition systems. *Psychophysiology, 40*, 106-114.

Crews, William D. / Harrison, David W. 1994. Sex differences and cerebral asymmetry of facial affect perception as a function of depression. *Psychobiology, 1*, 55-64.

Damasio, Antonio R. 1998. Emotion in the perspective of an integrated nervous system. *Brain Research Reviews, 26*, 83-86.

Davidson, Richard J. 1984. Affect, cognition, and hemispheric specialization. In C. E. Izard / J. Kagan / R. Zajonc (eds), *Emotion, cognition, and behavior* (320-365). New York, NY: Cambridge University Press.

Davidson, Richard J. 1995. Cerebral asymmetry, emotion, and affective style. In Richard. J. Davidson / Kenneth Hugdahl (eds), *Brain asymmetry* Cambridge: MIT Press, 361-399.

Demaree, Heath. A. / Everhart, Daniel E. / Youngstrom, Eric. A. / Harrison, David W. 2005. Brain Lateralization of Emotional Processing: Historical Roots and a Future Incorporating "Dominance". *Behavioral and Cognitive Neuroscience Reviews, 4*(1), 3-20.

Denney-Brown, Derek. / Meyer, J. S. / Horenstein, S. 1952. The significance of perceptual rivalry resulting from parietal lesions. *Brain, 75*(434-471).

Ehrlichman, Howard 1987. Hemispheric asymmetry and postive-negative affect. In D. Ottoson (ed.), *Duality and unity of the brain*. Hampshire, En: Macmillan.

Erhan, Hulya. / Borod, Joan C. / Tenke, Craig E. / Bruder, Gerald E. 1998. Identification of emotion in a dichotic listening task: event-related brain potential and behavioral findings. *Brain and Cognition, 37*(2), 286-307.

Etcoff, Nancy 1986. The neuropsychology of emotional expression. In G. Goldstein / R. E. Tarter (eds), *Advances in Clinical Neuropsychology* New York: Plenum Press, 127-175.

Everhart, Daniel E. / Carpenter, Michael D. / Carmona, Joseph E. / Ethridge, Amy J. / Demaree, Heath A. 2003. Adult sex-related P300 differences during the perception of emotional prosody and facial affect. *Psychophysiology, 40*, S39-S39.

Everhart, Daniel E. / Demaree, Heath A. / Shipley, Amy 2006. Perception of Emotional Prosody: Moving Toward a Model That Incorporates Sex-Related Differences. *Behavioral and Cognitive Neuroscience Reviews, 5*(2), 92-102.

Everhart, Daniel E. / Shucard, Janet L. / Quatrin, Teresa /Shucard, David W. 2001. Sex-related differences in event-related potentials, face recognition, and facial affect processing in prepubertal children. *Neuropsychology, 15*(3), 329-341.

Everhart, Daniel E. / Shucard, Janet L. / Quatrin, Teresa / Shucard, David W. 2004. Tone probe event-related potential differences during a face recognition task in prepubertal children and Turner Syndrome girls. *Psychoneuroendocrinology, 29* (10), 1260-1271.

Fleck, Karen M. / Polich, John 1988. P300 and menstrual cycle. *Electro-encephalography and Clinical Neurophysiology, 71*, 157-160.

George, Mark S. / Parekh, Priti I. / Rosinsky, Ned / Ketter, T. A. / Kimbrell, T. A. / Heilman, Kenneth M. 1996. Understanding emotional prosody activates right hemisphere regions. *Archives of Neurology, 53*, 665-790.

Gerding, Alan L. / Everhart, Daniel E. / Davis, Claude E. 2007. Patterns of P300 laterality observed during the presentation of emotional prosodic utterances and emotional prosodic words. *Psychophysiology, 44*, S58-S58.

Geschwind, Daniel H. / Boone, Kyle B. / Miller, Bruce. L. / Swerdloff, Ronald S. 2000. Neurobehavioral phenotype of Klinefelter syndrome. *Mental Retardation and Developmental Disabilities Research Reviews, 6*(2), 107-116.

Goldstein, Jill M. / Seidman, Larry J. / Horton, Nicholas. J. 2001. Normal sexual dimorphism of the adult human brain assessed by in vivo magnetic resonance images. *Cerebral Cortex, 11*(490-497).

Gray, Jeffrey A. 1982. Precis of the neuropsychology of anxiety: An enquiry into the functions of the septo-hippocampal system. *The Behavioral and Brain Sciences, 5*, 469-534.

Grunwald, Ilana. S. 1999. The Effects of Age and Gender on the Perception of Lexical Emotion. *Applied Neuropsychology,* 6(4), 226.

Gur, R. C. / Gunning-Dixon, F. / Bilker, W. B. / Gur, R. E. 2002. Sex differences in temporo-limbic and frontal brain volumes of healthy adults. *Cerebral Cortex, 12*, 998-1003.

Gur, Ruben. C. / Turetsky, Bruce. I. / Matsui, Mie / Yan, Michelle / Bilker, Warren / Hughett, Paul et al. 1999. Sex differences in brain gray and white matter in healthy young adults: correlations with cognitive performance. *Journal of Neuroscience, 19*, 4065-4072.

Haggard, Mark P. / Parkinson, Alan M. 1971. Stimulus and task factors as determinants of ear advantages. *Quarterly Journal of Experimental Psychology, 23*, 168-177.

Hall, Jay A. 1978. Gender effects in decoding nonverbal cues. *Psychological Bulletin, 4*, 845-857.

Hamann, Stephan / Canli, Turhan 2004. Individual differences in emotion processing. *Current Opinions in Neurobiology, 14*, 233-238.

Hampson, Elizabeth 1990. Variations in sex-related cognitive abilities across the menstrual cycle. *Brain and Cognition, 14*, 26-43.

Handa, Robert J. / Connolly, Paul. B. / Resko, John A. 1988. Ontogeny of cystolic androgen receptors in the brain of the fetal rhesus monkey. *Endocrinology, 122*, 1890-1896.

Handa, Robert J. / Roselli, Charles / Resko, John. 1988. Distribution of androgen receptor in microdissected brain areas of the female baboon. *Brain Research, 445*, 111-116.

Harmon-Jones, Eddie / Allen, John J. B. 1997. Behavioral activation sensitivity and resting frontal EEG asymmetry: Covariation of putative indicators related to risk for mood disorders. *Journal of Abnormal Psychology, 106*(1), 159-163.

Harrison, David W. / Demaree, Heath A. / Everhart, Daniel E. / Shenal, Brian V. 1998. QEEG assisted neuropsychological evaluation of autism. *International Journal of Neuroscience, 93*, 133-140.

Harrison, David W. / Gorelczenko, Paul. O. / Cook, J. 1990a. Functional asymmetry for facial affect perception. *International Journal of Neuroscience, 52*, 11-16.

Harrison, David W. / Gorelczenko, Paul O. / Cook, J. 1990b. Sex differences in the functional asymmetry for facial affect perception. *International Journal of Neuroscience, 52*, 11-16.

Heilman, Kenneth M. / Bowers, Dawn 1990. Neuropsychological studies of emotional changes induced by right and left-hemisphere lesions. In N. Stein, B. Leventhal / T. Trabasso (eds), *Psychological and biological approaches to emotion* Hillsdale: Erlbaum, 99-114.

Heister, Gabriele / Landis, Theodor / Regard, Marianne / Schroeder-Heister, Peter 1989. Shift of functional cerebral asymmetry during the menstrual cycle. *Neuropsychologia, 27*, 871-880.

Imaizumi, Satoshi / Mori, Koichi / Kiritani, Shigeru / Kawashima, Ryuta / Sugiura, Motoaki / Fukuda, Hiroshi 1997. Vocal identification of speaker and emoton activates different brain regions. *Neuroreport, 8*, 2809-2812.

Itti, E. / Gonzalo, I. T. G. / Pawlikowska-Haddal, A. / Boone, K. B. / Mlikotic, A / Itti, L. et al. 2006. The structural brain correlates of cognitive deficits in adults with Klinefelter's syndrome. *Journal of Clinical Endocrinology and Metabolism, 91*(4), 1423-1427.

Janowsky, Jeri S. / Chavez, Bambi / Orwoll, Eric 2000. Sex steroids modify working memory. *Journal of Cognitive Neuroscience, 12*, 407-414.

Jordan, Amy L. / Everhart, Daniel E. / Demaree, Heath A. 2004. Luteal and follicular phase related P300 changes during the perception of emotional prosody and affective faces. *Psychophysiology, 41*, s60.

Kestenbaum, Roberta / Nelson, Charles A. 1992. Neural and behavioral correlates of emotion recognition in children and adults. *Journal of Clinical and Experimental Neuropsychology, 54*, 1-18.

Kimura, Doreen 1992. Sex differences in the brain. *Scientific American, 267*, 119-125.

King, F. Laurain / Kimura, Doreen 1972. Left ear superiority in dichotic perception of vocal and nonverbal sounds. *Canadian Journal of Psychology, 26*, 111-116.

Knickmeyer, Rebecca / Baron-Cohen, Simon 2006. Fetal Testosterone and Sex Differences in Typical Social Development and in Autism. *Journal of Child Neurology, 21*(10), 825-845.

Kolb, Bryan. / Wishaw, Ian 1990. *Fundamentals of Human Neuropsychology*: WH Freeman and Company.

Kotz, Sonja A. / Meyer, Martin / Alter, Kai / Besson, Mireille / von Cramon, D. Yves. / Friederici, Angela D. 2003. On the lateralization of emotional prosody: An event-related functional MR investigation. *Brain and Language, 86*(3), 366-376.

Landis, Theodor / Assal, Gil / Perret, Etienne 1979. Opposite cerebral hemispheric superiorities for visual associative processing of emotional facial expressions and objects. *Nature, 278*, 739-740.

Laurian, S. / Bader, M. / Lanares, J. / Oros, L. 1991. Topography of event-related potentials elicited by visual emotional stimuli. *Psychophysiology, 10*, 231-238.

Lawrence, Kate / Kuntsi, Joanna / Coleman, Michael / Campbell, Ruth / Skuse, David 2003. Face and emotional recognition deficits in Turner syndrome: A possible role for X-linked genes in amygdala development. *Neuropsychology, 17*, 39.

Ley, Robert G. / Bryden, Mark P. 1979. Hemispheric differences in processing emotions and faces. *Brain and Language, 7*(127-138).

Maccoby, Eleanor. E / Jacklin, Carol N. 1974. *The psychology of sex differences*. Stanford: Stanford University Press.

Maki, Pauline / Rich, Jill. / Rosenbaum, R. Shayna 2002. Iimplicit memory varies across the menstrual cycle: Estrogen effects in young women. *Neuropsychologia, 40*, 518-529.

Maki, Pauline / Zonderman, Alan B. / Resnick, Susan M. 2001. Enhanced verbal memory in non-demented elderly women receiving hormone replacement therapy. *American Journal of Psychiatry, 158*, 227-233.

Manning, J. T. / Baron-Cohen, Simon / Wheelright, S. / Sanders, G. 2001. The 2nd to 4th digit ration and autism. *Developmental Medicine and Child Neurology, 43*, 160-164.

Matthews, Karen / Cauley, Jane / Yaffe, Kristine / Zmuda, Joseph M. 1999. Estrogen replacement therapy and cognitive decline in older community women. *Journal of the American Geriatrics Society, 47*, 518-523.

Mazzucchi, Anna / Biber, Carol 1983. Is prosopagnosia more frequent in males than females? *Cerebral Cortex, 9*, 431-444.

McCauley, Elizabeth / Kay, Thomas / Ito, Joanne / Treder, Robert 1987. The Turner syndrome: Cognitive deficits, affective discrimination, and behavior problems. *Child Dev, 58*, 464-473.

McGee, Mark G. 1979. Human spatial abilities: Psychometric studies and environmental, genetic, hormonal, and neurological influences. *Psychological Bulletin, 86*, 889-918.

McKeever, Walter F / Dixon, Michael 1981. Right-hemisphere superiority for discriminating memorized and nonmemorized faces: Affective imagery, sex, and perceived emotionality. *Brain and Language, 12*, 246-260.

Mills, C. K. 1912a. The cerebral mechanisms of emotional expression. *Transactions of the College of Physicians of Philadelphia* (34), 381-390.

Mills, C. K. 1912b. The cortical representation of emotion, with a discussion of some points in the general nervous mechanism of expression in its relation to organic nervous disease and insanity. *Proceedings of the American Medico-Psychological Association, 19*, 297-300.

Mitchell, Rachel L. C. 2007. fMRI delineation of working memory for emotional prosody in the brain: Commonalities with the lexico-semantic emotion network. *NeuroImage, 36*(3), 1015-1025.

Mitchell, Rachel. L. C., Elliott, Rebecca / Barry, Martin / Cruttenden, Alan / Woodruff, Peter. W. R. 2003. The neural response to emotional prosody, as revealed by functional magnetic resonance imaging. *Neuropsychologia, 41*(10), 1410-1421.

Monrad-Krohn, G. H. 1947. Dysprosody or altered "melody of language". *Brain, 70*, 405-423.

Munte, Thomas F. / Brack, Martina / Gootheer, Olaf. / Wieringa, Bernardina / Matzke, Mike / Johannes, Sonke 1998. Brain potentials reveal the timing of face identity and expression judgements. *Neuroscience Research, 30*, 25-34.

Murphy, G. M. 1986. The human medial amygdaloid nucleus: No evidence for sex difference in volume. *Brain Research, 365*, 321-324.

Natale, Michael / Gur, Raquel E. / Gur, Ruben C. 1983. Hemispheric asymmetries in processing emotional expressions. *Neuropsychologia, 21*, 555-565.

New, M. I. 2003. Inborn errors of adrenal steroidgenesis. *Molecular and Cellular Endocrinology, 211*, 75-83.

Orozco, Sara. / Ehlers, Cindy L. 1998. Gender differences in electrophysiological responses to facial stimuli. *Biological Psychiatry, 44*, 281-289.

Pell, Mark D. 1999. The temporal organization of affective and non-affective speech in patients with right-hemisphere infarcts. *Cortex, 35*, 455-477.

Pell, Mark D. 2006. Cerebral mechanisms for understanding emotional prosody in speech. *Brain and Language, 96*(2), 221-234.

Pennington, B. F. / Heaton, Robert K / Karzmark, P / Pendleton, M. G. / Lehman, R. / Shucard, David W. 1985. The neuropsychological phenotype in Turner Syndrome. *Cortex, 21*, 391-404.

Penton-Voak, Ian S. 1999. Menstrual cycle alters face preference. *Nature, 399*, 741-742.

Phillips, Krista / Silverman, Irwin 1997. Differences in the relationship of menstrual cycle phase to spatial performance on two and three dimensional tasks. *Hormones and Behavior, 32*, 167-175.

Pihan, Hans. / Altenmuller, Eckart. / Ackermann, Hermann 1997. The cortical processing of perceived emotion: A DC-potential study on affective processing. *Neuroreport, 8*(623-627).

Pihan, Hans / Altenmuller, Eckart / Hertrich, Ingo. Ackermann, Hermann 2000. Cortical activation patterns of affective speech processing depend on concurrent demand on the subvocal rehearsal system: A DC potential study. *Brain, 123*, 2338-2349.

Postma, Albert / Izendoorn, Roeland / De Haan, Edward H. 1998. Sex differences in object location memory. *Brain and Cognition, 36*, 334-345.

Rosenburg, L. / Park, S 2002. Verbal and spatial funcions across the menstrual cycle in healthy young women. *Psychoneuroendocrinology, 27*, 835-841.

Ross, Elliott D. 1981. The aprosodias: functional anatomic organization of the affective components of language in the right hemisphere. *Archives of Neurology, 38*, 561-569.

Ross, Elliott D. 1985. Modulation of affect and nonverbal communicaiton by the right hemisphere. In M. M. Mesulam (ed.), *Principles of Behavioral Neurology*. Philadelphia: Davis.

Ross, Elliott D. / Monnot, Marilee 2008. Neurology of affective prosody and its functional-anatomic organization in right hemisphere. *Brain and Language, 104*, 51-74.

Ross, Elliott D. / Thompson, Robin D. / Yenkosky, Joseph 1997. Lateralization of affective prosody in brain and the callosal integration of hemisphere language funtions. *Brain and Language, 56*(27-54).

Ross, Judit L. / Stefanatos, Gerry A. / Roeltgen, H. K. / Cutler, G. B. 1995. Ulrich-Turner Syndrome: Neurodevelopmental changes from childhood through adolescence. *American Journal of Medical Genetics, 58*, 74-82.

Rovet, Joann F. 1991. The cognitive and neuropsychological characteristics of females with Turner Syndrome. In B. Bender / D. Birch (eds), *Sex chromosome abnormalities and behavior: Psychological Studies* Westview Press, 39-77.

Rymarczyk, Krystyna / Grabowska, Anna 2007. Sex differences in brain control of prosody. *Neuropsychologia, 45*(5), 921-930.

Sander, Kerstin / Roth, Patricia / Scheich, Hennig 2003. Left-lateralized fMRI activation in the tmeporal lobe of high repressive women during the identification of sad prosodies. *Cognitive Brain Research, 16*, 441-456.

Schirmer, Annett / Kotz, Sonja A. 2003. ERP evidence for a sex-specific stroop effect in emotional speech. *Journal of Cognitive Neuroscience, 15*(8), 1135-1148.

Schirmer, Annett / Kotz, Sonja A. 2006a. Beyond the right hemisphere: Brain mechanisms mediating vocal emotional processing. *Trends in Cognitive Sciences, 10*(1), 24-30.

Schirmer, Annett / Kotz, Sonja A. 2006b. Beyond the right hemisphere: Brain mechanisms mediation vocal emotional processing. *Trends in Cognitive Sciences, 10*, 24-30.

Schirmer, Annett / Kotz, Sonja A. / Friederici, Angela D. 2002. Sex differentiates the role of emotional prosody during word processing. *Cognitive Brain Research, 14*(2), 228-233.

Schirmer, Annett / Kotz, Sonja A. / Friederici, Angela D. 2005. On the role of attention for the processing of emotions in speech: Sex differences revisited. *Cognitive Brain Research, 24*(3), 442-452.

Schirmer, Annett / Striano, Tricia / Friederici, Angela D. 2005. Sex difference in the preattentive processing of vocal emotional expressions. *Neuroreport, 16*(6), 635-639.

Sholl, S. A. / Goy, R. W. / Kim, K. L. 1989. 5 Alpha-reductase, aromatase, and androgen receptor levels in the monkey brain during fetal development. *Endocrinology, 124*, 627-634.

Sholl, S. A. / Kim, K. L. 1990. Androgen receptors are differentially distributed between right and left cerebral hemispheres of the fetal male rhesus monkey. *Brain Research, 516*, 122-126.

Shucard, David W. / Shucard, Janet L., / Clopper, Richard R. / Schachter, Mark 1992. Electrophysiological and neuropsychological indices of cognitive processing deficits in Turner syndrome. *Developmental Neuropsychology, 8*, 229-323.

Shucard, Janet L. / Shucard, David W. 1990. Auditory evoked potentials and hand preference in 6-month-old infants: Possible gender related differences in cerebral organization. *Developmental Psychology, 26*(923-930).

Shucard, Janet L. / Shucard, David W. / Cummings, Jay L. / Campos, Jeff J. 1981. Auditory evoked potentials and sexl-related differences in brain development. *Brain and Language, 13*, 91-102.

Silberman, Edward K. / Weingartner, Herbert 1986. Hemispheric lateralization of functions related to emotion. *Brain and Cognition, 5*, 322-353.

Silverman, Irwin / Phillips, Krysta 1993. Effects of estrogen changes during the menstrual cycle on spatial performance. *Ethology and Sociobiology, 14*, 257-270.

Slabbekoorn, Ditte / van Goozen, Stephanie H. / Megens, Jos / Gooren, Louis J. / Coehn-Kettenis, Peggy T. 1999. Activating effects of cross-sex hormones on cognitive functioning: A study of short-term and long-term hormon effects in transsexuals. *Psychoneuroendocrinology, 24*, 424-447.

Smith, Laurel L. / Hines, Melissa 1987. Language lateralization and handedness in women prenatally exposed to diethylstilbestrol (DES). *Psychoneuroendocrinology, 2000*, 497-512.

Suberi, Max / McKeever, Walter F. 1977. Differential right hemisphere memory storage of emotional and non-emotional faces. *Neuropsychologia, 15*, 757-768.

Sutton, Steven K. / Davidson, Richard J. 1997. Prefrontal brain asymmetry: A biological substrate of the behavioral approach and inhibition systems. *Psychological Science, 8*(3), 204-210.

Sybert, V. P. / McCauley, E. 2004. Turner's syndrome. *New England Journal of Medicine, 351*(12), 1227-1238.

Tordjman, Sylvie / Ferrari, Pierre / Sulmont, Veronique 1997. Androgenic activity in autism. *American Journal of Psychiatry, 1997*, 1626-1627.

Tucker, Don M. 1981. Lateral brain function, emotion, and conceptualization. *Psychological Bulletin, 89*(1), 19-46.

van Rijn, Sophie / Aleman, Andre / Swaab, Hanna / Krijn, Tessell / Vingerhoets, Guy / Kahn, Rene S. 2007. What it is said versus how it is said: Comprehension of affective prosody in men with Klinefelter (47, XXY) syndrome. *Journal of the International Neuropsychological Society, 13*(6), 1065-1070.

Vanderploeg, Rodney D. / Brown, Warren S. / Marsh, James T. 1987. Judgments of emotion in words and faces: ERP correlates. *International Journal of Psychophysiology, 5*, 193-205.

Verghese, Joe. / Kuslansky, Gail / Katz, Mindy J. / Sliwinski, Martin / Crystal, H. A. / Buschke, H. 2000. Cognitive performance in surgically menopausal women on estrogen. *Neurology, 55*, 872-874.

Vingerhoets, Guy / Berckmoes, Celine / Stroobant, Nathalie 2003. Cerebral hemodynamics during discrimination of prosodic and semantic emotion in speech studied by transcranial doppler utrasonography. *Neuropsychology, 17*, 93-99.

Walpurger, Verena / Pietrowsky, Reinhard / Kirschbaum, C. / Wolf, O. T. 2004. Effects of the menstrual cycle on auditory event-related potentials. *Hormones and Behavior, 46*(5), 600-606.

Weathers, Monica D. / Frank, Elaine M. / Spell, Leigh A. 2002. Differences in the communication of affect: Members of the same race versus members of a different race. *Journal of Black Psychology, 28*(1), 66-77.

Wildgruber, Dirk / Pihan, H. / Ackermann, Hermann / Erb, Michael / Grodd, Wolfgang 2002a. Dynamic Brain Activation during Processing of Emotional Intonation: Influence of Acoustic Parameters, Emotional Valence, and Sex. *NeuroImage, 15*(4), 856-869.

Wildgruber, Dirk. / Pihan, Hans / Ackermann Hermann / Erb, M. / Grodd, Wolfgang 2002b. Dynamic brain activation during processing of emotional intonation: Influence of acoustic parameters, emotional valence, and sex. *NeuroImage, 15*, 856-869.

Wildgruber, Dirk / Riecker, Axel. / Hertrich, Ingo./ Erb, Michael / Grodd, Wolfgang / Ethofer, T. 2005. Identification of emotional intonation evaluated by fMRI. *NeuroImage, 24*(4), 1233-1241.

ANNETT SCHIRMER / QINGYANG LI

Electrophysiological Correlates of Vocal Emotional Processing in Male and Female Listeners

1. Introduction

The capability for abstract thought and language is believed to be the driving force of human evolutionary success (Pinker 2003; Corballis 2004). Moreover, as abstractly thinking individuals, humans typically consider verbal information to be of key importance in interactions with conspecifics. However, such interactions also always engage phylogenetically older, nonverbal channels. Rather than being superfluous evolutionary artifacts, these nonverbal channels play an important role in human communication. They often unconsciously tinge the perception and evaluation of the words that have been exchanged (Schirmer/Kotz 2003). For example, a speaker's prosody may both reinforce and contradict verbal content. Moreover, in cases such as sarcasm or irony it may completely negate the interpretation of the verbal message. Aside from supporting and guiding the interpretation of spoken language, nonverbal signals also serve functions that were already relevant for our pre-linguistic ancestors. Specifically, they represent a means of alerting and informing group members about significant events in the environment. Additionally, they help facilitate social exchange and foster the relationship of group members. For example, individuals jointly engaged in an activity may concurrently vocalize to reinforce their social bond (e.g., Mithen 2005).

Like other facets of personality, human interest in social bonds is characterized by interindividual variation. Specifically, women have been found to be more socially oriented than men (Kashima/Kokubo/ Kashima/Boxall/Yamaguchi/Macrae 2004; Fahrenberg/Hampel/Selg 1994). Starting at a young age, girls tend to be more interested than boys in toys and games (e.g., dolls) that imitate social interactions (Pasterski/Geffner/Brain/Hindmarsh/Brook/Hines 2005). Furthermore, as young adults, women score higher than men in questionnaires that test social orientation (Fahrenberg et al. 1994). Women are also more likely than men to seek social support in stressful situations (Ptacek/Smith/Zanas 1992; Zivotofsky/Koslowsky 2005) – a behavior that is believed to be mediated by estrogen and oxytocin (Taylor/Klein/Lewis/Gruenewald/Gurung/Updegraff 2000). While clearly pointing towards sex differences in social interests, this evidence also hints that the 'social bonding' function of nonverbal expressions may be more important in women than in men.

In line with this latter assertion, research suggests greater sensitivity to nonverbal cues in women than in men. Women typically outperform men in the recognition of emotion from facial or vocal cues (Hall 1978, Schirmer/Kotz 2003; Scholten, Aleman/Kahn 2008; Vaskinn/Sundet/Friis et al. 2007). Furthermore, sex differences have been reported in the neurophysiological response to emotional expressions (Guntekin/Basar 2007; Schirmer/Kotz 2003; Schirmer/Zysset/Kotz/von Cramon 2004). Of particular interest here is an event-related potential (ERP) study that investigated vocal emotional processing using an auditory oddball paradigm (Schirmer/Striano/Friederici 2005). In this study, participants watched a silent movie with subtitles while passively listening to syllables spoken with emotional or neutral prosody. In one block, neutrally spoken syllables (i.e., standards) were presented frequently and interrupted rarely by angrily or happily spoken syllables (i.e., deviants). In another block, angrily and happily spoken syllables served as standards and were rarely interrupted by a neutral deviant. Both emotional and neutral deviants elicited a negative component in the ERP termed mismatch negativity (MMN). This component peaked at around 200 ms following stimulus onset with a central scalp distribution. In line with prior research on sex differences, this MMN was larger for emotional as compared to neutral deviants in women, but not in men.

Given the common belief that women are the more emotional sex, one may argue that rather than being a reflection of differential social interests, sex differences in vocal processing may be due to a generally increased emotional responsiveness in women as compared to men. That this is not the case was demonstrated by a more recent ERP study (Schirmer/Escoffier/Simpson 2007). In this study, participants listened to two types of oddball sequences. One sequence consisted of spoken syllables that rarely and unpredictably increased in amplitude. Another sequence consisted of synthesized sounds whose envelope matched that of the spoken syllables. Like the first sequence, this one contained rare increases in sound amplitude. Typically, an increase in sound amplitude is associated with an emotional response and heightened subjective arousal. Moreover, drastic changes in sound amplitude are known to elicit a startle response (Bradley/Codispoti/Sabatinelli/Lang 2001) – a reflexive protection of the body. As both the spoken and synthesized sequences contained amplitude increases, both should trigger an emotional response. Thus, if sex differences found for vocal emotional processing are not specific to social information, increases in sound amplitude should elicit sex differences for both types of material. However, if the previously observed female enhancement of vocal emotional processing is a function of the social significance of the stimulus, sex differences should show for spoken syllables and be smaller or non-significant for the synthesized sounds. In line with this latter hypothesis, the MMN measured in response to amplitude changes showed sex differences for the spoken syllables but not for the synthesized sounds. Moreover, as predicted, subjective ratings of the sounds indicated that an increase in sound amplitude was associated with increased emotional arousal in both men and women. However, while male and female ratings were comparable for the synthesized sounds, women rated the spoken syllables as more emotionally arousing than men.

Taken together, research on vocal processing suggests that emotional expressions engage more mental resources than neutral expressions. Moreover, women seem to discriminate emotional and neutral expressions more readily than men do and are more likely to respond with changes in emotional arousal. Given that these sex differences show for vocalizations but not for comparable nonvocal sounds (Schirmer et al. 2007), one may conclude that they are a function of a sound's social significance. Due to a heightened social interest, women may be more sensitive than men to the emotional connotation of social signals. As both nature and nurture are known to shape the human mind, one may speculate as to which of these mechanisms accounts for the findings reviewed here. Nature may enhance vocal emotional processing through the actions of steroids or neuropeptides, which are known to have sex-specific functions. Nurture on the other hand may act top-down, by encouraging women more than men to value social signals. Specifically, due to upbringing and cultural norms, women may be more likely than men to *attend* to vocalizations even if these vocalizations are irrelevant for the task at hand.

To address this latter possibility, the present study aimed at replicating prior work on vocal emotional processing while controlling for participant attention. To this end, we again presented syllables spoken with angry or neutral prosody in an oddball paradigm. In two different blocks, participants either attended to the auditory stimuli (i.e., active oddball condition) or to a visual task (i.e., passive oddball condition). In the active oddball condition, the syllable sequences were task relevant. Participants were asked to count rare deviants that differed from standards in emotional tone. The passive oddball condition was adopted from research by Escera and colleagues (Escera/Alho/Winkler/Näätänen 1998; Escera/Corral/Yago 2002). It required participants to indicate with a button press whether visually presented numbers were odd or even. Unlike auditory subsidiary tasks, this task directed attention to another modality and thus reduced the likelihood of attentive deviance detection. Moreover, hit rates of about 90 percent indicated that the task was difficult enough to require participants to attend to the visual information in order to maintain a reasonable performance. Performance could then be compared to determine whether men and women engaged differently in the task leaving different attentional resources available for processing the task-irrelevant auditory input. If true, this would indicate that sex differences in vocal emotional processing are a function of the attention male and female listeners direct to the auditory information. However, if performance in the subsidiary task is comparable between men and women, one must conclude that both have comparable resources available for processing the vocalizations. Moreover, sex differences then likely reflect automatic processes instead of controlled direction of attention.

2. Methods

Participants. Forty-two participants were invited for the study. Two participants were excluded from data analysis due to excessive EEG artifacts. Twenty of the remaining participants were male with a mean age of 25.3 (sd 2.11) years. Female participants were on average 24.6 (sd 3.05) years old. All participants were right handed, had normal hearing and vision or corrected to normal vision.

Stimulus Material and Task. A female speaker produced the syllables *dada* several times with angry and neutral prosody. A group of 6 listeners (3 males) classified each stimulus as very angry, angry, neutral, or emotional (with the emotion not being anger). Two stimuli that had been uniquely identified as 'very angry' and 'neutral', respectively, were selected for the study. The angry and neutral stimuli were equally long (i.e., 557 ms) and loud (i.e., 67 dB max, 56 dB mean), but differed with respect to other acoustic parameters (e.g., F_0, spectral energy). Equal stimulus length was achieved by sampling several vocalizations for each category and by instructing the speaker to keep an equal rhythm. Minor differences in stimulus duration were then edited using the CoolEdit 2000 Software from Syntrillium. Equal mean stimulus amplitude was achieved by employing the CoolEdit 2000 Normalization algorithm. Maximum and mean amplitude were determined with Praat (Boersma/Weenik 2005).

Each condition comprised two blocks with 700 standards ($P=0.875$) and 100 deviants ($P=0.125$) in each block. There was a minimum of 3 and a maximum of 11 standards between deviants. The emotional and the neutral stimuli served as standards and deviants in two separate blocks. In one block, neutral syllables were presented as standards and emotional syllables as deviants. In the other block, emotional syllables were presented as standards and neutral syllables as deviants. Presenting the same syllables as both standards and deviants allowed us to investigate the MMN by comparing physically identical stimuli, thereby reducing the influence of acoustic differences between the neutral and the emotional conditions on

MMN amplitude (Jacobsen/Schröger/Horenkamp/Winkler 2003). Block order was counterbalanced across participants. The syllable onset to syllable onset interval in each block was 1200 ms.

In the passive oddball condition, each spoken syllable was followed by a number that appeared on the computer screen in front of the participant. The numbers ranged from 1 to 8 and were equiprobably odd or even. There was a 300 ms interval between the onset of the syllable and the onset of the number. Numbers stayed on the screen for 200 ms and were followed by a blank screen for 700 ms. Then the next trial started. During the passive condition, participants were asked to ignore auditory input and to focus on the numbers presented on the screen in front of them. They had to indicate via button press as fast and accurately as possible, whether a given number was odd or even. The assignment of 'odd' and 'even' response buttons to left and right hand was counterbalanced across participants. During the active oddball condition, spoken syllables were presented without additional visual input. The two blocks were divided into four sub-blocks each and participants were asked to write down the number of auditory deviants that they detected in each sub-block.

Procedure. Participants were seated in a comfortable chair facing a computer monitor at a distance of 1.15 m. Syllables were presented over loudspeakers positioned to the left and right of the monitor. The electroencephalogram (EEG) was recorded from 58 scalp electrodes positioned according to the modified expanded 10-20 system. Two electrodes were positioned at the mastoids. Those and the scalp electrodes were referenced to the nose. Two bi-polar recordings were used to measure horizontal and vertical eye movements. Electrode resistance was kept below 5 kOhm. ERP averages were computed for deviants and immediately preceding standards (i.e., 100 per condition) with a 150-msec baseline and an 800-msec ERP time window. Trials where participants responded incorrectly or that contained eye blink and movement artifacts were omitted from the data analysis. Across participants, an average of 76.5 (sd 10.15) trials per condition was available for statistical analysis of the passive task and an average of 77.34 trials (sd 19.11) per condition was available for statistical analysis of the active task. The EEG was filtered off-line with a 0.5 to 15 Hz bandpass filter.

Data analysis. Visual inspection of the ERP waveforms elicited by deviants revealed an MMN that peaked between 170 to 270 ms following stimulus onset. The exact MMN peak was determined by searching for the minimum voltage in this time window. Computing a mean minimum across electrodes revealed a value of 216 ms. Mean voltages of a 100 ms time window centred around this value were subjected to an ANOVA with *Stimulus Type* (standard/deviant), *Prosody* (angry/neutral), *Task* (passive/active), *Hemisphere* (left/ middle/right) and *AP* (anterior/posterior) as repeated measures factors and *Sex* as a between subjects factor. The factors *Hemisphere* and *AP* comprised the following subgroups of electrodes: anterior-left: AF7 F5 FC5 C5; anterior-middle: AFZ FZ FCZ CZ; anterior-right: AF8 F6 FC6 C6; posterior-left: CP5 P5 PO7 O1; posterior-middle: CPZ PZ POZ OZ; posterior-right: CP6 P6 PO8 O2. For planned and post-hoc comparisons that exceeded the number of degrees of freedom associated with the treatment source of variance a corrected p-value was used according to the modified Bonferroni procedure (see Keppel, 1991). Where appropriate we report p-values corrected for violations of sphericity using the Greenhouse-Geisser procedure.

3. Results

i) *Behavioral measures*

Passive Oddball Task. The behavioral findings are presented in Figure 1. Reaction time and accuracy data from the visual task in the passive oddball condition were analyzed using separate ANOVAs with *Prosody* (angry/neutral) and *Stimulus Type* (standard/deviant) as repeated measures factors and *Sex* as a between subjects factor. Analysis of reaction times revealed a tendential *Prosody***Stimulus Type* interaction (F[1,38] = 3.31, p = .07), suggesting that these factors were not completely independent. All other main effects and interactions were nonsignificant (p > .1). Analysis of accuracy revealed a significant *Stimulus Type* main effect (F[1,38] = 5.07, p < .05) indicating that participants responded more accurately to numbers that followed the presentation of auditory deviants as compared to standards. All other main effects and interactions were nonsignificant (p > .1).

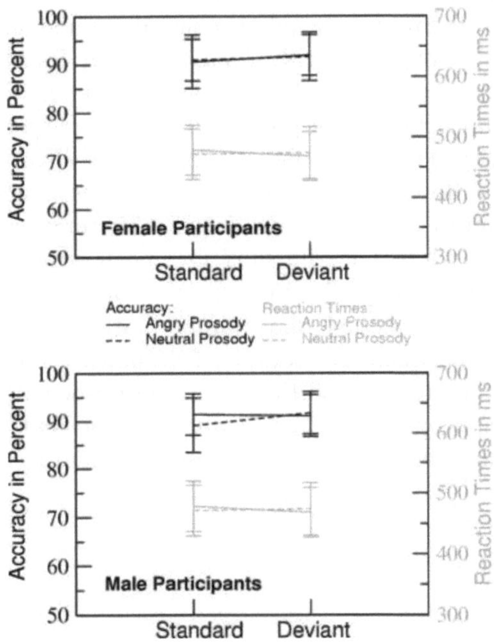

Figure 1: Behavioral measures and standard deviations obtained for the number judgment task in female (top row) and male (bottom row) participants. Accuracy is presented in black lines and scaled according to the left y-axis. Reaction times are presented in gray lines and scaled according to the right y-axis. Solid lines represent syllables spoken with angry prosody. Dotted lines represent syllables spoken with neutral prosody.

Active Oddball Task. Performance in the auditory deviant detection task was assessed by comparing participants' count of deviants in the two blocks (i.e., emotional deviant/neutral standard and neutral deviant/emotional standard) with the number of presented deviants. Note that each block was divided into four sub-blocks following which participants were asked to write down their count of deviants on a sheet of paper. In some sub-blocks, participants counted more whereas in other sub-blocks they counted fewer deviants than were presented. Additional counts were treated as false alarms and missing counts were treated as misses. An ANOVA with *Block* as a repeated measures factor and *Sex* as a between subjects factor was conducted for false alarms and misses separately. This analysis revealed only non-significant main effects and interactions (all *p*s>.1). On average, performance was very accurate with approximately one false alarm or miss per block for each listener.

ii) *Electrophysiological measures*

The electrophysiological findings are presented in Figure 2. The MMN peaked at 212 and 221 ms following stimulus onset for emotional and neutral stimuli, respectively. Statistical analysis for mean amplitudes revealed a *Stimulus Type*Prosody*Sex* interaction ($F[1,38] = 4.74$, $p < .05$) indicating sex differences in the influence of emotional prosody on the MMN. Women (*Stimulus Type*Prosody*, $F[1,19] = 14.72$, $p < .01$), but not men (*Stimulus Type*Prosody*, $p > .1$), showed a significantly larger MMN in response to emotional (*Stimulus Type*, $F[1,19] = 135.49$, $p < .0001$) as compared to neutral deviants (*Stimulus Type*, $F[1,19] = 30.87$, $p < .05$). No interactions with *Task* reached significance ($p > .1$).

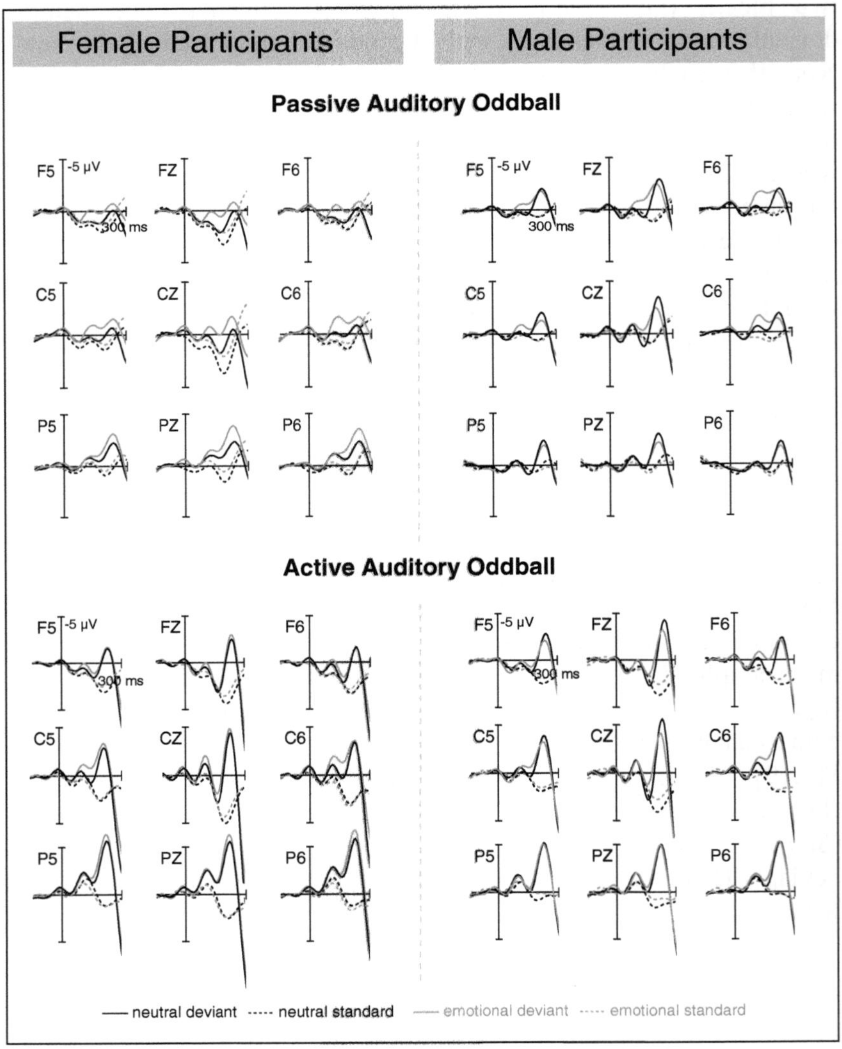

Figure 2: ERP results for the passive and active oddball conditions time locked to the onset of standards (dotted lines) and deviants (solid lines). Black lines represent syllables spoken with neutral prosody and gray lines represent syllables spoken with angry prosody.

4. Discussion

Previous work indicated that, compared to male listeners, female listeners are more sensitive to task-irrelevant vocal emotional expressions (Schirmer et al. 2005, 2007). In the present study, we asked the question whether this sex difference can be attributed to a difference in the allocation of attentional resources. Women, due to cultural norms and upbringing, may be more inclined than men to attend to social signals. Moreover, if presented with a subsidiary task and task-irrelevant vocal expressions, they may choose to direct more attentional resources than men at monitoring the task-irrelevant sounds. As a consequence, women may be more likely than men to respond to sudden changes in emotional connotation.

The present findings contradict this proposition. We found that when asked to respond to a subsidiary task, accuracy and reaction times were comparable in men and women. Moreover, concurrently recorded MMN responses to rare vocal change nevertheless revealed sex differences. Women but not men showed increased MMN amplitudes to emotionally as compared to neutrally spoken deviants. This processing difference, albeit visibly smaller, extended to the active oddball task during which participants had to count auditory deviants. Together, these results indicate that attentional allocation to the subsidiary task and task-irrelevant vocal sounds was comparable in men and women. Moreover, controlled allocation of attention cannot account for sex differences in the processing of task-irrelevant emotional expressions. Instead one has to conclude that enhanced MMN amplitudes to emotional vocalization observed in women reflect an automatic detection of emotionally significant social cues and that this occurs relatively independently of attentional focus.

This interpretation is in line with the presumed nature of the MMN. Specifically, it has been proposed, that the MMN reflects the automatic updating of a sensory memory trace in response to a change in the environment (Näätänen/Gaillard/Mäntysalo 1978; Sams, Paavilainen/Alho/Näätänen 1985). The assumption that this mechanism is triggered automatically rests on the finding that it can be elicited in sleeping participants (Loewy/Campbell/Lugt/Elton/Kok 2000) and that, under wakefulness, it occurs independently of the subsidiary task (Muller-Gass/Stelmack/Campbell 2005). Here we show that also the emotional modulation of the MMN amplitude is fairly automatic.

That such an emotional modulation occurs in women but not in men is intriguing and raises the question as to whether it is a result of biological or cultural pressures. Given its automaticity, one may speculate that innate differences in the neurophysiological make-up of men and women are at the heart of the observed sex differences. However, such a speculation would be poorly justified as humans demonstrate automaticity not just for innate mechanisms. With sufficient practice, learned processes such as bicycling or reading can become automatic. This can be demonstrated experimentally in studies that employ interference paradigms. For example, in the Stroop paradigm (Stroop, 1935), participants are presented with color words (e.g., red) printed in a matching (e.g., red) or mismatching (e.g., green) color ink. Naming the color of the ink is associated with reduced response time and more errors than reading the word suggesting that reading is more automatic than color naming. However, this interference pattern can be changed and even reverted if subjects practice the less familiar task (MacLeod 1998; MacLeod/Dunbar 1988) thus indicating that automaticity is not fixed but subject to an individual's interaction with the environment.

With this in mind, it is easy to conceive that the automaticity with which individuals respond to social emotional signals could be a function of their upbringing and cultural context. In line with this, research suggests that certain emotional displays, which are of particular importance for a specific culture, are also best recognized by individuals from that culture (Beaupre/Hess 2005). Furthermore, there is evidence that Asian listeners with a collectivistic cultural background process vocal emotional signals more automatically than Western listeners with an individualistic cultural background (Ishii/Reyes/Kitayama 2003). When presented with emotional words spoken in an incongruous emotional voice, Asian listeners show greater interference effects than Western listeners.

Extending these cross-cultural comparisons, there is evidence for a modulation of emotional processing by environmental influences within a given culture. For example, parental involvement in infant care has been identified as a determining factor for how quickly infants advance with respect to their emotion recognition skills (Montaque/Walker-Andrews 2002). Moreover, differences in the way parents interact with boys and girls have been linked to the development of sex differences in emotional processing as observed in young adults (for a review see Maccoby 1998).

However, as not every parental intervention is successful in shaping children's perception and behavior (Pasterski et al. 2005), it is necessary to consider additional biological factors. Moreover, especially in the context of emotion it is now well established that certain processing and response patterns are largely innate. For example, primates learn to fear potentially dangerous objects such as snakes or spiders more readily than they would learn to fear objects that were irrelevant during their evolutionary history (Mineka/Cook 1993; Mineka/Davidson/Cook/Keir 1984). Furthermore, it has been demonstrated that threatening stimuli engage specifically dedicated emotion circuits that automatically activate stimulus relevant psychophysiological and behavioral response patterns (e.g., startle; Bradley/Codispoti/Sabatinelli/Lang 2001; LeDoux 1998). Given sex-specific evolutionary pressures in the detection and response to social threat (Taylor et al. 2000), one may conclude that women evolved more sensitive mechanisms for monitoring the emotional state of their social environment. Past research has highlighted estrogen as a potential agent by which nature could enhance emotional sensitivity in women. For example, estrogen has been linked to a better accuracy in the recognition of fear from faces (Pearson/Lewis 2005). Additionally, estrogen appears to be involved in the differential processing of unattended emotional and neutral vocalization (Schirmer/Escoffier/Li/Li/Strafford-Wilson/Li 2008). A larger MMN in response to emotional as compared to neutral vocal deviants has been associated with high estrogen in both men and women. Moreover, estrogen appears to reduce listener distractibility by neutral but not emotional events.

Taken together these results implicate both nature and nurture in shaping listener sensitivity to vocal emotional signals. Moreover, they corroborate the observations made in the present experiment that emotional expressions have an advantage over neutral expressions in engaging the auditory change detection mechanism reflected by the MMN. As such an advantage was observed in women only, we can conclude that women are more sensitive than men to the emotional significance of social signals. Furthermore, as women demonstrated an enhanced MMN to emotional as compared to neutral vocalization independently of the task, the processing advantage for emotional expressions appears to be fairly automatic and not simply a function of conscious allocation of attention to social signals. This is in accordance with the idea that vocal emotional information is more important to women than to men and provides insights into potential mechanisms that increase women's risk for developing fearful conditioned responses to these and other social stimuli (Hettema/ Prescott/Myers/Neale/Kendler 2005).

Acknowledgments

The authors want to express their gratitude to Carles Escera and Risto Näätänen for insightful discussions of the present experiments. We also thank Trevor Penney for comments on earlier drafts of the manuscript. This research was supported by the National University of Singapore Young Investigator Award conferred to Annett Schirmer (R-581-000-066-123).

References

Beaupre, Martin G. / Hess, Ursula 2005. Cross-cultural emotion recognition among Canadian ethnic groups. *Journal of Cross-cultural Psychology* 36, 355-370.

Boersma, Paul / Weenink, David 2005. Praat: doing phonetics by computer (Version 4.3.14) [Computer program]. Retrieved from <http://www.praat.org/>.

Bradley, Margaret M. / Codispoti, Maurizio / Sabatinelli, Dean / Lang, Peter J. 2001. Emotion and motivation II: Sex differences in picture processing. *Emotion* 1, 300-319.

Corballis, Michael C. 2004. The origins of modernity: Was autonomous speech the critical factor? *Psychological Review* 111, 543-552.

Escera, Carles / Alho, Kimmo / Schröger, Erich / Winkler, Istevan 2000. Involuntary attention and distractibility as evaluated with event-related brain potentials. *Audiology and Neuro-Ootology* 5, 151-166.

Escera, Carles / Corral, Maria-Jose / Yago, Elena 2002. An electrophysiological and behavioral investigation of involuntary attention towards auditory frequency, duration and intensity changes. *Cognitive Brain Research* 14, 325-332.

Fahrenberg, Jochen / Hampel, Rainer / Selg, Herbert 1994. *Das Freiburger Persönlichkeitsinventar FPI: Revidierte Fassung FPI-R und teilweise geänderte Fassung FPI-A1*. Göttingen: Hogrefe.

Guntekin, Bahar / Basar, Erol 2007. Gender differences influence brain's beta oscillatory responses in recognition of facial expressions. *Neuroscience Letters* 424, 94-99.

Hall, Judith A. 1978. Gender effects in decoding nonverbal cues. *Psychological Bulletin* 4, 845-857.

Hettema, John M. / Prescott, Carol A. / Myers, John M. / Neale, Michael C. / Kendler, Kenneth S. 2005. The structure of genetic and environmental risk factors for anxiety disorders in men and women. *Archives of General Psychiatry* 62, 182-189.

Ishii, Keiko / Reyes, Jose A. / Kitayama, Shinobu 2003. Spontaneous attention to word content versus emotional tone. *Psychological Science* 14, 39–46.

Jacobsen, Thomas / Schröger, Erich. / Horenkamp, Thorsten / Winkler, Istevan 2003. Mismatch negativity to pitch change: varied stimulus proportions in controlling effects of neural refractoriness on human auditory event-related potentials. *Neuroscience Letters* 344, 79-82.

Kashima, Yoshihisa / Kokubo, Teruyoshi / Kashima, Emiko S. / Boxall, Diane / Yamaguchi, Susumu / Macrae, Kristina 2004. Culture and self: are there within-culture differences in self between metropolitan areas and regional cities? *Personality and Social Psychology Bulletin* 30, 816-823.

Keppel, Geoffrey 1991. *Design and analysis: A researcher's handbook.* New Jersey: Prentice Hall.

Loewy, Derek H. / Campbell, Kenneth B. / Lugt, Duncan R. / Elton, Martin / Kok, Albert 2000. The mismatch negativity during natural sleep: intensity deviants. *Clinical Neurophysiology* 111, 863–72.

LeDoux, Joseph 1998. *The emotional brain. The mysterious underpinnings of emotional life.* New York: Touchstone.

MacLeod, C.M. 1998. Training on integrated versus separated Stroop tasks: the progression of interference and facilitation. *Memory and Cognition* 26, 201-211.

MacLeod, Colin M. / Dunbar, Kevin 1988. Training and Stroop-like interference: evidence for a continuum of automaticity. *Journal of Experimental Psychology: Learning, Memory and Cognition* 10, 304–315.

Maccoby, Eleanor E. 1998. The socialization component. In Maccoby, Eleanor. E. (ed.) *Growing up apart, coming together.* London: Harvard University Press, 118–152.

Mineka, Susan / Cook, Michael 1993. Mechanisms involved in the observational conditioning of fear. *Journal of Experimental Psychology: General* 122, 23–38.

Mineka, Susan / Davidson, Mark / Cook, Michael / Keir, Richard 1984. Observational conditioning of snake fear in rhesus monkey. *Journal of Abnormal Psychology* 93, 355–372 .

Mithen, Steven J. 2005. *The singing neanderthals: The origin of music, language, mind and body*. London: Harvard University Press.

Montaque, Diane P.F. / Walker-Andrews, Arlene S. 2002. Mothers, fathers, and infants: The role of person familiarity and parental involvement in infants' perception of emotion expressions. *Child Development* 73, 1335-1352.

Näätnen, Risto / Gaillard, Anthony W. K. / Mäntysalo, Sirkka 1978. Early selective-attention effect on evoked potential reinterpreted. *Acta Psychologica* 42, 313-329.

Pasterski, Vickie L. / Geffner, Mitchell E. / Brain, Cariline / Hindmarsh, Peter / Brook, Charles / Hines, Melissa 2005. Prenatal hormones and postnatal socialization by parents as determinants of male-typical toy play in girls with congenital adrenal hyperplasia. *Child Development* 76, 264-278.

Pearson, Rebecca / Lewis, Michael B., 2005. Fear recognition across the menstrual cycle. *Hormones and Behavior* 47, 267-271.

Pinker, Steven 2003. Language as an adaptation to the cognitive niche. In Christiansen, M. / Kirby, S. (eds) *Language evolution: States of the Art*. New York: Oxford University Press, 16-37.

Ptacek, John T. / Smith, Ronald E. / Zanas, John 1992. Gender appraisal and coping: a longitudinal analysis. *Journal of Personality* 60, 747-768.

Sams, Mikko. / Paavilainen, Petri / Alho, Kimmo / Näätänen, Risto. 1985. Auditory frequency discrimination and event-related potentials. *Electroencephalography and Clinical Neurophysiology* 62, 437-448.

Schirmer, Annett / Escoffier, Nicolas / Simpson, Elisabeth 2007. Listen up! Processing of intensity change differs for vocal and nonvocal sounds. *Brain Research* 1176, 103-112.

Schirmer, Annett / Escoffier, Nicholas / Li, Qing Y. / Li, Hui / Strafford-Wilson, Jennifer / Li, Wan-I. 2008. What grabs his attention but not hers? Estrogen correlates with neurophysiological measures of vocal change detection, 33, 718-727.

Schirmer, Annett / Kotz, Sonja A. 2003. ERP evidence for a gender specific Stroop effect in emotional speech. *Journal of Cognitive Neuroscience* 15, 1135-1148.

Schirmer, Annett / Kotz, Sonja A. / Friederici, Angela D. 2005. On the role of attention for the processing of emotions in speech: Sex differences revisited. *Cognitive Brain Research* 24, 442-452.

Schirmer, Annett / Striano, Tricia / Friederici, Angela D. 2005. Sex differences in the pre-attentive processing of vocal emotional expressions. *Neuroreport* 16, 635-639.

Schirmer, Annett / Zysset, Stefan / Kotz, Sonja A. / von Cramon, D. Yves. 2004. Gender differences in the activation of inferior frontal cortex during emotional speech perception. *NeuroImage* 21, 1114-1123.

Scholten, Marton R. / Aleman, Andre / Kahn, Rene S. 2008. The processing of emotional prosody and semantics in schizophrenia: relationship to gender and IQ. *Psychological Medicine*, 38, 887-898.

Stroop, J. Ridley 1935. Studies of interference in serial verbal reactions. *Journal of Experimental Psychology* 18, 643–662.

Taylor, Shelley E. / Klein, Laura C. / Lewis, Brian P. / Gruenewald, Tara L. / Gurung, Regan A.R. / Updegraff, John A. 2000. Biobehavioral responses to stress in females: Tend-and-befriend, not fight-or-flight. *Psychological Review* 107, 411-429.

Vaskinn, A. / Sundet, K. / Friis, S. / Simonsen, C. / Birkenaes, A.B. / Engh, J.A. / Jonsdottir, H. / Ringen, P.A. / Opjordsmoen, S. / Andreassen, O.A. 2007. The effect of gender on emotion perception in schizophrenia and bipolar disorder. *Acta Psychatria Scandinavia* 116, 263-270.

Zivotofsky, Ari Z. / Koslowsky, Meni 2005. Gender differences in coping with the major external stress of the Washington D.C. sniper. Stress and Health: *Journal of the International Society for the Investigation of Stress* 21, 27-31.

Implementation and analysis
of emotion recognition
in synthesis systems

RODDY COWIE / ELLEN DOUGLAS-COWIE

Prosodic and Related Features that signify Emotional Colouring in Conversational Speech

1. Introduction

Contemporary research on speech and emotion involves several distinct streams, which have many of the characteristics of Kuhn's paradigms. A relatively mature tradition in the human sciences is well represented in the review by Juslin and Laukka (2003). In contrast, a stream based in engineering, represented for instance by the CEICES project (Batliner et al. 2006), has been developing rapidly. The paradigm differences between the two are quite wide ranging. For example, human scientists are typically concerned with identifying individual speech variables whose values depend on the speaker's emotional state; instead, engineers are typically concerned with the recognition rates achieved using a particular array of speech variables. Human scientists try to reduce differences to a small number of speech variables, whereas the CEICES project regards hundreds of speech variables as significant. Human scientists tend to look for relationships that hold for emotion in general, whereas engineers target particular application scenarios. The list goes on.

It may be that the paradigms are an example of what Kuhn called incommensurability: there are too many differences for comparison to be meaningful. However, it makes sense to withhold that conclusion until other options have been explored. This chapter explores the possibility that the engineering stream does incorporate new insights that are of interest to both communities, even if they are not immediately easy to disentangle from the paradigm differences.

The method that the chapter uses is reanalysis of data that was generated in an engineering context. Material that was acquired in the context of recognition is used to describe how humans appear to communicate and decipher emotional colouring. The material derives from two European projects, ERMIS <www.image.ntua.gr/ermis/> and HUMAINE <http://emotion-research.net/>. The technicalities of feature extraction are several years old, and therefore distinctly dated by the internal standards of the paradigm. However, the technical limitations are not critical. Old systems are less refined than more recent ones in terms of the detail that they capture, but they deal in broadly similar kinds of overall structure. In some respects, it is an advantage that less technical detail is needed to achieve a basic sense of what is happening.

Both ERMIS and HUMAINE set out to develop techniques for recognising speakers' emotional states. The methods followed the standard pattern in the area. Recognisers are trained by applying learning rules to examples drawn from a database. Each example involves features extracted from a recording, together with a label describing the emotional state that was associated with that combination of features. The learning rules build up statistical summaries of the relationships between features and states, and those can then be used to infer what state a new combination of features is likely to indicate. Recognisers developed using the material described here achieved some of the highest recognition rates reported in the literature on emotion, which reflects well on both the features selected and the learning methods used (Fragopanagos/Taylor 2005; Kollias et al. 2008).

The key feature of this chapter is that it considers the kind of feature set that is typically used for recognition, but explores how it translates into a description of differences between styles. It tries to indicate that there are interesting questions about the way emotion colours speech implicit in the choice of material, the choice of features, the choice of emotion descriptors, the statistics of their relationships, and various other aspects of the work. Engineering papers typically leave them implicit, and emphasise recognition rate. This chapter aims to draw out the features of the work that are usually left implicit, but that are potentially interesting to the human sciences.

2. Recordings

The recordings to be considered use a paradigm called SAL (short for Sensitive Artificial Listener, see Douglas-Cowie et al. 2008). It involves a person talking to a partner who behaves in a stereotyped way that is designed to elicit emotion in the recipient. The partner – the 'SAL agent' – is modelled on a chat show host. His or her conversation consists of a fixed repertoire of phrases, from which he/she selects in the light of the state the person currently appears to be in and his/her own emotional agenda – which at any given moment may be to make the person happy, angry, sad, or reasonable. In the material considered here, the agent was played by a person who had been given a suitable repertoire of phrases (and ways to navigate through the repertoire). Research is under way on the construction of a fully automated SAL (see SEMAINE project <http://www.semaine-project.eu/>): the point is that it offers a testbed for developing a range of 'soft' communicative skills.

The SAL format was developed as a way of meeting requirements that are important from an engineering point of view. First and foremost, the material is relatively naturalistic. Of course, the easiest way to elicit 'emotional' speech is for actors to be given a target emotion and to speak in a way that is supposed to convey that emotion. Almost all of the material reported in Juslin and Laukka is of that kind. But acted emotional speech was used to train recognisers, transfer to real tasks involving spontaneous emotional speech was poor (Batliner et al 2003). Not a great deal is known about the phonetic differences between acted and spontaneous speech (Frigo, in progress), but the fact that they are different should not be surprising given that most people can tell within seconds whether material on TV involves acting or people expressing their own feelings relatively spontaneously (Cowie et al. forthcoming). SAL does not produce absolute authenticity: there is an element of play about the situation, and an element of stiffness associated with the recording. But people express feelings that emerge from the situation in their own words, and the stiffness and playfulness are not outside the range that occurs in real interactions with (for instance) a neighbour who wants to be friendly, but is not terribly well known.

Partial authenticity is part of a compromise, because machine analysis requires benign recording conditions and quite large amounts of data that is not effectively neutral; and in both ERMIS and HUMAINE, there was a commitment to multimodal data. The issue of multimodality will not be elaborated on, but it is the case that speech is usually part of a multimodal interaction, and analysing how it conveys emotion without referring to the other modalities is rather like analysing chorales without referring to the lower parts.

The SAL format was one of several responses to these requirements that ERMIS and related projects explored. It emerged as pragmatically the most satisfying way of generating data. People do respond to the SAL agent's provocation with a reasonable amount and variety of emotional colouring, in a reasonably natural way, and it is possible to make good recordings, audio and visual.

The effort put into developing appropriate sources is a very characteristic feature of contemporary engineering approaches to emotion. The point is illustrated by special sessions at the main conference on databases, Language Resources and Evaluation Conference (Devillers et al. 2006, 2008). That marks a point of contact with linguistics, which has a tradition of developing corpora. Psychology, in contrast, has traditionally focused on ensuring that observations could be replicated rather than storing records of them.

3. Description of emotion

Emphasising natural emotion has implications for description. What occurs in relatively natural interaction is emotional colouring that is quite hard to capture in terms of the categories that people automatically use to describe emotions (Cowie/Cornelius 2003). Various alternatives exist, such as using 'soft vectors' to describe the proportion of standard categories (happiness, anger, sadness, etc) that are present in a given state or theoretical primitives derived from appraisal theory (Devillers et al. 2006). ERMIS used the option that is technically simplest, which is describing states in terms of the two dimensions routinely used to describe 'core affect' (Russell/Feldman Barrett 1999), valence (how positive or negative the person feels) and activation (how inclined or disinclined to take action). The two dimensions can be thought of as defining a space whose origin is a default state of alert neutrality. It will be called affect space from now on.

Descriptions in that format were assigned using FEELtrace (Cowie et al. 2000). FEELtrace is designed to capture the perceived flow of affect – that is, the broad kind of state an observer would be expected to infer given the signs that are present. Raters move a cursor as they watch and listen to a recording to indicate where the speaker appears to lie at any given moment in affect space. The output of that process is a trace giving instant-by-instant values of the speaker's perceived valence and activation. Using that kind of trace to train recognisers means that they should end up 'reading' signs of emotion as a human observer would. That includes being misdirected if the human is, which is appropriate if the aim is a machine that will react much as humans do.

Individual differences are part of that story. It has become clear that although FEELtrace raters agree rather well on examples that are selected to be clear-cut, subtler material gives rise to systematic individual differences. These reflect the fact that humans may 'read' the same emotional signs in rather different ways. These differences need to be understood rather than averaged out, and mathematical techniques designed for that purpose are beginning to emerge (Steidl et al. 2005).

4. Speech variables

It is natural to suppose that the key to recognising emotion in speech is discovering a core set of variables that are used to signal it. Some of the reasons for making that kind of assumption are conceptual. It fits neatly with the assumption that vocal expression of emotion involves superimposing emotion-related signals on the other elements of the speech stream: using a few well-defined variables makes for effective signalling. The assumption also fits with accounts that emphasise the physiological correlates of emotion, since one might expect changes in voice to reflect a few key physiological changes (e.g. Banse/Scherer 1996). Statistically, it is devoutly to be wished that the problem can be reduced to a few variables, because if there are too many the 'curse of dimensionality' comes into play.

The speech analysis reported here uses a system called ASSESS (Cowie et al. 2000), which developed over a decade or so. ASSESS began by extracting continuous descriptors – contours of pitch and intensity, and a spectrum divided into four broad bands. These were divided at two main levels. 'Tunes' were identified using one of the standard definitions: a silence of over 150ms is classified as a pause, and taken to mark a break between tunes. Points of inflection (peaks and troughs) were also identified in each of the contours, allowing each to be 'stylised' as a series of rises and falls. That analysis laid the groundwork for extracting features. The extraction used tunes as the main unit of analysis: each tune had a vector of features associated with it.

It quickly became apparent that a very large number of features could very easily be generated. Because that was a problem for recognition technology, statistical techniques for reducing the number were explored (McGilloway et al 2000). But as technology has developed, it has become standard to accept that very large numbers of features are genuinely worth considering (see, e.g. the CEICES project, Batliner et al. 2006).

The feature set considered in this chapter is a compromise. It uses 80 measures that previous work had suggested were potentially useful. Brief descriptions of the individual features are given in the Appendix. The body of the chapter refers only to the groups of features, but the individual features can be identified by comparison with the table in the Appendix if need be.

5. Structure of analysis

The speech analysed came from eight speakers, four male and four female. From each, 20 clips were selected for analysis. A clip is a recording of a period in which the speaker talks relatively continuously with little or no intrusion from the SAL agent. Clips were on average 17 seconds long, and contained 9 tunes.

The question behind the analysis is: which of the variables under consideration is systematically associated with perceived affect? And to what extent can variables that are associated be ignored because they duplicate effects that others capture more directly? The core technique is correlation. A significant correlation between values associated with a feature F and a measure of affect A indicates that F is systematically associated with A. Of course, there are relationships that correlations do not detect (curvilinear ones), and significant correlations may be spurious (reflecting statistical accidents rather than real relationships). The analysis that follows is sensitive to those issues, but they are generally not discussed explicitly.

The correlations consider three measures of emotionality per tune. They are the mean rating of valence associated with it; the mean rating of activation associated with it; and the mean distance from the origin of valence-activation space, which will be called net affect. Work has been done on other measures, including the standard deviation of each measure within the tune and the square of each measure (that provides a way of capturing some kinds of curvilinearity); but the results do not radically affect the picture given here.

The measures of affect were generated by two FEELtrace raters (both female psychology graduates engaged in research). Each rated the whole dataset, and a separate set of correlation was calculated for each.

6. Correlations for the group as a whole

If the key to recognising emotion in speech were discovering a core set of variables that are used to signal it, then the natural strategy would be to consider the data as a whole, so that local noise would be smoothed out. That kind of procedure was applied to data from the more traditional ASSESS measures (55 in all), by taking the clip as a unit of analysis, and relating average affect ratings per clip to average to speech properties calculated over the clip as a whole.

That procedure revealed 80 correlations significant beyond the traditional 0.05 level, spread over 40 of the 55 measures considered. As might be expected from the literature, most of the correlations were with activation (n=44), and rather few with valence (n=11). Less predictably, a substantial number of correlations (n=25) were with net affect (i.e. distance from the centre of the affect space, irrespective of direction).

Pursuing the logic of looking for a robust core of signs, factor analysis was applied to the variables that correlated with affect ratings. That identified nine factors, most reasonably easy to describe intuitively by looking at the variables that contributed strongly to the factor. Names are given in Table 1. The factors are ordered from those that account for most variance in the set of speech measures to those that account for least. Scores for the underlying factors were reconstructed in the standard way, and correlated with affect ratings. Table 1 shows the results in a way that conveys the broad picture.

Description of factor (intuitive summary of associated variables)	*Activation*		*Net affect*	
	Rater 1	Rater 2	Rater 1	Rater 2
Global variation in pitch	0.39	0.35	0.18	(0.05)
Slope of vowel spectrum	(0.13)	0.18		
Raised pitch, reduced frication	0.28	(-0.1)		
Length of pauses	-0.20	-0.21		
Global variation in intensity	-0.22	(0.00)		
Subdivision (pitch infections, short silences)			(-0.03)	-0.27
Intensity			-0.22	(-0.05)
Complex F_0 contour shape (lack of smoothness, tunes end high & vary in length)	-0.24	(-0.12)		
Curvature of F_0 contours			(-0.11)	-0.19

Table 1 Correlation coefficients for significant correlations ($p<0.05$) between recovered factors and affect measures. Coefficients in brackets show non-significant correlations in cases where there was a significant relationship with measures from the other rater.

The picture that the table presents is broadly consistent with a good deal of literature. Only two types of information seem to be used by both raters: global variation in pitch and pause length. In two more cases, the second rater might be said to show a trend in the same direction as the significant effect: these are slope of the vowel spectrum and complex F_0 contour shape. All of those relationships involve activation. The other relationships, including all those that involve net affect, are specific to one rater – suggesting cues that some people use and others do not.

There is an argument for stopping at that point, and concluding that essentially the data boil down to a small number of trends. However, that amounts to assuming that any information worth recovering can be extracted by a very restricted type of mathematical technique. In engineering terms, that amounts to considering only a very basic type of recogniser. In fact, the high recognition rates that have been reported have used recognisers capable of using contexts and relationships between features in quite complex ways. With that in mind, the next sections explore distinctions that are averaged out in the kind of analysis represented by Table 1.

7. Using more complex relationships

This section considers two ways of extending the approach taken in the previous section. One is using more complex features, the other is using tune characteristics to identify context-sensitive relationships.

The complex measures target specific attributes that might be considered relevant to emotion rather than general-purpose descriptors: recognisable voice qualities, irregularity in F_0 (creak and jitter); rates of occurrence for various types of feature (intensity peaks, brief silences, fricatives); relationships between the duration of a tune and its range of pitch or intensity, or curvature of the pitch contour; and features that describe a tune's relationship to its immediate predecessors.

The feature used to distinguish contexts is tune duration. It has been shown that recognition improves when short tunes were taken out of the analysis (Kollias et al. 2008). The natural assumption is that they represent noise: they are too short to be rated reliably. In fact, though, the correlations between raters tell a very different story. For both valence and net affect, the subset of tunes that show the highest correlations between the two raters ($r=0.77$ and $r=0.64$ respectively) are those that last 250ms or less (i.e. about one or two syllables). The implication is that different lengths of tune may carry different kinds of information, and should be analysed differently.

Table 2 summarises analysis based on those considerations. The presentation is designed to convey a visual impression of pattern. Cells are coloured dark grey if neither rater showed a significant correlation between the relevant affect and speech variables; light grey if one of the raters showed a significant correlation; and white if both correlations were significant. In the white cells, the correlation coefficients are in normal type if both relationships are in the same direction, and grey italic if the relationships are significant but in opposite directions. The discussion below concentrates on the white cells where both relationships are in the same direction – 'simple agreements'.

The immediate impression is that relationships between speech variables and perceived affect are much more complex than Table 1 and similar analyses would suggest. Several patterns go to make up that impression.

First, separating tune lengths seems to be illuminating. There are many measures for which it seems true to say 'this variable conveys X in tunes of length Y, but not elsewhere'. Aggregating tunes of all lengths simply obscures these relationships.

The most immediately striking effect of length is that there are far more simple agreements in the longer tunes. That explains why excluding shorter tunes improves recognition rates. However, that is not the whole story by any means. Note that the short tunes seem to offer good indicators of net affect, without reference to the character of the emotion. There are eight simple agreements of that kind, with quite high correlation coefficients. Though it is less clear cut, it is also noticeable that measures involving durations of elements, both intensity- and pitch-based, seem to be more informative in the intermediate length tunes than in the longest. It seems at least worth considering that the different lengths of tune should be thought of as offering different kinds of information, not simply different amounts.

The second broad pattern is that particularly with the longer tunes, the complex measures do seem to be useful. It is noticeable that three of the four simple agreements involving valence come from complex measures – one of the measures of jitter, and two voice quality measures from the set described by Hammarberg et al. (1980), which involve comparisons between energy levels in different spectral bands. The features relating pitch and intensity range to duration also come through consistently. They are designed to detect, for instance, tunes that are long but have a narrow pitch range, or show a wide intensity range relative to their duration. In one sense, the information that these features use is already there in the general measures. However, it makes perfect sense mathematically that the information sources may not be useful unless they are combined in specific ways. The feature sets used in projects like CEICES become very large partly because they include various ways of recombining simpler measures. The data here illustrate the reasons why that kind of strategy makes sense.

A final point is made more directly by the right hand columns in the full table of variables in the Appendix. They show the number of significant correlations in Table 2, summing across the different tune durations. It is clear that correlations do exist in one context or another for almost all of these variables. That is not surprising in the sense that the variables were selected on the basis of previous studies. However, looking at the numbers in conjunction with the descriptions of variables, it does not look as if the shifts with emotion involve a few broad effects: rather that emotion affects speech in a great many distinguishable ways.

The nature of the effects is linked to the level of correlation that is generally present. The effects involve properties that vary from tune to tune in unemotional speech. What a correlation means is that tunes at one extreme of a particular range become slightly, but noticeably likelier if the speaker is in the relevant emotional state. It is because relatively extreme values in any one dimension of variation are relatively rare that using multiple variables makes sense as a recognition strategy.

Table 2 Significant correlations between speech and emotion ratings for each rater and tune length

	Tunes with duration < 250ms						Tunes with duration > 250ms <1.25s						Tunes with duration > 1.25s					
	evaluation		activation		emotionality		evaluation		activation		emotionality		evaluation		activation		emotionality	
	R1	R2	R1	R2	R1	R2	R1	R2	R1	R2	R1	R2	R1	R2	R1	R2	R1	R2
Global shape of tune F0 contour					0.33													
			0.3					0.09										
							0.08	0.08	0.1	0.1					0.08			-0.11
attributes of tune beginnings and ends												-0.11						
		-0.29				-0.29									0.08			
					-0.44	-0.43					-0.11	-0.09						
							-0.12		-0.18	-0.12						-0.14		-0.15
								-0.09	-0.1	-0.11		-0.09				-0.11		-0.1
distribution of energy across the spectrum			-0.31	-0.36			-0.1		-0.11	-0.11				0.1	-0.22	-0.16		
												0.13		0.11	-0.26	-0.21	-0.16	
									0.14		0.11				0.19		0.17	
								-0.13	0.14	0.09				-0.1	0.25	0.17	0.14	
								-0.1				-0.11	-0.12	-0.17	0.24	0.12	0.24	
															-0.18			
								-0.1				-0.13		-0.14	0.23	0.16		-0.12
																		-0.07
intensity levels and changes										-0.11		-0.08			-0.14	-0.11	-0.2	-0.15
												-0.14						-0.18
										-0.12	-0.08	-0.12			-0.15	-0.11	-0.22	-0.16
										-0.09								-0.15
											0.13						0.11	
												-0.08					-0.11	
durations of intensity-based features									0.12					-0.11				
								-0.1	-0.16	-0.12		-0.09				-0.1	-0.09	-0.13
									-0.1	-0.08	0.08			0.1				0.08
									-0.13		-0.12				-0.14		-0.15	
									-0.11		-0.13						-0.14	
						-0.22			-0.09	-0.11	-0.13						-0.1	
									-0.15		-0.08			0.09	-0.1		-0.08	

Table 2 (cont) Significant correlations between speech and emotion ratings for each rater and tune length

	Tunes with duration < 250ms						Tunes with duration > 250ms <1.25s						Tunes with duration > 1.25s					
	evaluation		activation		emotionality		evaluation		activation		emotionality		evaluation		activation		emotionality	
	R1	R2	R1	R2	R1	R2	R1	R2	R1	R2	R1	R2	R1	R2	R1	R2	R1	R2
F0 levels and changes			0.51					-0.18	0.36	0.11	0.18			-0.2	0.37		0.23	-0.11
					-0.31	-0.35			0.18			-0.12		-0.09	0.3	0.11		-0.11
			0.52	0.25				-0.17	0.33	0.11	0.19			-0.18	0.31		0.19	-0.1
			0.51					-0.19	0.35	0.1	0.19			-0.21	0.37		0.24	-0.12
			0.48					-0.14	0.35	0.1	0.12	-0.08		-0.18	0.37	0.1	0.19	-0.1
									-0.1	-0.12							0.11	0.09
									0.16					-0.09	0.21	0.09	0.08	
									0.12						0.24	0.1		-0.08
									0.15					-0.08	0.26	0.11	0.1	
					-0.47				0.16			-0.08		-0.11	0.21	0.13		-0.09
									0.17						0.21	0.1		-0.08
durations of pitch-based features								-0.1	-0.16	-0.13		-0.1				-0.13		-0.18
								-0.11		-0.08		-0.09						-0.18
											0.08						0.09	
				0.38					-0.09									
																	-0.11	
														0.08				
										0.08								
local pitch irregularity					-0.45	-0.43	0.12		0.14					-0.09	0.23	0.14	0.1	
							0.1				-0.1		0.13	0.17	-0.1	0.12	-0.09	0.1
									0.12		0.16			-0.17	0.22	0.1	0.19	-0.09
								-0.09	0.2		0.14			-0.15	0.26		0.15	-0.11
spectrum-based measures of voice quality										-0.08				0.1	-0.29	-0.22	-0.18	
													0.18	0.08	0.1	0.2		
								0.09					0.14	0.18	-0.22	-0.07	-0.21	
										-0.09	-0.08		-0.1		-0.24	-0.25	-0.1	
								-0.08			0.1			-0.1	0.26	0.21	0.13	-0.09

Table 2 (cont) Significant correlations between speech and emotion ratings for each rater and tune length

	Tunes with duration < 250ms						Tunes with duration > 250ms <1.25s						Tunes with duration > 1.25s					
	evaluation		activation		emotionality		evaluation		activation		emotionality		evaluation		activation		emotionality	
	R1	R2	R1	R2	R1	R2	R1	R2	R1	R2	R1	R2	R1	R2	R1	R2	R1	R2
rate at which features occur									0.13		0.1			-0.08	0.09		0.1	
														-0.07				-0.08
																	-0.08	-0.09
multi-tune crescendo & sustained high level									0.13		0.26				0.14	0.09	0.13	0.11
															0.09	0.13		
	0.34				0.32	0.34										0.11		
features incorporating range & duration												-0.09			-0.1	-0.08	-0.15	-0.1
											-0.12				0.11	0.09	0.12	
											-0.12				0.13	0.1	0.16	
								-0.08				-0.13			-0.12			
					-0.27	-0.32			0.15			-0.09		-0.11	0.26	0.1	0.09	
					-0.29	-0.28			0.14		-0.09	-0.13		-0.1	0.29	0.13	0.12	-0.08
			0.3					-0.09	0.24						0.21	0.13	0.2	
features using curvature & duration		0.28			0.38	0.29		0.1										
similarity to previous tune												-0.09						-0.16

Figure 1 illustrates the point using a relationship that is present at various levels, the relationship between pitch change at the end of a tune and net affect. With the short tunes, the correlation coefficients are high, and the relationship is very clear visually: it is only when speakers are rated effectively neutral that there is final pitch movement of any size. The intermediate length tunes show the same kind of relationship, but much less strongly. Substantial final pitch movement, particularly upwards, is common when speakers give the impression of neutrality, but it does happen elsewhere; and neutral speakers share the usual tendency for final movement to be very small.

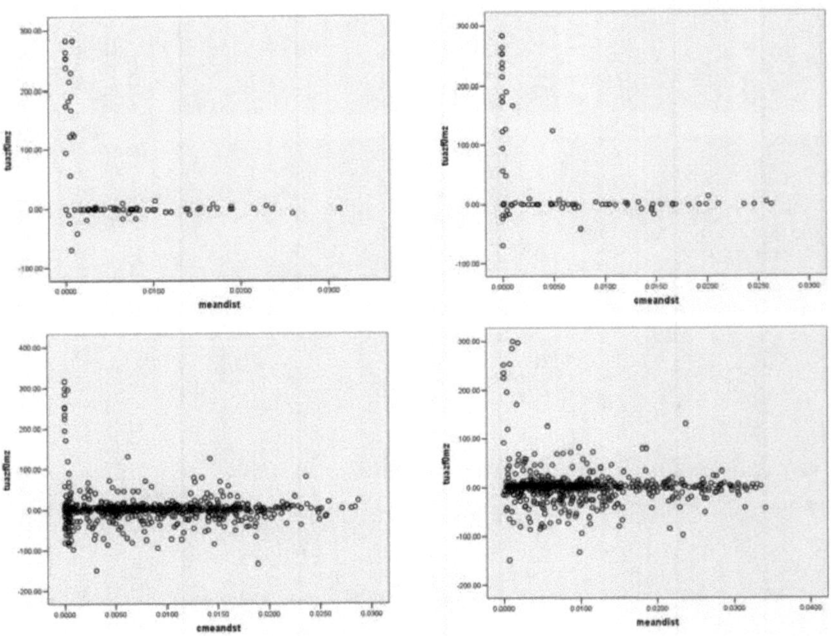

Figure 1 Size of closing pitch movement (in Hertz) plotted against net emotionality for the two raters, for short tunes (upper panels) and intermediate tunes (lower panels).

Figure 1 provides a convenient context to make some technical points. First, note that correlation is not ideally suited to picking up the relationships that are present. The sheer convenience of correlation makes it the default technique for detecting that variables are related, but examples like this indicate why finding comparably convenient alternatives is a major issue. Second, it is a recurring problem for work in this area that automatic extraction of F_0 is notoriously difficult with spontaneous speech, and doubly so with spontaneous emotional speech. It is very likely that that problem explains the strings of near-zero values for short tunes involving any degree of emotionality. ASSESS interpolates when it does not have robust local estimates of F_0; and the near-zero values probably mean that it did not recover good local estimates of F_0, and therefore interpolated more or less flat F_0 contours. If so, the relationships do not mean what they appear to at first sight. They probably mean that short tunes with easily recovered F_0 are diagnostic for absence of emotion. However, that does not alter the fact that the relationships concerned are informative.

8. Gender effects

In addition to the distinctions that have already been drawn, there are good reasons to expect that males and females may signal emotion in different ways. Table 3 uses essentially the same format as Table 2, but separates the genders. Inspection suggests that the differences are quite substantial.

It is immediately striking that males show strong effects for the variables involving level and change of level for both F_0 and intensity, whereas they are much less marked for females, particularly for intensity.

Conversely, females show more simple agreements than males in most areas where timing is critical – the beginnings, ends and global shapes of tune contours; durations of elements involving both intensity and F_0 (males show almost no consistent effects here).

Table 3 Significant correlations between speech and emotion ratings for each rater and tune length, separating males (left half) and females (right half)

	Duration <250ms						Duration >250ms <1.25sec						Duration > 1.25 sec					
	valence		activ		net aff		valence		activ		net aff		valence		activ		net aff	
	R 1	R 2	R 1	R 2	R 1	R 2	R 1	R 2	R 1	R 2	R 1	R 2	R 1	R 2	R 1	R 2	R 1	R 2
Global shape of tune F0 contour																-0.1		
								0.1										
									0.2						0.2			-0.2
attributes of tune beginnings and ends												-0.2						
		-0.4				-0.4												
						-0.4			-0.2	-0.1						-0.1		
											-0.1	-0.1						
distribution of energy across the spectrum				-0.6											-0.2	-0.2	0.2	
			0.5			0.5								0.2	-0.2	-0.1	0.1	0.2
											0.1				0.1		0.2	
								-0.1							0.1	0.1		
	-0.4		-0.5					-0.1						-0.2	0.2			-0.2
									0.2	0.1	0.2	0.2					0.2	
											-0.1	-0.1		-0.2	0.2	0.1	-0.3	-0.3
															0.1			-0.1
intensity levels and changes								-0.1		-0.1	-0.2	-0.2	-0.1	-0.2	-0.1	-0.2	-0.3	-0.3
								-0.2				-0.2					0.1	-0.2
								-0.1		-0.1	-0.2	-0.3	-0.1	-0.2	-0.1	-0.2	-0.3	-0.3
								-0.1		-0.1		-0.2	-0.1	-0.1		-0.1	-0.1	-0.3
											0.2							
											-0.1	-0.2						
durations of intensity-based features																	0.2	
												-0.1						
																	-0.1	
											-0.2						-0.1	
											-0.2						-0.1	
											-0.2						-0.1	
					0.3				-0.1		-0.1							
F0 levels and changes	0.4	0.4	0.4	0.4			0.1		0.3	0.1				-0.2	0.3	0.2		-0.2
									0.1			-0.1		-0.1	0.2	0.1		
	0.4	0.4	0.4	0.4					0.2				0.1		0.2			-0.2
	0.4	0.4	0.4	0.4			0.2		0.3	0.1				-0.2	0.3	0.1		-0.3
	0.4	0.3	0.4	0.4			0.1		0.3	0.1				-0.1	0.2	0.2		-0.1
									-0.3	-0.1				0.1	-0.2			0.2
									0.1					-0.1	0.1	0.1		
									0.2						0.2			
									0.1						0.1			
								-0.1	0.1					-0.1	0.2	0.2		
															0.1	0.2		

	Duration <250ms						Duration >250ms <1.25sec						Duration > 1.25 sec					
	valence		activ		net aff		valence		activ		net aff		valence		activ		net aff	
	R 1	R 2	R 1	R 2	R 1	R 2	R 1	R 2	R 1	R 2	R 1	R 2	R 1	R 2	R 1	R 2	R 1	R 2
Global shape of tune F0 contour																		
								0.1	0.1	0.1	0.1							
attributes of tune beginnings and ends																		
			-0.3		-0.5	-0.5					-0.1	-0.2						
							-0.2		-0.2	-0.1					-0.2	-0.2		-0.2
						-0.5	-0.1	-0.1	-0.2	-0.1						-0.1		-0.1
distribution of energy across the spectrum							-0.2			-0.1						-0.2		
	-0.4										0.1	0.2			-0.1	-0.3	-0.2	-0.1
															0.1			
										0.2		0.2	0.1		0.2	0.2	0.2	0.1
	0.4											-0.1				0.2	0.2	
							-0.1								-0.2			
							0.1			0.1		-0.1			0.1	0.2		
				-0.6														
intensity levels and changes																		
																	-0.1	-0.2
										-0.1								
											0.1							
durations of intensity-based features									0.1									
							-0.2	-0.2	-0.2	-0.2						-0.1		-0.2
										-0.1	0.1						0.2	
								-0.1										
F0 levels and changes							0.2		0.2	0.1			0.2		0.2	0.1		
					-0.4	-0.4		0.1			-0.2				0.3		-0.1	-0.1
							0.2		0.2	0.1								-0.1
							0.1		0.2				0.2		0.2			-0.1
							0.2		0.2				0.2		0.3	0.1		
										-0.1								
											-0.2				0.2			
											-0.2				0.2	0.1		
											-0.2				0.2	0.1		
															0.1		-0.1	
															0.2		-0.1	-0.1

Table 3 (cont) Significant correlations between speech and emotion ratings for each rater and tune length, separating males (left half) and females (right half)

	Duration <250ms						Duration >250ms <1.25sec						Duration > 1.25 sec						Duration <250ms						Duration >250ms <1.25sec						Duration > 1.25 sec					
	valence		activ		net aff		valence		activ		net aff		valence		activ		net aff		valence		activ		net aff		valence		activ		net aff		valence		activ		net aff	
	R1	R2	R1	R2	R1	R2	R1	R2	R1	R2	R1	R2	R1	R2	R1	R2	R1	R2	R1	R2	R1	R2	R1	R2	R1	R2	R1	R2	R1	R2	R1	R2	R1	R2	R1	R2
durations of pitch-based features												-0.1				-0.1		-0.1							-0.2	-0.2	-0.2	-0.2					-0.2	-0.2	-0.1	-0.2
																		-0.1								-0.2									-0.1	-0.2
											0.2																									
																		-0.1											0.2							0.1
							-0.1							-0.1				-0.1						-1.0					0.2							
									0.2	0.1																					0.1					
									0.1					-0.1	0.2			-0.1											0.2							
														-0.2	0.2			-0.1																		
local pitch irregularity	-1.0		-1.0		-1.0													-0.1							0.2			0.1			0.2		0.2	0.2		
													0.1	0.1	0.2	0.2									0.2								-0.2		0.2	0.1
							0.1		0.1		0.2			-0.2	0.2		0.1	-0.2								-0.1								0.2		
										0.1	0.1			-0.2	0.1		0.1	-0.2									0.1						0.1			
spectrum-based measures of voice quality						0.6								0.2	-0.2	-0.2		0.2			-0.4							-0.1			-0.2		-0.2	-0.3	-0.2	-0.2
	0.5		0.5												0.1	0.2		-0.2													0.3	0.2	0.1	0.2		
	0.5		0.5			0.5							0.1	0.1	-0.2			0.1	-0.5															-0.1	-0.2	-0.1
						0.5								0.2	-0.2	-0.2		0.2			-0.5							-0.1			-0.2	-0.2	-0.2	-0.3	-0.1	-0.1
								-0.1				-0.1		-0.2	0.2	0.2		-0.3			0.4							0.2	0.1		0.1		0.1	0.3	0.1	
rate at which features occur											0.2																									
																	0.2																		-0.2	
																																				-0.2
multi-tune crescendo & sustained high level																																				
											0.2		0.2	0.1		0.1	0.2	0.2						-0.6					0.2							
																0.1							0.6					0.1					0.2			
	0.4																																	0.2		
features incorporating range & duration												-0.2		-0.1				-0.2																	-0.1	
											-0.1	-0.1																					0.1	0.2	0.2	
											-0.1																						0.1	0.2	0.2	
		0.4	0.4			0.4		-0.2				-0.2																							-0.2	-0.1
									0.1					-0.1	0.2	0.1																	0.1		-0.1	
									0.1			-0.1		-0.1	0.2	0.1													-0.3	-0.1			0.2	0.2		
		0.4		0.4					0.2						0.2			-0.1											-0.1				0.2	0.2	0.2	
features using curvature & duration																-0.1																			0.1	
								0.1								-0.1																			0.1	
																				0.3	0.3		0.4				0.2									
similarity to previous tune																																				
						0.4												-0.1																		-0.2

A quite unexpected pattern is that males show more variables that are consistently associated with valence, which is the aspect of affect that is classically difficult to recover from speech. Among the longest tunes, six variables, of different types, correlate consistently with valence. Even more surprisingly, variables involving F_0 level show a cluster of simple agreements with valence, with rather high correlation coefficients, in the context of the short tunes spoken by males.

9. Rater effects

Looking at the data indicates that the raters behaved differently, but it is not easy to formulate the differences. Part of the difference lies in the numbers of variables that related to particular kinds of judgment. For rater 1, the number of variables linked to valence (21) was rather lower than the number linked to activation (36) or net affect (38). For rater 2, there was a cross-over with gender. For males, her ratings of valence and net affect were linked to quite large numbers of variables (31 and 33 respectively). For females, they were linked to much lower numbers of variables (6 and 13 respectively).

Numbers like these suggest different perceptual strategies – selective (focusing on a few relevant variables) or inclusive (using a wide range). It is interesting that rater 2, who seems to have used fewer variables with females, tended to report less variation in their emotional states. The standard deviations for her measures of valence and activation respectively were 0.25 and 0.19 respectively: the corresponding values for rater 1 were 0.32 and 0.21 respectively. Perhaps raters who detect few relevant variables discriminate states less. The data do not support strong conclusions about issues like that. What is worth noting is that they invite questions of that kind, about different ways of using potential information.

10. Relationship to machine recognition and psychological theory

The point of the discussion so far has been to convey broadly the kind of data that is considered in research on automatic recognition of emotion from speech, and the level at which it is considered. Above all, it aims to convey the kind of complexity that the research assumes it is appropriate to consider – the variety and specificity of variables, and their sensitivity to context.

The mechanics of recognition in recent research is a very different matter. ASSESS is a generation old, and a great deal has changed since it was developed. MFCCs tend to be used rather than direct spectral measures, and much more phonetic detail is recovered (vowel centres, formants, etc). Effects that span appreciable time intervals are often handled implicitly, by using recognition techniques that learn to take account of preceding units, rather than explicitly, by creating features that involve tunes and sequences of tunes. Nevertheless, what the techniques do is to engage with patterns that are at least comparable in complexity to those that have been discussed here. They do not assume that any useful information can be recovered by placing individual units relative to a comparatively small number of general-purpose dimensions.

A key part of that strategy is embedded in an emphasis on context which is different in form from the discussion here, but which reflects the same underlying issue. It is assumed that to be effective, machines should be trained on data that reflect the application as closely as possible. That is because the features and the balances that are important in one context may not be those that are important in another. That would not be the case if the essence of the story were captured by a few dimensions that always carry signals of emotion. Rather, the variables by which emotion may be recognised are many, and dependent on context.

Research on speech recognition has faced similar issues before, and the parallels are interesting. Bailey and Summerfield (1980) noted that voiced/voiceless distinctions could be conveyed by a great many different features, apparently of different kinds, depending on context. They asked why such diverse features might be associated with the same distinction. The answer that they proposed was that all of the acoustic features could be byproducts of the same kind of action; and that they are grouped functionally because perceptual processes relate them to a model of the underlying mechanical events, rather than treating them as sound patterns *per se.*

Applying the same logic, it makes sense to ask whether the multiple kinds of change that are associated with emotional speech have a common origin in pressures on the mechanisms of speech production, to which those mechanisms may respond in diverse ways, depending on the individual and the context.

If so, some of the effective factors may involve rather straightforward physiological shifts, such as tense or lax settings. Others may involve global shifts at a planning level, such as impatience reflected in rapid speech, with the various other effects that that brings. More subtly, some theorists view synchronisation as central to emotion (Sander et al. 2005). Speech may also be pulled towards rhythms that are set internally as part of the emotion. Another range of possible effects involve competition for resources that would otherwise be allocated to speech production – either sustained or in the form of intrusions that disrupt planning at some level. Since emotion is almost by definition unstable, all of these effects would be expected to come and go, and different coping mechanisms would be expected to come into play.

Of course, purposeful communicative factors may also be involved. If so, some may be as crude as raising pitch or intensity (apparently among males more than females). However, linguists have long pointed out that what seem to be the most clearly signal-like indicators of emotion are contextual (Scherer et al. 1984; Mozziconacci 1998). The tune contour measures in ASSESS (such as the one illustrated in Figure 1) were developed with that in mind, and behave roughly as would be expected from linguistics: certain kinds of pattern become marginally commoner as emotion moves in certain directions. It is not a one-to-one relationship, but regular enough to contribute to the task of recognising emotion.

11. Conclusion

This chapter has tried to draw out the implications of material collected and analysed in the context of research on machine recognition. The findings suggest that understanding the emotional colouring of speech is a challenge on a large scale. There are major issues to be faced in a range of areas, from collection of appropriate data, to pure statistics and robust recovery of features such as F_0, to the selection of psychological models that bring the alternatives into the open rather than obscuring them.

At the core of the work are the automatic feature detection techniques that are now standard in machine recognition. The features may be complex and/or extended in time. These techniques allow research to form images of the events involved in emotionally coloured speech that are both fine grained and cover substantial bodies of material. With that, though, comes the problem of seeing how to structure the mass of information, in terms of both numerical techniques, statistical and representational; and conceptual models. This chapter offers an approach to dealing with that problem which may be a useful model.

References

Bailey, Peter / Summerfield, Quentin 1980. Information in speech: observations on the perception of [s]-stop clusters *Journal Exp Psychol Hum Percept Perform* 6(3): 536-563.

Banse, Rainer / Scherer, Klaus 1996. Acoustic profiles in vocal emotion expression. *Journal of Personality and Social Psychology* 70 (3), 614-636.

Batliner, Anton / Fischer Kerstin / Huber, Richard / Spilker, Jorg / Nöth, Elmar 2003. How to find trouble in communication. *Speech Communication* 40, 117-143.

Batliner, Anton / Steidl, Stefan / Schuller, Bjorn / Laskowski, Kornel / Seppi, Dino / Vogt, Thurid / Devillers, Laurence / Vidrascu,

Laurence / Amir, Noam / Kessous, Loic / Aharonson, Vered 2006. Combining efforts for improving automatic classification of emotional user states. In Erjavec, Tomaz / Gros, Jerneja (eds), *Language Technologies*, IS-LTC 2006 Ljubljana, Slovenia: Infornacijska Druzba (Information Society), 240-245.

Cowie, Roddy / Cornelius, Randy 2003. Describing the emotional states that are expressed in speech. *Speech Communication* 40, 5-32.

Cowie, Roddy / Douglas-Cowie, Ellen / Savvidou, Susie / McMahon, Edelle / Sawey, Martin / Schröder, Marc 2000. 'Feeltrace': an instrument for recording perceived emotion in real time. Proceedings of the ISCA Workshop on Speech and Emotion, 19–24.

Cowie, Roddy / Douglas-Cowie, Ellen / Sawey, Martin 1995. A new speech analysis system: ASSESS (Automatic Statistical Summary of Elementary Speech Structures). Proceedings ICPhS, vol. 3, 278-281.

Cowie, Roddy / Douglas-Cowie, Ellen / McRorie, Margaret / Sneddon, Ian / Devillers, Laurence / Amir, Noam, forthcoming. Issues in Data Collection. HUMAINE Handbook.

Devillers, Laurence / Cowie, Roddy / Martin, Jean-Claude / Douglas-Cowie, Ellen / Abrilian, Sarkis / McRorie, Margaret 2006. Real life emotions in French and English TV video clips: an integrated annotation protocol combining continuous and discrete approaches. 5th international conference on Language Resources and Evaluation (LREC 2006), Genoa, Italy.

Devillers, Laurence / Martin, Jean-Claude / Cowie, Roddy / Douglas-Cowie, Ellen / Batliner, Anton 2006/2008. Workshop on Corpora for research on emotion and affect. LREC 2006 and 2008.

Douglas-Cowie, Ellen / Cowie, Roddy / Cox, Cate / Amir, Noam / Heylen, Dirk 2008. The Sensitive Artificial Listener: an induction technique for generating emotionally coloured conversation. Proceedings LREC 2008.

ERMIS. Emotionally Rich Man-machine Intelligent System. 5th Framework EC funded project no. IST-2000-29319 <www.image.ntua.gr/ermis/>.

Frigo, Stefanie, ongoing. A comparison of the speech of acted and naturalistic data. PhD project, Queen's University Belfast.

Fragopanagos, Nickolaos / Taylor, John 2005. Emotion recognition in human-computer interaction. *Neural Networks* 18, 389-405.

Hammarberg, Britta / Fritzell, Bjorn / Gauffin, Jan / Sundberg, Johan / Wedin, Lage 1980. Perceptual and acoustic correlates of abnormal voice qualities. *Acta Otolaryng*. 90, 441-451.

HUMAINE. Human-Machine Interaction Network on Emotion. 6th Framework EC funded Network of Excellence no. 507422. <http://emotion-research.net/projects/humaine/aboutHUMAINE>.

Juslin, Patrik / Laukka, Petri 2003. Communication of emotions in vocal expression and music performance: different channels, same code? *Psychol Bull*, 129(5), 770-814.

Kollias, Stefanos et al. 2008. HUMAINE Deliverable no. D4h, Final Report on WP4 <http://emotion-research.net/projects/humaine/aboutHUMAINE>.

McGilloway, Sinead / Cowie, Roddy / Douglas-Cowie, Ellen / Gielen, Stan / Westerdijk, Machiel / Stroeve, Sybert 2000. Automatic recognition of emotion from voice: a rough benchmark, 5-7 September 2000, Textflow, Belfast, 207-212.

Mozziconacci, Sylvie 1998. Speech variability and emotion: Production and perception. Ph.D thesis, Technical University Eindhoven, Eindhoven.

Russell, James / Feldman Barrett, Lisa 1999. Core Affect, Prototypical Emotional Episodes, and Other Things Called Emotion: Dissecting the Elephant *Journal of Personality and Social Psychology* 76, 805-819.

Sander, David / Grandjean, Didier / Scherer, Klaus 2005. A systems approach to appraisal mechanisms in emotion. *Neural Networks*, 18(4), 317-352.

Scherer, Klaus / Ladd, D. Robert / Silverman, Kim 1984. Vocal cues to speaker affect: Testing two models. *Journal of the Acoustical Society of America* 76, 5, 1346-1356.

SEMAINE Sustained Emotionally coloured Machine-human Interaction using Nonverbal Expression. 7th Framework EC funded project <http://www.semaine-project.eu/>.

Steidl, Stefan / Levit / Michael / Batliner, Anton / Noth, Elmar / Niemann, Heinrich 2005. 'Of all things the measure is man'. Automatic classification of emotions and inter-labeler consistency. Proc. ICASSP, 2005.

Appendix

ASSESS variables and the numbers of significant correlations with each affective variable associated with each.

GROUP OF VARIABLES	MEASURE	Valen		Activn		N Aff	
	RATER	1	2	1	2	1	2
Global shape of tune (from quadratic fitted to F_0 contour)	Linear coefficient					1	
	Quadratic coefficient		1	1			
	Goodness of fit	1	1	2	1		1
Attributes of tune beginnings and ends	Size of opening rise in intensity						1
	Size of opening pitch movement		1	1			1
	Size of closing pitch movement					2	2
	Length of pause before tune	1		1	2		1
	Length of pause after tune		1	1	2		2
Distribution of energy across the spectrum (using average vowel spectrum except cases marked FS, which use average spectrum of periods with frication)	% of total energy in region 0-250Hz	1	1	3	3		
	% of total energy in region 0-2000Hz		1	1	1	1	1
	Sample-to-sample change region 0-2000Hz			2		2	
	Sample-to-sample change region 2000-5000Hz		2	2	2	1	
	% of total energy in region 5000-10000Hz	1	2	1	1	1	1
	FS: % of total energy in region 5000-10000Hz			1			
	Slope of average spectrum		2	1	1		2
	FS: slope of average spectrum						1
Intensity levels and changes	Mean intensity			1	2	1	2
	SD of intensity						2
	Median intensity			1	2	2	2
	Maximum intensity				1		1
	Number of rises in intensity					2	
	Mean size of rises in intensity					1	1
Durations of intensity-based features. A break is a silence of over 25 ms: a burst is a stretch of speech with no internal breaks.	Number of breaks		1	1			
	Mean duration of breaks		1	1	2	1	2
	Number of 'bursts'		1	1	1	1	1
	Mean duration of bursts			2		2	
	Median duration of bursts			1		2	
	Mean duration of rises in intensity			1	1	2	1
	Mean duration of falls in intensity		1	2		2	
F_0 levels and changes	F_0 Mean		2	3	1	2	1
	F_0 SD		1	2	1	1	3
	F_0 Minimum		2	3	2	2	1
	F_0 Median		2	3	1	2	1
	F_0 Maximum		2	3	2	2	2

	Number of rises in F_0			1	1	1	1
	Mean size of rises in F_0		1	2	1	1	
	SD of rises in F_0			2	1		1
	Maximum rise in F_0		1	2	1	1	
	Mean size of falls in F_0		1	2	1	1	2
	SD of falls in F_0			2	1		1
Durations of pitch-based features. A pause is a silence of over 150ms: a tune is a stretch of speech with no internal pauses: a plateau is a region on either side of a peak where F_0 is relatively stable.	Mean duration of pauses		1	1	2		2
	SD duration of pauses		1		1		2
	Mean duration of tunes					2	
	SD duration of tunes						
	Median duration F_0 plateaux			1	1		
	SD duration F_0 plateaux					1	
	Mean duration F_0 rises						
	SD duration F_0 rises		1				
	Mean duration F_0 falls				1		
	SD duration F_0 falls						
Local pitch irregularity	Frequency of creak	1	1	2	1	2	1
	Conservative measure of jitter	2	1	1	1	2	1
	Inclusive measure of jitter		1	2	1	2	1
	mean of absolute pitch change		2	2		2	1
Spectrum-based measures of voice quality (using indices from Hammarberg et al. (1980)	Coarse voice Hammarberg index		1	1	2	1	
	Stable voice Hammarberg index	1	1	1	1		
	Head voice Hammarberg index	1	2	1	1	1	
	Breathy voice Hammarberg index	1		1	2	2	
	Vocal effort Hammarberg index		2	1	1	2	1
Rate at which features occur	Rate of intensity maxima		1	2		2	
	Rate of silences over 25ms		1				1
	Rate of pauses					1	1
	Rate of intervals with frication present						
Multi-tune crescendo & sustained high level	Sequential increase in duration						
	High maximum intensity in successive tunes			2	1	2	1
	Rising maximum intensity in successive tunes						
	High maximum F_0 in successive tunes			1	1		
	Rising maximum F_0 in successive tunes	1			1	1	1
Features incorporating range & duration	Intensity range			1	1	1	2
	Short with wide intensity range			1	1	2	
	Short with high peak intensity			1	1	2	
	Intensity jump from one tune to next		1	1			1
	Pitch range		1	2	1	2	2
	Short with wide f_0 range		1	2	1	3	3
	Short with high peak f_0		1	3	1	1	
	F_0 jump from 1 tune to next						

Features using curvature & duration	Rate of change in fitted pitch line						
	Start-to-end change in fitted pitch line						
	Rise or fall in fitted pitch quadratic		2			1	1
Prosodic repetition	Similarity to previous tune						2

PETRI LAUKKA / NICOLAS AUDIBERT / VÉRONIQUE AUBERGÉ

Exploring the Graded Structure of Vocal Emotion Expressions

1. Introduction

Traditionally, research on vocal expressions of emotion has relied on actors, who are asked to produce expressions of a few emotion categories (e.g., anger, fear, happiness, sadness). Recent reviews of studies in this tradition have shown that vocal expressions of discrete emotions are generally recognized with accuracy above chance, also cross-culturally, and that different emotions are associated with relatively distinct patterns of acoustic cues (e.g., Cowie et al. 2001; Juslin/Laukka 2003; Laukka 2008; Scherer 2003). In contrast, research on spontaneous affect expression in everyday speech often claims that clear-cut expressions of discrete emotions are rarely encountered in normal day-to-day conversations (Campbell 2005; Cowie/Cornelius 2003; Devillers/Vidrascu/Lamel 2005). Thus, there seem to exist prototypical expressions that are easily recognizable and have unique acoustic characteristics (e.g., Laukka 2005), but these prototypical expressions may be rare in everyday speech. This chapter presents work-in-progress exploring this seeming contradiction using methods from cognitive psychology, especially work on categorization by Barsalou (1985). A central question is to consider what determines the typicality of an expression.

Not all members of a category are equally good members; for instance in the category of 'birds', a robin is generally considered to be more typical than an ostrich (e.g. Rosch/Mervis 1975; Smith/Shoben/Rips 1974). Similarly, one vocal expression of, for example, happiness can be more typical than another expression of the same emotion, though both expressions are clearly perceived as 'happy'. The continuum of category representativeness begins with the most representative members of a category and continues through its atypical members. In the words of Barsalou (1987), categories have *graded structure*. Among the possible determinants of graded structure, three candidates stand out: (a) the category members' *similarity to ideals* associated with the goals served by its category, (b) the category members' *frequency of instantiation* (how often they are encountered as category members), and (c) the category members' *similarity to the central tendency* of their category (Barsalou 1985; 1987; see also Lakoff 1986).

Categories can further be divided into common taxonomic categories (i.e., categories that exist in the natural world, for example 'birds'), and goal-derived categories (i.e., categories that involve human activities of various sorts, for example 'things to do for weekend entertainment'). These two types of categories have different characteristic properties (see Barsalou 1987). For example, members of common taxonomic categories often share co-occurring properties that rarely occur outside the category. For example, most birds have feathers, but also have wings and a beak. Thus common taxonomic categories are said to reflect the correlational structure of the environment (i.e., they are representative of the ways given properties generally co-occur in our environment). Members of goal-derived categories, on the other hand, may be very dissimilar to each other in some respects and may even be similar to non-members in others. Because goal-derived categories do not represent the correlational structure of the environment, they are less salient than common taxonomic categories and appear to become salient only when they are relevant to currently pursued goals. Relatedly, common taxonomic categories are usually highly familiar, culturally transmitted biological or artifactual categories, whereas goal-derived categories often are less familiar and less central to cultural knowledge. The uses of the two types of categories also seem to differ. Common taxonomic categories are often used for classification of things in the environment, whereas goal-derived categories are instead used to facilitate the instantiation of goals. Though the differences between common taxonomic and goal-derived categories are not clear-cut or defining, they do suggest that, in general, different factors may determine their graded structures. In a series of experiments, Barsalou

(1985) found that the typicality of members of common taxonomic categories was determined predominantly by their frequency of instantiation as a category member and their similarity to the central tendency of the category. The typicality of members of goal-derived categories instead was determined by similarity to ideal category members. Ideals can be thought of as those characteristics that a category member should possess in order to best serve the goals associated with its category. From this it follows that ideal values are often true only of a few actual category members (or none at all) which entails that they may be infrequently occurring. Also, ideal values are not confined to the centre of categories, and can thus often be quite extreme.

Theoretically, vocal expressions could belong to either of the above category types. For one thing, vocal expressions represent quite familiar, perceptually salient clusters of co-occurring properties, which can be used for classification. As an example, anger expressions are characterized by high pitch, large pitch variability, high voice intensity, much high-frequency components in the energy spectrum, and fast speech rate, whereas sadness expressions are characterized by low pitch, small pitch variability, low voice intensity, little high-frequency components in the energy spectrum, and slow speech rate (see Juslin/Laukka 2003, for a detailed summary on the characteristic cue patterns for anger, fear, sadness, happiness and love/tenderness). Thus vocal expressions could very well be common taxonomic categories. However, vocal expressions (like emotion expressions in general) also serve the *goal* of emotional communication. By expressing emotions it is possible for us to communicate vital information to others and we can infer others' probable behaviours by recognizing their expressions. Also, emotion expressions may regulate social behaviour by inducing affective responses in the perceiver (e.g. Darwin 1872/1998; Ekman 2003; Russell/Bachorowski/Fernández-Dols 2003).

If vocal expressions are structured like common taxonomic categories, typicality should be best predicted by frequency of instantiation and similarity to central tendency. If, in contrast, they are structured like goal-derived categories, typicality should instead be best predicted by similarity to ideals. Most importantly, if typicality is determined by frequency of instantiation and/or similarity to central tendency, we should expect prototypical vocal expressions to be frequently occurring in everyday spontaneous conversations. Because this seems not to be the case as noted earlier (e.g., Cowie/Cornelius 2003), this would imply that the posed prototypical expressions of discrete emotions – which make up the bulk of the literature on vocal expression – have limited ecological validity. Ideals, however, need not be frequently occurring and need not represent the central tendency of categories. Therefore, if the typicality of vocal expressions is best predicted by similarity to ideals, this could help to explain why prototypical expressions are easily recognizable and have unique acoustic characteristics, while at the same time they do not occur frequently in everyday conversations.

In this chapter we present results from an on-going series of investigations that aim to examine which factor (similarity to ideals, frequency of instantiation, or similarity to central tendency) best determines the typicality of different kinds of vocal expressions. Preliminary results have been reported in Laukka/Audibert/Aubergé (2007). We include three kinds of vocal expressions in order to get an expressive corpus that includes lots of variation with respect to typicality: acted prototypical expressions, acted non-prototypical expressions, and spontaneous expressions. Similar work has recently been performed by Horstmann (2002), who investigated the determinants of typicality in line drawings of facial expressions. His results indicated that prototypical facial expressions are goal-derived categories, instead of common taxonomic categories. Research using other types of social stimuli (e.g., personality traits) has also concluded that goals play an important role in determining the typicality of social categories (e.g., Borkenau 1990; Read/Jones/Miller 1990). Based on the fact that both facial and vocal expressions are social stimuli and serve the same functions (i.e., facilitating social communication and interaction; Juslin/Laukka 2003) we hypothesize that prototypical vocal expressions may also be best characterized as goal-derived categories.

2. Study 1

2.1 Methods

2.1.1 Stimuli

The stimuli used in this study were extracted from the French expressive corpus E-Wiz (Aubergé/Audibert/Rilliard 2004), in which subjects participated in a Wizard of Oz experiment under the pretext of taking part in an easy task of learning phonetics of a foreign language. Subsequently, different affective states were induced in the subjects by manipulating their performances on the learning task. The utterances collected in the E-Wiz corpus, apart from free commentaries, are monosyllabic utterances of the French colour names *brique* [bʁik], *jaune* [ʒon], *vert* [vɛʁ], *rouge* [ʁuʒ], and *sable* [sabl], as well as utterances of *page suivante* [paʒ sɥivɑ̃t]. The affective values carried by these utterances were labelled by the subjects themselves from the video recordings of the experiment. For a more detailed description of the E-Wiz corpus, see Aubergé/Audibert/Rilliard (2006).

The productions of six speakers (three male and three female) were retained for the present study. All six speakers were actors who were asked, immediately after having participated in the Wizard of Oz experiment, to portray expressions of the same affects they had just been experiencing, using the same utterances. In addition, the actors were asked to portray expressions of six basic emotions (happiness, anger, fear, sadness, disgust, and surprise), still using the same utterances (French colour names). The collected expressions subsequently fall into three categories, which will be referred to as spontaneous, acted non-prototypical and acted prototypical expressions. Three broad classes of emotion, for which there were a sufficient number of utterances, were selected for the present study: anger, fear, and joy.

As the number of utterances in each emotion x condition category was not equal, a subset had to be pre-selected following two consecutive steps. First, expert ratings by the authors came up with a set of 193 stimuli that were considered to be expressive of each emotion class, with as much variation as possible in activation level and prosodic morphology. Second, these 193 stimuli were evaluated in a pre-test by 15 French-speaking naïve listeners (eight male and seven female, mean age = 29.8 years), who were allowed to listen to the stimuli as many times as they wanted and had to select for each one either an emotion class among the three proposed (anger, fear, or joy) or an 'other emotion' label. Moreover, the listeners were asked to rate the perceived emotion intensity of each stimulus (see Juslin/ Laukka 2001), using a scale ranging from 0 (very weak intensity) to 10 (very strong intensity). Stimuli were presented in a different random order for each listener, and presentation and recording of answers was automated using a graphical interface. Among stimuli identified with accuracy above chance, the authors retained twelve stimuli in each emotion x condition subcategory, for a total of 108 stimuli, using variation in identification score and emotion intensity as main criteria. We also strived for a balanced stimulus set regarding the speakers' gender and the prosodic morphologies of the expressions.

2.1.2 Design and procedure

The purpose of the listening experiments was to have the 108 stimuli rated by three distinct groups of naïve listeners with regard to typicality, ideal (suitability to express the respective emotion), and frequency of instantiation. The listeners were asked the following questions:

- *Typicality*: How typical is this expression of anger/fear/joy? (not at all typical 0-10 very typical).
  [A quel point le mot que vous venez d'entendre vous semble-t-il typique d'une expression de la colère/peur/joie? (pas du tout typique 0-10 très typique).]
- *Ideal*: If someone were trying to express anger/fear/joy, how effectively would this particular vocalization express it? (not at all effectively 0-10 very effectively).
  [Si quelqu'un tentait d'exprimer de la colère/peur/joie, avec quelle efficacité la manière de prononcer que vous venez d'entendre exprimerait-elle cette émotion? (pas du tout efficacement 0-10 très efficacement).]

- *Frequency of instantiation*: How often would you observe such a vocalization in another person, when this person is angry/fearful/joyful? (not frequently at all 0-10 very frequently).
  [Avec quelle fréquence pourriez-vous entendre cette manière de prononcer chez d'autres personnes, lorsque ces personnes ressentent de la colère/peur/joie? (pas du tout fréquemment 0-10 très fréquemment).]

Stimuli were presented grouped by emotion class, and sorted in a different random order for each listener within each emotion class. The order of presentation of the emotion classes was also systematically alternated within each listener group. 16 French speaking naïve listeners rated the stimuli in each of the three groups (eight male and eight female in the typicality group, mean age = 27.0 years; eight male and eight female in the ideal group, mean age = 27.9 years; and seven male and nine female in the frequency of instantiation group, mean age = 27.9 years; overall mean age = 27.6 years).

An approximation of *similarity to central tendency* was obtained by calculating a family resemblance score for each stimulus. In research on similarity it is of great importance to clearly define the specific stimulus properties the similarity of which one is interested in (e.g., Goldstone & Yu, 2005). Because we were mainly interested in how similar the different stimuli were with regard to their expression, we used the decoding accuracy scores from the pre-test to calculate a similarity measure. By comparing the recognition accuracies of the stimuli, we get an estimate of how similarly they were perceived by the listeners with regard to their expression. Because an individual category member's similarity to other members is at least roughly the same as its similarity to the central tendency of the category (Barsalou 1985), we calculated the absolute difference between the decoding accuracy of each stimulus and the mean decoding accuracy of its respective emotion category. This absolute difference was then subtracted from 1 for each stimulus (so that a greater value would represent a greater similarity), and these values were subsequently used as approximations of similarity to central tendency.

2.2 Results

The mean and standard deviation of the ratings of typicality, similarity to ideals, frequency of instantiation (FI), and central tendency (CT) together with decoding accuracy and emotion intensity are shown in Table 1 for the different types of expression (acted prototypical, acted non-prototypical, and spontaneous expressions). As intended, all variables were fairly equally distributed among the expression types and the variability within each expression group was also quite large. Some differences between groups also occurred, for example, we can note that the acted expressions received significantly higher typicality and intensity ratings than the spontaneous expressions, as expected. However, contrary to our expectations, the acted expressions were also rated higher on FI than the spontaneous ones (*t*-tests, all *p*'s < .0001). There were no significant differences between different emotion classes (anger, fear, and joy) for any of the variables in Table 1 (*t*-tests).

	Overall	*Acted proto-typical*	*Acted non-prototypical*	*Spontaneous*
Typicality	3.30 (1.79)	3.61 (1.78)	3.93 (1.85)	2.36 (1.35)
Ideal	3.41 (1.66)	3.57 (1.53)	4.08 (1.73)	2.60 (1.37)
FI	3.62 (1.59)	3.98 (1.46)	4.23 (1.54)	2.63 (1.32)
CT	0.83 (0.10)	0.85 (0.07)	0.82 (0.11)	0.82 (0.11)
% correct	0.77 (0.20)	0.83 (0.16)	0.80 (0.22)	0.70 (0.20)
Emotion intensity	4.76 (1.76)	4.93 (1.77)	5.54 (1.75)	3.82 (1.31)

Table 1. Descriptive statistics (mean and standard deviation) of judges' ratings of (a) typicality, (b) ideal, (c) frequency of instantiation, (d) similarity to central tendency, (e) accuracy of emotion recognition, and (f) emotion intensity, for all groups of stimuli.

The further analyses intended to determine which variable best predicted the typicality ratings. We used a similar methodology as described in Barsalou (1985) and Horstmann (2002). First, the mean rating of each variable (typicality, ideal, and FI) was calculated for each stimulus, across all listeners. Then, we calculated the partial correlations between (a) typicality and ideal (controlling for FI and CT), (b) typicality and FI (controlling for ideal and CT), and (c) typicality and CT (controlling for ideal and FI). The results are shown in Table 2, and show similar patterns of correlations for all three types of expression.

	r_p*(ideal)*	r_p*(FI)*	r_p*(CT)*
Overall	.56 ***	.49 ***	-.13 ns
Acted prototypical	.59 ***	.53 ***	-.32 ns
Acted non-prototypical	.58 ***	.36 *	.02 ns
Spontaneous	.55 **	.46 *	-.13 ns

*** $p < .0001$, ** $p < .001$, * $p < .05$, ns = non significant.

Table 2. Partial correlations between (a) typicality and ideal (controlling for FI and CT), (b) typicality and FI (controlling for ideal and CT), and (c) typicality and CT (controlling for ideal and FI).

The partial correlation between typicality and ideal accounted for more unique variance (31%) than did the correlations between typicality and FI (24%) or typicality and CT (2%). This mirrors the pattern of results obtained by Horstmann (2002) regarding facial expressions, but the amount of explained variance was smaller in our study. To substantiate the findings, we also conducted a multiple regression analysis with the listeners' mean ratings of typicality as the dependent variable and ratings of ideal, FI and CT as independent variables. In other words we wanted to investigate which were the best predictors of typicality: ideal, FI or CT. The multiple correlation was high ($R^2 = .87$) with significant beta-weights for ideal ($\beta = .53$) and FI ($\beta = .44$; all p's $< .0001$). Again, similarity to ideals turned out to be the most important predictor of typicality, followed by FI.

3. Study 2

The results from Study 1 indicated that typicality of vocal expressions was mainly determined by similarity to ideals. However, the differences in predictive power between ideals and FI were smaller than in previous studies (e.g., Horstmann 2002). One possible reason for this may have been that the listeners confused FI (how often a particular vocalization would be observed in another person when this person is angry/fearful/joyful) with ideal (how effectively a particular vocalization expresses anger/fear/joy). We thus conducted a follow-up study where we altered the wording of the instructions for the FI question in such a way as to avoid confusion with ideals, to see if similar results would be obtained.

3.1 Methods

Sixteen French-speaking naïve listeners rated the same 108 stimuli as in Study 1 with regard to their frequency of instantiation (eight male and eight female, mean age = 28.9 years). The methodology was identical to Study 1, with the exception that we used the following new wording of the FI instructions:

- *Frequency of instantiation*: How often would you observe such a vocalization in another person, when this person is angry/ fearful/ joyful? Note that we are interested in how frequent-ly various expressions occur, and not in how clearly they express particular emotions. It is possible that a frequently occurring expression expresses a particular emotion very clearly, but it is also possible that a frequently occurring expression is not easily recognized. (not frequently at all 0-10 very frequently).
  [Avec quelle fréquence pourriez-vous entendre cette manière de prononcer chez d'autres personnes, lorsque ces personnes ressentent de la colère/peur/joie? Notez bien que nous cherchons à évaluer la fréquence d'apparition de différentes expressions, et non la clarté avec laquelle elles expriment des émotions particulières. Il est possible qu'une expression fréquente exprime très clairement une emotion particulière, mais une expression fréquente peut aussi ne pas être facilement reconnue. (pas du tout fréquemment 0-10 très fréquemment).]

3.2 Results

The mean and standard deviation of the listeners' ratings of frequency of instantiation using the new instructions (FI2) for the different types of expression were: overall (M = 4.13, SD = 1.16), acted prototypical (M = 4.28, SD = 1.14), acted non-prototypical (M = 4.32, SD = 1.21), and spontaneous expressions (M = 3.78, SD = 1.07). When compared to the results for the old frequency of instantiation measure (FI) from Study 1, the new frequency of instantiation measure (FI2) received significantly higher ratings for spontaneous expressions ($p < .001$), but not for acted expressions, as revealed by t-tests. Thus, the added clarification did lead to an increase in the ratings of frequency of instantiation for the spontaneous expressions. Also, like in Study 1 the acted expressions still received higher frequency ratings than the spontaneous ones, but the differences were not statistically significant for FI2 as revealed by t-tests. There were further no significant differences between different emotion classes for FI2 (t-tests).

Next we wanted to investigate which variable best predicted the typicality ratings. The analyses were conducted in a similar fashion as in Study 1. First, we calculated the mean rating of FI2 for each stimulus across all listeners. In the next step, we calculated the partial correlations between (a) typicality and ideal (controlling for FI2 and CT), (b) typicality and FI2 (controlling for ideal and CT), and (c) typicality and CT (controlling for ideal and FI2). For typicality, ideal, and CT, we used the same mean ratings as in Study 1. The results are shown in Table 3, and show that the partial correlation between typicality and ideal overall accounted for much more unique variance (62%) than did FI2 (5%). Ideals were further the most important predictor for all types of expression. However, inspection of Table 3 also shows that FI2 was a relatively more important predictor of the typicality of spontaneous expressions, than of acted expressions. A multiple regression analysis with listeners' mean ratings of typicality as the dependent variable and ratings of ideal, FI2 and CT as independent variables further yielded a high multiple correlation (R^2 = .84, $p < .0001$) with significant beta-weights for ideal ($\beta = .76$, $p < .0001$) and FI2 ($\beta = .21$, $p < .05$). To summarize, like in Study 1, similarity to ideals turned out to be the best predictor of typicality. The results of Study 2 further indicated that the rephrasing of the frequency instructions made the distinction between ideals and frequency of instantiation clearer to the listeners. Thus we will use FI2 as our preferred index of frequency of instantiation in the subsequent analyses.

	r_p(ideal)	r_p(FI2)	r_p(CT)
Overall	.79 ***	.22 *	-.04 ns
Acted prototypical	.80 ***	.18 ns	-.31 ns
Acted non-prototypical	.81 ***	.19 ns	.12 ns
Spontaneous	.65 ***	.42 *	-.04 ns

*** $p < .0001$, ** $p < .001$, * $p < .05$, ns = non significant.

Table 3. Partial correlations, using the rephrased frequency of instantiation instruct-tion, between (a) typicality and ideal (controlling for FI2 and CT), (b) typicality and FI2 (controlling for ideal and CT), and (c) typicality and CT (controlling for ideal and FI2).

Next we wanted to investigate the correlations (Pearson *r*) among our different variables of interest and the ratings of emotion intensity. Emotion intensity was most strongly correlated with typicality (r = .86), followed by ideal (r = .81), and FI2 (r = .61; all p's < .001), whereas emotion intensity and CT were not significantly correlated. These findings suggest that prototypical, and ideal, vocal expressions are fairly intense expressions, whereas frequently occurring expressions are less intense.

4. Discussion

To summarize, similarity to ideals turned out to be the best predictor of the judged typicality of vocal expressions. In other words, the typicality of vocal expressions varied according to their suitability of obtaining the goal of conveying emotional information as effectively as possible. In contrast, typicality judgments did not seem to reflect the relative frequency with which particular vocal expressions are encountered in everyday conversations, or similarity to the central tendency of such expressions. Because ideals depend on the goals people have, they can be independent of the particular exemplars (category members) that a person usually encounters. As hypothesized, vocal expressions may thus best be characterized as goal-derived categories, instead of common taxonomic categories. If vocal expressions are indeed goal-derived categories, whose typicality is determined by similarity to ideals, this may help to explain why prototypical expressions are highly recognizable and have unique acoustic characteristics, while at the same time they may occur infrequently in everyday conversations.

The results further indicated that typical expressions generally are intense (i.e., have high emotion intensity). This finding also makes sense when vocal expressions are viewed as goal-based categories, rather than common taxonomic categories. Previous research has shown that intense vocal expressions are easier to recognize than less intense expressions (e.g., Juslin/Laukka 2001), so intense expressions better serve the goal of accurately communicating emotional information. However, because intense emotions occur less frequently than mild and moderately intense affective states in our daily lives, expressions of intense states should consequently also occur less frequently than expressions of milder states. The high emotion intensity of typical expressions could thus also help explain why prototypical expressions may be rare in everyday speech.

The findings also showed that ratings of both similarity to ideals and frequency of instantiation accounted for unique variance in ratings of typicality of vocal expressions. This underlines the findings of Barsalou and others that graded structure is a highly flexible phenomenon and that the boundaries between goal-derived and common taxonomic categories are not clear-cut (e.g., Barsalou 1987). Even though the present results suggest that vocal expressions are best characterized as goal-derived categories, they seem to belong to a special type of goal-derived categories which shares many features with common taxonomic categories. For example, like common taxonomic categories, vocal expressions represent familiar, perceptually salient clusters of co-occurring properties, which can be used for classification (but unlike common taxonomic categories, the graded structure of vocal expressions is best predicted by similarity to ideals). Horstmann (2002) found a similar pattern of results for facial expressions, and speculated that this "pattern may be characteristic for evolved signals which are naturally occurring and are used by receivers to regulate their actions in biologically relevant domains" (2002: 303). The present results tentatively support this suggestion by providing evidence also from vocal emotion expressions. Also, recent research has suggested that ideals become more important predictors of typicality judgments when the judges have relevant knowledge and experience of the category in question, as compared to when judges rate stimuli that are not meaningful to them (e.g., Burnett/Medin/Ross/ Blok 2005; Lynch/Coley/Medin 2000). Because emotion expressions make up meaningful stimuli, this could also help to explain the current results.

Further, we would like to point out that the present findings do not render prototypical expressions an unimportant topic of study – when prototypical expressions do occur in spontaneous conversations they are likely to efficiently capture the attention of the perceiver (e.g., Laukka 2005). Also, the study of prototypical expressions in itself warrants interest for theoretical reasons. However, if one aims at capturing the essence of expression in spontaneous conversational speech, it may be better to look for less prototypical expressions because spontaneous expressions are often masked, and/or strategically posed, and thus may convey quite complex affective states (e.g., Cowie/Cornelius 2003; Devillers et al. 2005; Laukka et al. 2008). The present results also indicated that acted expressions are more intense than spontaneous expressions, which is in agreement with some previous findings (e.g., Wilting/Krahmer/Swerts 2006). Our results further indicated that acted expressions received higher typicality ratings than spontaneous expressions. The bulk of research conducted on acted expressions has so far focused on prototypical expressions of basic emotions, but it is of course also possible to ask actors to portray more subtle affective states (see Bänziger/Scherer 2007). In the present study, acted expressions of both basic emotions (acted prototypical expressions) and more subtle affective states (acted non-prototypical expressions) received higher typicality and intensity ratings than did spontaneous expressions. This suggests that acted expressions may turn out more typical and intense than spontaneous expressions, even if the actors try to act out more subtle states. Moreover, results from a discrimination task conducted on speech stimuli from the same corpus as in the present study suggest that listeners are able to discriminate acted from spontaneous expressions even when they are perceived as expressing similar levels of emotion intensity (Audibert/Aubergé/Rilliard 2008).

Finally, this study also has several limitations that need to be discussed. Before any strong conclusions are drawn, the results of this study need to be replicated. Replication is particularly important because the present study is, to the best of our knowledge, the first to have addressed these questions applied to vocal expression. Further work also needs to be done in order to disentangle how various factors (e.g., the type of speech stimuli used, the emotion labels used, the context in which the expressions are perceived, and speaker and listener characteristics) may affect the graded structure of vocal expressions. Another limitation of the present study is that we, unlike earlier studies, did not collect similarity judgments in order to get an estimate of similarity to central tendency. Because of this it is unclear how our measure of similarity to central tendency compares with those utilized in previous studies. Work also needs to be directed toward developing measures of frequency of instantiation and similarity to central tendency that are independent of subjective judgments, because subjective judgments may not perfectly represent the actual frequencies and central tendencies. We are currently conducting studies which address several of the above limitations. In particular we are further investigating the effects of different contexts on graded structure, and we are also working on developing a measure of similarity to central tendency which is based on acoustical measurements. Limitations aside, we propose that this study may present a useful framework through which to view similarities and differences between prototypical and spontaneous expressions.

Acknowledgments

This study was supported by the Swedish Foundation for International Cooperation in Research and Higher Education (STINT) and the Ryoichi Sasakawa Young Leaders Fellowship Fund (SYLFF) through grants to Petri Laukka. The authors would like to thank all listeners who kindly participated in the experiments.

References

Aubergé, Véronique / Audibert, Nicolas / Rilliard, Albert 2004. E-Wiz: A trapper protocol for hunting the expressive speech corpora in lab. In *Proceedings of the 4th International Conference on Language Resources and Evaluation (LREC 2004)*. Paris: European Language Resources Association, 179-182.

Aubergé, Véronique / Audibert, Nicolas / Rilliard, Albert 2006. De E-Wiz à C-Clone: Recueil, modélisation et synthèse d'expressions authentiques. *Revue d'Intelligence Artificielle* 20/4-5, 499-527.

Audibert, Nicolas / Aubergé, Véronique / Rilliard, Albert 2008. How we are not equally competent for discriminating acted from spontaneous expressive speech. In Barbosa, Plínio A. / Madureira, Sandra / Reis, César (eds) *Proceedings of the Speech Prosody 2008 Conference.* Campinas, Brazil: Editora RG/CNPq, 693-696.

Bänziger, Tanja / Scherer, Klaus R. 2007. Using actor portrayals to systematically study multimodal emotion expressions: The GEMEP corpus. In Paiva, Ana / Prada, Rui / Picard, Rosalind W. (eds) *Affective Computing and Intelligent Interaction.* Berlin: Springer, 476-487.

Barsalou, Lawrence W. 1985. Ideals, central tendency, and frequency of instantiation as determinants of graded structure in categories. *Journal of Experimental Psychology: Learning, Memory, and Cognition* 11/4, 629-654.

Barsalou, Lawrence W. 1987. Concepts and conceptual development: Ecological and intellectual factors in categorization. In Neisser, Ulric (ed.) *Concepts and Conceptual Development: Ecological and Intellectual Factors in Categorization.* Cambridge: Cambridge University Press, 101-140.

Borkenau, Peter 1990. Traits as ideal-based and goal-derived social categories. *Journal of Personality and Social Psychology* 58/3, 381-396.

Burnett, Russell C. / Medin, Douglas L. / Ross, Norbert O. / Blok, Sergey V. 2005. Ideal is typical. *Canadian Journal of Experimental Psychology* 59/1, 3-10.

Campbell, Nick 2005. Getting to the heart of the matter: Speech as the expression of affect; rather than just text or language. *Language Resources and Evaluation* 39/1, 109-118.

Cowie, Roddy / Cornelius, Randolph R. 2003. Describing the emotional states that are expressed in speech. *Speech Communication* 40/1-2, 5-32.

Cowie, Roddy / Douglas-Cowie, Ellen / Tsapatsoulis, Nicolas / Votsis, George / Kollias, Stefanos / Fellenz, Winfried / Taylor, John G. 2001. Emotion recognition in human-computer interaction. *IEEE Signal Processing Magazine* 18/1, 32-80.

Darwin, Charles 1998. *The Expression of the Emotions in Man and Animals.* New York: Oxford University Press. (Original work published 1872).

Devillers, Laurence / Vidrascu, Laurence / Lamel, Lori 2005. Challenges in real-life emotion annotation and machine learning based detection. *Neural Networks* 18/4, 407-422.

Ekman, Paul 2003. *Emotions revealed.* New York: Henry Holt.

Goldstone, Robert L. / Son, Ji Y. 2005. Similarity. In Holyoak, Keith J. / Morrison, Robert G. (eds) *Cambridge Handbook of Thinking and Reasoning.* Cambridge: Cambridge University Press, 13-36.

Horstmann, Gernot 2002. Facial expressions of emotion: Does the prototype represent central tendency, frequency of instantiation, or an ideal? *Emotion* 2/3, 297-305.

Juslin, Patrik N. / Laukka, Petri 2001. Impact of intended emotion intensity on cue utilization and decoding accuracy in vocal expression of emotion. *Emotion* 1/4, 381-412.

Juslin, Patrik N. / Laukka, Petri 2003. Communication of emotion in vocal expression and music performance: Different channels, same code? *Psychological Bulletin* 129/5, 770-814.

Lakoff, George 1986. *Women, Fire and Dangerous Things: What Categories Tell Us about the Nature of Thought.* Chicago: University of Chicago Press.

Laukka, Petri 2005. Categorical perception of vocal emotion expressions. *Emotion* 5/3, 277-295.

Laukka, Petri 2008. Research on vocal expression of emotion: State of the art and future directions. In Izdebski, Krzysztof (ed.) *Emo-*

tions in the Human Voice. Vol 1: Foundations. San Diego: Plural Publishing, 153-169.

Laukka, Petri / Audibert, Nicolas / Aubergé, Véronique 2007. Graded structure in vocal expression of emotion: What is meant by "prototypical expressions"? In Schröder, Marc / Batliner, Anton / d'Alessandro, Christophe (eds) *Proceedings of the International Workshop on Paralinguistic Speech – between Models and Data (ParaLing'07).* Saarbrücken, Germany: Deutsches Forschungszentrum für Künstliche Intelligenz, 1-4.

Laukka, Petri / Linnman, Clas / Åhs, Fredrik / Pissiota, Anna / Frans, Örjan / Faria, Vanda / Michelgård, Åsa / Appel, Lieuwe / Fredrikson, Mats / Furmark, Tomas 2008. In a nervous voice: Acoustic analysis and perception of anxiety in social phobics' speech. *Journal of Nonverbal Behavior* 32/4, 195-214.

Lynch, Elizabeth B. / Coley, John D. / Medin, Douglas L. 2000. Tall is typical: Central tendency, ideal dimensions, and graded category structure among tree experts and novices. *Memory and Cognition* 28/1, 41-50.

Read, Stephen J. / Jones, David K. / Miller, Lynn C. 1990. Traits as goal-based categories: The importance of goals in the coherence of dispositional categories. *Journal of Personality and Social Psychology* 58/6, 1048-1061.

Rosch, Eleanor / Mervis, Carolyn B. 1975. Family resemblances: Studies in the internal structure of categories. *Cognitive Psychology* 7/4, 573-605.

Russell, James A. / Bachorowski, Jo-Anne / Fernández-Dols, José-Miguel 2003. Facial and vocal expressions of emotion. *Annual Review of Psychology* 54, 329-349.

Scherer, Klaus R. 2003. Vocal communication of emotion: A review of research paradigms. *Speech Communication* 40/1-2, 227-256.

Smith, Edward E. / Shoben, Edward J. / Rips, Lance J. 1974. Structure and process in semantic memory: A featural model for semantic decisions. *Psychological Review* 81/3, 214-241.

Wilting, Janneke E. / Krahmer, Emiel / Swerts, Marc 2006. Real vs. acted emotional speech. In *Proceedings of the 9th International Conference on Spoken Language Processing (Interspeech 2006).* Pittsburgh, PA, 805-808.

GRÉGORY BELLER

Transformation of Expressivity in Speech

1. Introduction

The need to express and understand emotions is a fundamental part of human communication. This level of information does not always inform us of the emotional state the person is in. Even if the actors are driven by their emotions, they can also be simulated. From reviewing different theories on the control of emotional reactions and of several emotional data collecting methods, it appears necessary to separate the inner emotional state from the corresponding outer perceived expression, by the introduction of the term 'expressivity'.

With regard to speech, expressivity is presented here as a level of information in the spoken message which gathers the expression of emotions, simulated or not, attitudes and moods. It is different from speaker identity, speaking style, modality and prominence, which justifies the interest in defining a state reference called 'neutral'. Expressivity is accessible beyond words because it is also conveyed by paralinguistic indices such as restructurings, non-verbal sounds, and prosody.

Since it is an essential level of information, human-machine interfaces try to manage it by recognising and synthesising expressive speech; indeed, current speech synthesis methods provide natural and intelligible speech. Art directors, film studios and video game producers are now interested in the many possibilities of a system which offers analysis, synthesis, and transformation of the expressivity of the voice, as demonstrated by the VIVOS project.

Statistical models of emotional prosody have been used by voice conversion systems (Hsia *et al.* 2007) as well as by concatenative (Bulut *et al.* 2007) and HMM-based (Yamagishi *et al.*

2005) speech synthesizers. Our approach consists of splitting the problem into two parts: firstly, we establish a neutral synthesis from a neutral corpus of excellent quality; then we transform the expressivity of this synthesis. This does not prevent us from using expressive targets in the stage of synthesis, and it also allows us to transform recorded and non-synthesised sentences. The second part of this chapter focuses on transformation of the expressivity of an utterance.

2. Emotion and expressivity

A growing community of researchers study emotional data to infer or confront theories on emotions. A commonly recognised difficulty expressed in these studies is evaluating the degree of control/ spontaneity over the emotional data. The acted emotional data from long studies in laboratories is now widely criticised by those who wish to observe the demonstrations of the felt emotional states.

However, it must be acknowledged that several techniques employed by actors, for example, self-induction of an emotional state, can lead to real emotional expressions. Furthermore, this difficulty shows that a clear boundary has to be drawn between inner emotional state studies and outer expression observations. That is why we provide an attempt at defining expressivity.

2.1. Theoretical background on emotions

Different topics related to emotions have motivated theories. Many theories have been designed on the function, the role and the mechanism of emotions, though few of them deal with the control of emotions and related emotional reactions. Here we try to provide a chronological view of such theories.

From Aristotle to the Middle Ages, emotions were considered as reflecting the animal part of the human kind. To get to perfection, one has to control them (Saint Thomas d'Aquin). At rebirth, Descartes describes emotions as bodily responses to external stimuli (Descartes 1664). They are thus uncontrollable since they are part of rational determinism. LeBrun draws a dictionary of composed and basic facial emotional responses. They both related the existence of an emotion organic centre, called the pineal gland.

In 1872, Charles Darwin characterises emotions as vestiges of patterns of actions for the survey, designed by evolutionary development (Darwin 1872). This description of systematic emotional responses, which are considered as universals (for mammals), does not allow for any control, as they are biologically defined. Shortly after, James (1884) agrees with Darwin, but changes the causal relations. Emotions are appraisals of emotional reactions which are direct responses to external stimuli.

During the past century, cognitivists aim at describing this appraisal (Frijda 1986). Scherer especially describes two parallel processes that occur in vocal expression of emotions (Scherer 2006). The 'push' effect underlies psycho-physiological activations displayed by uncontrollable paralinguistic signs. The 'pull' effect is shown by the use of socio-cultural codes. Each of these two effects affects the prosody of emotional speech. The 'push-pull' distinction aims to distinguish between the controlled part (pull) and the uncontrolled one (push). This distinction can be seen in other theories as making a difference between the spontaneous part and the symbolic/acted part of the expression of an emotional state (Buck 1985). The argument for totally, culturally designed emotional response is central in the social-constructivist perspective that claims that emotional responses are not biologically but culturally motivated (Averill 1980).

Nowadays neuroscientists aiming at localizing the pineal gland refresh the debate. On the one hand, emotional stimuli seem to be directly managed by the limbic system and then interpreted by the cortex (LeDoux 2005). On the other hand, somatic effects related to emotions can be activated consciously (Changeux 1983), that is to say, one can self-induce emotional reactions without the need of external stimuli. This debate about our ability to control emotional response is at the heart of methods for collecting emotional data.

2.2. Collecting emotional data

Emotional data is, by nature, rare and heterogeneous. Nevertheless, some experimental protocols allow their acquisition (Douglas-Cowie *et al.* 2003). These methods are generally divided into three adopted classes:

- Naturalistic data:
  - Free context: All emotions can occur. The difficulty remains in the lack of knowledge about the context and consequently, in the variability of recording conditions (Chung 2000).
  - Constrained context: A service is dedicated to specific scenarios where a limited number of emotional states can occur. As the emotional state is not the goal of one who is under it, this method is part of the category of indirect measurements, using the perception test terminology (indirect method). It provides naturalistic emotional data with a stable recording process (Vidrascu/Devillers 2005).
- Induced data: An emotional situation is artificially created in a predefined context with good recording conditions. Again, it involves indirect methods, the subject of which is not aware of what data is really observed (Aubergé *et al.* 2004).
- Acted data: Actors simulate desired emotions while speaking a chosen text and are recorded in ideal conditions (direct method).

A review on techniques employed by actors reveals that some can generate naturalistic data, e.g self-induction methods (Beller *et al.* 2008c), though these techniques have not been involved in a scientific study yet. All recorded emotional data by use of direct or indirect methods handle a compromise between their spontaneity and their controllability (or the knowledge about their context). The case of acted versus spontaneous emotional expression is even harder to define taking into account that the person in an emotional state cannot measure the degree of control he has on his own expression. From a perceptual point of view, it is also difficult when regarding an emotional expression, to infer whether the speaker is in the corresponding emotional state. Nevertheless, an emotional expression simulated or not, often contains enough information for people to agree on the inner emotional state, i.e. on a supposition about the inner emotional state. Even if we do not know that the emotion is true or acted (felt or not), we can observe the same emotional expression and then reproduce it in order to give the information of the corresponding inner motional state. Thus, it seems that a clear boundary needs to be defined between an emotional state and its expression. To distinguish the emotional (inner) state, i.e., what one can feel, from the (outer) expression of this state, i.e., what people can perceive, we specify this last phenomenon by the term 'expressivity'.

2.3. A definition of expressivity

Expressivity is a level of information in communication. This level groups together the external demonstrations, controlled or not, which can be attributed to uncontrolled internal states. These internal states include the emotions, feelings, attitudes, moods, and psychological states which make up the actor's performance style. Expressivity is thus a part of the communication system, defined as a demonstrator of an internal state which is inaccessible, by definition, in others. This internal state can be present or not, and its demonstration can be thus feigned or not. In every case, the expressivity refers only to the internal states which we can suppose are uncontrollable.

As for any common perceptual category, a significant number of people should agree on the term used to define expressivity. Since the perception of expressivity is dependent on the context in which it occurs, and since the way one perceives it is influenced by its proper experienced inner emotional states (neural perception-action theory (LeDoux 2005)), a large number of items compose the panel of expressivity. Actually, the literature reveals a lot of related terms that can be said to be components of a heterogeneous field with ambiguous and badly determined words. Even if standardisations have been proposed by the observation of the universal emotional responses (Ekman 1999), perceptive tests (Devillers *et al.* 2003) still show that people prefer to use more than one of these words for labeling emotional data. Furthermore, one can consider anger as a category, yet others will differentiate cold anger from hot anger since involved taxonomy is strongly application-driven. Thus, it is hard to define explicitly a closed set of linguistic categories that compose expressivity. That is why we attempt to define this information level by using 'the opposite definition paradigm'. In other words, we report here information levels that cannot be considered as part of expressivity (see Figure 1).

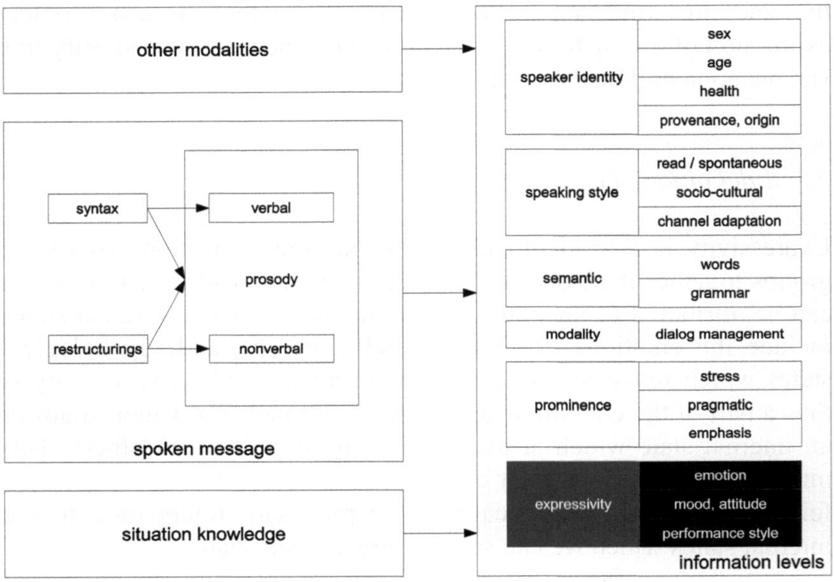

Figure 1. Presentation of various levels of information involved in verbal communication (right part). Expressivity refers to a hypothetical internal state. The spoken message, which conveys this information, can be decomposed into several supports (left part).

2.3.1. Speaker identity

First of all, in any act of vocal communication there is a speaker involved. The various information relative to the identity of this speaker is then implicit in communication. In the case of spoken communication, the identity of a speaker is conveyed by its voice. The sex, age, health, origin (foreign status, regional accent, social standing, level of language) all contain a wealth of information relative to the personality of the speaker made accessible to the others by the voice.

2.3.2. Speaking style

Numerous contextual factors can affect the manner in which an individual speaks. First of all, physical constraints can bring them to speak louder or to repeat words they have said, for example, in the case of a noisy environment (Garnier 2007). Social constraints also come into play. The professional constraints especially bring complex speaking styles as is the case in political speech or in a teaching environment. Finally, important differences appear between spontaneous speech, speech read from a text and speech recited 'off by heart'.

2.3.3. Semantic message

A speaker taking into account external constraints communicates a semantic message. Interestingly, expressivity can only be perceived by the way words are pronounced and flourished by non-verbal sounds. This means that semantically non-expressive texts (said neutrally) can be spoken in a way that people can perceive an intended expressivity. By non-expressive texts, we rely on sentences that can be pronounced in any expressivity without losing any sense. To a larger extent, musical performance can carry expressivity without using any word. Furthermore, universal emotions can be perceived by foreign listeners that do not understand the language of the expressive speaker (Burkhardt *et al.* 2006). Expressivity can thus be explicitly recognized by means of the semantic message, but is not dependent on it.

2.3.4. Modality

Modality is a special part of the vocal communication due to its important role in dialog management. Modality is generally defined by three common categories: question, assertion and exclamation. In normal dialogical situations, modality governs the tour of word. At some point of a discussion, it reflects the position of the speaker on the issue being discussed. He can then adopt the opposite position, generally called case irony, scepticism and doubt. Irony and doubt are commonly classified as an instance of expressivity. But, unusually, we leave it to the reader to classify them as a part of the modality group.

This is because of the strong relationship between the linguistic message and the way it is uttered. This does not prevent the message from being accompanied by any expressivity such as confusion or embarrassment.

2.3.5. Prominence

Prominence is the perceptive result of controlled acoustic contrasts (culmination, distinction, demarcation) performing several functions. First of all, it is evident in the accentuation of certain syllables which can be defined by linguistic rules (Lacheret-Dujour/Beaugendre 1999) and which is thus language-dependent. Prominence sometimes plays a role in the disambiguation of the sense, as in pragmatic accent. Finally, prominence also serves to emphasise certain elements (accent of focus, accent of emphasis, and accent of instigation). It seems that prominence plays a particular role in verbal communication, because its realisation requires a more important part of control during its production. That is why prominence distinction is very important for expressivity analysis (see Section 4.1.2). In a certain way, the 'push-pull' theory can be scaled down to a local and dynamic version: the non prominent, obvious syllables, which are brought about by the 'push' effect vs. the prominent, more elaborated syllables, the realisations of which are marked by the 'pull' effect.

2.4. Neutral as a reference

In this chapter, expressivity is explicitly presented as a level of information among others, within a vocal message. An individual (speaker identity) pronounces (modality and prominence) a linguistic message (semantic message), in a certain physical environment and under certain social constraints (speaking style) and according to his internal state, which he decides to express or suppress (expressivity). To observe the variations due to this last level of information, that is, due to expressivity, it is necessary to marginalise the variations due to the other levels of information. If it has not been demonstrated yet that there is a neutral internal emotional or psychological state, in which neither emotion, nor mood, nor feeling, nor attitude exists, the existence of a level of zero expressivity, in which the speaker gives no information about his internal state, seems widely accepted by those who address this absence of information by the case: neutral. This is why researchers and engineers usually compare two versions of the same sentence, pronounced by the same person and in the same conditions, and containing two different expressivities, in order to analyse, measure and compare them (Tao *et al.*, 2006). This empirical and widely used process seems evident here because it neutralizes the variations due to the other information levels in order to enlighten the variations relative to the change of expressivity. The measured variations can be reused for the other speakers pronouncing other texts and so lead towards general, generative models of expressivity. The realised corpus is based on this process (see Section 4).

3. Expressivity in speech

The 'double coding of speech' framework (Fónagy 1983) differentiates the linguistic channel from the paralinguistic channel. The linguistic channel contains the semantic information level of words structured by syntax. The paralinguistic channel handles nonverbal sounds, restructuring and prosody that describe not only the way words are pronounced but also the way nonverbal sounds are uttered. From a perceptual point of view, the listener perceives an acoustic signal where information is expressed, through syntax and restructuring, in a structured sequence of verbal and non-verbal sounds, all modulated by prosody. Previous information levels and their relationships are retrieved by the listener decoding the spoken message together with other modalities such as visual, and with internal and situational knowledge.

3.1. Non-verbal sounds

Non-verbal sounds are a common phenomenon in speech. This category groups all sounds produced during speech that do not handle any linguistic function. For instance, fillers (laughter, scream, etc.), and respiration (breaths, pauses, etc.) are important information for expressivity but not for semantic sense. In fact, nonverbal sounds act as a semantic mark-up of expressivity. One can infer sadness only from a cry, and fear only from a scream. The importance of nonverbal sounds can be emphasized by the fact that they are often written in a text, in a phonetic-spelling way. For instance, *ha ha ha* is often used to write laughter in comic strips. Despite a formal textual representation, non-verbal sounds appear to be of first importance for expressivity. That is why expressive text-to-speech systems start to synthesise nonverbal sounds such as laughter (Beller Forth.).

3.2. Restructuring

Another part of the paralinguistic channel relies on possible restructuring cases that are commonly considered as disfluencies in neutral speech (Piu/Bove 2007). Repetitions, resettings, and other a-syntactical restructuring of speech are informative and appear a lot in expressive speech (Beller *et al.* 2008c). An efficient and common language needs to be defined in order to annotate these expressive non-verbal phenomena (both restructuring and non-verbal sounds) and to compare them among corpora. Several transcriptions have been proposed (Aubergé *et al.* 2006). They almost all consist in extensions of the SSML[1] (Eide *et al.* 2004) (Blankinship/Beckwith 2001).

1 SSML: Speech Synthesis Markup Language: <http://www.w3.org/TR/speech-synthesis>.

3.3. Prosody

The verbal and non-verbal sounds of speech are ordered in a sequential way. At the same time, the acoustic realization of these sound elements is modulated by prosody. Prosody deals with phonological features, known as suprasegmental features, which apply to groups larger than a single segment (e.g. the phoneme), such as the syllable, the word, or the breath group. Five features are cited in literature as the five dimensions of prosody (Pfitzinger 2006):

- intonation: fundamental frequency, pitch, F_0;
- loudness: intensity, energy;
- speech rate: speed of delivery;
- articulation degree: pronunciation, vocal tract configuration, formant dynamics;
- phonation: glottal excitation, relaxation (pressed / normal / breathy), vibration mode, voicing.

4. Prosody analyses

The significant variation of these features, allotted to the change of expressivity, makes it possible to build models of actors' performance styles. The recording of the latter provides sound examples which are both symbolically and acoustically analysed. The machine then learns the existing relationships between the expressivities and the configurations from acoustic parameters such as intonation (for example), whilst taking into account contextual information. Lastly, these generative statistical models are able to propose parameters of transformation for new sentences from outside of the corpus, and more importantly from a different speaker. The use of these transformation parameters by speech processing algorithms makes it possible to confer a desired degree of expressivity to recorded or synthesised neutral speech. Therefore, we build an expressive corpus involving actors that utter expressivity. After presenting the corpus, we shall offer some prosodic analyses to prepare the design of a context-dependent generative model of the prosody of expressivity in speech.

4.1. IrcamCorpusExpressivity

IrcamCorpusExpressivity contains recordings of four French actors (two males and two females for a varying speaker identity) each with a duration of approximately one hour and a half (Beller *et al.* 2008c). They were all recorded in the same professional conditions and followed the same procedure. Ten neutral sentences extracted from a phonetically balanced French corpus (Combescure 1981) were uttered with expressivities: introvert and extrovert anger, introvert and extrovert happiness, introvert and extrovert fear, introvert and extrovert sadness, and, positive and negative surprises, disgust, discretion, excitation, confusion, and, of course, neutral. Moreover, six repetitions per sentence occurred for basic emotions (written in italics), starting from the neutral version and afterwards with an increasing degree of the expressive level (power, intensity, activation). The corpus was composed of approximately 550 utterances per actor. Each utterance was phonetically hand-segmented (to discard semantic level) and prominence was hand-labelled (to discard prominence level). Some non-verbal sounds for each emotion were also recorded. All these data and their interrelationships were managed by a relational database management system (Beller *et al.* 2008b).

4.1.1. Intonation and loudness

The first analysis of the corpus focuses on intonation and loudness. Pitch has been estimated with the Yin algorithm (De Cheveigné/ Kawahara 2002) and loudness with a perceptual measurement (Peeters 2004). Jitter and shimmer are related to the spectral centre of gravity of windowed pitch and loudness respectively. Pitch is modifiable, using dynamic transposition, just as loudness is modifiable, using dynamic gain, thanks to SuperVP, a phase vocoder technology (Bogaards *et al.* 2004). The known results in agreement with the literature set apart (a strong correlation between pitch and loudness), show that extrovert emotions often distinguish themselves by a pitch the average of which is situated an octave or two over that of the neutral case (see Figure 3). So, a simple estimation of the average does not allow distinguishing between extrovert happiness and extrovert anger. This leads us to investigate other prosodic dimensions such as speech rate.

4.1.2. Speech rate

Speech rate is often defined as the average number of syllables per second in a whole sentence (Chung 2000, Pereira/Watson1998). Because the most prominent syllables often have a longer duration, we prefer to define speech rate by the sequence of individual syllable durations. The speech rate curve is thus represented by an interpolation of the durations of syllables (see Figure 2). A deceleration corresponds to a rising of the curve and an acceleration is represented by a falling of the curve. These movements can be simulated using SuperVP by locally time-stretching (compressing or dilating) the speech signal. Figure 2 shows that the final accent is more distinguishable in the speech rate curve than in the F_0 curve. Indeed, it has been shown that speech rate analysis with prominence care performs a better discrimination between extrovert happiness and extrovert anger than pitch analysis only (Beller *et al.* 2006). The author emphasises here the need for prominence information level to analyse expressivity (see Section 2.3.5) since prominent parts of the speech are more controlled than others.

Another advantage of the dynamic speech rate estimation is the facilitation of the study of rhythm. In fact, Figure 2 shows clearly that the actor emphasises the sentence with an increase of the prominent syllable duration which gives a certain rhythm to his performance. Research is now focused on rhythm extraction so as to measure the metricity of the speech, that is to determine whether it possesses an inherent perceptual rhythmical structure or not.

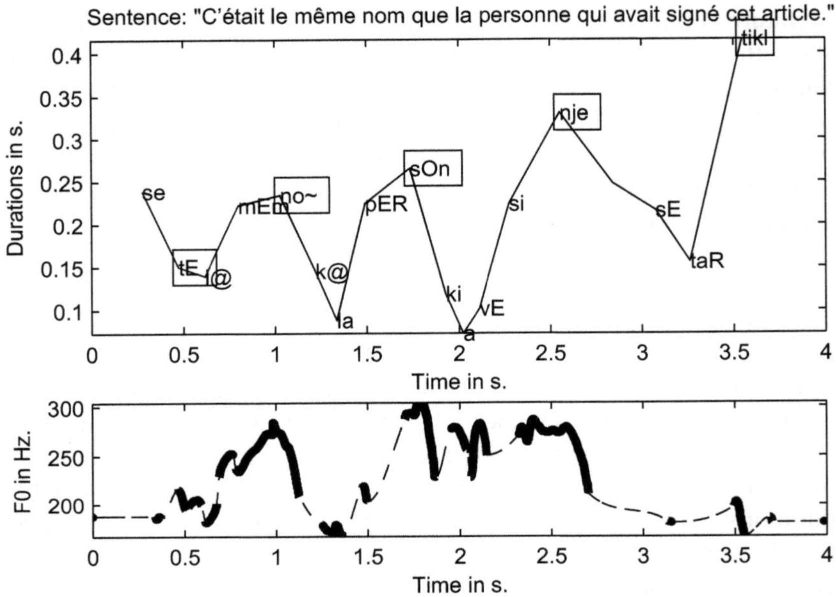

Figure 2. Duration of syllables and F_0 curve of a French sentence uttered by a male actor with extrovert happiness: "C'était le même nom que la personne qui avait signé cet article". Squared syllables are perceived as prominent.

4.1.3. Articulation degree

Articulation degree (Lindblöm 1983) originates from interactions between phonetic context, speech rate, and spectral dynamics (which correspond to speed changes in the configuration of the vocal tract). A study concerning the influence of segment duration on the vocalic triangle in neutral speech (Gendrot/Adda-Decker 2004) shows that formants aim towards a central vowel for segments of short duration, resulting in a diminishing of the vocal triangle area (neutral natural tendency). A major difference exists between neutral and other expressivities. Given a phonetic context, the articulation degree is not only dependent on the speech rate variable but also on expressivity.

Indeed, we conducted a statistical analysis on the influence of expressivity on the articulation degree (Beller *et al.* 2008a). Using phonetic segmentation, previous dynamic speech rate estimation and a proposed robust formant analyser, articulation degrees for different expressivities were computed. The neutral natural tendency is clearly not designed for expressivities like extrovert sadness, introvert fear, and surprises which show a reduction of the vocalic triangle despite slower speech (see Figure 3). Conversely, extrovert anger shows an expansion of the vocalic triangle area which exceeds that of the neutral natural tendency. Dynamic frequency warping manages articulation degree modifications by moving dynamically formant frequencies. Again, expressivity analysis and transformation require phonetic information derived from the semantic message information level (see Section 2.3.3).

4.1.4. Voice quality

Voice quality has been recently introduced as a prosodic dimension (Campbell/Mokhtari 2003), especially for expressive speech (Gobl/ Chasaide 2003). This recent and exciting framework groups several analyses aimed at describing phonation. Several problems arise as this approach intrinsically involves an inverse problem – the separation of the effects of the glottis excitation signal and of the vocal tract filter. Nevertheless, some features already exist and allow for an analysis, such as the four parameters Liljencrants-Fant (LF) model together with the Rd relaxation coefficient (Fant *et al.* 1985). Our first step in voice quality analysis thus involves an ARX-LF model estimation of the speech signal (Vincent *et al.* 2005). From the parameters of the LF models, the Rd coefficient is computed (Henrich *et al.* 2002) to estimate the relaxation degree of the speech (pressed/normal/breathy). To change this coefficient and to transform voice quality, a filter is designed by the ratio of the corresponding spectral envelope of the glottis models and applied by SuperVP. Voice quality analysis also investigates other phonation phenomena such as voicing (dynamic spectro-temporal voicing frequency), vibratory modes (falsetto, normal, fry), abnormalities (asymmetry of the vocal folds) and micro-temporal variations (jitter, shimmer, growl).

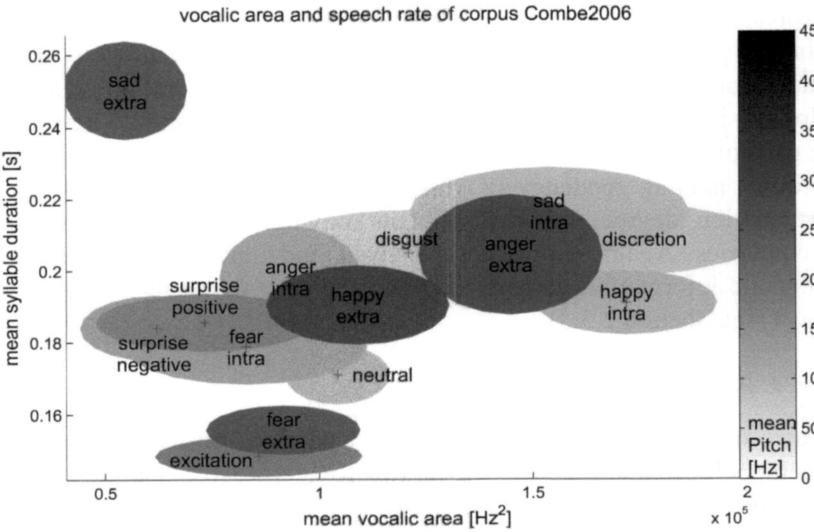

Figure 3. Expressivities performed by a male actor, represented according to their vocalic area (X axis), to their syllabic duration (Y axis) and to their mean pitch (Z axis -colours). Ellipsoids show mean values (centre coordinates) and variances (widths).

4.2. Paralinguistic paradox

Interestingly, voice quality parameters (open quotient) seem to be dependent on the pronounced vowel (probably due to production efficiency). Similarly, in order to analyse the articulation degree (to draw a vocalic triangle; for instance), we need at least the phonetic labels of the vowels. This level of annotation offers a categorisation in phonetic classes in which the spectra of the corresponding vowels can be compared. Thus the articulation degree can be estimated for all utterances independently of the phonetic context and then used to compare expressivity. Again, the study of speech rate has shown the importance of the prominence level of syllables.

Indeed, one major difficulty in the analysis of paralinguistic features is the acoustical influence of the verbal/segmental content. The realization of phonetic segment sequences driven by a text implies a co-articulation phenomenon and other physiological constraints that may affect pitch course and other prosodic features. The produced infra-segmental variations can falsely be attributed to prosody if the linguistic context is unknown. In order to observe supra-segmental features, segmental effects need to be removed. That is the paradox of paralinguistic analysis that requires linguistic information to be achieved. This is done by adding contextual information at each step: analysis, transformation and synthesis.

5. Prosody model and transformation

Our system is aimed at transforming a given neutral source utterance into a target utterance with the same sentence, from the same speaker, in the same speaking style, and with respect to original modality and prominence, but with a given expressivity *E* and a given expressive power *P*. First, linguistic information is derived from the text for each syllable of the neutral sentence (see Section 4). This provides a temporal sequence of contexts C^{N}_{src}. Then two corresponding acoustic descriptor sets are predicted, one using expressivity neutral A^{N}_{model} and the other using expressivity *E* A^{E}_{model}. Inferred acoustic parameter distributions are then compared so as to provide transformation factors. Hence the problem becomes to infer acoustic data A^{X}_{model} corresponding to a given context $C^{X}_{model} = C_i$, i.e. to evaluate:
$P(A^{X}_{model} \mid C^{X}_{model} = C_i)$

5.1. Context-dependent model

The recordings divided in syllables can be classified according to symbolic information such as expressivity, prominence level, syllable type (V, CV, CVC...), or other linguistic annotation (relative to other information levels). A context is defined as a set of symbolic variables that can take different states in closed vocabularies. An example of such a context is given in Table 1. The syllable produced in context C_1 is a non-prominent syllable made of a consonant (CV) and of a vowel /a/, uttered by a male expressing extrovert anger with an expressive power of three (third repetition of the sentence in the database).

Variable	*Information level*	*State description*	*Example C_1*
Gender	speaker identity	female or male	"male"
expressivity	expressivity	see section 4	"extrovert anger"
Power	expressivity	degree or power of expressivity	"3"
prominence	prominence	non-secondary, primary prominent	"non-prominent"
type	semantic message	V, CV, CVC, VC	"CV"
vowel	semantic message		"/a/"

Table 1. Context definition: symbolic variables of different information levels and their state descriptions. C1 is an example

5.2. Model parameters: stylization of acoustic features

Once the context $C^X_{model} = C_i$ is defined, temporal evolution of the acoustic signals related to prosodic dimensions can be modelled: e.g. F_0, loudness, local speech rate, articulation degree, relaxation coefficient. At this point there were many attempts at stylizing intonation contours. Different stylization models were proposed and tested on the data. They could briefly be summed up using Legendre polynomial family, starting from mean value on the segment (order 0), by way of linear model (first order), to higher order stylization models like quadratic (second order) or cubic (third order) contours. This family is generally used since it confers the model a specific scalability on its fitting precision (Schwarz 2004), providing controllable complexity to the model. Every syllable of expressivity *X* is modelled by the stylization parameter values of its acoustic features A^X_{model}(*syllable*) together with its corresponding context C^X_{model}(*syllable*). These are the parameters of the proposed prosodic model of expressivity.

5.3. Model robustness: statistics

The power of a model is not only in its capacity to fit well and infer real data, but also in its simplicity (reduction of complexity) and its generality. Therefore, statistics are used to evaluate part of the model parameters that remain stable and robust in a significant amount of data. Again, contextual information is used to group syllables into classes. Statistics of model parameter values can be estimated in each context, leading to smoother, more robust, and more significant model parameter values.

5.4. Model generalness: marginalized decision tree

A new sentence to transform can present a context which was not observed during the recording phase. In that case, our generative model has the ability to propose a solution and supply parameters for the transformation. Several solutions exist depending on the knowledge about the context relationships. Firstly, the ability to compare contexts (needing a definition of a symbolic distance) can lead to a choice of the closest context to infer model parameter values or to interpolate values of the neighbouring contexts. Secondly, unobserved cases can be filled by model parameter distributions that are given a priori, using a Bayesian paradigm (Beller 2007). Finally, and as presented in more detail here, knowledge about context can be defined by hierarchical relationships between contextual variables. We view the order of the presentation of contextual variables (see Section 1) as a hierarchical order (expressivity is more important than prominence which is more important than syllable type, and so on). Figure 4 represents this hierarchy by means of a decision tree. Each variable can take as many states as labels in its dictionary. Each node groups leaf syllables the context of which is the same as described by the path of the node.

Let us suppose that the new sentence to transform presents a context C_1 that was unobserved during the learning phase. For instance, it may happen because none of the syllables of the database contains the desired syllable type ("CV"). That part of this too specific request can be eliminated by marginalising context with regard to the variable type. This modified request is then applied to find syllables from the database which correspond less to our initial contextual request C_1, but which correspond to the most important part of that request (to the sense of the predefined hierarchy). Successive marginalisation of the initial request can be repeated until a syllable is found, or until a significant number of syllables have been accumulated. This procedure leads to a prediction of acoustic transformation parameters for any symbolic context even if it was not observed before; it allows the model to become general.

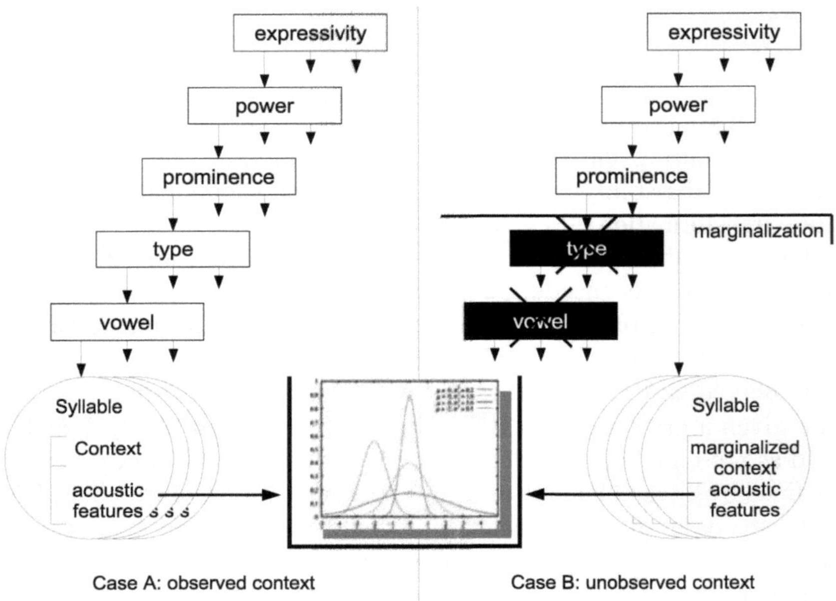

Figure 4. Decision tree involving a hierarchy of contextual variables. Left: Observed case of the database. Right: Unobserved case that requires recursive context marginalisation until it reaches an observed case.

5.5. Prosody transformation

After the two inference phases, the proposed prosodic model, fed by the input sequence of contexts ($C^N{}_{src}$), provides two sequences of acoustic parameters: $A^N{}_{model}$ (neutral) and $A^E{}_{model}$ (desired expressivity). Significant differences can be seen as effects of changing from one expressivity to another (see Section 2.4). These two sequences are compared in order to provide dynamic speaker-independent transformation controls that drive signal processing algorithms (SuperVP and ARX-LF model). Some examples can be listened to at the following address: <http://www.ircam.fr/anasyn/-beller>.

6. Conclusion

In this chapter, we have presented a review of theories that deal with control of emotional reactions. They raise the difficulty of evaluating the degree of spontaneity in an emotion by observing only its external expression. Although empirical methods involving direct and indirect measurements have been used to collect emotional data, it is difficult for them to identify the inherent degree of control the speaker has on his emotional reaction, whether it is simulated or not. Therefore, emotions and their corresponding expressions have to be distinguished.

We have provided an attempt at defining expressivity as an information level of communication. This involves all perceivable demonstrations, controlled or not, of an internal state that can be interpreted as uncontrolled. Expressivity can formally be separated from other information levels, e.g. speaker identity, speaking style, modality and prominence. In practice, the task is harder since all these information levels share the same paralinguistic channel composed of restructurings of verbal words and non-verbal sounds, all modulated by prosody. This problem can be solved by discarding prosodic variations due to other information levels, e.g. involving the so-called neutral case.

By contextually clustering an expressive French corpus, significant prosodic variations can be attributed to the change of expressivity. A statistical context-dependent method has been described. The resulting speaker independent model of expressivity has been used to modify the expressivity of a neutral utterance, either recorded or synthesised. The proposed method is aimed at artistic ends, but can also be applied to the analysis of anthropomorphisation of Human-machine interfaces.

Acknowledgments

This work was partially funded by the French RIAM network project VIVOS (http://www.vivos.fr). The authors thank the actors involved in this study for their performances.

References

Aubergé, Véronique / Audibert, Nicolas / Rilliard, Albert 2004. E-Wiz: A trapper protocol for hunting the expressive speech corpora, *LREC04*, Lisbon, 179-182.

Aubergé, Véronique / Audibert, Nicolas / Rilliard, Albert 2006. Auto-annotation: an alternative method to label expressive corpora, *LREC06*, Workshop on Emotional Corpora, Genova, 45-46.

Averill, James R. 1980. A constructivist view of emotion, In *Theory, Research and Experience*, New York: Academic Press, 1/305-339.

Beller, Grégory 2007. Context Dependent Transformation of Expressivity in Speech Using a Bayesian Network, *ParaLing*, Saarbrücken.

Beller, Grégory, Forthcoming. Semi-Parametric Synthesis of Speaker-Like Laughter, *The Phonetics of Laughing*. Berlin: de Gryuter.

Beller, Grégory / Obin, Nicolas / Rodet, Xavier 2008a. Articulation Degree as a Prosodic Dimension of Expressive Speech, *Speech Prosody 2008*, Campinas.

Beller, Grégory / Schwarz, Diemo / Hueber, Thomas / Rodet, Xavier 2006. Speech Rates in French Expressive Speech, *Speech Prosody 2006*, Dresden 2006.

Beller, Grégory / Veaux, Christophe / Degottex, Gilles / Obin, Nicolas / Lanchantin, Pierre / Rodet, Xavier 2008b. IRCAM Corpus Tools: Système de Gestion de Corpus de Parole, In *TAL*.

Beller, Grégory / Veaux, Christophe / Rodet, Xavier 2008c. IrcamCorpusExpressivity: Nonverbal Words and Restructurings, *LREC workshop on emotions*.

Blankinship, Eric / Beckwith, Richard 2001. Tools for expressive text-to-speech markup, *UIST'01,* New York, 159-160.

Bogaards, Niels / Roebel, Axel / Rodet, Xavier 2004. Sound Analysis and Processing with AudioSculpt 2, *ICMC*, Miami.

Buck, Ross 1985. The Communication of Emotion, *Paperback Edition.* New York: Guilford Press.

Bulut, Murtaza / Lee, Sungbok / Narayanan, Shrikanth 2007. A statistical approach for modelling prosody features using pos tags for emotional speech synthesis, *ICASSP*, Hawaï.

Burkhardt, Felix / Audibert, Nicolas / Malatesta, Lori / Turk, Oytun / Arslan, Levent / Aubergé, Valérie 2006. Emotional Prosody – Does Culture Make A Difference?, *Speech Prosody*, Dresden.

Campbell, Nick / Mokhtari, Parham 2003. Voice quality: the 4th prosodic dimension, *XVth Int. Congress of Phonetic Sciences*, Barcelona, 3/2417-2420.

Changeux, Jean-Pierre 1983. *L'Homme neuronal*, Paris : Odile Jacob.

Chung, Soo-Jung 2000. L'expression et la perception de l'émotion extraite de la parole spontannée : évidences du coréen et de l'anglais, phonétique, *PhD thesis Université PARIS III*, Paris.

Combescure, Pierre 1981. 20 listes de dix phrases phonétiquement équilibrées, *Revue d'Acoustique*, 56/34-38.

Darwin, Charles 1872. *Expression of Emotion in Man and Animal.* Oxford: Oxford University Press.

De Cheveigné, Alain / Kawahara, Hideki 2002. YIN, a Fundamental Frequency Estimator for Speech and Music, *JASA*, 111/1917-1930.

Descartes, René 1664. *Les passions de l'Âme*. Paris : Michel Bobin et Nicolas Le Gras.

Devillers, Laurence / Lamel, Lauri / Vasilescu, Ioana 2003. Emotion detection in Task-oriented spoken dialogs. *IEEE ICME*.

Douglas-Cowie, Ellen / Campbell, Nick / Cowie, Roddy / Roach, Peter 2003. Emotional speech: towards a new generation of databases, *Speech Communication*., 40/1-2/33-60.

Eide, E. / Aaron, A. / Bakis, R. / Hamza, W. / Picheny, M. / Pitrelli, J. 2004. A Corpus-Based Approach to <Ahem/> Expressive Speech Synthesis, *5th ISCA Speech Synthesis Workshop*.

Ekman, Paul 1999. Basic Emotions, In *The Handbook of Cognition and Emotion*, John Wiley & Sons, Ltd.

Fant, Gunar / Liljencrants, Johan / Lin, Qiguang 1985. A four-parameter model of glottal flow, *STL-QPSR*, 4/1-13.

Fónagy, Ivan 1983. *La vive voix : essais de psychophonétique*. Paris ; Payot.

Frijda, Nico H. 1986. *The emotions*. Cambridge: Cambridge University Press.

Garnier, Maëva 2007. Communiquer en environnement bruyant : de l'adaptation jusqu'au forçage vocal, *PhD thesis University of Paris 6*.

Gendrot, Cédric / Adda-Decker, Martine 2004. Analyses formantiques automatiques de voyelles orales: évidence de la réduction vocalique en langues française et allemande, *MIDL*.

Gobl, Christer / Ni Chasaide, Ailbhe 2003. The role of voice quality in communicating emotion, mood and attitude, *Speech Communication*. 40/1-2/189-212.

Henrich, Nathalie / d'Alessandro, Christophe / Doval, B. 2002. *Glottal Flow Models: Waveforms, Spectra And Physical Measurements*.

Hsia, Chi-Chun / Wu, Chung-Hsien / Wu, Jian-Qi 2007. Conversion function clustering and selection for expressive voice conversion, *ICASSP*, Hawaï.

Lacheret-Dujour, Anne / Beaugendre, Frédéric 1999. *La prosodie du Français*, Paris : CNRS langage.

LeDoux, Joseph 2005. *Le Cerveau des émotions,* Paris : Lavoisier.

Lindblom, Bjorn 1983. Economy of Speech Gestures, In *The Production of Speech*, New York: Spinger-Verlag.

Peeters, Geoffroy 2004. A large set of audio features for sound description (similarity and classification) in the CUIDADO project, *Technical report IRCAM.*

Pereira, Cecile / Watson, Catherine 1998. Some acoustic characteristics of emotion, *Fifth International Conference on Spoken Language Processing*, Sydney.

Pfitzinger, Helmut 2006. Five Dimensions of Prosody: Intensity, Intonation, Timing, Voice Quality, and Degree of Reduction, In H. Hoffmann, R.; Mixdorff (eds), *Speech Prosody*, Dresden, 40/6-9.

Piu, Marie / Bove, Rémi 2007. Annotation des disfluences dans les corpus oraux, *RECITAL.*

Scherer, Klaus R. 2006. The Affective and Pragmatic Coding of Prosody, In *Chinese Spoken Language Processing*, 4274/13-14.

Schwarz, Diemo 2004. Data-Driven Concatenative Sound Synthesis, *PhD thesis Université Paris 6.*

Tao, Jianhua / Kang, Yongguo / Li, Aijun 2006. Prosody conversion from neutral speech to emotional speech, *IEEE Transactions on Audio, Speech, and Language Processing*, 14/4/1145-1154.

Vidrascu, Laurence / Devillers, Laurence 2005. Detection of Real-Life Emotions in Call Centers, *Interspeech.*

Vincent, Damien / Rosec, Olivier / Chonavel, Thierry 2005. Estimation of LF glottal source parameters based on an ARX model, *Interspeech.*

Yamagishi, Junichi / Onishi, Koji / Masuko, Takashi / Kobayashi, Takao 2005. Acoustic modelling of speaking styles and emotional expressions in HMM-based speech synthesis, *IEICE Trans. on Inf. & Syst.*, E88-D/503-509.

BJÖRN SCHULLER / MARTIN WÖLLMER / FLORIAN EYBEN /
GERHARD RIGOLL

Prosodic, Spectral or Voice Quality? Feature Type Relevance for the Discrimination of Emotion Pairs[1]

As for every automatic pattern recognition task, the performance of emotion recognition is strongly dependent on the suitability of the used features. Therefore, determining optimal features provides the basis for reliable emotion classification. Prosodic features such as energy or pitch are widely used for emotion recognition since they are highly correlated to emotion. Together with voice quality, spectral features, and statistic functionals, they are extracted to form high dimensional feature vectors which often contain redundant information. Consequently, it is necessary to select the features which best reflect emotion. However, the question which features to use for what emotion or speaker group has not been answered so far. To get an insight into the relevance of specific feature types for different emotion discrimination tasks, three different databases of English emotional speech, which contain different types of emotion, were used for recognition experiments in this chapter: the 'Big Six' emotions as named by Ekman (1972), different stress-levels, and different interest-levels. A large set of 1,406 acoustic features was used. The features were grouped into three different categories: prosodic, spectral, and voice quality features. The performance of an emotion recogniser using exclusively certain feature groups or types (such as duration, energy, pitch, formants, cepstral coefficients, jitter, shimmer, or harmonics-to-noise ratio) was evaluated with and without subsequent

1 The research leading to these results has received funding from the European Community's Seventh Framework Programme (FP7/2007-2013) under grant agreement No. 211486 (SEMAINE).

automatic feature selection. Thereby 24 different combinations of emotion pairs were considered and experiments were conducted speaker-independently. The overall goal was to answer the question which features best signal which emotion type. Further, redundancy would be reduced in order to operate in a lower dimensional feature space and save computational power while simultaneously improving recognition performance.

1. Introduction

Opposing related speech recognition tasks, the predominant question of optimal features is still an open issue for recognition of affect (McGilloway *et al.* (2000: 207-212), Cowie *et al.* (2001: 32-80), Pantic/Rothkrantz (2003: 1370-1390), Schuller *et al.* (2007b: 2253-2256)). It is well known that prosodic features based on speech rate, loudness, and pitch, as well as voice quality or articulatory information are highly correlated to emotion. Yet, it is not fully researched and determined which attributes best signal affect in general (Batliner *et al.* (2006: 240-245), Schuller *et al.* (2007b: 2253-2256)), let alone specific emotions, or speaker groups. In order to provide additional research and input to answer this yet unsolved issue, effects of features on emotion recognition performance have been investigated on multiple databases of English emotional speech.

Three sets were chosen to overcome singular effects arising from typical use of single sets. The sets covered a broad variety of emotions and situations reaching from elicited 'Big Six' emotions as named by Ekman (by the eNTERFACE set) to real-life stress-levels (by the SUSAS set), and to levels of interest (by the AVIC set) in spontaneous human conversational speech. Conditions throughout experiments were kept constant by the use of one systematically and fully automatically extracted large feature set. As a starting point, 37 acoustic Low-Level-Descriptors, which are well known to carry information about paralinguistic effects, were chosen. Following the typical static classification strategy, 19 statistical functionals were employed for each Low-Level-Descriptor. Hence, the obtained multivariate time series of variable length was projected onto a single 1,406 dimensional feature vector as used among others in Batliner *et al.* (2008: 4497-4500), Schuller *et al.* (2008), and Vlasenko *et al.* (2007: 139-147). The functionals included the first four statistical moments, quartiles, extremes, ranges, positions, and zero-crossings. The obtained features were grouped into the following types: prosodic (duration, energy, and pitch), spectral (formants and cepstral), and voice quality (jitter, shimmer, and harmonics-to-noise ratio). The results were reported for the performance of each feature group individually, with respect to the aforementioned specific emotion pairs. The relevance of single features was revealed by additional employment of popular closed-loop floating search, and correlation analysis. To cope with current challenges and prepare for the future generation of emotion recognition, all experiments have been carried out speaker-independently.

The knowledge obtained can be used to design recognition engines more efficiently due to lower extraction effort and compact feature space representation. Additionally, sets tailored for emotion pairs can boost recognition performance by layer-wise optimised two-class decisions as in Support-Vector-Tree construction or Boosting.

The rest of this chapter is structured as follows: first, the emotional speech corpora are introduced in Section 2, following the acoustic features and their grouping in Section 3. In Section 4 the classification and selection of features is explained in detail and in Section 5 experimental findings with respect to feature type relevance are presented. A final conclusion is drawn in Section 6.

2. Emotional speech corpora

In this section, the three databases used for the investigation of feature type relevance with respect to the discrimination of emotion pairs are introduced. All speech samples in the databases are spoken in English.

The sets contain Ekman's six basic emotions, stress levels, and interest in spoken language. They were chosen to cover a broad range of emotions and user states. Additionally, weight has been laid on spontaneous emotions, which is in particular true for two of the three databases. Finally, large and popular sets were preferred.

2.1. Basic Emotions – The eNTERFACE Corpus

The eNTERFACE corpus is a public audio-visual emotion database introduced by Martin *et al.* (2000: 207-212). Emotions covered are Ekman's basic emotions (1972: 207-283), often referred to as the 'Big Six' and standardised in MPEG-4. 44 subjects from 14 nations are contained in the database. It consists of studio recordings of pre-defined spoken content whereas each subject was instructed to listen to six successive short stories, each of them eliciting a particular emotion. Further, they had to react to each of the situations and two experts judged whether the reaction expressed the emotion in an unambiguous way. Only then was the sample added to the database. The audio sample rate is 48 kHz; the bit depth is 16 bit. Overall, the database consists of 1,170 samples distributed among emotions as shown in Table 1.

Anger	*Disgust*	*Fear*	*Joy*	*Sadness*	*Surprise*	*Sum*
200	189	189	205	195	192	1170

Table 1. Distribution of speaker-turns among emotions in the eNTERFACE database.

2.2. Stress – The SUSAS Corpus

Next, the Speech Under Simulated and Actual Stress (SUSAS) audio database by Hansen *et al.* (1997: 1743-1746) was considered for the experiments presented here. These are spontaneous recordings in field noise. Herein, the 3,593 stress speech samples were used as shown in Table 2. These were recorded in fear and stress tasks in a helicopter and rollercoaster environment. Seven speakers, three of them female, in free fall stress situations are contained. Two different stress conditions were collected: medium and high stress. Further samples cover neutrality, fear, and screaming as classes. However, neutrality is too sparsely represented to be included. The SUSAS samples are constrained to a 35 words vocabulary of short aircraft communication commands. All files are sampled in 8 kHz at 16 bit. The recordings are partly overlaid with heavy noise and background over-talk. This resembles realistic acoustic recording conditions as given in many application scenarios.

High Stress	*Med. Stress*	*Neutrality*	*Fear*	*Sum*
1202	1276	701	414	3593

Table 2. Distribution of speaker-turns among emotions in the SUSAS database.

2.3. Interest – The AVIC Corpus

Finally, the evaluation of feature type relevance is provided on the Audiovisual Interest Corpus (AVIC) covering interest types as further classes (Schuller *et al.* (2007a: 3037-3041)). In the recording scenario setup an experimenter and a subject were sitting on opposite sides of a desk. The experimenter played the role of a product presenter and led the subject through a commercial presentation. The subject's role was to listen to explanations and topic presentations of the experimenter, ask several questions of her/his interest, and to actively interact with the experimenter considering his/her interest to the addressed topics without respect to politeness. Voice data was recorded using two microphones, one headset – used in the experiments presented here – and one far-field microphone. The audio was sampled at 44.1 kHz with 16 bit. 21 subjects (ten of them female) were contained, three of them Asian, the others European. The language throughout the recordings was English as in the other two databases, and all subjects were very experienced English speakers. Three age categories were defined for balancing: younger than 30 years, younger than 40 years, and older than 40 years. The average age of male subjects was 32.7 years; the average age of female subjects was 30.1 years. The total recording time for males was 5:14:30 h, for female 5:08:00 h. In order to acquire reliable labels for the level of interest, the entire video material was segmented into speaker and sub-speaker turns and subsequently labelled independently by four male annotators. The level of interest was annotated for every sub-speaker turn.

Five Levels of Interest were distinguished in the first place: *disinterest* (the subject is bored, listening and talking about the topic, is very passive, and does not follow the discourse), *indifference* (the subject is passive, does not give much feedback to the product presenter's explanations, and asks unmotivated questions, if any), *neutrality* (the subject follows and participates in the discourse; it cannot be determined, if she/he is interested or indifferent in the topic), *interest* (the subject wants to discuss the topic, closely follows the explanations, and asks some questions), *curiosity* (strong wish of the subject to talk and learn more about the topic). However, due to sparse occurrences, disinterest and indifference instances were combined with neutrality ones. Table 3 shows the distribution of sub-speaker-turns used for the results presented here. For details on original audiovisual class distribution, annotation and fusion of these levels of interest to a master level of interest, the reader is referred to Schuller *et al.* (2007a: 3037-3041).

Neutrality	*Interest*	*Curiosity*	*Sum*
316	510	170	996

Table 3. Distribution of speaker-turns among levels of interest in the AVIC database.

3. Acoustic features

A strictly systematic generation of features was used for the construction of a large feature space as a starting point for the subsequent selection of relevant features. Such an approach generally leads to more than 1,000 features (Vogt/Andre (2005: 474-477), Batliner *et al.* (2006: 240-245)). The basis is a set of 37 typical acoustic Low-Level-

Descriptors that are known to carry information about paralinguistic effects (Batliner *et al.* (2006: 240-245), Schuller *et al.* (2007b: 2253-2256)). These descriptors are shown in Table 4. The features are split into the six commonly used types: duration (DUR), energy (NRG), pitch (F_0), formants (FX), cepstral (CEP), and voice quality (VQ). The latter is covered by jitter and shimmer (J+S), and Harmonics-to-Noise Ratio (HNR), resulting in a total of seven feature types that are investigated here. These seven types can be further grouped into three meta-groups: prosodic features, spectral features and voice quality features. The following listing provides a detailed overview regarding these three groups and explains each of the seven feature types briefly:

Prosodic features:

- *Duration (DUR):* these features model temporal aspects. Normally the basic unit is milliseconds for the 'raw' values. Thereby different types of normalisation techniques are used. The relative positions on the time axis of features like energy or pitch (maxima, on-/off-set positions, etc.) also represent duration rather than energy and pitch as such, since they are measured in milliseconds and were proven to be highly correlated with duration features in Batliner *et al.* (2001: 2781-2784). Therefore, the duration features can be distinguished regarding their extraction nature: features representing temporal properties of other acoustic base contours, and those that exclusively represent the duration of high level linguistic units such as phonemes, words, pauses, or utterances.
- *Energy (NRG):* these features model intensity, based on the amplitude, with implicit or explicit normalisation. They can model intervals or characteristic points. Since the sensation of loudness increases logarithmically as the intensity of a stimulus grows, the decibel scale is used for energy measures. The spectral distribution and the duration of a stimulus also influence loudness perception (Zwicker/Fastl 1990). A sequence of short-term loudness values, which are extracted framewisely, is called a loudness contour.

- *Pitch (F_0):* this is the acoustic equivalent to the perceptual unit pitch. It is measured in Hertz (Hz) and is often transformed to a perceptually more adequate representation, e.g. by mapping onto semi-tone intervals. Pitch is detected by applying a frame-based time or spectral analysis. After dividing the speech sequence into overlapping frames, the autocorrelation method, as used herein, or spectral analysis can be applied to derive the pitch value for each frame.

Spectral features:

- *Formants (FX):* formants (i.e. spectral maxima) are known to model spoken content. This is especially true for lower order formants. Higher order formants, however, also represent speaker characteristics. Each formant is fully represented by its centre frequency, amplitude, and bandwidth. Their spectral position thereby is independent of the perceived fundamental frequency. Methods like Linear Prediction Coding (Boersma (1993: 97-110)), as used here, or cepstral analysis can be applied to estimate formant frequencies and bandwidths.
- *Cepstral (CEP):* Mel-Frequency-Cepstral-Coefficient (MFCC) features – homomorphically transformed with equidistant band-pass-filters on the Mel-frequency-scale – tend to strongly correlate with the spoken content. Yet, they have proven beneficial in practically any speech processing task. The Mel-Frequency-Cepstral-Coefficients are calculated from the logarithm of Mel-filter bank amplitudes using the discrete cosine transform.

Voice Quality features:

- *Harmonics-to-Noise Ratio (HNR):* the harmonics-to-noise ratio is a measure of the quality of the speech signal. It is estimated from voiced parts of speech and can be calculated as the ratio between the signal power in periodic parts and the signal power of the noise components. For the experiments reported here, autocorrelation was used for this calculation.
- *Jitter and Shimmer (J+S):* jitter and shimmer are micro-perturbations based on pitch and intensity reflecting voice quality.

In order to calculate Low-Level-Descriptors for the following analyses of features signalling emotion, the speech signal was transformed to 16 kHz sampling rate and 16 bit precision in the first step. In general, a Hamming window function was used, except for the calculation of pitch and Harmonics-to-Noise Ratio, where a Hanning window was chosen. Frames were sampled at a rate of 100 Hz with 50% overlap. Thus, the effective frame length is 20 milliseconds. Energy resembles logarithmic frame energy. Pitch and Harmonics-to-Noise Ratio calculation bases on a time-signal autocorrelation with window correction. Formant calculation uses 18-point Linear Prediction Coding with root-solving and a pre-emphasis factor of 0.7. The pitch and formant trajectories were globally optimised by the use of Dynamic Programming. The Low-Level-Descriptors were smoothed by techniques such as semi-tone-interval filters or simple moving average low-pass filtering to eliminate outliers. As a next step delta (i.e. differential over time) coefficients for each Low-Level-Descriptor were added to the feature set.

Low-Level-Descriptors (2x37)	*Functionals (19)*
Pitch	Mean
Energy	Standard Deviation
Envelope	Zero-Crossing-Rate
Formant 1-5 Amplitude	Quartile 1
Formant 1-5 Bandwidth	Quartile 2
Formant 1-5 Frequency	Quartile 3
MFCC Coefficient 1-16	Quartile 1 - Minimum
Harmonics-to-Noise-Ratio	Quartile 2 - Quartile 1
Shimmer	Quartile 3 - Quartile 2
Jitter	Maximum - Quartile 3
Δ Pitch	Centroid
Δ Energy	Skewness
Δ Envelope	Kurtosis
Δ Formant 1-5 Amplitude	Maximum Value
Δ Formant 1-5 Bandwidth	Relative Maximum Position
Δ Formant 1-5 Frequency	Minimum Value
Δ MFCC Coefficient 1-16	Relative Minimum Position
Δ Harmonics-to-Noise-Ratio	Maximum Minimum Range
Δ Shimmer	Position of 95% Roll-Off-Point
Δ Jitter	

Table 4. Low-Level-Descriptors and Functionals considered for emotion pair discrimination.

Next, the typical static classification strategy commonly used in emotion recognition, e.g. by Batliner *et al.* (2006: 240-245), was employed: a total of 19 statistical functionals was applied to each of the 2x37 Low-Level-Descriptors. Thus, the obtained multivariate time series of variable length was projected onto a single 1,406 dimensional feature vector. A typical selection of common functionals covering the first four statistical moments, quartiles, extremes, ranges, positions, and zero-crossings, was chosen, as depicted in Table 4. The three position related functionals lead to a sub-group of features with the physical unit of milliseconds which were treated as duration features, though being based on a number of diverse Low-Level-Descriptors as described above. Further, duration related features such as those based on e.g. lengths of pauses or syllables were not included because this information cannot be easily integrated in the strictly systematic generation approach (they are modelled in a general value series rather than in a time series).

Table 5 shows the obtained distribution of features among the introduced types. As can be seen, considerably more spectral than prosodic features were extracted. The fewest features were extracted for voice quality. However, this reflects the standard situation (Batliner *et al.* (2006: 240-245)): cepstral coefficients and formants result in a higher number of Low-Level-Descriptors as compared to pitch and energy, for example.

Group	*DUR*	*NRG*	F_0	*FX*	*CEP*	*HNR*	*J+S*
Features [#]	222	64	32	480	512	32	64
Relative [%]	15.8	4.6	2.3	34.1	36.4	2.3	4.6
Type	*Prosodic*			*Spectral*		*Voice Quality*	
Features [#]	318			992		96	
Relative [%]	22.6			70.6		6.8	

Table 5. Distribution of frequency of acoustic features among types. DUR: duration, NRG: energy, F_0: pitch, FX: formants, CEP: cepstral, HNR: Harmonics-to-Noise Ratio, J+S: jitter and shimmer.

The next section deals with the technique used to automatically find relevant features to distinguish affect/emotion pairs. The results, i.e. the features found to be most relevant, are discussed in Section 5.

4. Classification and feature selection

In order to automatically recognise affect using acoustic features, advanced classification algorithms are required. The classification method used in this chapter is called Support-Vector-Machines (SVM). The model for the Support-Vector-Machines is built using a Sequential Minimal Optimisation (SMO) Algorithm (Witten, 2005). The Support-Vector-Machine classifier is a binary classifier, i.e. only two classes can be separated with one model. However, as can be seen in Section 2, usually more than two classes are required for recognition of emotion/affect. For multi-class problems a technique called Round Robin, i.e. one-against-one, classification is used (Fürnkranz (2002: 721-747)). If n is the total number of classes there are $n(n-1)/2$ class pairs. For each pair a model is built that is able to distinguish only between these two classes. This classification technique was used for the work described herein.

Classification and modelling techniques are only the second part of the two essential parts of machine learning. The first part is the selection of appropriate features. "Appropriate" in this context refers to being highly predictive, i.e. attributes that are highly correlated with the classes that are to be separated. For emotion recognition based on large sets of acoustic features the attribute selection, besides improving classifier performance, also serves the purpose of reducing the number of required features, which results in faster processing. The selected attributes are furthermore of interest in paralinguistic and prosodic studies since they are clues as to how affect and emotion is encoded in spoken language. Given a set of more than a thousand statistical features computed from the acoustic Low-Level-Descriptors as introduced in Section 3, feature selection is not straight forward; preferably, automatic feature selection methods are used (Schuller *et al.* (2005: 805-809)).

Generally, a target function is required as optimisation criterion for reduction of the feature space, meaning the reduction of the dimensionality of the feature vector (the number of features). An attribute evaluator based on Correlation-based Feature Subset Selection was used (Witten 2005).

Correlation-based Feature Subset Selection evaluates the worth of a subset of attributes by considering the individual predictive ability of each feature along with the degree of redundancy between them. Subsets of features that are highly correlated with the class while having low inter-correlation are preferred. Since the feature set is very large, not all possible combinations of feature subsets can be evaluated in a reasonable amount of time. Therefore – as also stated in other works on speech emotion recognition (Ververidis/Kotropoulos (2005: 1500-1503), (2006: 1162-1181)) – an exhaustive search is not an efficient and applicable option. Instead, a Sequential Forward Floating Search (SFFS) (Pudil *et al.* (1994: 1119-1125)) – the most commonly used search function in this field (Lee/Narayanan (2005: 293–303), Ververidis/Kotropoulos (2005: 1500-1503), Vogt/Andre (2005: 474-477)), Schuller *et al.* (2005: 805-809)) which is also highly competitive in general feature selection (Zongker (1997: 18-22)) – was applied. This approach refers to the space of feature subsets being processed by greedy hill climbing augmented with a backtracking facility. Setting the number of consecutive non-improving nodes allows for control of the level of backtracking being done. Generally, Sequential Forward Floating Search may start with the empty set of features and search forward (known as best first), start with the full set of features and search backward, or start at any point and search in both directions (by considering all possible single attribute additions and deletions at a given point). Here, the forward search direction was chosen since a small number of final features were expected in order to keep the complexity low and increase the processing speed.

Since Correlation-based Feature Subset Selection is an automatic and unsupervised feature selection method based on statistical properties of the data, the resulting feature sets are potentially not the general best set for every possible classifier or the overall most representative sets of attributes that encode affect in speech communication. To evaluate which feature types are essential for detecting specific affective states or emotions, binary classification test-runs were conducted for every possible class pair in each database using only one of the seven feature type sets described in Section 3. These test-runs were performed using a) the full (not reduced) set of 1,406 features and b) a set reduced by Correlation-based Feature Subset Selection. Both sets were split into subsets containing one of the seven feature types.

The evaluations of the test-runs were performed in a Leave-One-Speaker-Out speaker independent cross validation. 'Speaker independent' implies that the speaker of the classified utterances is not included in the training data set. She is unknown to the classifier and the deduced learning rules (Lugger/Yang (2007: 2149-2152)), which is important for realistic use-cases (Schuller *et al.* (2007c: 941-944)). The results are reported in form of mean accuracy (RR), non-weighted mean recall (CL) and the harmonic mean F of mean accuracy and mean recall as given by equation 1.

$$F = \frac{2RR \cdot CL}{RR + CL}$$

Equation 1. Harmonic mean F.

These three different measures are necessary in case the number of instances per class is not distributed equally among the classes, as is usually the case for emotional speech corpora (see Section 2). Results for classes with fewer instances tend to be below the actual achievable result for that class. This is due to insufficient amount of training data and low a-priori probability for the class. Likewise, the classes with more instances have a higher a-priori probability and a more robustly estimated model due to the higher amount of available training data. The recognition performance for such a class is usually over-estimated. Classes with many instances have a substantial influence on the RR measure, whereas smaller classes have very little influence. Thus, the RR measure tends to over-estimate performance when the instance numbers of the classes are very unbalanced. In the same way, not weighting the mean recall rate with the number of instances in each class increases the influence of classes with very few instances, thus under-estimating overall performance. Therefore, the F-measure is commonly used to give an estimate of a balanced result even if the size of the classes is not balanced (Batliner *et al.* (2006: 240-245), Schuller *et al.* (2007c: 941-944)).

5. Feature type relevance

This section presents the results for the experiments described in the previous section. As mentioned in the last section, Leave-One-Speaker-Out evaluation is used for subject independent testing. Mean results over all subjects are provided. In Table 6 the relevance of the non-reduced feature types (i.e. using all 1,406 features split into the seven types) for all possible emotion pairs can be seen. In addition to the performance measures RR and CL, the F-measure is given as described in Section 4. Further, emotion pairs are listed in Table 6 for the three cases 'Big Six', stress, and interest levels, covered by the databases eNTERFACE, SUSAS, and AVIC. The part on the right of the Table 6 shows the absolute difference between the mean F-measure and the F-measure for each Low-Level-Descriptor type, which is referred to as ƒF here.

For 11 out of 24 possible emotion pairs, the best performance can be obtained when using formant features (FX). Cepstral features (CEP) outperformed all other Low-Level-Descriptor types in 12 cases. Only in one case (emotion pair fear/surprise, eNTERFACE database) did the usage of pitch features (F_0) yield the best results. Considering the emotion pairs of the eNTERFACE database, the performance gain with respect to the mean F-value varied between 1.7% and 12.4% when using formant features as Low-Level-Descriptors, and between 0.9% and 12.8% when using cepstral features. When classifying the emotion pairs of the SUSAS database, cepstral features outperformed formant Low-Level-Descriptors for all emotion pairs. Contrariwise formant Low-Level-Descriptors prevailed for interest-related affect in the AVIC database.

Consequently, in 23 out of 24 cases the best emotion recognition performance could be obtained with spectral features alone. Averaged over all emotion pairs, the F-measure for all prosodic and voice quality Low-Level-Descriptors was lower than the mean F-measure (negative mean ƒF), while the mean ƒF was 6.9% for formant features and 7.1% for cepstral features respectively.

[%]	*RR*	*CL*	*F*	*ƒF*						
	Mean			*DUR*	*NRG*	F_0	*FX*	*CEP*	*HNR*	*J+S*
anger/disgust	73.4	71.2	72.1	0.8	-3.0	-5.5	**8.1**	7.6	-3.0	-5.0
anger/fear	72.4	71.7	72.1	0.1	2.3	-3.0	**8.0**	6.8	-6.0	-8.2
anger/happiness	75.1	71.0	74.8	-3.3	0.6	-2.2	**7.5**	5.3	-3.7	-4.2
anger/sadness	76.4	69.3	76.0	-6.6	-2.1	0.9	10.5	**12.8**	-7.7	-7.7
anger/surprise	74.8	73.2	73.8	0.5	2.5	-6.9	8.9	**9.7**	-9.7	-5.0
disgust/fear	66.4	63.2	66.0	-2.4	-2.9	6.4	**6.8**	0.9	-0.6	-8.2
disgust/happiness	62.2	59.7	61.4	-1.0	1.4	-1.1	3.1	**3.5**	-2.1	-3.8
disgust/sadness	69.4	61.1	68.3	-5.8	-1.6	4.3	5.6	**12.2**	-7.3	-7.4
disgust/surprise	65.6	62.2	64.7	-0.6	-7.1	-0.4	6.0	**10.6**	-4.3	-4.3
fear/happiness	69.3	67.1	69.3	-2.7	-0.3	1.4	**7.0**	6.0	-3.1	-8.5
fear/sadness	66.0	65.1	65.0	1.0	-1.7	2.0	**10.3**	4.6	-5.1	-11.1
fear/surprise	63.7	64.2	63.4	1.4	-8.0	**6.3**	1.7	5.1	-1.7	-4.9
happiness/sadness	72.5	67.6	71.6	-3.6	0.7	3.5	**12.4**	8.1	-12.0	-9.1
happiness/surprise	65.8	64.4	65.5	-0.7	-2.1	-1.7	6.3	**8.2**	-7.8	-2.3
sadness/surprise	70.1	69.5	68.8	2.3	-5.1	5.1	**9.5**	4.9	-9.2	-7.4
high stress/med.	58.3	57.0	58.3	-1.4	2.0	0.1	-0.7	**3.5**	-4.0	0.7
high stress/neutral	59.7	53.4	56.5	-0.7	-1.0	-4.0	-2.5	**8.3**	-0.6	0.1
high stress/fear	89.3	80.1	86.0	-3.1	5.5	-4.5	11.1	**11.4**	-18.3	-3.0
med.stress/neutral	61.5	56.0	56.9	2.3	1.0	-0.4	-0.3	**4.5**	-8.1	-0.2
med.stress/fear	90.6	82.9	87.4	-1.9	6.0	-4.9	10.7	**11.1**	-14.1	-7.5
neutral/fear	87.8	82.3	87.0	-3.8	4.7	-2.5	10.7	**11.5**	-13.8	-6.9
neutral/interest	74.5	75.2	73.4	1.9	3.1	-1.2	**2.4**	1.2	-3.0	-3.5
neutral/curiosity	75.2	73.2	74.1	-0.2	1.5	-4.2	**14.6**	10.7	-13.3	-9.4
interest/curiosity	73.9	60.0	64.5	0.9	-1.4	-2.9	**8.4**	2.5	-4.5	-4.7
mean	71.4	67.5	69.9	-1.1	-0.2	-0.6	6.9	**7.1**	-6.8	-5.5

Table 6. Relevance of non-reduced Low-Level-Descriptor types for all emotion pairs by mean accuracy (RR), non-weighted recall (CL) and harmonic mean of these two (F). Further the absolute difference for each Low-Level-Descriptor type to the mean is provided (ƒF). Databases in order of appearance: eNTERFACE (top), SUSAS (middle), AVIC (bottom). Speaker-independent Leave-One-Speaker-Out evaluation. Support-Vector Machine classification.

Using only voice quality features (HNR and J+S) led to the worst performance (ƒF of -6.8% and -5.5% respectively).

For the emotions in the eNTERFACE database no relation between the emotion pair and whether cepstral or formant features are more relevant could be found. However, an interesting fact can be observed when looking at the ƒF measure of pitch. If sadness or fear is one part of the emotion pair (except for anger/fear), the pitch features performed better than the mean (i.e. ƒF is greater than zero), yet still worse than the spectral features. The latter can be explained because information about pitch can also be interpreted as spectral information. It can be assumed that the spectral features to some extent contain the same information as carried by the pitch features alone, but add more information about higher level harmonics. The fact that for fear and especially sadness pitch performed better than the average may indicate that pitch variations make a person sound uneasy. When a person is described as speaking fearfully or sadly, the term 'trembling voice' is often used to refer to pitch modulations.

[%]	*DUR*	*NRG*	F_0	*FX*	*CEP*	*HNR*	*J+S*	*Pros*	*Spec*	*VQ*
'Big Six'	13.6	3.4	3.4	33.0	45.5	0.0	1.1	20.4	78.5	1.1
Stress	1.2	7.0	5.9	31.8	48.2	0.0	5.9	14.1	80.0	5.9
Interest	4.1	7.3	1.6	37.4	49.6	0.0	0.0	13.0	87.0	0.0

Table 7. Relevance of Low-Level-Descriptor types and groups (Pros: prosodic, Spec: spectral, VQ: voice quality) averaged over all emotion pairs by percentage within the final selected subset after Correlation-based Feature Subset Selection with Sequential Forward Floating Search. Databases in order of appearance: eNTERFACE (top), SUSAS (middle), AVIC (bottom).

The importance of spectral features for affect recognition can also be seen in Table 7, which shows the results of feature selection. Averaged over all emotion pairs, the percentage within the final feature subset after Sequential Forward Floating Search is given for every database as well as for every Low-Level-Descriptor type (on the left) and Low-Level-Descriptor group (on the right). In the case where feature selection was carried out for every Low-Level-Descriptor type, between 45.5% and 49.6% of the remaining features were cepstral Low Level Descriptors. The percentage of remaining formant features varied between 33% and 37.4%, depending on the database. Only a small fraction of the selected features were prosodic or voice quality Low Level Descriptors. The Harmonics-to-Noise Ratio features were found not to be relevant at all for signalling affect, regardless of the database.

[%]	*DUR*	*NRG*	*F_0*	*FX*	*CEP*	*HNR*	*J+S*	*Pros*	*Spec*	*VQ*	*All*
'Big Six'											
without Feature Selection											
RR	68.3	67.6	70.2	77.2	76.6	63.9	62.9	72.8	80.3	65.0	81.9
CL	66.7	66.6	68.7	75.5	75.3	62.7	61.9	70.0	79.0	62.7	80.6
F	67.5	67.1	69.4	76.3	75.9	63.3	62.4	71.4	79.6	63.8	81.2
with Feature Selection											
RR	69.9	68.3	69.3	75.5	76.6	63.1	62.9	76.5	81.4	63.9	83.1
CL	68.7	67.1	68.0	74.1	75.7	61.8	61.9	75.1	80.2	62.8	81.8
F	69.3	67.7	68.6	74.8	76.1	62.4	62.4	75.8	80.8	63.3	82.4
Stress											
without Feature Selection											
RR	72.8	76.8	72.6	77.1	80.8	67.8	73.7	77.1	79.3	74.5	80.2
CL	68.6	73.5	66.5	76.6	80.0	57.7	65.5	75.2	79.0	68.4	80.2
F	70.6	75.1	69.4	76.8	80.4	62.3	69.4	76.1	79.1	71.3	80.2
with Feature Selection											
RR	73.7	77.8	73.5	77.3	82.1	67.4	74.4	78.2	80.5	73.1	80.5
CL	67.2	72.3	66.6	75.6	80.2	55.8	61.4	74.9	79.1	65.1	79.0
F	70.3	74.9	69.9	76.4	81.1	61.1	67.3	76.5	79.8	68.9	79.7
Interest											
without Feature Selection											
RR	74.0	76.1	73.5	80.1	77.0	70.8	71.1	78.2	79.2	70.6	69.5
CL	69.5	68.3	63.7	78.3	74.1	58.7	60.3	75.8	76.5	60.3	69.3
F	71.7	72.0	68.3	79.2	75.5	64.2	65.3	77.0	77.8	65.0	69.4
with Feature Selection											
RR	76.2	76.7	71.0	83.3	81.6	68.8	69.0	78.3	84.2	69.9	74.1
CL	66.4	68.2	58.1	80.1	77.9	56.1	55.9	70.1	81.8	57.1	75.8
F	71.0	72.2	63.9	81.7	79.7	61.8	61.8	74.0	83.0	62.9	74.9

Table 8. Relevance of Low-Level-Descriptor types and groups and accuracies of all features (Pros: prosodic, Spec: spectral, VQ: voice quality) averaged over all emotion pairs by mean accuracy (RR), non-weighted recall (CL) and harmonic mean of these two (F) with and without Feature Selection. Databases in order of appearance: eNTERFACE (top), SUSAS (middle), AVIC (bottom).

Feature selection was also carried out for each Low-Level-Descriptor type. Again, the majority of the selected features were spectral attributes (between 78.4% and 87%). Compared to the recognition of the 'Big Six' emotions of the eNTERFACE database, prosodic features seem to be slightly more relevant for interest-related user states as in the AVIC database. Here, 20.5% of the remaining features were prosodic Low-Level-Descriptors. In this respect the initially different amount of features per group to pick from has to be considered.

Table 8 shows the recognition results for the three emotion sets with and without feature selection. As before, best results could be obtained when using spectral features. Thereby, feature selection carried out with the spectral Low Level Descriptors, slightly improved recognition performance. Using only spectral features resulted in a performance almost as good as obtained when incorporating all features. For the interest-related emotions the usage of spectral features alone even outperformed classification with all features. This demonstrates that non-exhaustive feature selections simply are sub-optimal and can lead to lower performance in rare cases.

6. Conclusion

Aiming to determine features in the speech signal which are optimally suited to represent affect in human speech, several experiments were performed to automatically discriminate between varieties of emotion pairs. In total, 1,406 features were extracted from the audio data taken from three databases (eNTERFACE, SUSAS, AVIC). The experiments proved that spectral features contain the most relevant information about emotion within speech for almost every pair of emotions and independent of the dataset. When using only formant features for emotion recognition, performance was shown to be 6.9% higher compared to the average. Cepstral features performed even 7.1% better than the average feature type. Pitch, as a prosodic Low-Level-Descriptor, prevailed only for the emotion pair fear/surprise where it performed 6.3% better than the average. Considering the different emotion sets, cepstral features were proved to be best suited for the discrimination of stress related emotions whereas formants out-performed all other feature types for emotions expressing interest. Emotion pairs like high stress/medium stress, medium stress/neutral, or fear/surprise were more difficult to classify than pairs such as neutral/fear or anger/sadness.

The importance of spectral features cannot only be seen in recognition performance but also in the outcome of Correlation-based Feature Subset Selection: depending on the database, between 78.4% and 87% of the remaining features were spectral attributes whereas voice quality features were almost completely rejected. Thereby it has to be considered that spectral features also encode linguistic information. This is not of importance in the case of the eNTERFACE and SUSAS sets, where the spoken content is predefined and fixed for different emotions. However, in the case of the AVIC set this may well play a further important factor.

The feature selection could slightly improve recognition results when using only spectral features. Thereby the usage of spectral features performed almost as well as a classifier operating with all feature types – even better for interest related emotions.

All conducted emotion recognition experiments highlight the high importance of spectral features such as formants and cepstral coefficients and prove that most information about emotion within speech can be found directly in the spectrum of the speech signal and in prosodic features – as opposed to many earlier works in which the first type plays only a secondary role (e.g. Ang *et al.* (2002: 2037-2040)). At the same time voice quality-based features were not found to be of high importance, as opposed to e.g. Scherer (1986: 143-165). However, works in favour of voice quality features often derive their findings from listening experiments with acted or synthesised data (cf. Gobl *et al.* (2003: 189-212)). Speaker-independent automatic recognition of affect clearly differs from these settings. Finally, prosodic features clearly helped to improve overall performance, though on their own they were not the best choice. Similar to the voice quality features, their assumed importance often stems from emotional voice synthesis and listening experiments. Thereby these parameters are easier to edit, better understood and intuitive for listeners than the more abstract and complex spectral characteristics.

While future research efforts will have to verify these findings in further corpora, the discussed findings clearly support the trends towards expecting that among other current changes in the field of emotional speech analysis (e.g. Wöllmer *et al.* (2008: 597-600), Schuller *et al.* (2007c: 1500-1503)) a shift in the preferred feature type will be observable.

References

i) books

Witten, Ian H. / Frank, Eibe. 2005: *Data Mining: Practical Machine Learning Tools with Java Implementations*, 2nd edition. San Francisco: Morgan Kaufmann.

Zwicker, Eberhard. / Fastl, Hugo 1990. *Psychoacoustics. Facts and Models.* Series in Information Sciences, Volume 22. Berlin: Springer-Verlag.

ii) articles in books:

Ang, Jeremy / Dhillon, Rajdip / Krupski, Ashley / Shriberg, Elizabeth / Stolcke, Andreas 2002. Prosody-Based Automatic Detection of Annoyance and Frustration in Human-Computer Dialog, In *Proceedings of ICSLP 2002*. Denver, Colorado. 2037-2040.

Batliner, Anton / Steidl, Stefan / Schuller, Björn / Seppi, Dino / Laskowski, Kornel / Vogt, Thurid / Devillers, Laurence / Vidrascu, Laurence / Amir, Noam / Kessous, Loic / Aharonson, Vered 2006. Combining Efforts for Improving Automatic Classification of Emotional User States. In *Proceedings of IS-LTC 2006*. Ljubliana, 240-245.

Batliner, Anton / Schuller, Björn / Schaeffler, Sonja / Steidl, Stefan 2008. Mothers, Adults, Children, Pets – Towards the Acoustics of Intimacy. In *Proeedings of Int. Conf. on Acoustics, Speech, and Signal Processing ICASSP 2008,* Las Vegas, Nevada. Washington: IEEE, 4497-4500.

Boersma, Paul 1993. Accurate Short-Term Analysis of the Fundamental Frequency and the Harmonics-To-Noise Ratio of a Sampled Sound. In *Proceedings of the Institute of Phonetic Sciences*, Volume 17. Amsterdam. 97-110.

Ekman, Paul 1972. Universals and Cultural Differences in Facial Expressions of Emotion. In Cole, J. (eds) *Nebraska Symposium on Motivation 1971, Volume 19.* Lincoln: University of Nebraska Press, 207-283.

Hansen, John H. L. / Bou-Ghazale, Sahar 1997. Getting Started with SUSAS: A Speech Under Simulated and Actual Stress Database. In *Proceedings of EUROSPEECH-97, Volume 4. Rhodes, Greece*. Lisbon: ISCA, 1743-1746.

Lugger, Marco / Yang, Bin 2007. An Incremental Analysis of Different Feature Groups in Speaker Independent Emotion Recognition. In *Proceedings of the 16th International Congress of Phonetic Sciences, Saarbruecken, Germany*. Washington: IEEE, 2149-2152.

Martin, Olivier / Kotsia, Ioannis / Macq, Benoît / Pitas, Ioannis 2006. The Enterface'05 Audio-Visual Emotion Database. In *Proceedings of the IEEE Workshop on Multimedia Database Management, Atlanta*. Washington: IEEE. 207-212.

McGilloway, Sinéad / Cowie, Roddy / Douglas-Cowie, Ellen / Gielen, Stan / Westerdijk, Machiel / Stroeve, Sybert 2000. Approaching Automatic Recognition of Emotion from Voice: a Rough Benchmark. In *Proceedings of the ISCA Workshop on Speech and Emotion*. Lisbon: ISCA, 207-212.

Schuller, Björn / Müller, Ronald / Lang, Manfred / Rigoll, Gerhard 2005. Speaker Independent Emotion Recognition by Early Fusion of Acoustic and Linguistic Features within Ensembles. In *Proceedings of the 9th Eurospeech – 6th Interspeech 2005.* Lisbon: ISCA, 805-809.

Schuller, Björn / Müller, Ronald / Hörnler, Benedikt / Höthker, Anja / Konosu, Hitoshi / Rigoll, Gerhard 2007a: Audiovisual recognition of Spontaneous Interest within Conversations. In *Proceedings of the 9th Int. Conference on Multimodal Interfaces (ICMI)*, Special Session on Multimodal Analysis of Human Spontaneous Behaviour. Nagoya, Japan: ACM SIGCHI. 3037-3041.

Schuller, Björn / Batliner, Anton / Seppi, Dino / Steidl, Stefan / Vogt, Thurid / Wagner, Johannes / Devillers, Laurence / Vidrascu, Laurence / Amir, Noam / Kessous, Loic / Aharonson, Vered 2007b. The Relevance of Feature Type for the Automatic Classification of Emotional User States: Low Level Descriptors and Functionals. In *Proceedings 8th Interspeech 2007, Antwerp*. Lisbon: ISCA, 2253-2256.

Schuller, Björn / Seppi, Dino / Batliner, Anton / Maier, Andreas / Steidl, Stefan 2007c. Towards More Reality in the Recognition of Emotional Speech. In *Proceedings of ICASSP 2007, Honolulu, Hawaii*. Washington: IEEE. 941-944.

Schuller, Björn / Rigoll, Gerhard / Can, Salman / Feussner, Hubertus 2008. Emotion Sensitive Speech Control for Human-Robot Interaction in Minimal Invasive Surgery. In *Proceedings 17th Intern. Symposium on Robot and Human Interactive Communication RO-MAN 2008, Munich.* Washington: IEEE, 453–458.

Ververidis, Dimitrios / Kotropoulos, Constantine 2005. Emotional Speech Classification Using Gaussian Mixture Models and the Sequential Floating Forward Selection Algorithm. In *Proceedings of ICME 2005, Amsterdam.* Washington: IEEE, 1500-1503.

Vlasenko, Bogdan / Schuller, Björn / Wendemuth, Andreas / Rigoll, Gerhard 2007. Frame vs. Turn-Level: Emotion Recognition from Speech Considering Static and Dynamic Processing. In *Proceedings 2nd Int. Conf. on Affective Computing and Intelligent Interaction ACII 2007, Lisbon, Portugal*, volume LNCS 4738. Berlin/Heidelberg: Springer. 139-147.

Vogt, Thurid / Andre, Elisabeth 2005. Comparing Feature Sets for Acted and Spontaneous Speech in View of Automatic Emotion Recognition. In *Proceedings of ICME 2005*, Amsterdam. Washington: IEEE, 474–477.

Wöllmer, Martin / Eyben, Florian / Reiter, Stephan / Schuller, Björn / Cox, Cate / Douglas-Cowie, Ellen / Cowie, Roddy 2008. Abandoning Emotion Classes – Towards Continuous Emotion Recognition with Modelling of Long-Range Dependencies. In *Proceedings 9th Interspeech 2008, Brisbane*. Lisbon: ISCA. 597–600.

Zongker, Douglas / Jain, Anil 1996. Algorithms for Feature Selection: An Evaluation. In *Proceedings of the International Conference on Pattern Recognition* (ICPR 96)*, Vienna, Austria*. Washington: IEEE, 18-22.

iii) articles in journals:

Cowie, Roddy / Douglas-Cowie, Ellen / Tsapatsoulis, Nicolas / Votsis, George / Kollias, Stefanos / Fellenz, Winfried / Taylor, John G. 2001. Emotion Recognition in Human-Computer Interaction. *IEEE Signal Processing magazine* 18/1. 32-80.

Fürnkranz, Johannes 2002. Round Robin Classification. *Journal of Machine Learning Research* 2. 721-747.

Gobl, Christer / Ní Chasaide, Ailbhe 2003. The Role of Voice Quality in Communicating Emotion, Mood and Attitude. *Speech Communication* 40, 189-212.

Lee, Chul Min / Narayanan, Shrikanth 2005. Toward Detecting Emotions in Spoken Dialogs. *IEEE Transactions on Speech and Audio Processing* 13(2), 293-303.

Pantic, Maja / Rothkrantz, Leon J. M. 2003. Toward an Affect-Sensitive Multimodal Human-Computer Interaction, *Proceedings of the IEEE* 91, 1370-1390.

Scherer, Klaus R. 1986. Vocal Affect Expression: a Review and a Model for Future Research. *Psychological Bulletin* 99, 143-165.

Ververidis, Dimitrios / Kotropoulos, Constantine 2006. Emotional Speech Recognition: Resources, Features, and Methods. *Speech Communication* 48/9, 1162-1181.

CARLOS BUSSO / MURTAZA BULUT / SUNGBOK LEE / SHRIKANTH NARAYANAN

Fundamental Frequency Analysis for Speech Emotion Processing

Let's not forget that the little emotions are the great captains of our lives and we obey them without realizing it. (Vincent Van Gogh 1889)

1. Introduction

Experiencing and expressing emotions are the fundamental characteristics of human beings. Conveyed through different modalities, such as speech, facial expressions, and body language, emotions play a crucial role in decision making, action taking, and interactions for the self and for the others. Identifying and characterizing various emotions continue to be a challenging research topic for many disciplines, including but not limited to psychology, sociology, philosophy and engineering (Cowie/Cornelius 2003; Ekman *et al.* 1987; Izard 1977; Picard 1997; Scherer 2003).

Recent findings suggest that rational and intelligent communication between humans is closely related to emotions. Therefore, it is essential that emotions be integrated into human-machine interface (HCI) designs so that they will be more in tune with the users' emotional state and attitudes. Fortunately, recent advances in technologies such as speech recognition and computer vision are making HCIs that accommodate natural human communication modalities increasingly possible. As a result, it has added one more reason to study and model how emotions modulate and enhance the verbal and non-verbal channels of human communication.

Representation of emotions in speech in terms of measurable signal properties has been a central theme in the literature. It has been found that speech prosody is one of the most important communicative aspects that is susceptible to emotional modulation. The intonation, tone, timing, and energy of speech are jointly modified in non-trivial manner to add emotion to the spoken utterance. Now it is well established that emotion expression can be associated with changes in prosodic and spectral characteristics of speech signals. The focus has been mainly on the statistical evaluation of pitch, duration and energy with significant emphasis on the F_0. These parameters are usually treated to be independent of each other and their relation to the emotional content of speech is described using terms showing the directional change (i.e., increase or decrease) in their value. Some of the previous research results are summarized in Table 1, which is adapted from Cowie *et al.* (2001).

The focus of this chapter is to study the effect of emotions on fundamental frequency (F_0) characteristics, as well as the effect of F_0 changes on emotion perception. Specifically, it presents results of a detailed analysis on the F_0 contour properties for understanding the emotion dependent pitch modulation observed in expressive speech. The purpose is to identify how F_0 characteristics are manipulated in expressive natural speech and to show how they can be used in the implementation of emotion recognition and synthesis systems. The results present a useful reference for the design of human-machine interaction interfaces that better incorporate expressive content. The content of this chapter is based on work drawn from our previous studies, especially those reported in Bulut and Narayanan (2008), and Busso *et al.* (2008).

	Anger	Happiness	Sadness
Pitch Statistics	Higher in mean, median, range and variability	Higher in mean, median, range and variability	Lower in mean and range
Pitch Changes	Abrupt on stressed	Smooth, upward inflections	Downward inflections
Pitch Contour	Angular frequency curve, stressed syllables ascend frequently and rhythmically, irregular up and down inflection, level average pitch except for jumps of about a musical fourth or fifth on stressed syllables	Descending line, melody ascending frequently and at irregular intervals	Downward inflections

Table 1. Relations between F_0 and emotions. Neutral speech is considered as a reference for the presented relative descriptions (from Cowie *et al.* 2001).

The present chapter is organized as follows. In Section 2, fundamental frequency analysis methods and results reported in the literature are summarized. Also, our approach to compare the F_0 properties of emotional and neutral speech are presented (Bulut *et al.* 2007; Busso *et al.* 2008; Yildirim *et al.* 2004). In the next section (Section 3), pitch features are investigated in terms of their usefulness for emotion recognition, by analyzing their performance in the binary emotion classification tasks between neutral and emotional speech (Busso *et al.* 2008). Next, in Section 4, the F_0 characteristics of emotional utterances are modified, and their effect on emotional content and speech quality perception is investigated (Bulut/Narayanan 2008). Finally, discussion and conclusions are presented in Section 5.

2. Analysis of fundamental frequency

It is well accepted that F_0 contour conveys emotional information, especially for certain emotional categories. For instance, many studies have found that recorded happy or angry utterances have relatively higher and more variable pitch level accompanied by a wider pitch range. In contrast, for subdued emotional categories such as sadness, the pitch average is lower relative to neutral speech (Banse/Scherer 1996; Juslin/Laukka 2003; Murray/Arnott 1993; Scherer 1986). This section discusses previous efforts toward identifying the emotionally salient aspects from speech and presents the results of our analyses.

Lieberman and Michaels (1962) analyzed whether perturbations of fundamental frequency convey emotional information. They performed subjective experiments, in which the participants were asked to assess the emotional content of semantically neutral sentences recorded over different emotions. Using an analysis by synthesis approach, they manipulated the pitch, and the intensity values; for example, smoothing the F_0 contour using 40-msec and 100-msec windows. Combinations of these modifications were presented to the labelers. The results indicated that the identification of the emotional content decreased when the F_0 contour is smoothed, suggesting that small localized perturbations are indeed important in the perception of emotions. Similar perceptual experiments were presented by Breitenstein *et al.* (1986). Although their results showed that small pitch variations were not the most important cues in the perception of emotion, they did influence the emotional percepts.

Paeschke *et al.* (1999) studied several features, derived from the F_0 contour, that could be used to characterize expressive speech. Their results suggested that the shape of the fundamental frequency contour conveys emotional information. They found that the slope, and the steepness of rising and falling of F_0 present different patterns for the targeted emotional categories (anger, fear, happiness, boredom, disgust and sadness).

In several languages, the values of the F_0 contour gradually decrease at the end of the sentences, a phenomenon known as pitch declination. Wang *et al.* (2005) analyzed whether the patterns in pitch declination is affected by emotional modulation. They focused on contrasting happy and neutral sentences, using 4-word sentences in Mandarin. They concluded that the declination degree was lower for happy sentences, especially in the last part of the sentence. These results agree with our previous study, in which we showed that the first and second part of a sentence present different F_0 patterns, which are also emotionally dependent (Fig. 1) (Bulut *et al.* 2005). The study presented by Paeschke (2004) also indicates that declination is an important emotional cue, especially for emotional categories such as boredom and sadness.

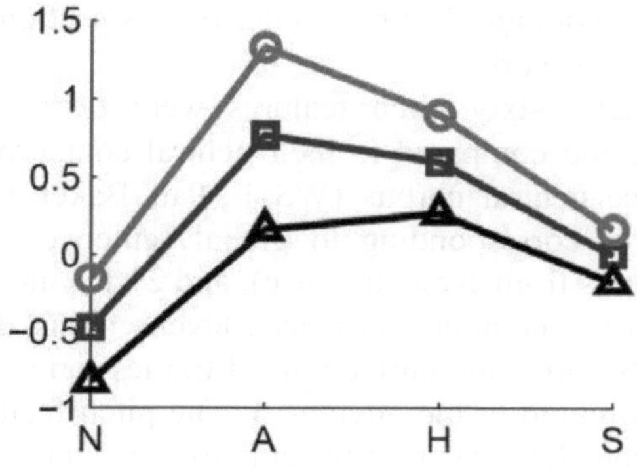

Fig. 1. Main effects of emotion and position in the sentence for F_0 median. Results for the first and second part of the sentence are marked with ○ and △, respectively. The values over the entire sentence are marked with □. Symbols N, A, H and S represent neutral, anger, happiness and sadness (from Bulut *et al.* (2005)).

Although the aforementioned aspects of the F_0 contour convey emotional information, some studies have suggested that gross statistics from pitch such as mean and range conveyed most of the emotional information (Bänziger/Scherer 2005; Ladd *et al.* 1985). For example, the analysis presented by Bänziger and Scherer (2005) indicates that mean levels and the range of the F_0 contour account for most of the important emotional variation found in the pitch. In contrast, the shape of the F_0 contour was only slightly affected by emotional modulation. Scherer *et al.* (1984) suggested that different aspects of the pitch are associated with linguistic and paralinguistic communicative goals. They suggested that the shape of the F_0 con-tour is associated with the grammatical structure of the sentence. Therefore, the interplay between affective and linguistic goals in the pitch shape is tighter compared to the degree of freedom observed in the manipulation of gross patterns in the F_0 contour.

Our recent experiments were designed to identify the most emotionally salient features of fundamental frequency (Busso *et al.* 2008). The approach was based on contrasting the F_0 features derived from neutral and expressive speech. The data support the idea that the gross statistics from the pitch are the most emotionally prominent aspects of the F_0 contour. The remainder of this section will discuss the results from this work.

In the study, sixty pitch features were extracted from expressive speech and compared to their neutral counterpart extracted from a reference neutral corpus (WSJ1 (Paul/Baker 1992)). There were 39 features corresponding to global sentence-level statistics (one set of features from each utterance), and 21 features corresponding to local statistics computed at voiced-level regions, defined as the speech segments with consecutive voiced frames (one set of features for each voiced region in the utterance). The pitch features included the most common statistics used for emotion recognition such as the mean, range, minimum, and maximum of the pitch contour. They also contained information about the F_0 shape, such as the inflection, curvature and slope, which were parameterized by fitting a first, second and third order polynomial, respectively. In the analysis, three emotional corpora were used: the electromagnetic articulography (EMA) database (Lee *et al.* 2005), the German emotional speech (GES) database (Burkhardt *et al.* 2005), and the emotional prosody speech and transcripts (EPSAT) database (Liberman *et al.* 2002). These corpora that were used in the original work include different speakers, emotional categories, and also different languages (English and German). In this chapter, we limit the analysis to English speech. Therefore, the results reported here and in Section 3 were recomputed without the GES database.

Instead of comparing the mean values of the expressive pitch features and their neutral counterpart, we proposed to compare their distributions by using Kullback-Leibler Divergence (KLD) (Cover/Thomas 2006). For a given emotional corpus, we estimated the ratio between the KLD from its emotional set and the KLD from its neutral set. A high value of this ratio would indicate that the distribution of this pitch feature changes during expressive speech. This allows us to rank the pitch features according to their emotional prominence, when compared to neutral speech.

Figures 2(a) and 2(b) provide the most salient pitch features in terms of the average KLD ratio across emotional categories and databases, for sentence- and voiced-level features, respectively. The figures show that mean (median), range (interquartile range), maximum (upper quartile) and minimum (lower quartile) are the most emotionally prominent pitch features. The average inflection, curvature and slope are not included among the top 15 most prominent sentence-level features. This result indicates that the F_0 shape is not as emotionally salient as gross pitch statistics. As suggested by Scherer *et al.* (1984), the linguistic aspects of the utterance may have stronger influence in the resulting pitch shape. Further discussion is given in Section 5.

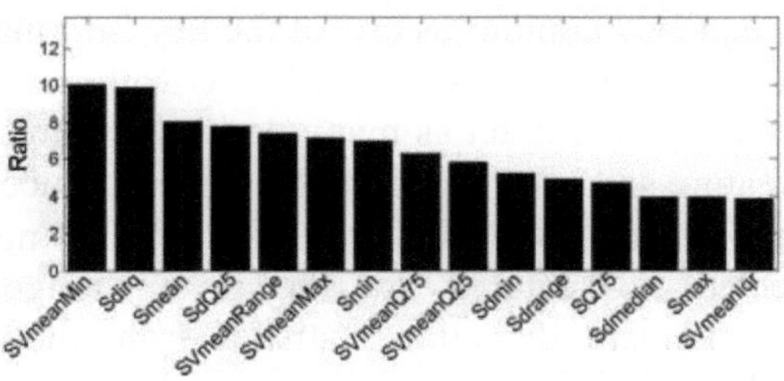

(a)

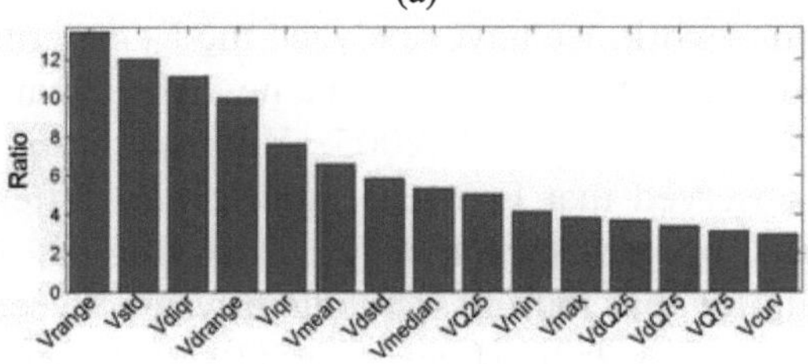

(b)

Fig. 2. Most emotionally prominent features according to the average KLD ratio between features estimated from expressive and neutral speech. (a) sentence-level features, (b) voiced-level features (from Busso *et al.* 2008).

The results from this analysis also indicate that variations within voice segment regions are emotionally salient. Figure 2(b) shows that the patterns of the standard deviation in voiced regions, *Vstd*, changes during expressive speech. This result agrees with the work presented by Lieberman and Michaels (1962). While these variations are useful for emotion recognition (Section 3), they do not significantly change the (human) emotional perception of the sentence, as discussed in Section 4.

3. Automatic emotion recognition from F_0 features

Many studies have proposed the use of features derived from the fundamental frequency contour as one of the key information sources for automatic emotion recognition (Pantic/Rothkrantz 2003). A common approach is to extract as many derived features as possible, and then use feature selection techniques to find a reduced subset that maximizes the performance (Schuller *et al.* 2007). Some of the most common selected F_0 features are the mean, range, minimum, maximum and standard deviation statistics from the F_0 utterance contour (Clavel *et al.* 2008).

In previous work, we have analyzed the F_0 patterns at different segmental and linguistic levels (phoneme, word, part of speech) (Bulut *et al.* 2005; Lee *et al.* 2005; Yildirim *et al.* 2004). For example, we observed that F_0 mean significantly differs for angry, happy, sad and neutral speech (Fig. 3). Using F_0 features, the recognition rate for this four-class problem was between 50.9% and 55.7% (chance level is 25%) (Lee *et al.* 2004; Yildirim *et al.* 2004). Most of the errors in the classifier came from the confusion between happiness and anger, and sadness and neutral state. These emotional categories are similar in the activation domain (calm-excited), but they differ in the valence (positive-negative) domain (Fig. 6).

Bänziger and Scherer (2005) suggested that the fundamental frequency is mainly affected by the arousal level of the utterance.

They analyzed changes in the F_0 contour in terms of the degree of activation in the sentences. They also analyzed the change of F_0 contour in terms of emotional categories. They found that changes in the arousal level change fundamental frequency. However, they did not find evidence for the qualitative changes in the F_0 contour among different emotions. These observations agree with the confusion between emotional categories observed in our aforementioned experiments.

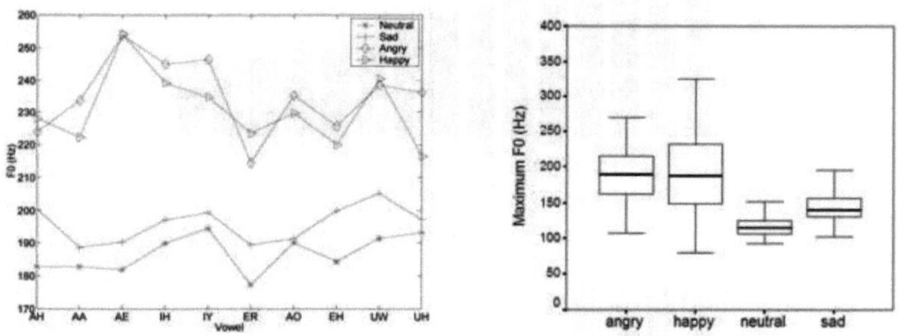

(a) (b)

Fig. 3. Emotional differences observed in F_0. (a) Pitch mean in terms of vowels (from Yildirim *et al.* 2004). (b) Maximum pitch distribution (from Lee *et al.* 2005).

An alternative approach to identify useful pitch features for emotion recognition is to perform binary classification between each individual emotional category and neutral speech (e.g., neutral-happiness, neutral-anger). This approach also provides insights into the emotional categories that can be accurately recognized from F_0 patterns. In our previous work, logistic regression models were proposed for this binary classification problem (Busso *et al.* 2008). A nice property of this framework is that the significance of the contribution of the features in the model can be quantified with the use of log-likelihood ratio tests.

Figures 4(a) and 4(b) show the pitch features, which on average have the highest impact in terms of log-likelihood, when individually included in the logistic regression models (one feature at a time). The top sentence-level features are the median (Smedian), and mean (Smean). The top voiced-level features are the upper quartile (VQ75), median (Vmedian), and mean (Vmean). The features depicting the pitch shape were not among the top features according to this criterion. These results support the idea that gross pitch statistics are the most emotionally salient aspect of the F_0 contour.

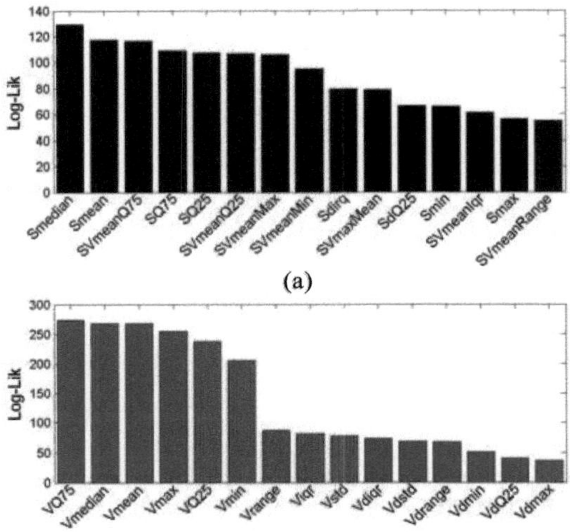

(b)

Fig. 4. Most emotionally prominent features according to the average log-likelihood score in logistic regression analysis, when a single feature is entered at a time in the model. (a) sentence-level features, (b) voiced-level features (from Busso *et al.* (2008)).

In Figures 4(a) and 4(b), the logistic regression models contain only a single feature. Therefore, the best features under this criterion may provide redundant information or be highly correlated. A second experiment was also proposed in this study to address this question. Instead of including one feature at a time, *Sequential Forward Feature* (SFF) selection was used to add pitch features until the improvement in the model was not significant. This procedure was performed for each emotional category in each emotional database

(EMA and EPSAT). Figures 5(a) and 5(b) show the pitch features that were most frequently selected. Under this criterion, the top features are the median (Smedian), and the derivative of the median (Sdmedian) for the sentence level features, and the minimum (Vmin), and curvature (Vcurv) for the voiced-segment features.

Although Vcurv and SVmaxCurv are not among the most prominent emotional features (Figs. 2 and 4), the results indicate that the pitch curvature provides complementary information that is important for emotion recognition purposes. Notice that the pitch mean value at sentence-level (Smean), which was the second best feature when a single feature was included in the model (Fig. 4(a)), does not appear in Figure 5(a). Given that the mean and median are highly correlated ($\rho \approx 0.96$), it is not surprising that these two features were almost never selected together.

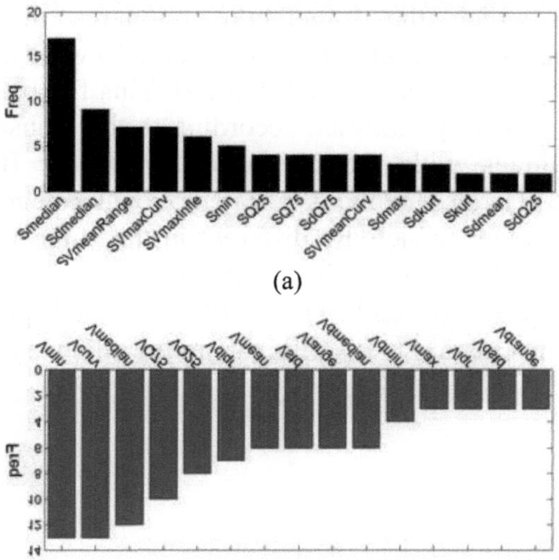

(a)

(b)

Fig. 5. Most frequently selected features in logistic regression models, when the features are added using sequential feature selection. (a) sentence-level features, (b) voiced-level features (from Busso *et al.* 2008).

Table 2 gives details of the logistic regression models built with sequential forward feature selection. The results are separately presented for each emotional category and database considered. The results indicate that certain emotional categories such as sadness and boredom cannot be discriminated from neutral speech using the investigated pitch features.

An interesting observation is that emotional categories with similar activation level cannot be easily recognized from each other using the proposed F_0 features. Table 2 shows that the performance of the logistic regression models for the emotional categories with neutral activation level is low (Nagelkerke R2 $<$ 0.5). For better visualization, Figure 6 presents the approximate location of different emotional categories in the activation-valence space. The locations determined were based on the Feeltrace snapshots presented by Cowie and Cornelius (2003) and Cowie *et al.* (2001). The emotional categories in which the Nagelkerke r-squares of the logistic regression models were higher than 0.5 (Table 2) were highlighted in black (otherwise they were plotted in gray). This figure suggests that pitch contour is mainly modified according to the arousal level. This observation agrees with the conclusion made by Bänziger and Scherer (2005). It also explains why emotional categories such as happiness and anger, which are different in the valence domain, are usually confused when only pitch features are used (Yildirim *et al.* 2004). As suggested by Ladd *et al.* (1985), voiced quality features may provide information to discriminate in the valence domain.

		Sentence-level features				Voiced-level features			
		Classification		Power of the model		Classification		Power of the model	
		Acc	Bas	-2 Log likelihood	Nagelkerke R2	Acc	Bas	-2 Log likelihood	Nagelkerke R2
EMA	Anger	91.9	58.1	66.6	0.901	75.9	50.9	1730.7	0.426
EMA	Happiness	96.0	64.0	16.6	0.976	83.2	51.4	1429.9	0.565
EMA	Sadness	68.2	59.1	314.7	0.166	59.5	51.2	2371.0	0.057
EMA	Emotional	87.1	82.2	370.3	0.491	76.5	75.9	3286.9	0.246
EPSAT	Happiness	87.6	75.1	156.1	0.795	82.3	72.2	1120.6	0.413
EPSAT	Sadness	80.9	77.5	452.2	0.130	74.7	73.3	1487.1	0.065
EPSAT	Boredom	77.3	76.2	426.5	0.285	70.6	71.3	1594.8	0.023
EPSAT	Disgust	84.0	73.8	356.5	0.466	72.4	68.5	1558.7	0.186
EPSAT	Fear	74.7	75.8	480.1	0.192	72.0	72.2	1677.9	0.034
EPSAT	Panic	97.1	81.2	46.8	0.946	88.6	76.1	581.3	0.707
EPSAT	Hot anger	97.1	79.8	37.7	0.954	91.3	75.2	720.3	0.672
EPSAT	Cold anger	79.0	74.2	218.4	0.683	77.4	73.2	1340.4	0.243
EPSAT	Despair	79.3	69.7	276.4	0.553	77.1	72.7	1368.5	0.216
EPSAT	Elation	94.5	75.4	62.5	0.927	89.8	71.8	719.4	0.668
EPSAT	Interest	85.6	70.8	254.2	0.634	77.4	69.9	1276.6	0.303
EPSAT	Shame	73.4	75.0	438.2	0.115	76.7	76.7	1530.3	0.015
EPSAT	Pride	83.3	76.7	318.5	0.446	76.9	74.8	1332.7	0.200
EPSAT	Contempt	76.4	70.8	465.0	0.214	75.3	73.2	1576.1	0.112
EPSAT	Emotional	80.5	82.6	1371.4	0.305	83.8	83.9	4980.5	0.167

Table 2. Details of the logistic regression models using SFF (from Busso *et al.* (2008).

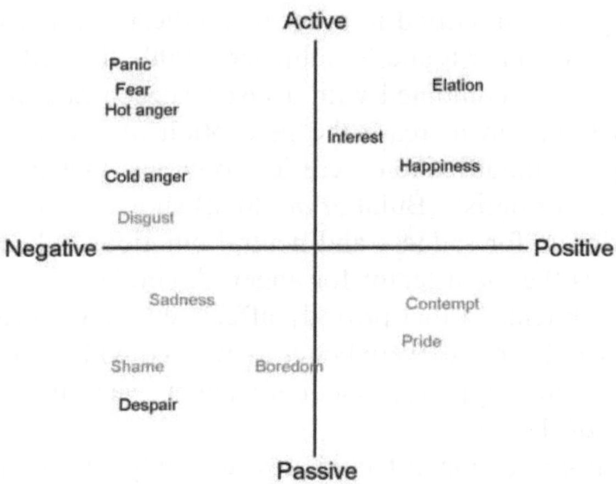

Fig. 6. Location of the emotional categories in the activation-valence space. For the emotional categories in gray, the power of the logistic regression model was inadequate to accurately recognize emotional from neutral speech ($r^2 < 0.5$). The figure was adapted from Cowie/Cornelius (2003) and Cowie *et al.* (2001).

4. Analysis by synthesis: emotional effects of F_0 feature modifications

Section 2 suggests that the gross statistics from the fundamental frequency contour are the most emotionally prominent F_0 features. However, the results presented in Section 3 indicate that F_0 features that were not among the most emotionally prominent features (i.e., F_0 curvature) were also useful for other applications such as automatic emotion recognition. In this section, we address the following question: What aspects of the F_0 contour have stronger influence on the human perception of expressive speech?

In the literature, the synthesis of emotional speech has been studied from different perspectives using formant (Burkhardt *et al.* 2000; Cahn 1990; Murray/Arnott 1995) and concatenative (Bulut *et al.* 2002; Bulut *et al.* 2005; Montero *et al.* 1999; Murray *et al.* 2000; Raux/Black 2003) synthesis techniques. These studies provide useful information about how different prosody and spectral parameters need to be jointly modified in order to synthesize emotional speech. For example, Burkhardt and Sendlmeier (2000) showed that broader pitch range, when combined with a faster speech rate and modal or tense phonation, can increase the perception of joy. For anger, the effects of pitch modification were less obvious. Our copy synthesis experiments on English (Bulut *et al.* 2002) showed that prosody was more descriptive for sadness and neutral emotions, while segmental inventory was the main factor for anger. A similar approach applied for Spanish concluded that prosody affects emotions differently and that sadness and surprise were better associated with supra-segmental variations, while happiness and cold anger were more segmental (Montero *et al.* 1999).

The aforementioned techniques for studying emotions have a powerful value. However, they do not specifically address how important the F_0 characteristics are for the perception and synthesis of emotions. The main reason is that many different parameters are jointly modified.

The analyses presented in the previous sections indicate which F_0 features are the most emotionally prominent features. In this section, we explore whether these aspects of the F_0 contour can be individually manipulated to change the human emotional perception of an utterance. Following an experimental methodology, we systematically modified the F_0 contour characteristics of natural emotional utterances to observe their influence in the perception of the emotions (Bulut/Narayanan 2008). This simple procedure allowed us to infer the role of F_0 properties in emotion perception. It also provided important insights into the limits within which the F_0 characteristics of the utterances can be modified without significantly altering the original emotion. The remainder of this section presents the results from this study.

To reduce the number of modifications, we limited the analysis to the mean, range and shape of the fundamental frequency contour. We proposed an analysis by synthesis approach. Two sentences, "She told me what you did" (sentence 1) and "This hat makes me look like an aardvark" (sentence 2) were recorded by a female (speaker 1) and a male speaker (speaker 2). The sentences were uttered portraying the following emotions: anger, happiness, sadness and neutral state. In total, 16 utterances were considered (two speakers, two sentences, four emotions).

Several modifications manipulating the mean, range and shape of the natural F_0 contours were applied to all of the recorded emotional utterances. These three parameters were chosen because of their common usage in emotion analysis and recognition studies as explained in the previous sections. The modifications were done using the Time Domain Pitch Synchronous Overlap and Addition (TD-PSOLA) algorithm (Moulines/Charpentier 1990) as implemented in the Praat software (Boersma/Weeninck 1996).The applied modifications can be categorized into three groups: mean, range and stylization modifications (summarized in Table 3). The details are given below.

- Modifications in F_0 mean: The mean was modified by shifting the F_0 contour up or down. The following modifications were applied: (1) Increasing/decreasing the original F_0 mean by 10%, 15%, 25% and 50%, (2) Making the F_0 mean equal to 50, 100, 150, 200, 250 and 300 (Hz).

- Modifications in F_0 range: The range was modified by multiplying the F_0 contour with a constant and then shifting the contour up or down so that the mean will be the same as the original mean value. The following modifications were applied: (1) Scaling the range by 0.5, 0.75, 1.5 and 2, (2) Making the F_0 range equal to 10, 30, 50, 80, 110 and 150 (Hz).
- Stylization modifications: The shape of the F_0 contour of the utterances was altered by stylizing the F_0 contour. The following modifications were applied: Stylizing the F_0 contour by a 2, 5, 10, 15, and 40 semitone frequency resolution. Stylization of the F_0 contour was performed using the Praat software. The logic behind the stylization algorithm is to try to represent the F_0 contour using linear segments. The length of the linear segments was determined by the frequency resolution component. For instance, while a 2 semitone resolution corresponds to fairly short linear segments, thus preserving the general contour shape, 40 semitone resolution may cause the whole utterance F_0 contour to be a line.

F0	Mean	Range	Stylization
Increase	m1: 0.10	r3: +50%	
	m2: 0.15	r4: +100%	
	m3: 0.25		
	m4: 0.50		
Decrease	m5: -0.10	r1: -50%	
	m6: -0.15	r2: -25%	
	m7: -0.25		
	m8: -0.50		
Value	m9: =50	r5: 10	s1: =2
	m10: =100	r6: 30	s2: =5
	m11: =150	r7: 50	s3: =10
	m12: =200	r8: 80	s4: =15
	m13: =250	r9: 110	s5: =40
	m14: =300	r10: 150	

Table 3. Summary of the performed F_0 contour modifications. The values for mean and range are in Hz and the values for stylization are in semitones.

All natural and resynthesized utterances were evaluated by listening experiments with naïve listeners that included both native and non-native American English speakers. Before evaluation, all speech files were normalized so that the maximum digitized waveform amplitude was 1. In the listening tests – conducted in a quiet room, using headphones and with a single rater at a time – first the speech file was presented and then the raters were asked to choose among the following options: Happy, angry, sad, neutral, and other. The raters were particularly instructed to choose *other* if their choice of emotion was not listed, or if they could not decide on the emotional content, or if the speech sounded to them as a mixture of several emotions. They were allowed to listen to each utterance as many times as they liked before making their decision. After the raters had chosen the emotional content label, they were asked to rate the naturalness (i.e., quality) of the utterance on a scale from 1 to 5, with five corresponding to the most natural. They were specifically instructed to give low values if the speech was perceived to be different from natural human speech in terms of quality. Again, the raters were able to listen to the speech as many times as they liked. The files were presented in a different random order for each rater.

In order to limit the time of any single test to around 20 minutes the test set was divided into 10 groups of 48 utterances, each consisting of three variations (which were chosen randomly) of the 16 original utterances. Average number of raters per set was 9.2 and each set was evaluated by at least seven raters. In total, there were 14 different people that participated.

A summary of the listening tests results is presented in Tables 4, 5, and 6. The average values of percentage, quality, and similarity variables are displayed in the tables. The percentage variable represents the percentage of listeners that perceived the same emotion as the original emotion. The quality variable is a measure of speech quality as determined by the responses of the listeners. Five represents excellent quality, while four, three, two, and one correspond to good, fair, poor, and bad quality ratings, respectively.

	m1 10%	m2 15%	m3 25%	m4 50%	m5 -10%	m6 -15%	m7 -25%
Similarity	0.97	0.97	0.93	0.8	0.96	0.97	0.92
Percentage	0.74	0.76	0.71	0.59	0.74	0.74	0.65
Quality	4.29	4.29	4.07	3.57	4.27	4.09	3.4
	m8 -50%	m9 =50	m10 =100	m11 =150	m12 =200	m13 =250	m14 =300
Similarity	0.88	0.81	0.88	0.95	0.93	0.92	0.82
Percentage	0.63	0.57	0.63	0.73	0.73	0.74	0.63
Quality	2.2	1.99	2.73	3.18	3.63	3.49	3.42

Table 4. Summary of the F_0 mean modification effects.

The difference between the perception of original (unmodified) utterances, and resynthesized utterances was quantified using the similarity measure defined in Equation 1. To do that, first, the utterances were represented by normalized vectors (i.e., all entries sum to 1) consisting of fractions of each emotion as determined by human raters. For example, a vector $y = [0.5\ 0.3\ 0.1\ 0\ 0.1]$ was used for an utterance that was perceived as happy, angry, sad, neutral and other by 50%, 30%, 10%, 0% and 10% of human raters, respectively. Then, these vectors were used to calculate the similarity value. Technically, the similarity function is a simple nonmetric measure that is the cosine of the angle between two vectors and that has a large value (i.e., close to 1) when the vectors point in the same direction (Duda *et al.* 2000). In our case, a large similarity value indicates that the effect of modification was minimal and that the subjective recognition percentages of the original and its modified version were similar. In contrast, a low similarity value indicates that the performed modification changed the emotional content of the original utterance.

(1) $$s(x, y) = \frac{x^t y}{\|x\| \cdot \|y\|}$$

The results show that although F_0 modification caused new emotional nuances to be perceived, the major emotion perception was not significantly affected in many cases. In other words, even the significant variations in F_0 parameters did not mask the original emotion perception. In general, it was observed that the F_0 modifications caused sad, neutral, or other emotion perception to increase, and angry, or happy emotion perception to decrease. The effects of the F_0 range modifications on emotion perception were more prominent than the F_0 mean modifications. Also, for the F_0 range modifications, the drop in the perceived speech quality was less than the F_0 mean modifications. These results suggest that one should focus on F_0 range and not F_0 mean modifications during the synthesis of emotional speech. The results also indicate that eliminating the small prosodic variations (s1, s2, s3) in the F_0 contour shape did not significantly decrease the perception of the original emotions. It was only when the F_0 contour at the sentence level was fully linearized – eliminating any accents and foot patterns (Klabbers and Van Santen, 2004) – the percentages of emotions changed significantly. This is an important result which has implications for emotional speech synthesis. It indicates that during the emotion synthesis, priority should be given to the other modifications (such as overall F_0 contour shape, F_0 range, and spectral characteristics), but not to the small prosodic variations in the F_0 contour shape. Later, in order to improve the naturalness of the synthesized speech, small prosodic variations may be considered. As a final point, it is also important to note that the results were significantly dependent on the speaker and the original utterance characteristics. The readers are referred to (Bulut/Narayanan 2008) for a detailed discussion of the results presented in this section.

	r1 (-50%)	r2 (-25%)	r3 (+50%)	r4 (+100%)	r5 (=10)
Similarity	0.91	0.97	0.94	0.93	0.73
Percentage	0.63	0.76	0.74	0.65	0.51
Quality	3.95	4.35	4.13	3.56	3.45

	r6 (=30)	r7 (=50)	r8 (=80)	r9 (=110)	r10 (=150)
Similarity	0.69	0.76	0.83	0.91	0.84
Percentage	0.47	0.51	0.58	0.69	0.61
Quality	3.52	3.76	3.84	3.9	4.08

Table 5. Summary of the F_0 range modification effects.

	s1 (=2)	s2 (=5)	s3 (=10)	s4 (=15)	s5 (=40)
Similarity	0.97	0.97	0.91	0.83	0.65
Percentage	0.78	0.72	0.6	0.58	0.48
Quality	4.51	4.35	3.73	3.44	3.01

Table 6. Summary of the F_0 stylization effects.

5. Discussion and conclusions

According to the results presented in this chapter, we conclude that the most prominent features are gross (overall phrase/utterance level) statistics from the F_0 contour such as the mean, minimum, maximum, and range. In contrast, the F_0 shape features were not among the most emotionally salient features. Since affective and linguistic goals are simultaneously conveyed in the pitch, some kind of interplay needs to regulate these two production processes. It seems that the shape of the fundamental frequency is constrained by the lexical content of the utterance, as suggested by Scherer *et al.* (1984). Therefore, emotional information seems to be mainly encoded by modulating the global patterns in the pitch. As an aside, a similar interplay is observed in the face, in which the upper face area is less constrained by the articulatory process, and therefore, it has more degrees of freedom to convey emotions (Busso/Narayanan, 2006).

Although this study indicates that major acoustic correlates of emotion expression are global pitch parameters such as mean and range, it is possible that these observations are the surface phenomena of the underlying dynamics associated with the shape of the pitch contour and the rate of pitch change. Therefore, further attention should focus on the dynamic aspects of pitch modulation in expressive speech.

From an automatic emotion recognition perspective, it is interesting to note that emotional categories which exhibit neutral level of activation were not accurately discriminated from neutral speech using F_0-based features. This result supports the studies that indicate that fundamental frequency is affected by the arousal level, rather than by emotional categories (Bänziger/Scherer, 2005). Therefore, F_0 features may not be adequate by themselves for performing multi-class emotional categorization. Other aspects of the speech also convey important emotional information (Lieberman/Michaels, 1962). For instance, in our previous work, the performance of an automatic emotion classifier increased from 50%, when only pitch-related features were used, to 67%, when duration and energy were included (for a similar task, human recognition was only 68.3%) (Yildirim *et al.* 2004). Likewise, other aspects of speech such as voice quality features may provide information to discriminate expressive speech in the valence domain, as suggested by Ladd *et al.* (1985).

Although F_0 shape features were not emotionally salient compared to global F_0 patterns, they do provide supplementary information that can be used to recognize expressive from neutral speech, which agrees with the analysis presented by Paeschke (1999). Even though some features are not emotionally prominent, they may still provide additional emotional cues. Notice that features that are good to discriminate expressive speech types are not necessarily useful to modify the emotional content of an utterance. For example, the pitch shape needs to be dramatically modified to significantly change the emotional content of the speech. Likewise, changes in the F_0 mean (median), which was one of the most emotional prominent features in our analysis, do not influence the emotion perception as much as the F_0 range modifications, which was always ranked below the mean. These results indicate that relevant features for synthesis and recognition of expressive speech need to be studied separately.

From an expressive speech synthesis perspective, the results discussed here suggest that, in general, modifications in the mean, range and shape of fundamental frequency introduce new emotional nuances, and therefore change the perception of emotions. However, in order for the (emotional) change to be significantly different than the perception of emotions of the input speech, the modifications should be performed in larger scales. This result indicates that the emotion content is not affected by the small variations in F_0 mean, range, and shape values.

In light of the presented analyses, we suggest the following improvements for systems analyzing the variations of F_0 characteristics in emotional speech, following Bulut and Narayanan (2008). These suggestions can be easily generalized to other parameters as well.

- *Use of more descriptive linguistic labels:* A hybrid labeling scheme combining categorical and attribute descriptions can be utilized. For example, considering the findings showing that valence, activation and intensity dimensions are correlated with the acoustic features of emotional speech (Grimm *et al.* 2007; Schröder *et al.* 2001), an angry utterance can be described as angry, high (low, medium) activation, high (low, medium) valence, high (low, medium) intensity, instead of just angry. As a recent example, this technique was used by Bänziger and Scherer (2005) to study F_0 variations in emotional speech.

- *Clear definitions of the labeling specifications:* Each of the chosen emotional labels should be described in detail in terms of what type of emotions they represent. For example, emotional adjectives such as annoyed, hostile, impatient, intolerant, nervous, etc. can all be used to describe angry emotion. This is important because, due to the subjective nature of emotions, identical labels used by different research studies may correspond to very different emotions.

- *Careful design of sentence structure for corpus collection:* Concepts such as constituency, grammatical relations, and sub-categorization and dependencies (Jurafsky/Martin 2000) can be employed to restrict the 'text space'. Sentences can be chosen to have similar syntax and grammar, for example. In addition, the lexicon can also be restricted, because different words may have different effects as suggested by 'The dictionary of affect' (Whissel 1989). Note that imposing such restrictions on text may be difficult to generalize, but it will be helpful for modeling the acoustical correlates of emotional speech. Once successful parameterization is achieved, the models can be adapted to more general datasets.

These suggestions are in line with the four main issues, the scope, naturalness, context of the content, and the kinds of descriptor it is appropriate to use, emphasized by Douglas-Cowie *et al.* (2003) for more systematic database construction and analysis. They also support the idea that acoustic parameters should be studied in connection with the human perception of prosodic and paralinguistic features (Roach 2000).

Perception of information present in speech signals is dependent on linguistic, expressive, physiological, and perspectival quality factors (Modulation Theory (Traunmüller 2005)). The first three of these factors have significant effects on the acoustic features of speech and therefore should be accounted for during the analysis of emotional information in speech.

The Facial Action Coding System (FACS) developed by Ekman, Friesen and their colleagues (Ekman/Friesen 1978; Ekman *et al.* 1987) consists of rules for reading and interpreting facial emotions. It is desirable to have a similar system for speech. The emotional labels used for facial expressions can be too restrictive to represent all possible variations in speech. For example, they may not be adequate to represent different levels of activation, valence, and intensity that is present in emotional speech. Therefore, more expressive emotional labels, combining dimensionality approaches can be developed. Our hope is that there will be more research on defining expressive descriptors particular to emotional speech.

Acknowledgments

This research was supported in part by funds from the National Institutes of Health (NIH), National Science Foundation (NSF), and the Army. The authors thank colleagues in the emotion research group for their support and valuable comments. Thanks go to Emily Mower, Serdar Yildirim, Chul Min Lee, Abe Kazemzadeh, Matthew Black, Chi-Chun Lee, Angeliki Metallinou, Jeannette Chang, and Samuel Kim.

References

Banse, Rainer / Scherer, Klaus R. 1996. Acoustic profiles in vocal emotion expression. *Journal of Personality and Social Psychology*, 70/3, 614-636.

Bänziger, Tanja / Scherer, Klaus R. 2005. The role of intonation in emotional expressions. *Speech Communication*, 46/3-4, 252-267.

Boersma, Paul / Weeninck, David 1996. Praat, a system for doing phonetics by computer. Technical Report 132, Institute of Phonetic Sciences of the University of Amsterdam, Amsterdam, Netherlands. <http://www.praat.org>.

Breitenstein, Caterina / Van Lancker, Diana / Daum, Irene 1986. The contribution of speech rate and pitch variation to the perception of vocal emotions in a German and an American sample. *Cognition & Emotion*, 15/1, 57-79.

Bulut, Murtaza / Narayanan, Shrikanth S. / Syrdal, Ann K. 2002. Expressive speech synthesis using a concatenative synthesizer. In *7th International Conference on Spoken Language Processing (ICSLP 2002)*, 1265-1268, Denver, CO, USA, September 2002.

Bulut, Murtaza / Busso, Carlos / Yildirim, Serdar / Kazemzadeh, Abe / Lee, Chul Min / Lee, Sungbok / Narayanan, Shrikanth S. 2005. Investigating the role of phoneme-level modifications in emotional speech resynthesis. In *9th European Conference on Speech Communication and Technology (Interspeech'2005 – Eurospeech)*, 801-804, Lisbon, Portugal, September 2005.

Bulut, Murtaza / Lee, Sungbok / Narayanan, Shrikanth S. 2007. Analysis of emotional speech prosody in terms of part of speech tags. In *Interspeech 2007 – Eurospeech*, 626-629, Antwerp, Belgium, August 2007.

Bulut, Murtaza / Narayanan, Shrikanth S. 2008. On the robustness of overall F_0-only modification effects to the perception of emotions in speech. *Journal of the Acoustical Society of America*, 123/6, 4547-4558, June 2008.

Burkhardt, Felix / Paeschke, Astrid / Rolfes, Miriam / Sendlmeier, Walter F. / Weiss, Benjamin 2005. A database of German emotional speech. In *9th European Conference on Speech Com-munication and Technology (Interspeech'2005 – Euro-speech)*, 1517-1520, Lisbon, Portugal, September 2005.

Burkhardt, Felix / Sendlmeier, Walter F. 2000. Verification of acoustical correlates of emotional speech using formant-synthesis. In *ISCA Tutorial and Research Workshop (ITRW) on Speech and Emotion*, 151-156, Newcastle, Northern Ireland, UK, September 2000.

Busso, Carlos / Narayanan, Shrikanth S. 2006. Interplay between linguistic and affective goals in facial expression during emotional utterances. In *7th International Seminar on Speech Production (ISSP 2006)*, 549-556, Ubatuba-SP, Brazil, December 2006.

Busso, Carlos / Lee, Sungbok / Narayanan, Shrikanth S. 2008. Analysis of emotionally salient aspects of fundamental frequency for emotion detection. *IEEE Transactions on Audio, Speech and Language Processing*, In press 2008.

Cahn, Janet E. 1990. The generation of affect in synthesized speech. *Journal of the American Voice I/O Society*, 8, 1–19, July 1990.

Clavel, Chloé / Vasilescu, Ioana / Devillers, Laurence / Richard, Gaël / Ehrette, Thibaut 2008. Fear-type emotion recognition for future audio-based surveillance systems. *Speech Communication*, 50/8, 487-503, June 2008.

Cover, Thomas M. / Thomas, Joy A. 2006. *Elements of Information Theory*. Wiley-Interscience, New York, USA, 2006.

Cowie, Roddy / Douglas-Cowie, Ellen / Tsapatsoulis, Nicolas / Votsis, George / Kollias, Stefanos / Fellenz, Winfried / Taylor, John G. 2001. Emotion recognition in human-computer interaction. *IEEE Signal Processing Magazine*, 18/1, 32-80, January 2001.

Cowie, Roddy / Cornelius, Randolph R. 2003. Describing the emotional states that are expressed in speech. *Speech Communication*, 40/1-2, 5–32, April 2003.

Douglas-Cowie, Ellen / Campbell, Nick / Cowie, Roddy / Roach, Peter 2003. Emotional speech: Towards a new generation of databases. *Speech Communication*, 40/1-2, 33-60, April 2003.

Duda, Richard O. / Hart, Peter E. / Stork, David G. 2000. *Pattern Classification*. Wiley-Interscience, New York, USA, 2000.

Ekman, Paul / Friesen, Wallace V. / O'Sullivan, Maureen / Chan, Anthony / Diacoyanni-Tarlatzis, Irene / Heider, Karl / Krause, Rainer / LeCompte, William A. / Pitcairn, Tom / Ricci-Bitti, Pio E. / Scherer, Klaus R. / Tomita, Masatoshi / Tzavaras, Athanase 1987. Universals and cultural differences in the judgments of facial expressions of emotion. *Journal of Personality and Social Psychology*, 53:712–717, October 1987.

Ekman, Paul / Friesen, Wallace V. 1978. *Facial Action Coding System: A Technique for Measurement of Facial Movement.* Consulting Psychologists Press, Palo Alto, CA, USA.

Grimm, Michael / Kroschel, Kristian / Mower, Emily / Narayanan, Shrikanth S. 2007. Primitives-based evaluation and estimation of emotions in speech. *Speech Communication*, 49/10-11, 787-800, October-November 2007.

Izard, Carroll E. 1977. *Human Emotions*. Plenum Press, New York, 1977.

Jurafsky, Daniel / Martin, James H. 2000. *Speech and Language Processing: An introduction to natural language processing, computational linguistics, and speech recognition*. Prentice-Hall, Inc., Upper Saddle River, New Jersey, 2000.

Juslin, Patrik N. / Laukka, Petri 2003. Communication of emotions in vocal expression and music performance: different channels, same code? *Psychological Bulletin*, 129/5, 770-814, September 2003.

Klabbers, Esther / Van Santen, Jan P.H. 2004. Clustering of foot-based pitch contours in expressive speech. In *5th ISCA Speech Synthesis Workshop*, 73-78, Pittsburgh, PA, USA, June 2004.

Ladd, D. Robert / Silverman, Kim E. / Tolkmitt, Frank / Bergmann, Günther / Scherer, Klaus R. 1985. Evidence for the independent function of intonation contour type, voice quality, and F_0 range in signaling speaker affect. *Journal of the Acoustical Society of America*, 78/2, 435-444, August 1985.

Lee, Chul Min / Yildirim, Serdar / Bulut, Murtaza / Kazemzadeh, Abe / Busso, Carlos / Deng, Zhigang / Lee, Sungbok / Narayanan, Shrikanth S. 2004. Emotion recognition based on phoneme classes. In *8th International Conference on Spoken*

Language Processing (ICSLP 04), 889-892, Jeju Island, Korea, October 2004.

Lee, Sungbok / Yildirim, Serdar / Kazemzadeh, Abe / Narayanan, Shrikanth S. 2005. An articulatory study of emotional speech production. In *9th European Conference on Speech Communication and Technology (Interspeech'2005 – Eurospeech)*, 497-500, Lisbon, Portugal, September 2005.

Liberman, Mark / Davis, Kelly / Grossman, Murray / Martey, Nii / Bell, John 2002. Emotional prosody speech and transcripts, 2002. Linguistic Data Consortium.

Lieberman, Philip / Michaels, Sheldon B. 1962. Some aspects of fundamental frequency and envelope amplitude as related to the emotional content of speech. *Journal of the Acoustical Society of America*, 34/7, 922-927, July 1962.

Montero, Javier M. / Gutierrez-Arriola, Juana M. / Colás, José / Enriquez, Emilia / Pardo, José Manuel 1999. Analysis and modelling of emotional speech in Spanish. In *International Congress of Phonetic Sciences (ICPhS 1999)*, 957-960, San Francisco, CA, USA, August 1999.

Moulines, Eric / Charpentier, Francis 1990. Pitch-synchronous waveform processing techniques for text-to-speech synthesis using diphones. *Speech Communication*, 9/5-6, 453-467, December 1990.

Murray, Iain R. / Arnott, John L. 1993. Toward the simulation of emotion in synthetic speech: A review of the literature on human vocal emotion. *Journal of the Acoustical Society of America*, 93/2,1097-1108, February 1993.

Murray, Iain R. / Arnott, John L. 1995. Implementation and testing of a system for producing emotion-by-rule in synthetic speech. *Speech Communication*, 16/4, 369-390, June 1995.

Murray, Iain R. / Edgington, Mike D. / Campion, Diane / Lynn, Justin 2000. Rule-based emotion synthesis using concatenated speech. In *ISCA Tutorial and Research Workshop (ITRW) on Speech and Emotion*, 173-177, Newcastle, Northern Ireland, UK, September 2000.

Paeschke, Astrid 2004. Global trend of fundamental frequency in emotional speech. In *Speech Prosody (SP 2004)*, 671-674, Nara, Japan, March 2004.

Paeschke, Astrid / Kienast, Miriam / Sendlmeier, Walter F. 1999. F_0-contours in emotional speech. In *Proceedings of the 14th International Conference of Phonetic Sciences (ICPh 1999)*, 929-932, San Francisco, CA, USA, August 1999.

Pantic, Maja / Rothkrantz, Leon J.M. 2003. Toward an affect-sensitive multimodal human-computer interaction. *Proceedings of the IEEE*, 91/9, 1370-1390, September 2003.

Paul, Douglas B. / Baker, Janet M. 1992. The design for the Wall Street Journal-based CSR corpus. In *2th International Conference on Spoken Language Processing(ICSLP 1992)*, 899-902, Banff, Alberta, Canada, October 1992.

Picard, Rosalind W. 1997. *Affective Computing*. MIT Press, Cambridge, MA, USA.

Raux, Antoine / Black, Alan W. 2003. A unit selection approach to F_0 modeling and its application to emphasis. In *IEEE Automatic Speech Recognition and Understanding Workshop (ASRU 2003)*, 700-705, St Thomas, US Virgin Islands, November-December 2003.

Roach, Peter 2000. Techniques for the phonetic description of emotional speech. In *ISCA Tutorial and Research Workshop (ITRW) on Speech and Emotion*, 53-59, Newcastle, Northern Ireland, UK, September 2000.

Scherer, Klaus R. / Ladd, D. Robert / Silverman, Kim E. 1984. Vocal cues to speaker affect: Testing two models. *Journal of the Acoustical Society of America*, 76/5, 1346-1356, November 1984.

Scherer, Klaus R. 1986. Vocal affect expression: A review and a model for future research. *Psychological Bulletin*, 99/2, 143-165, March 1986.

Scherer, Klaus R. 2003. Vocal communication of emotion: A review of research paradigms. *Speech Communication*, 40/1-2, 227-256, April 2003.

Schröder, Marc / Cowie, Roddy / Douglas-Cowie, Ellen / Westerdijk, Machiel / Gielen, Stan 2001. Acoustic correlates of emotion dimensions in view of speech synthesis. In *European*

Conference on Speech Communication and Technology (Eurospeech), volume 1, 87-90, Aalborg, Denmark, September 2001.

Schuller, Bjorn / Seppi, Dino / Batliner, Anton / Maier, Andreas / Steidl, Stefan 2007. Towards more reality in the recognition of emotional speech. In *International Conference on Acoustics, Speech, and Signal Processing (ICASSP 2007)*, volume 4, 941-944, Honolulu, HI, USA, April 2007.

Traunmüller, Hartmut 2005. Speech considered as modulated voice. revised manuscript (last retrieved March 9, 2008).

Van Gogh, Vincent 1889. Letter 603 to Theo van Gogh written on 6 July 1889. Retrieved, July 7th, 2008. Web site: <http://www.vggallery.com/>.

Wang, Haibo / Li, Aijun / Fang, Qiang 2005. F_0 contour of prosodic word in happy speech of Mandarin. In Tao, J. / Tan, T. / Picard, R.W. (eds), *Affective Computing and Intelligent Interaction (ACII 2005), Lecture Notes in Artificial Intelligence 3784*, 433-440. Springer-Verlag, Berlin, Germany, November 2005.

Whissel, Cynthia M. 1989. The dictionary of affect in language. In R. Plutchik and H. Kellerman, editors, *Emotion: Theory, research and experience: Vol.4, The measurement of emotions*. Academic Press, New York, NY, USA.

Yildirim, Serdar / Bulut, Murtaza / Lee, Chul Min / Kazemzadeh, Abe / Busso, Carlos / Deng, Zhigang / Lee, Sungbok / Narayanan, Shrikanth S. 2004. An acoustic study of emotions expressed in speech. In *8th International Conference on Spoken Language Processing (ICSLP 04)*, 2193-2196, Jeju Island, Korea, October 2004.

OLIVIER PIOT

Using Klatt Synthesis to Study the Expression of Affects by Prosody

1. Introduction

Speech is generally considered as the output of two components. A linguistic component – transforming a meaning into a sequence of phonemes – and a paralinguistic component – determining how this phonemic sequence is to be produced. This dichotomy is named *encodage double de la parole* (double encoding) by Fónagy (1986), who considers paralinguistic encoding as a quantitative modulation of linguistic encoding (the latter including the shape of intonation contours, or intonation patterns). But this widespread conception is partly contradicted by Studdert-Kennedy *et al.* (1973) who, for the English one word phrase 'November', observe that the recognition rate of the interrogative modality depends continuously on pitch range of the final rise. According to the double encoding model, a purely quantitative variation should not influence the linguistic modality.

Hence the interrogative modality is not purely linguistic, because the recognition of linguistic units is categorial. In this respect, it behaves more like an attitude or an affect, the perception of which is gradient (Ladd *et al.* 1985, Scherer 1986). The study of Studdert-Kennedy *et al.* thus invites to consider the interrogative modality as the expression of one or several attitude(s). But which one(s)? To fully answer this question demands elaborating a theory, which is not the purpose of the present study. But it contributes to giving it a partial answer. Indeed, interrogation brings forward two affects or attitudes of the speaker: ignorance, and the desire to know. Both underlie any true interrogation, and one may wonder if and how they can be expressed by prosody. One purpose of this chapter is to provide some answers for French.

We may ask similar questions regarding the assertive modality. Couldn't it be that this modality relies on the expression and recognition of a set of attitudes or affects? And then which ones? Just like interrogation, assertion basically involves two affects: an evaluation of the hearer as being 'more or less' ignorant, and a desire to inform him/her. Can they be expressed by prosody, and how? We answer these questions in the second part of the study.

2. Experiment 1: Yes-no questions

2.1. Presentation

In the first experiment, prosodic variants of one yes-no question are rated on a common semantic scale. We chose the most typical intonation pattern (cf. 2.2.1.), which involves a rise on the accented last syllable of the utterance. Two semantic scales were used in two subsequent parts within the experiment: "L'ignorance exprimée" (expressed ignorance) on the one hand (part I), and "l'envie de savoir exprimée" (expressed desire to know) on the other hand (part D). Before going on with this presentation, the following point deserves discussion. Desire can be considered as continuous, just as arousal, the former being a typical cause of the latter (Scherer 1986). Being continuous, its expression can be expected to be continuous as well. This justifies the evaluation of the expressed desire to know on a scale of more than just two levels. But the case of ignorance is different. Because basically, a piece of information is either known or unknown by the speaker. Of course this is not as simple as that. The speaker may well think that a proposition is certainly true, or else that it is certainly false, but not be sure of it. In either case the proposition is neither known nor unknown. Hence, even if ignorance is certainly not a gradient parameter, it can be considered (and rated) as either *faible* (weak), *moyenne* (average), *forte* (great) or *très forte* (very great) (cf. 2.2.2.).

We wanted to have a total control over the acoustic parameters of the stimuli, so as to be sure, when changing one parameter, not to have another one being altered. More precisely we planned to change, within one given utterance, one or more of three prosodic parameters – namely F_0, intensity and speech rate – while leaving all other parameters unchanged. The only known way to achieve that goal was to use Klatt synthesis. We therefore used it to produce our stimuli, in a way that is described below.

2.2. Method

2.2.1. Stimuli

The prosodic variants were built from the one word phrase 'Natacha' (/nataʃa/). This forename was used with the same meaning as "This is Natacha" which, provided that the context is clear enough, may be reduced to "Natacha". The choice of this particular forename results from several decisions or constraints: (1) We wanted a three syllables stimulus because this was necessary to ensure a good and clear perception of the intended nuances in prosody (the results of the experiments confirm that the variants were perceived as dissimilar). (2) Fewer syllables mean less to handle by the short term memory, which is preferable in a rating experiment. (3) Three similar vowels make it simpler to deal with the difficulty of taking into account their intrinsic pitch and loudness. (4) Fewer syllables also lower the quantity of non-informative input to the subjects' ears, and makes it easier and less time consuming for them to listen to the stimuli several times.

For this experiment the stimuli were prosodic variants of the yes-no question "Natacha?". The intonation contour was low-flat on /nata/, thus providing a reliable reference for the perception of the following F_0-rise on /ʃa/. A final F_0 rise is, according to Faure (1973), the only intonative feature to be able to trigger the perception of a yes-no question, while the melody on the preceding syllables can be either rising, falling or flat.

We used several recordings of yes-no questions as a basis for the intonation contours of the stimuli, in order to remain as close as possible to ecological stimuli. This resulted in the values mentioned in Table 1. They include:

- Two different speech rates: one of them was perceived as rather 'low' by our informants, while the other one was perceived as 'high'.
- Two different trajectories of speech intensity over the accented final syllable /ʃa/: the lower of the two corresponded to an unmarked yes-no question – according to the criteria of Fónagy and Bérard (1973: 78), while the higher intensity was clearly perceived as 'emphatic'.
- Four different trajectories of F_0 over the accented final syllable /ʃa/: the pitch values shown in Table 1 (154, 192, 240 and 300 Hz) form a geometric progression, i.e. the differences between two successive values are perceptively similar.

All three conditions stated by House (1990) for an optimal perception of the final rise of the contours are fulfilled: (1) F_0 rises over a spectrally stable zone of the speech signal, all the more as the sigmoidal F_0 pattern moves the start of the rise away from the ʃ-a transition; (2) This start coincides with a decrease of new spectral information; (3) The final /a/ is always longer than 100 milliseconds (it lasts 120 ms with the faster speech rate). Moreover, the smallest difference in the amplitude of an F_0 rise is 3.8 ST (semi-tones). This is superior to the 3 ST threshold ensuring that two different F_0 rises are regularly and robustly discriminated (t'Hart 1980). The resulting 16 stimuli are perceptually easy to differentiate, and they cover the major part of an F_0-register within which 123 Hz is a non-terminal low value.

In an informal experiment, we asked two informants whether each stimulus was or was not an admissible yes-no question. They gave a confirmation in each case, as later did the subjects (see Faure 1973: 14, for an independent experimental justification).

The stimuli were synthesized using Compost, an implementation of Klatt synthesis for PCs equipped with an OROS™ DSP card. We preferred Klatt synthesis to PSOLA-type resynthesis, because only the former allows to tune prosodic parameters independently from all other speech parameters (spectral ones in particular), and without altering them.

F0	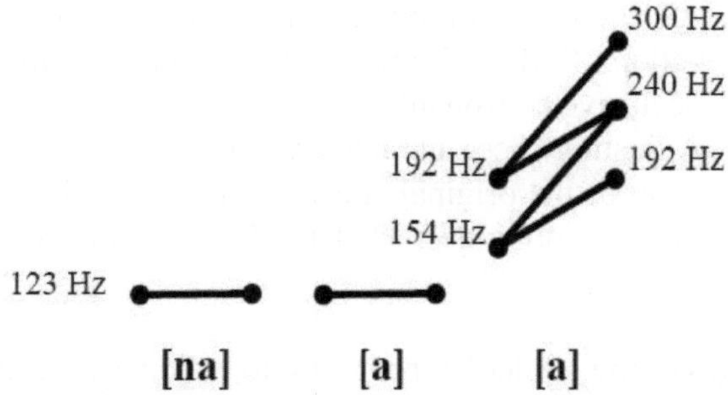
Intensity	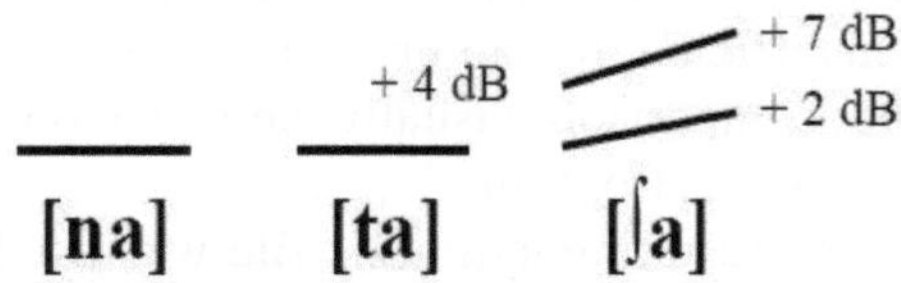
Speech Rate	Original dates and durations or multiplied by 0.8

Table 1: Prosodic characterization of the 16 stimuli used in experiment 1.

The synthesis of the first version of the forename ‘Natacha’ was performed using the following method, which is inspired by Klatt *et al.* (1989):

- Recording of a male speaker, uttering this forename as ‘neutrally’ as possible, as an answer to the question: “What is this woman’s name?”. After several recordings, we kept the most convincing and clear-sounding of all renditions.

- Set the phoneme durations to be those of the recording. Then do the same thing for (in the following order) F_0, formants' frequencies F1 to F5, voicing amplitude U0 (Klatt's AV), formants' bandwidths B1 to B5, formants' amplitudes A1 to A5, nasal pole-zero frequency and bandwidth, and the amplitudes of frication AF and of aspiration AH on consonants (the temporal synchronization of AF with the other parameters is difficult, especially for occlusive consonants).
- Adjusting these parameters until obtaining a perceptually close copy of the original speech signal, with differences of +/- 1 to 2 dB for amplitudes, +/- 1 to 3% for frequencies, and +/- 5 ms for durations.

We used the Unice™ program to calculate temporal and spectral values, and to perform the synthesis/recording comparison. However, the program's LPC spectrum is limited to the 0-4 kHz range, which is often insufficient to capture the 5th formant. Consequently we carried out the comparison visually between both 5th formants, using the program's spectrogram.

The resulting synthesis file was used as a common basis to the synthesis of the 16 stimuli of the experiment (see Table 1). These files were digitalized on Macintosh™, using the analogical input of a professional sound card, as well as the Sound Designer II™ program. The format of the resulting sound files, (48kHz, 16 bits), was chosen so as to keep the original quality of the synthesis, whose format was (10kHz, 16 bits). Within each sound file, we imposed a silence of 200 ms before the start of the sound wave (while the end of the latter was the end of the file). After doing so, the sound of the mouse click did not interfere any more with the listening.

2.2.2. Procedure

2.2.2.1. Setup of the experiment

The experiment was carried out using a HyperCard stack (it could also be done using Powerpoint). The first card was a presentation of the task to the subjects (henceforth the Ss). Then followed eight cards allowing the Ss to get familiar with the task itself: four cards for the evaluation of *l'ignorance exprimée* (expressed ignorance), then four cards for the evaluation of *l'envie de savoir exprimée* (expressed desire to know). The stimuli presented in this initial phase were chosen so as to cover the whole prosodic range of the utterances. Then appeared a presentation card for the rating of expressed ignorance (part I). It was followed by two subsequent blocks of test cards, each one containing a randomized sequence of the 16 evaluations to be performed. The same was done for the expressed desire to know (part D). The randomization of the cards was performed again for each subject.

The presentation cards aimed at making clear which of both ratings the Ss were to perform. The aim was also to make it clear for them that ignorance and desire to know were not necessarily correlated with each other, but that they were a priori independent variables. To do that, examples were given of situations whereby one of them was high while the other one was high, and vice versa. The presentation card of the current part of the experiment was always accessible to the Ss during the experiment.

On each card, one button allowed to hear the stimulus, which could be heard several times by the Ss. On each card, also, the affect to be rated was written, the word *exprimée* (expressed) being underlined using capital letters. The reason was that we wanted the Ss to base their judgments on what was directly expressed: indeed, it seemed important that the Ss did not make inferences such as, for instance: "the speaker expresses low ignorance to hide the fact that his ignorance is high", or "the speaker refrains himself to express his desire to know". We therefore ensured that the expression itself was the target of the ratings.

The latter had to be made, for each part, between *très grande* (very high), *grande* (high), *moyenne* (moderate), and *faible* (low). The label *null* was not proposed to the Ss because in the chosen context of a casual interrogation, both ignorance and desire to know were supposed to be present; and since the stimuli were found by our informants and ourselves as ecological within this context – and none of the Ss cast doubts about this, a null value could reasonably not be considered by the Ss as being expressed.

2.2.2.2. *Realization of the experiment*

The experiment was performed in an anechoic room. The subject was told precisely what the task consisted in, which came in complement to the written explanation. Once the training cards had been performed, the subject was left alone. The experiment lasted between 10 and 25 minutes.

2.2.3. *Subjects*

20 Ss, 6 male and 14 female, aged between 20 and 35, performed the experiment. All were native speakers of French and students in linguistics. All of them could be considered as speakers of Standard French.

2.3. *Analysis of the data*

The labels used for the ratings (*très grande*, *grande*, *moyenne*, and *faible*) were converted into 4, 3, 2 and 1 (resp.). Mean ratings are shown in Tables 2 (part I) and 3 (part D). Stimuli are coded in the following way: the first letter stands for the speech rate (R: *rapide* tr. rapid, L: *lent* tr. low), and the subsequent three digits respectively designate the final /a/'s initial pitch (1: 154 hertz, 2: 192 hertz), final pitch (2: 192 hertz, 3: 240 hertz, 4: 300 hertz), and its intensity (0: rise from 0 to +2 dB, 1: rise from +4 to +7 dB).

The consistency of the Ss' ratings can be measured by the mean absolute difference between their two series of answers to the same questions. The value of this parameter is 0.62 on average for part I, and 0.51 for part D: this is less than 2/3 of the difference between two nearest ratings. Provided that the 'ideal' rating of a subject may stand at the midpoint between two labels, then some variability in the ratings is to be expected. This result thus appears to denote a fairly good global consistency. Moreover, the global means of the intra-block ratings were 2.34 versus 2.45 for part I, and 2.40 versus 2.50 for part D. A paired t-test gives $p>0.02$ in both cases. We thus have convergent indications of a good consistency of the Ss' ratings for both parts I and D.

The individual consistency of each subject was then measured for both parts. We calculated the rate of identical answers to the same question. The inter-Ss mean m and standard deviation s of this rate was first determined. Then we decided to reject Ss whose rate was inferior to m-2s. Among the whole $20 \cdot 2 = 40$ parts to consider, only one part (a part I) was thus rejected. Hence remain $(20-1) \cdot 2 = 38$ (instead of 40 originally) occurrences of each evaluation for part I.

For the following statistical tests we used Student's t-test as well as ANOVA. The use of these parametric tests is justified on the one hand by the four levels of the evaluation scale, which allows to 'reasonably' consider the dependent variable as continuous, and on the other hand by the shapes of the distributions of answers (to the same question) which, as we verified, can all be interpolated by Gaussian curves.

2.3.1. Part I: L'ignorance exprimée (expressed ignorance)

For part I, speech rate has no influence on the ratings: $F(1,296)=0.152$, $p>0.5$); moreover, this is still the case for all eight possible pairwise comparisons ($p>0.2$, except for L/R231: $0.05>p>0.02$). Final intensity also has no influence, either globally ($F(1,296)=0.73$, $p>0.2$), or after grouping together stimuli differing only by speech rate: $p>0.2$. There was also no influence of the initial pitch of the final /a/: a comparison between stimuli "13" and "23" gives $p>0.5$.

On the contrary, the final pitch of the final /a/ has a high influence, expressing *greater* ignorance when it is higher: $F(2,301)=77.7$, $p<0.0001$. This effect is confirmed for all pairwise comparisons made after grouping together stimuli differing only by speech rate and/or intensity: $p<0.0001$. The mean ratings for the four intonation contours are shown in Figure 1.

Part I: *Ignorance exprimée* (expressed ignorance)					
L_120	*1.88*	1.02	*R_120*	*1.88*	0.82
L_121	*1,88*	0.99	*R_121*	*1.85*	0.74
L_130	*2.20*	0.72	*R_130*	*2.23*	0.73
L_131	*2.25*	0.71	*R_131*	*2.38*	0.81
L_230	*2.35*	0.74	*R_230*	*2.15*	0.74
L_231	*2.15*	0.77	*R_231*	*2.60*	0.87
L_240	*3.10*	0.78	*R_240*	*3.10*	0.84
L_241	*3.20*	0.65	*R_241*	*3.18*	0.93

Table 2: Mean and standard deviation of the ratings for expressed ignorance.

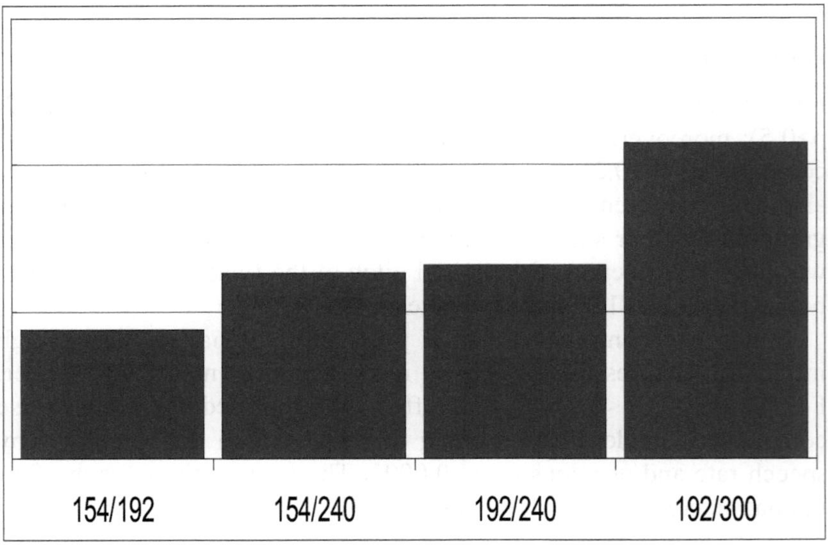

Figure 1: Mean ratings (Part I: *ignorance exprimée*) obtained by the four intonation contours, here named by the initial and final pitches of the final /a/. As can be seen, only the final pitch has an influence on the ratings.

2.3.2. Part D: L'envie de savoir exprimée (expressed desire to know)

The positive influence of intensity on mean ratings (see Table 3) is not significant: $F(1,316)=3.14$, $p>0.05$. But here speech rate has an influence (see Figure 2): $F(1,316)=22.9$, $p<0.0001$; Moreover this influence remains for all four intonation contours (after grouping together stimuli differing only in final intensity): $p<0.002$. This shows a posteriori that stimuli of different speech rates are correctly discriminated. Final /a/'s initial pitch has no influence at a low speech rate ($p>0.5$), but it does have one when the speech rate is high ($p<0.02$): a pitch contour starting higher on the final /a/ expresses greater desire to know (+0.28 on average). This effect may be caused by the necessity of a higher muscular tone to perform the F_0 transition between 123 Hz and 192 Hz during the 112 ms duration (at the higher speech rate) of the consonant /ʃ/. And here again, the final pitch has a high positive influence: $F(2,317)=183.0$, $p<0.0001$ (and $p<0.0001$ also for all possible pairwise comparisons between contours).

Part D: *Envie de savoir exprimée* (expressed desire to know)					
L_120	*1.40*	0.55	*R_120*	*1.83*	0.75
L_121	*1.48*	0.64	*R_121*	*1.98*	0.77
L_130	*2.05*	0.68	*R_130*	*2.33*	0.73
L_131	*2.08*	0.69	*R_131*	*2.58*	0.71
L_230	*1.95*	0.64	*R_230*	*2.63*	0.74
L_231	*2.20*	0.72	*R_231*	*2.83*	0.71
L_240	*3.23*	0.77	*R_240*	*3.50*	0.55
L_241	*3.38*	0.67	*R_241*	*3.75*	0.44

Table 3: Mean and standard deviation of the ratings for *l'envie de savoir exprimée*.

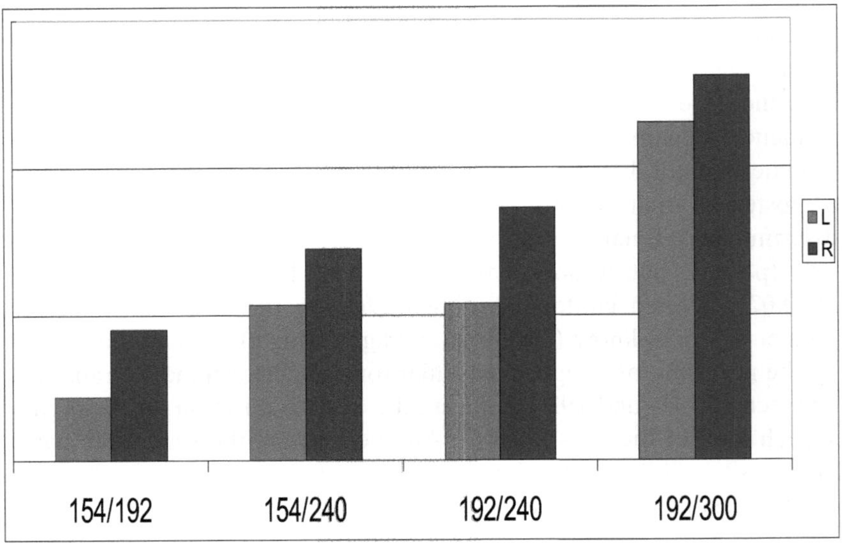

Figure 2: Mean ratings (Part D: *Envie de savoir exprimée*) obtained by the four intonation contours (named by the initial and final pitches of the final /a/), and two speech rates (L: 'low' and R: 'rapid). Initial F_0 has an effect only at a high speech rate.

2.4. Discussion

Let us first consider the question of what was evaluated in this experiment. The situation was one where the speaker felt both ignorance and a desire to know, the valence of which Ss had to judge from his expression. Conceivably, the speaker may express his ignorance either plainly, or just one part of it. He can also, why not, overplay it. The same, of course, goes for his desire to know. What is assessed here is their valence 'as the utterance expresses them', but it is not necessarily true feelings, according to how well Ss can decode their cultural biases intervening between affects and their expression. Some intra-linguistic variability in the ratings is thus expected. Besides, languages prescribe different organizations of physiological resources during speech; a consequence is that the relationships that we may find between affect expression and prosodic parameters cannot be expected to be universal. And to finish with, what is called *moderate* or *high* may well differ from one culture to another. Anyway these potential sources of variations in the ratings, for such an experiment, do not produce any bias in the experiment itself.

The instructions aiming at insuring that the Ss dissociated ignorance and desire to know, reached their goal: parts I and D led to fairly different results. For expressed ignorance, the only influence is that of final pitch. And since the initial pitch of the final vowel has no influence on the ratings ($p>0.5$), the mean pitch over this vowel cannot constitute a more accurate parameter than final pitch. Noteworthy, the general positive influence of F_0 peak was followed by 18 Ss out of 20 (hence by 90% of them), while two Ss displayed a negative one. A possible explanation is that these latter Ss interpreted higher final pitch as expressing surprise, which is greater when the speaker feels more confident that "this is not Natacha", hence when he feels less ignorant on that matter. If this hypothesis is correct, however, such an interpretation of the stimuli remained marginal enough to be neglected.

The linear regression formula for expressed ignorance is stated below, where E(qI) designates the expected ignorance expressed by the yes-no question stimuli, and $F_{0final}(ST)$ the final pitch expressed in semi-tones over the baseline of 123Hz:

$$E(qI) = 0.47 + 0.166 \cdot F_{0final}(ST)$$

predicting 89.8% of the variance. According to this formula, a moderate value of the expressed ignorance (E(qI)=2) is obtained for a final glissando of +9.2 ST. A high value corresponds to a glissando of +15.2 ST, a very high value to +21.3 ST, and a low value to +3.2 ST.

Now as regards the expressed desire to know, intensity has no significant influence either, although here a low and positive influence systematically appears (the p-value was close but superior to 0.05). On the contrary, both speech rate and final pitch have a highly significant positive influence. Despite the influence of the initial pitch of the final /a/ at a high speech rate, final pitch provides a closer estimation of the data than does mean pitch over the final /a/. We thus obtain the following formula, where E(qD) designates the expected desire to know for the yes-no question stimuli, and R the speech rate (R = 1 for the low speech rate, and R = 1/0.8 = 1.25 for the 'rapid' versions):

$$E(qD) = -2.292 + 1.825 \cdot D + 0.232 \cdot F_{0final}(ST)$$

predicting 94.0% of the variance. Let us note that for $F_{0final}(ST)$ = +9.2 ST, i.e. for moderate expressed ignorance, a moderate desire to know is obtained for R = 1.18, hence when the speech rate is close to the one labeled 'rapid' (R = 1.25). This is not surprising because perceptively, the 'low' speech rate (R = 1) seems close to the inferior limit for a yes-no question (the durations of the six phonemes of /nataʃa/ are then: 55, 90, 85, 80, 140 and 150 ms (resp.)). It can be seen also that the growth rate with respect to final pitch is greater for E(qD) than for E(qI). This underlies the importance of this parameter for the expressed desire to know: a difference of only 4.3 ST (to be compared to 6 ST for expressed ignorance) in the amplitude of the final glissando is enough to have its mean rating jump from one label to another (say from moderate to high).

3. Experiment 2: Assertions

3.1. Presentation

The aim of this second experiment was to conduct a comparable study on assertions. For that purpose we could work with an intonation pattern quite similar to the one used for yes-no questions: the first two syllables of the one word phrase 'Natacha' were left unchanged, while the pitch contour on the last accented syllable /ʃa/ was either high-flat or high-falling. Here we chose the two scales of *l'envie d'informer exprimée* (tr. the expressed desire to inform), and *l'ignorance d'autrui [l'allocutaire] exprimée* (tr. the expressed ignorance of the hearer). Both scales were chosen in concordance with those of the first experiment, of course, and also because both of them were supposedly present in the context of this experiment.

3.2. Method

3.2.1. Stimuli

They were synthesized on the basis of the Klatt file used for generating the stimuli of experiment 1. By using the same phonetic parameters (durations, formants, F_0, etc.), we ensured that we would be able to make a close comparison of the results of both experiments and, in particular, a comparison of the effect of a prosodic change on the 'dual' evaluation scales (for ex. ignorance of the speaker/hearer). The pitch contours used here are coded, according to Mertens (1987), as l..l/HH (high-flat contour) and l..l/HL (high-falling contour). The value of F_0 was left unchanged over the first two syllables. The stimuli are described in Table 4.

We again used recordings as models, here mainly for the design of the intonation contours. The modifications made on speech rate and final syllable intensity were similar to those made in the first experiment; in particular, versions with the lower intensity were judged by our informants as unmarked in this respect, while versions with the higher intensity were clearly perceived as emphatic. As can be noted by comparing Tables 1 and 4, F_0 values used as pitch targets were common to both experiments. Apart from facilitating comparisons between their results, this choice was again driven by the constraint of insuring perceptive similarity in the differences between two subsequent targets.

F_0	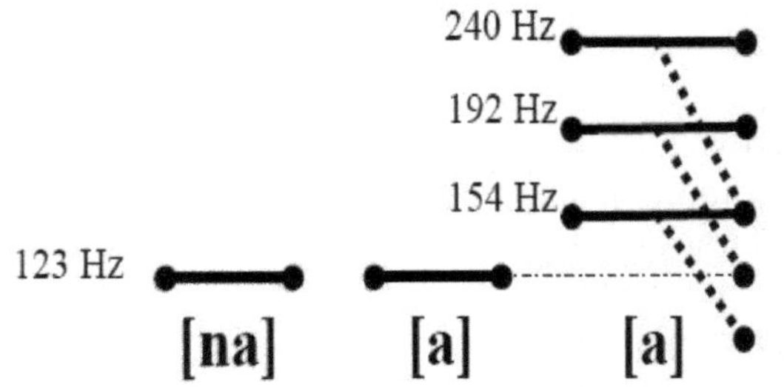
Intensity	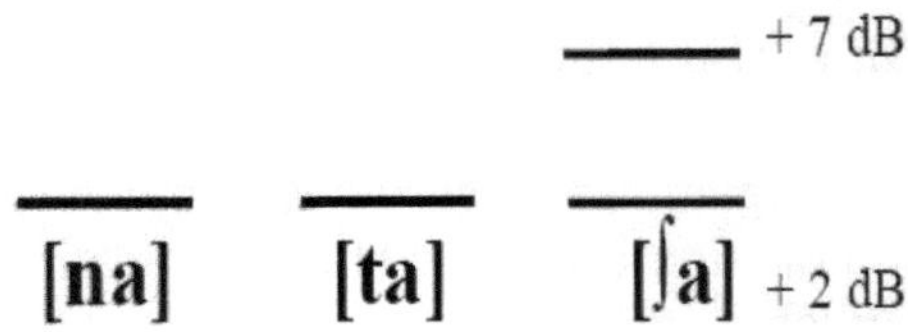
Speech Rate	Original dates and durations or multiplied by 0.8

Table 4: Prosodic characterization of the 24 stimuli used in experiment 2.

Here again, the three conditions of House (1990) for ensuring the optimal perception of the final pitch contour are fulfilled (see 2.2.1). And the distance between two successive pitch targets has a value of 3.8 ST, which is far above the tonal jnd (just noticeable difference) for speech (see Isacenko/Schädlich 1970, or Rossi/Chafcouloff 1972), estimated at 5% of the base value expressed in Hz (hence less than 1 ST). We thus obtain 24 easily discriminable stimuli, covering an important part of the tonal register of a speaker having his baseline at 123 Hz. In a preliminary phase, we ensured that the stimuli were possible realizations of an assertion, which was later confirmed by the Ss.

3.2.2. Procedure

3.2.2.1. Set up of the experiment

The stimuli were produced in the same way as for the first experiment, taking the same Klatt file as a common basis. The experimental design similarly included eight training cards – four cards for each of both parts, the prosody of which covering the entire range of values of the prosodic parameters. Then appeared a written explanation of the task for the expressed ignorance of the hearer, followed by 48 evaluation cards, composed of two randomized blocks of all 24 stimuli (part I). After that came the same sequence as the latter, but here for the expressed desire to inform (part D).

As for experiment 1, the word 'expressed' was underlined, in order to ensure that Ss made their ratings on the basis of the mere expression. Indeed, we wanted to avoid that the Ss ground their evaluations on unwanted inferences, such as: "the speaker expresses low ignorance because, actually, he feels like he is very ignorant, so this is what he is", or: "the speaker refrains from expressing his desire to inform the hearer". Expression was hence the target of the evaluations.

3.2.2.2. Realization

The experiment was performed in the same conditions, and using the same protocol as for the first experiment. The experiment lasted between 15 and 30 minutes.

3.2.3. Subjects

19 Ss, 7 male and 12 female, aged between 18 and 35, performed the experiment. All were native speakers of French, and students in linguistics. All of them could be considered as speakers of Standard French.

3.3. Analysis of the data

Mean ratings are shown in Tables 5 (part I) and 6 (part D). The labels used for the ratings (*très grande*, *grande*, *moyenne*, and *faible*) were again converted into 4, 3, 2 and 1 (resp.). Mean ratings are shown in Tables 2 (part I) and 3 (part D). Stimuli are coded in the following way: the first letter stands for the speech rate (R: *rapide* tr. rapid, L: *lent* tr. low), and the subsequent three characters respectively designate the initial pitch of the final /a/ (1: 154 Hz, 2: 192 Hz, 3: 240 Hz), its pitch contour (F: flat, D: descending), and its intensity (0: +2 dB, 1: +7 dB).

The consistency of the Ss' ratings was measured by the mean absolute difference between their two series of answers to the same questions. The value of this parameter was 0.65 on average for part I, and 0.60 for part D: this is, as for experiment 1, less than 2/3 of the difference between two nearest ratings. This result denotes a fairly good global consistency. Moreover, the global means of the intra-block ratings were 2.41 versus 2.32 for part I, and 2.43 versus 2.45 for part D. A paired t-test gives $p>0.05$ and $p>0.5$ (resp.). We thus have convergent indications of a good consistency of the Ss' ratings for both parts I and D. The individual consistency of each subject was measured for both parts, using the rate of identical answers to the same question (see 2.3. for an explanation). Among the $19 \cdot 2 = 38$ total number of parts to consider, no part could thus be rejected.

3.3.1. Part I: L'ignorance d'autrui exprimée (expressed ignorance of the hearer)

According to a research initiated by Halliday, the F_0 peak height on a word locates the information it provides on a 'given/new' scale (cf. Brown 1983, for a review): the higher the F_0 peak height, the newer the information. Of course, the information is new for the hearer (and not for the speaker). So the novelty comes from hearer's ignorance. One can therefore expect the latter, as it is evaluated by the speaker, to be expressed by his/her prosody through F_0 peak height.

Part I: *Ignorance d'autrui exprimée* (expressed ignorance of the hearer)					
L_1D0	*2.00*	0.87	*R_1D0*	*1.79*	0.93
L_1D1	*2.13*	0.96	*R_1D1*	*1.92*	1.08
L_1F0	*2.00*	0.99	*R_1F0*	*1.82*	0.95
L_1F1	*2.26*	1.13	*R_1F1*	*1.71*	0.96
L_2D0	*2.16*	0.72	*R_2D0*	*1.87*	0.81
L_2D1	*2.50*	0.86	*R_2D1*	*1.97*	0.88
L_2F0	*2.34*	0.71	*R_2F0*	*2.03*	0.79
L_2F1	*2.76*	0.91	*R_2F1*	*2.18*	0.95
L_3D0	*2.92*	0.75	*R_3D0*	*2.68*	0.93
L_3D1	*3.32*	0.70	*R_3D1*	*2.87*	1.07
L_3F0	*2.89*	0.89	*R_3F0*	*2.45*	1.13
L_3F1	*3.32*	0.87	*R_3F1*	*2.89*	1.03

Table 5: Mean and standard deviation of the ratings for the expressed ignorance of the hearer.

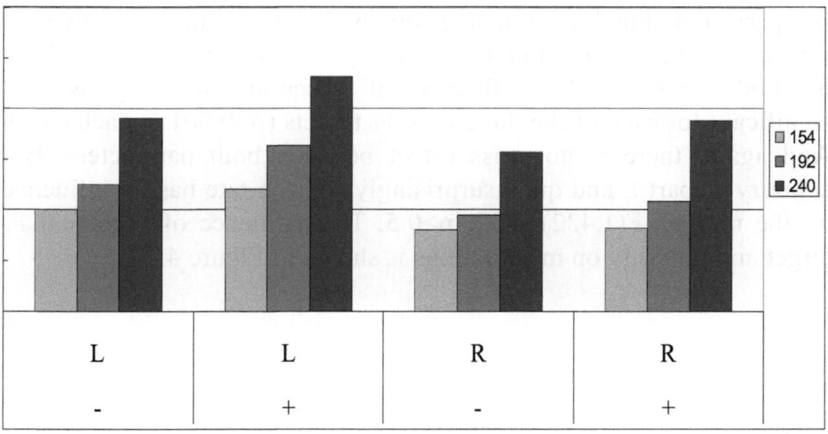

Figure 3: Mean ratings (Part I: *Ignorance d'autrui exprimée*) obtained for the three final F_0 targets – here named by the initial pitch of the final /a/, two speech rates (L and R), and two final intensities ('+' is for 1 – the higher intensity – and '-' for 0 – the lower intensity). Final F_0 target and intensity have a positive influence on the ratings, while the influence of speech rate is negative.

The final /a/'s F_0 contour (flat or falling) has no influence on the ratings: $F(1,432)=0.35$, $p>0.5$ (and $p>0.1$ for all 12 pairwise comparisons). We hence grouped together the results for stimuli differing only by this parameter. We obtained a positive influence of the final high F_0 target: $F(2, 432)=60.6$, $p<0.0001$, and also of intensity: $F(1,432)=10.7$, $p<0.005$. Speech rate has a significant negative effect: $F(1,432)=25.0$, $p<0.0001$. An ANOVA performed for each final high F_0 target shows that speech rate has an influence for all three of them (for F_0=**240 Hz:** $F(1,148)=8.8$, $p<0.001$; for F_0=**192** Hz: $F(1,148)=14.8$, $p<0.001$; for F_0=**154 Hz:** $F(1,148)=4.5$, $p<0.05$), but that intensity has no influence for F_0=**154** Hz (for F_0=**240 Hz:** $F(1,148)=7.7$, $p<0.001$; for F_0=**192** Hz: $F(1,148)=5.3$, $p<0.05$; but for F_0=**154 Hz:** $F(1,148)=0.6$, $p>0.1$). No cross effect was found between both parameters.

3.3.2. Part D: L'envie d'informer exprimée (expressed desire to know)

As for part I, the pitch contour (flat or descending) has no influence on the results: $F(1,432)=1.82$, $p>0.1$ (and $p>0.1$ for all 12 pairwise comparisons). Final F_0 and intensity both have a high positive influence on the ratings: $F(1,432)=50.0$, $p<0.0001$ and $F(1,432)=49.1$, $p<0.0001$ (resp.). The influence of accentual intensity is still significant for each of the three final F_0 targets ($p<0.001$ in each case). And again, there is no cross effect between both parameters. But contrary to part I, and quite surprisingly, speech rate has no influence on the ratings: $F(1,432)=0.02$, $p>0.5$. The influence of accentual F_0 target and intensity on mean ratings is shown in Figure 4.

Part D: *Envie d'informer exprimée* (expressed desire to inform)					
L_1D0	*1.71*	0.69	*R_1D0*	*1.89*	0.83
L_1D1	*2.34*	0.94	*R_1D1*	*2.39*	0.92
L_1F0	*1.63*	0.75	*R_1F0*	*1.84*	0.79
L_1F1	*2.18*	0.83	*R_1F1*	*2.34*	0.99
L_2D0	*2.18*	0.83	*R_2D0*	*2.21*	0.66
L_2D1	*2.74*	0.92	*R_2D1*	*2.63*	0.97
L_2F0	*2.11*	0.69	*R_2F0*	*2.11*	0.73
L_2F1	*2.66*	0.88	*R_2F1*	*2.50*	0.80
L_3D0	*2.74*	0.69	*R_3D0*	*2.61*	0.89
L_3D1	*3.24*	0.75	*R_3D1*	*3.11*	0.89
L_3F0	*2.68*	0.81	*R_3F0*	*2.66*	1.02
L_3F1	*3.08*	0.88	*R_3F1*	*2.89*	1.06

Table 6: Mean and standard deviation of the ratings for the expressed desire to inform.

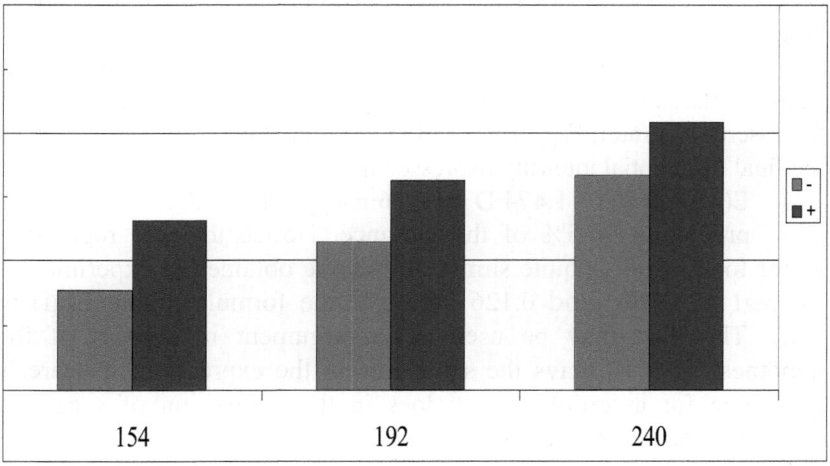

Figure 4: Mean ratings (Part D: *Envie d'informer autrui exprimée*) obtained for the three final F_0 targets – here named by the initial pitch of the final /a/, and two final intensities ('+' is for 1 – the higher intensity – and '-' for 0 – the lower intensity). Both final F_0 target and intensity have a positive influence on the ratings.

3.4. Discussion

As for experiment 1, 17 out of the 19 Ss followed a common tendency, judging that the expressed ignorance of the hearer was greater when the accented syllable had a higher target pitch. And in the same way, two Ss adopted the opposite scale. These two Ss are not the same as in the first experiment though, since the groups of Ss were different in both experiments. Here again, it is plausible that these two Ss misinterpreted the task, or did not actually make their judgment merely from what was expressed, but from some inferences on the speaker's strategy.

As for experiment 1, again, the instructions aiming at insuring that the Ss dissociated hearer's ignorance and speaker's desire to inform, reached their goal: parts I and D led to clearly different results. Each of the parameters tested here had an influence on the expressed ignorance of the hearer. The F_0 peak height in the final, accented syllable, appears again to be a major influence on the ratings, but speech rate also seems to play an important role. The influence of accentual intensity is not systematic, and is proportional to the F_0 peak height.

The linear regression formula for the expressed ignorance of the hearer is stated below, where E(aI) designates the expected ignorance for the assertive stimuli, $F_{0final}(ST)$ and D as defined before (see 2.4.), and I the final differential intensity expressed in dB – its value is +2 or +7:

$E(aI) = 2.837 - 1.474 \cdot D + 0.126 \cdot F_{0final}(ST) + 0.048 \cdot I$

predicting 90.5% of the variance. Notice that the regression factor for F_0 peak is quite similar to the one obtained in experiment 1 for part I (0.166, and 0.126 here; see the formula giving E(qI) in 2.4.). This fact may be used as an argument in support of the hypothesis that F_0 plays the same role in the expression of hearer's ignorance for assertions, as it does in the expression of speaker's ignorance for interrogations.

Regarding the expressed desire to inform, we obtain:

$E(aD) = 1.169 + 0.108 \cdot F_{0final}(ST) + 0.096 \cdot I$

predicting 95.0% of the variance. The coefficient of $F_{0final}(ST)$ in E(aD) is noticeably lower than the one obtained in experiment 1 for E(qD) (0.232, and 0.108 here). Noteworthy, this preeminence of interrogation over assertion is also found for the expression of the desire to know/inform. F_0 peak thus has a lower influence on the ratings for assertions than for interrogations. But this influence remains important for assertions. A possible explanation is that there is not one single scale of evaluation of ignorance here, but two different ones, through a bias: a desire to inform would seldom be great, and rarely be very great – because the self is not as much involved as it is when trying to solve one's own problems – while both adjectives would apply more often to a desire to be informed.

4. General discussion

The results obtained in this study do not seem to be explained by any theory of the expression of affects and/or attitudes by prosody. Concerning the expression of emotions, theories proposed for instance by Scherer (1986), or based on two or three dimensions (see Pereira 2000), generally consider emotions to induce some global changes in the vocal expression. In particular, they are often described as behaving like amplifiers either on mean F_0, intensity, speech rate, maximum F_0, and so on. These amplifications, whose gain factor may be either superior or inferior to 1, affect the characteristics of grammaticalized prosodic patterns. This view is justified by biological/physiological considerations, such as the fact that arousal enhances muscular activity as a whole, thus tending to increase speech rate (which depends on the speed of articulatory trajectories), and F_0 (see Titze 1993, or Farley 1994).

Such theories could possibly explain, for example, that higher speech rate expresses greater desire to know (in a yes-no question) while it does not express greater desire to inform (in an assertion): the arousal could be argued to decrease during an assertion, insofar as the assertion allows the speaker to progressively solve the problem at the origin of the utterance, which is not the case of an interrogation (whereby the problem is just 'shared' with the hearer); hence, a greater desire here would induce the speech rate to decrease more in the former case, and to be higher in the latter case (we discuss this interpretation further in the text). But the kind of explanations that these theories allow for cannot be invoked to explain the negative influence of speech rate on the expression of hearer's ignorance.

One can also consider more 'attitudinal' theories. Ohala's (1984) 'frequency code', for example, even though it can provide an explanation for the expression of speaker's ignorance, cannot explain the use of higher F_0 to express greater ignorance of the hearer, or greater desire to inform. Clearly, then, there is not only one frequency code, but several ones, providing that one such code does actually exist, which we will further discuss below. Another theoretical hypothesis is proposed by Vaissière (1995), who considers the inter-linguistic recurrence of rising F_0 patterns for yes-no questions as originating in the negation of an unmarked pitch contour, descending and assertive. But on this sole basis, it appears impossible to explain, for instance, the use of a bigger amplitude of the F_0 rise to express greater desire to know. Moreover, in experiment 2, the F_0 contour's shape (high-flat or high-falling) on the accented syllable has no influence on the ratings. But according to Vaissière's point of view, we could consider a more marked 'non-finality' to correlate with greater ignorance of the hearer; hence, we could have expected a high-falling contour to express lower hearer's ignorance than the high-flat one, which is not the case.

These 'attitudinal' theories do not provide any account for the shades of meaning conveyed by speech rate. And speech rate clearly plays an important role in both the experiments related in this chapter. Then, how can we interpret these results? Studies on the vocal expression of emotions agree that arousal is the main determinant. And for an ordinary yes-no question, arousal depends on speaker's ignorance and – above all – desire to know (see for example Scherer's model, 1986). This can be an explanation for the role of speech rate in experiment 1. Once the valence of arousal is set by both these parameters, among others, then it could well be expressed by prosody depending on some other cognitive parameters. But these parameters remain to be found.

If one considers that higher intensity may express greater desire to know, then all three prosodic parameters play a role here. But only final pitch plays a role for ignorance. Arousal, which is higher when the desire to know is greater, then provides an explanation in the former case. But this is not true in the latter case. This sole influence of F_0 may be interpreted, by a linguist, as a consequence of the reinforcement of interrogative modality, here through a more ample final F_0 rise. But then, how can we apply this affirmation to the results obtained for assertions (experiment 2)? Is higher final F_0 target a reinforcement of assertive modality? On the contrary, it seems to rather decrease the distance between our assertive and interrogative pitch contours. Conversely, the given/new dimension (Brown 1983) provides an interpretation of the influence of F_0 that we found for assertions, but not for interrogations.

An explanation could use Ohala's (1984) frequency code. According to the hypothesized code, higher final F_0 expresses higher submission – because of a higher dependence – of the speaker towards the hearer. This dependence is arguably greater for a more ignorant speaker, which explains the influence of F_0 for yes-no questions. But what about the use of higher accentual F_0 target to express greater ignorance of the hearer? Actually, the contrary could be expected, since hearer's ignorance contributes to lessen the speaker's dependence toward him/her. The 'frequency code' then needs to be modified to encompass hearer's dependence through a process of empathy of the speaker towards the hearer.

Syllable lengthening, besides facilitating perception through a more precise articulation, allows the speaker to highlight a word by making it stand salient for a longer duration; and hence to implicitly invite the hearer to localize his/her attention on this word. This could justify that lower speech rate / greater lengthening is a means for the speaker to ensure the transmission of a less expected content to a more ignorant speaker. This strategy, rated as *expressing* greater ignorance, would then result from its common and repeated use.

The role of intensity in the expression of hearer's ignorance is less clear, but it is more important when the F_0 peak is higher. Rossi (1978) showed that intensity has an influence on the perception of F_0; he found in particular that an intensity rise on a flat tone drives the audition to the perception of a slightly rising glissando. But this effect is too low to explain our results here, because the linear regression formula that we obtained indicates that a +8 dB rise is equivalent to an F_0 rise of 35 Hz, while for Rossi *et al.* (1972) a +8 dB rise, on a flat tone at 155 Hz, is perceived as a glissando having an amplitude of 17 Hz. Moreover, if our results came from a perception bias, we could expect the same kind of effect for yes-no questions, which is not the case since intensity does not play any role there.

Another possibility would be that intensity plays a role similar to the one proposed for duration, by facilitating hearer's perception: an intensity rise, even on one single syllable, makes a word appear as more salient to the hearer. Again here, the common use of a strategy would make it express its goal. Note that this interpretation is also compatible with the idea that the management of the speaker's energetic resources is in relation with the communication needs of the hearer at the perceptual level (Kohler 1990).

It is maybe more difficult to interpret the dependency of this influence to F_0 peak. One may suggest the following explanation: an F_0 peak height of 154 Hz expresses low ignorance of the hearer, according to the results. This means that the hearer considers the speaker's answer 'Natacha' as a possibility. Hence the hearer does not need this word to be very salient to recognize it without difficulty: the perception of this word is thus ensured. It can therefore be expected that lengthening and intensity will be quite useless here. According to the above hypothesis, since neither of both these parameters incorporates a strategy of communication under such conditions, then they should not influence the expression of hearer's ignorance. And indeed, both have a lower influence for lower F_0 peaks.

A greater desire to inform can be expressed by higher final F_0 peak and intensity, but not by higher speech rate, although the latter allows to express a greater desire to know (for yes-no questions). An explanation of this remarkable difference in the role of speech rate was proposed at the start of this section, and involved the possibility that the source of the motivation for informing could progressively disappear during the assertion. This interpretation is somehow reinforced after an experiment related by Piot (2002: ch. 7), which shows that a greater desire to inform can indeed be expressed by speech rate, through its higher decrease during the utterance (for a fixed total duration of this utterance).[1] However, both experimental results may be interpreted differently. Indeed, if it is correct that – as we proposed above – a lower speech rate favors information of the hearer, then it should preferably be used whenever the speaker has a great desire to inform the hearer. Thus in the second experiment, higher speech rate as well as lower speech rate would contribute to the expression of a higher desire to inform. The absence of influence of speech rate on the latter's ratings would result from the neutralization of both effects. And the above-mentioned influence of a higher decrease of speech rate would result either from such rhythmic pattern expressing a 'refrained' greater arousal, and/or from the corresponding lengthening of more informative last words.

One may be surprised, also, by the very significant influence of intensity in the expression of a greater desire to inform – an effect which is found for each final F_0 peak, while it plays no role in the expression of the desire to know (in yes-no questions). But if we suppose, as we did before, that accentual intensity belongs to a strategy aiming at making the accented word appear as more salient to the hearer, then this strategy is clearly a good one to get the hearer informed; but not so much for being informed through an interrogation, which basically rests on the hearer's intention to give information to the speaker. So here again, a common and repeated strategy may have shaped expression.

5. Conclusions

Klatt synthesis was chosen in order to independently manipulate three prosodic parameters (speech rate, F_0 and intensity) to generate a range of assertive as well as interrogative utterances. This allowed us to rigorously assess some influences of these parameters in the

1 This study, using a forced choice between two utterances, was made on just one single couple of stimuli, partly because of the difficulty of synthesizing a couple of auditorily distinct such stimuli.

expression of affects which are basic conditions for assertions or interrogations to be uttered: ignorance of the speaker or of the hearer, and desire to know or to inform. A preliminary outcome of the related experiments is the absence of cross-effects of the three prosodic parameters, showing that they influence the ratings independently from each other.

A first result of this study is the very significant positive influence of F_0 peak on the ratings for the four affects. If Ohala's 'frequency code' may be invoked concerning the expression of ignorance, a process of empathy has to be involved for it to explain that higher F_0 peak can be used to express greater ignorance of the hearer. And another influence has to be proposed to explain the use of higher F_0 peak to express greater desire to know or to inform, for which emotional arousal is most likely at stake.

A second important finding is that higher speech rate expresses greater desire to know in interrogations, but not greater desire to inform in assertions. If we consider the expected resolution of a 'problem' – here the one consisting roughly in sharing a piece of information with the hearer – as a source of the speaker's motor activity in speech, then it is not implausible that this problem be progressively solved during an assertion, while it is not during an interrogation. This interpretation is compatible with the reported influence of a larger diminution of the speech rate to express greater desire to inform. However there is another interpretation for both results, insofar as a lower speech rate favors information of the hearer – as it was proposed to explain the negative influence of speech rate on the expressed ignorance of the hearer. Then a lower speech rate should preferably be used whenever the speaker has a great desire to inform the hearer, which runs opposite to the influence of the resulting arousal of the speaker.

Another important result is that higher accentual intensity has a positive influence on the ratings for assertions, but that it has none for interrogations. It was suggested that higher intensity favored hearer's perception, and hence that it was well adapted to greater hearer's ignorance, or to ensure that the hearer got informed. It is also plausible that using higher intensity, by ensuring a more robust hearer's perception, is here less crucial in the context of an interrogation. We then proposed the hypothesis that a very common vocal strategy ended up being considered as a proper expression of its origin (i.e. of what motivated the choice of this strategy). This hypothesis provided an explanation for these findings.

One last result is that speech rate has a negative influence on the expression of hearer's ignorance. The above mentioned hypothesis that 'a common strategy becomes an expression' can also explain it, if we admit that a lowering speech rate favors hearer's perception. This latter proposition is comforted for instance by the use of higher speech rate for less informative speech, as in *l'incise intonative* (Gachet/ Avanzi 2008). So what is more important to the hearer (according to the speaker) would be uttered at a lower speech rate. Therefore lower speech rate would express greater hearer's ignorance, according to our hypothesis, which is experimentally confirmed.

This study shows how Klatt synthesis can be used to investigate the expression of affects and emotions, and in particular to better isolate the relevant acoustic parameters. It also sheds new light on the communication of some affects which are omnipresent in assertions and interrogations. Its methodology, exploiting Klatt synthesis or another tool (like diphone synthesis, which lowers the designing time but is less controllable), could be used to investigate further affect expression, but also, for instance, the validation or exploration of the tonal categories proposed by autosegmental-metric intonation models. Another field of application concerns the meaning of intonation, which stands between this research and the latter kind of studies. We believe that scientific method, in all these fields, asks for a more extended use of speech synthesis to rigorously evaluate the above mentioned models and theoretical predictions.

References

Brown, Gillian 1983. Prosodic structure and the given/new distinction. In Cutler, Anne / Ladd, D. Robert (eds) *Prosody: models and measurements.* Berlin: Springer, 67-78.

Farley, Glenn R. 1994. A quantitative model of voice F_0 control. *JASA* 95/2, 1017-1029.

Faure, Georges 1973. La description phonologique des systèmes prosodiques. In Grundstrom, Allan / Léon, Pierre (eds) *Interrogation et intonation en Français standard et Français Canadien.* Montreal: Didier (Studia Phonetica, *8*), 1-16.

Fónagy, Ivan 1986. Les langages de l'émotion. *Quaderni di Semantica* VII/2, 305-318.

Fónagy, Ivan / Bérard, Eva 1973. Questions totales simples et implicatives en français parisien. In Grundstrom, Allan / Léon, Pierre (eds) *Interrogation et intonation en Français standard et Français Canadien.* Montreal: Didier (Studia Phonetica, *8*), 53-98.

Gachet, Frédéric / Avanzi, Mathieu 2008. Le rôle de la prosodie dans l'identification des parenthèses. In *Journée CONSCILA*, Paris (see <http://www.atilf.fr/atilf/evenement/JourneeEtude/JourneeEtude_2008-03-14_Conscila.pdf>).

House, David 1990. *Tonal perception in speech.* Lund: Lund University Press.

Klatt, Dennis H. / Klatt, L. C. 1989. Analysis, synthesis, and perception of voice quality variations among female and male talkers. *JASA* 87/2, 820-857.

Kohler, Klaus 1990. Segmental reduction in connected speech in German: phonological facts and phonetic explanations. In Hardcastle, William J. / Marchal, Alain (eds) *Speech Production and Speech Modelling.* Dordrecht: Kluwer Academic Publishers, 69-92.

Ladd, D. Robert / Silverman, K. E. A. / Tolkmitt, F. / Bergmann, G. / Scherer, K. R. 1985. Evidence for the independant function of intonation contour type, voice quality, and F_0 range in signaling speaker affect. *J.A.S.A.* 78/2, 435-444.

Laver, John 1980. *The phonetic description of voice quality.* Cambridge: Cambridge University Press.

Mertens, Piet 1987. *L'intonation du français. De la description linguistique à la reconnaissance automatique.* Louvain: Université catholique de Louvain. (Ph. D.)

Ohala, John J. 1984. An ethological Perspective on common cross-language utilization of F_0 of voice. *Phonetica* 41, 1-16.

Pereira, Cécile 2000. Dimensions of emotional meaning in speech. In *Speech and Emotion, ISCA Tutorial and Research Workshop (ITRW). Newcastle, Northern Ireland, UK: ISCA Archive*, 25-28 (see <http://www.isca-speech.org/archive/archive_papers/speech_emotion/spem_025.pdf>).

Piot, Olivier 2002. *Vers une théorie unifiée de la prosodie du français et de l'anglais: des émotions à la phonologie.* Paris: Université Paris III (unpublished Ph. D., see <http://www.cavi.univ-paris3.fr/ilpga/ED/student/stop/>).

Rossi, Mario 1978. Interactions of intensity glides and frequency glissandos. *Language and speech* 21/4, 384-396.

Rossi, Mario / Chafcouloff, M. 1972. Recherche sur le seuil différentiel de fréquence fondamentale dans la parole. *Travaux de l'institut de phonétique d'Aix* 1, 179-185.

Scherer, Klaus R. 1986. Vocal affect expression: a review and a model for future research. *Psychol. Bulletin* 99, 141-165.

Studdert-Kennedy, Michael / Hadding, K. 1973. Auditory and linguistic processes in the perception of intonation contours. *Language and Speech* 16, 293-313.

Titze, Ingo R. 1993. *Principles of voice production.* Prentice Hall.

Vaissière, Jacqueline 1995. Phonetic explanations for cross-linguistic similarities. *Phonetica* 52, 123-130.

IOULIA GRICHKOVTSOVA / MICHEL MOREL / ANNE LACHERET

Perception of Affective Prosody in Natural and Synthesized Speech: Which Methodological Approach?

1. Introduction

Research on affective speech (cf. Johnstone/Scherer 2000; Murray/Arnott 1993) underlines the plural character of prosodic features involved in the expression of vocal emotions and attitudes. These prosodic features include, among others, voice quality, fundamental frequency, speech rate and intensity. Thus, speech prosody has a double function: linguistic and paralinguistic.

According to Ladd (1996), prosody realizes its linguistic and paralinguistic functions through two parallel channels tightly coordinated in time and used simultaneously in the interpretation of utterances with no effect on each other. Paralinguistic features are seen as modifications added to the linguistic features. Nevertheless, the question remains if these two types of prosody are separable for individual analysis of their roles and specific characteristics.

Even if studies into affective speech production have shown differences between emotions in the usage of prosodic parameters, difficulty is observed in determining a significant perceptive value of these parameters in the identification of affective states. Researchers come to an agreement on the importance of voice quality in the production and perception of emotions (d'Alessandro 2006). However, the definition of the perceptive role of other prosodic parameters remains a complex task. These prosodic parameters include pitch, rhythm, loudness, speech rate, and constitute the prosodic contour of an utterance. If voice quality generally realizes paralinguistic functions, prosodic contour plays two roles – linguistic and paralinguistic. The difficulty to analyze these two functions individually explains the importance of methodological choices in the corpus development of affective speech.

Two main types of corpus are usually used for perceptive analysis of affective speech: utterances with or without lexical content. Perceptive experiment on the basis of utterances with lexical meaning does not only establish the significant role of fundamental frequency in the identification of affective states, but also underlines cross-linguistic differences in the association of fundamental frequency with affective states in English and Dutch (Chen 2004). Studies on the basis of non-lexical utterances used an invented combination of syllables existing in the language (Bänziger/Scherer 2005) or an utterance in a foreign language unknown for the speakers and listeners (Yanushevskaya *et al.* 2006, Gobl/Ní Chasaide 2003). They aimed to neutralize lexical and syntactic constraints during the course of expression and identification of vocal affective states, as well as to facilitate cross-linguistic comparisons. These studies show the importance of the prosodic contour for certain affective states, and cross-linguistic differences for some associations between voice quality, fundamental frequency and affective states. Nevertheless, the absence of lexical meaning in the utterances used can engender bias in the analysis of the role played by intonation. Indeed, utterances devoid of lexical meaning do not permit chunking into syntactic and pragmatic units. We suggest that without distinction between words (function word/content word), without syntactic and information boundaries, gating points of prosodic contours encoding the expression of emotions are affected, and the role of intonation is minimized.

In order to study the role of prosody in the identification of affective states, a series of perception experiments were performed on the basis of two different corpora of affective speech. The first two experiments used a corpus of utterances with affective lexical meaning encoded by two French actors. The third experiment used a multi-speaker corpus of French neutral utterances. This report is organized as follows: the three experiments are described in the next two sections – 1) corpus with affective lexical meaning, 2) multi-speaker corpus with affectively neutral meaning – where research objectives and results are presented. In particular, our methodology for the corpus design and for the development of perception tests is discussed. Then, follow a general discussion and conclusive remarks.

2. Perception experiments based on the corpus with affective lexical meaning

A corpus of affective speech encoded by two French actors (a male and a female) was recorded in order to address our research questions concerning the role of prosody in the identification of affective states. This corpus contains six affective states: three emotions (anger, sadness, happiness) and three attitudes (obviousness, doubt, irony). We define emotion according to Scherer (2003) as a brief episode of synchronised response of all or most organismic subsystems in response to an external or internal event of major significance. Attitude is defined as affectively coloured stances, preferences or predispositions activated during an interpersonal interaction.

Utterances recorded for the corpus possess affectively charged lexical meaning, identifiable as such. In practice, even if the beginning of each utterance can be associated with different affective states, in the course of its production, little room is gradually left for interpretative manoeuvre. This approach allows to study utterances that are close to natural affective speech, as the expressed affect is in accordance with the lexical meaning. Examples of utterances from the corpus with affectively charged lexical meaning are given in Appendix 1.

Two perception experiments were realized with this corpus. The first experiment aimed to determine if affective states can be identified before the end of the utterances used for their expression. Our hypothesis was that emotions can be identified earlier in the flow of speech than attitudes, as voice quality specific to the expressed emotion is present from the beginning of the utterance. The second experiment was developed to compare the perceptive value of voice quality and prosodic contour for the studied affective states. Our hypothesis was that voice quality is privileged in the emotions, and prosodic contour in the attitudes. The methodology of the experiments and the obtained results are described in the two following subsections.

2.1. Experiment 1: gating paradigm

In the framework of experiment 1, the possibility to identify affective states before the end of the utterance was tested. According to our hypothesis expressed above, listeners may identify emotions earlier, in the beginning or at least clearly before the end of the utterance. Identification of attitudes requires the analysis of lexical, syntactic and prosodic structures of the utterance, and thus it may be realized later than for emotions.

The gating paradigm was chosen to test the proposed hypothesis. This paradigm allows understanding of how much phonetic information is needed for the optimal identification of affective states. This paradigm is based on the hypothesis that a gating point corresponds to the part of the utterance that triggers the identification of the encoded affective state. In order to localize the gating points in the utterance, our methodology was as follows: each stimulus was presented in segments increased progressively by time steps of 200 ms. Listeners were asked to identify the affective state at the end of each segment. The duration-blocked presentation format was chosen: first, all the stimuli of the particular segment size were presented to the listeners in a random order, then all the stimuli of the following segment size, and so on.

Twenty-four utterances were taken from the recorded corpus: two utterances for each studied affective state (anger, happiness, sadness, obviousness, irony and doubt) pronounced by an actress and two utterances by an actor. Thirteen subjects participated in the test. They were all native French speakers (average age – 31 years old). The Perceval software (Ghio *et al.* 2007), specially developed for psycholinguistic perception tests, was used. The experiment was run for about 40 minutes on a computer in a quiet laboratory room.

Three variables were selected for the analysis of correct responses: identification point, isolation point and final level of identification. Identification point refers to the gate of the stimulus where correct identification reaches at least 50%. Isolation point is the gate of the stimulus where the highest identification is achieved and maintained without any change in response thereafter. Finally, a general level of identification was calculated on the whole response data in percentage. Results are reported in Table 1.

Affective state	*Identification point (ms)*	*Isolation point (ms)*	*Identification level (%)*
ANGER	200/400	800/1600	74.9
SADNESS	400/1000	800/1600	70.1
OBVIOUSNESS	400/1200	800/complete	56.9
DOUBT	600/1400	800/complete	57.6
HAPPINESS	800/1800	1000/complete	54.1
IRONY	1600/1800	1600/complete	39.6

Table 1. Results for identification point, isolation point and the final level of identification. Two values show the observed range of gating points for each affective state across the four utterances.

The results observed for the three variables allow the differentiation of anger and sadness from the other affective states. For the identification point, we see that utterances encoded with anger are identified at the first or maximum at the second gate. Sadness too can be recognized as early as the second gate, but more variability is observed. The other affective states are identified later. Results for the isolation point also go in the same direction: angry and sad utterances are all successfully recognized before listeners hear the complete form. This is not true for the other expressive modalities.

Based on the gating paradigm, differences were shown in the identification of emotions and attitudes. Our hypothesis that emotions can be identified earlier than attitudes is confirmed for anger and sadness. Happiness follows the identification pattern observed for attitudes in our perception experiment. This observation can be explained by the specific communicative role played by happiness. Speakers may better control happiness; they may use it in inter-personal communication in the same way as attitudes. But it is also often the case with anger, which is identified early. Another explanation may be the difficulty to produce voluntarily specific 'smiling' voice quality by speakers, and thus they might privilege intonation more, like for attitudes.

2.2. Experiment 2: transplantation paradigm

Experiment 2 aimed to compare the perceptive value of voice quality and prosodic contour for six affective states: anger, happiness, sadness, obviousness, irony and doubt. More precisely, our objective was to investigate if intonation and voice quality are equally important for the perception of the studied affective states or whether one of them may be privileged. Our research hypothesis was that voice quality is privileged for marking emotions, while variation of prosodic contour is more used in the expression of attitudes.

Prosody transplantation paradigm (Garcia *et al.* 2006) was used to evaluate the corresponding perceptive roles of voice quality and prosodic contour in the identification of affective states. This method involves extraction and exchange of the prosodic contour between two utterances with the same segmental content: a natural utterance and a synthesized utterance with neutral intonation. Prosody transplantation acts on the fundamental frequency, intensity and temporal parameters, but it does not modify characteristics of voice quality (though degradation is sometimes observed).

Seventy-two utterances were chosen in the recorded corpus: six utterances for each studied affective state (anger, happiness, sadness, obviousness, irony and doubt) pronounced by a female, and six utterances pronounced by a male. The same utterances were synthesized with KALI, a French-speaking text-to-speech diphone synthesis system (Morel/Lacheret 2001). The synthesized utterances did not have any vocal affective meaning, as KALI does not perform this type of treatment. In the process of prosody transplantation, the prosody of Kali was mapped on the utterances encoded by actors, and the prosody of the actor was mapped on the utterance synthesized by Kali. Thus, four versions of each utterance were developed: version 1 – 'natural' (natural prosodic contour and voice quality encoded by the actor), version 2 – 'voice quality' (natural voice quality and prosodic contour from Kali), version 3 – 'prosody' (natural prosodic contour and voice quality from Kali), version 4 – 'lexical' (voice quality and prosodic contour of Kali without any vocal affective meaning). In total, 288 stimuli were designed for the perception test.

Experiment 2 was run in the same manner as Experiment 1, and it took about 40 minutes. All the stimuli were randomized. Twelve native French speakers (average age – 31 years old) participated in the test. The results of the perception test, displayed in Table 2, show the level of identification for the four versions of audio stimuli in percentage. Results for 'natural' stimuli show the best identification of the encoded affective state, as both natural voice quality and prosody of the actor are present. Identification of version 2 'voice quality' and version 3 'prosody' vary with the studied affective state. Version 4 'lexical' has the lowest identification level.

Affective state	*Natural (%)*	*Voice quality (%)*	*Prosody (%)*	*Lexical (%)*
ANGER	95	59	86	43
HAPPINESS	87	58	59	26
SADNESS	86	84	65	63
DOUBT	85	35	80	15
IRONY	74	46	61	43
OBVIOUSNESS	78	67	65	74

Table 2: Identification of affective speech stimuli. The correct responses are expressed in percentage.

The effect of the lexical meaning is present not only in the 'lexical' version of the stimuli, but also in all the other stimuli. Therefore, in order to compensate the influence of the lexical meaning in versions 1-3, a neutralization procedure was applied. The value of the identification level for 'lexical' stimuli is assigned to the role of lexical meaning in the identification of the affective states. The identification of the other versions is facilitated by the presence of specific voice quality and/or prosodic contour, which we aim to evaluate. The normalized values are calculated through the extraction of the 'lexical' value from the identification values received for 'natural', 'voice quality' and 'prosody' stimuli of the corresponding state. For example, 'natural' – 'lexical' for anger: 95% - 43% = 52%. Thus, the received value was judged as the contribution of voice quality and/or prosody in the affective speech perception. These results are displayed in Figure 1.

The results for anger show that both prosodic contour and voice quality are used in the process of identification. Nevertheless, 'prosody' stimuli are identified more successfully than 'voice quality' stimuli, and this difference is statistically significant. Doubt results show that prosody has the main role in its perception. Obviousness is identified exclusively on the basis of lexical meaning (but maybe it was not sufficiently well realized by the actors?). Voice quality and prosody play an equally important role in the identification of happiness. Lexical meaning is apparently very important in the perception of irony, but prosody also contributes to its better identification. Voice quality is privileged in the identification of sadness.

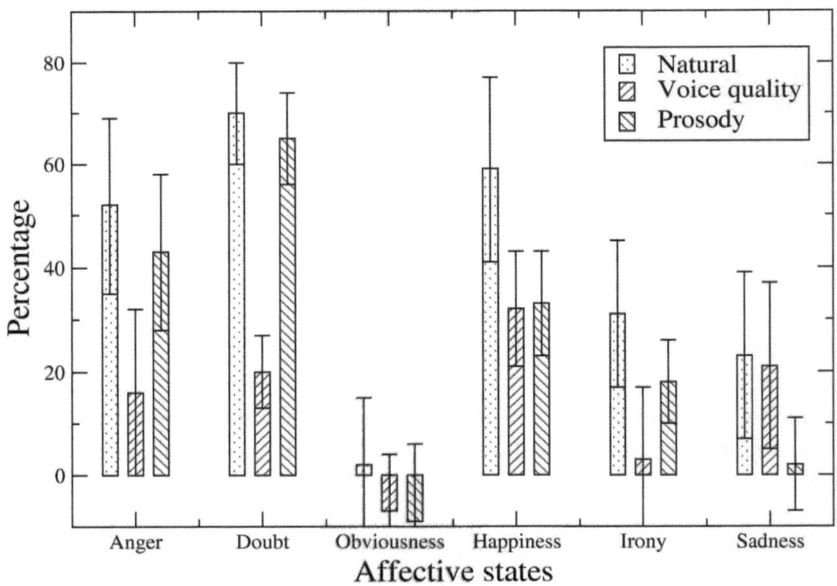

Figure 1: Neutralized values of successful identification.

This experiment investigated the perceptive value of voice quality and prosody for six affective states: anger, happiness, sadness, doubt, obviousness and irony. Previous studies (Yanushevskaya *et al.* 2006) suggest that voice quality has stronger and more consistent associations with affective meaning than intonation. And yet, these conclusions were drawn from the perception studies with non-sense utterances. Our choice to use natural utterances was motivated by our hypothesis that listeners have difficulty in interpreting the affective meaning of prosodic features without access to chunks, meaningful components of the utterance; as a consequence, results may become biased. Our results show the importance of prosodic contour in the identification of affective states, even if its level of identification is variable. The presence of natural prosody may even be crucial for the successful identification of some affective states, like doubt.

Even if it is not possible to separate completely emotions from attitudes based on the perceptive value of prosody and voice quality, some interesting observations can be made. They show certain distinctions between attitudes and emotions. Concerning attitudes, voice quality was not identified as important in their identification; lexical meaning played an important role for irony and obviousness; prosody was involved in the identification of doubt and irony. The results for emotions show that both prosody and voice quality carry an important perceptive value. While for happiness both prosody and voice quality are equally important, anger privileges prosody. Lexical meaning is generally less important for emotions than for attitudes.

2.3. Discussion of experiments 1 and 2

These two psycholinguistic tests on the perception of attitudes and emotions demonstrated differences between the affective states studied, and the important role played by prosody in the majority of cases. Nevertheless, two important issues were identified: the first concerns the number of speakers – the second, the type of the corpus used.

Our study shows important variability in the realization of affective states by the actors and its influence on their perception. In other words, some strategies may be easier for the identification of affective states than others. In parallel with this observation, it is important to remember that the corpus used for this experiment contains only two speakers. As a result, the question stands about the generalization of our results and the depth of understanding of the differences observed. In fact, other speakers may use other strategies for the expression of the same affective states; in this case, results of the acoustic and perceptive tests may differ significantly. At present, the level of inter- and intra-speaker variation in the realization of affective states is not known. Even if several multi-speaker speech corpora have appeared (Bänziger/Scherer 2005, Grichkovtsova 2008), the majority of the studies published in this research area use affective speech corpora with a small number of speakers (generally 1-4 subjects). This methodological weakness may explain the contradictory results observed in the studies on affective speech. This understanding of the variable character of affective speech motivated us to develop a multi-speaker corpus for sound and in-depth study in the field.

The neutralization of affective lexical meaning does not fully counterbalance its influence. Accentual prominence is generally realized on the informationally important words of the utterance, precisely those that are involved in the affective identification. By putting emphasis on these words, the prosodic contour facilitates the identification of affects, even in the absence of prosody specific to a particular affective state. It acts like a 'lexical amplifier'. Thus, there is an important risk that our results are overestimated concerning the role of prosodic contour. Our results do not distinguish the two functions realized by prosody: affective expression and lexical amplification. In comparison with experiments based on the corpora without lexical meaning, which may considerably underestimate the role of intonation, our experiments risk going to the opposite extreme. Here comes our motivation to run a new perception experiment on the basis of a corpus with neutral lexical meaning in order to evaluate the specific role of intonation in the identification of affective states without interference with prosodic amplification for affectively charged words.

3. Experiments on the basis of a multi-speaker corpus with neutral lexical meaning

The methodological issues brought up in the above section led us to develop a multi-speaker corpus on the basis of one affectively neutral utterance: *Je vais rentrer à la maison maintenant* / *I am going home now*. Twenty-two native French speakers (11 males and 11 females) were recorded. The total recording time of the corpus was seven hours. Six emotions (anger, sadness, happiness, disgust, fear and grief) and one neutral statement were selected for this study. Attitudes will make the subject of our future work.

A specific text was designed for each emotion investigated; the same neutral utterance was inserted in the middle of all the texts. Thus, it was possible to record the same lexically neutral utterance encoded in different emotional contexts. The underlying hypothesis was that the expression of emotions inducted from the beginning of the text with emotionally marked lexical meaning will propagate in the production of the neutral utterance. In such a way, the token utterance carries prosodic features of the emotion conveyed in the whole text, and speakers are not consciously aware of that. Each text is read three times by each speaker so that they imagine the context of the situation better and express the desired emotion in the most natural way.[1] The best realization of the token utterance was then extracted from the texts to constitute the corpus for experiment 3.

This corpus of lexically neutral utterances (154 stimuli presented in random order, test running time – 20 minutes) was first validated through an evaluation test with PERCEVAL software in order to filter out badly identified utterances. Ten French listeners (average age 30 years) participated in the test. We fixed the threshold of acceptance at 50% (at least 50% of listeners could identify the expressed emotion). This level of acceptance was chosen in order to exclude those utterances which are identified significantly above chance but which show important confusion with other affective

1 Examples of the texts used are given in Appendix 2.

states. We considered that a level of acceptance at 50% was necessary to increase the quality of the selected corpus. The results of this evaluation test are displayed in Table 3. Based on these results, we discarded disgust and fear, which did not give enough utterances at an acceptable identification level, and we kept the four following emotions: grief, sadness, anger and happiness.

Emotions	*Successful identification (%)*
ANGER	73
DISGUST	9
FEAR	14
HAPPINESS	36
GRIEF	32
SADNESS	68

Table 3: Rate of utterances identified by listeners with the level of acceptance at 50%. For example, 36% of happy utterances were identified by at least 50% of listeners.

The multi-speaker corpus was validated for the development of a new perception test (experiment 3) on the basis of two methodological paradigms: gating paradigm and transplantation paradigm. The methodology was the same as that described for experiments 1 and 2. As in experiment 2, prosodic transplantation allowed to develop four versions of each utterance: version 1 – 'natural' (natural prosody and voice quality encoded by the actor), version 2 – 'voice quality' (natural voice quality and prosody from Kali), version 3 – 'prosody' (natural prosodic contour and voice quality from Kali), version 4 – 'lexical' (voice quality and prosody of Kali without any vocal affective meaning). Then, according to the gating paradigm, vocal stimuli were cut in fragments increased progressively by steps of one or two syllables until the end of the utterance:

je vais | ren | trer | à la | mai | son | main | tenant |

We did not keep the classic method of durational segmentation largely used in gating studies (segments are increased by fixed steps – 200 ms in our experiment 1) in order to get around speech rate variability depending on individual speakers and affective states.

In total, 1,560 stimuli were designed. Considering the number of stimuli, the test was based on the Latin square method,[2] which allows reducing the number of stimuli presented to each speaker. Eight versions of the test were prepared based on this method. To have good statistical validity, 16 subjects were recruited (native French speakers, average age 25 years, test running time – 20 minutes). The stimuli were presented in duration-blocked groups of segments through the increasing presentation format. The order of stimuli was randomized in each group. Results for the perceptive value of prosodic contour and voice quality in the affective identification are presented in Figure 2. A more detailed analysis of our results, in particular an acoustic analysis of the stimuli linked to the gating points, will be the subject of our future work.

As five categories of affective states (anger, happiness, sadness, grief and neutral statement) were used for the perception experiment, the identification level of 20% stands for 'zero', which represents a value purely depending on chance which will serve as a reference for the significance evaluation of results. Grief and sadness are characterized by a good identification for the version 'voice quality'. This result is predictable, knowing that these are less controllable emotions, and therefore they modify first physiological parameters not coded in language and mainly influence voice quality. For anger, voice quality plays a less important role than prosodic contour. The importance of intonation for anger highlights a socially and linguistically controlled mechanism, comparable to the one used in attitudinal expressions. Happiness identification in its natural version is superior to the modified versions. Prosody is only just significant; voice quality does not go beyond the 'zero' level. The low identification level for the voice quality version is probably due to the prosodic transplantation, which alters the smiling voice in the 'voice quality' of version 2 and masks happiness. Even if this result shows limits in the transplantation

---

2 A Latin square is an $n \times n$ table filled with n different symbols in such a way that each symbol occurs exactly once in each row and exactly once in each column.

method, it highlights the role of intonation in the identification of happiness. The identification results for the neutral statement show no difference between version 1 'natural' and version 3 'prosody'. Voice quality participation is hardly significant. Thus, a neutral statement is well differentiated from the other emotional modalities, especially by its prosodic contour.

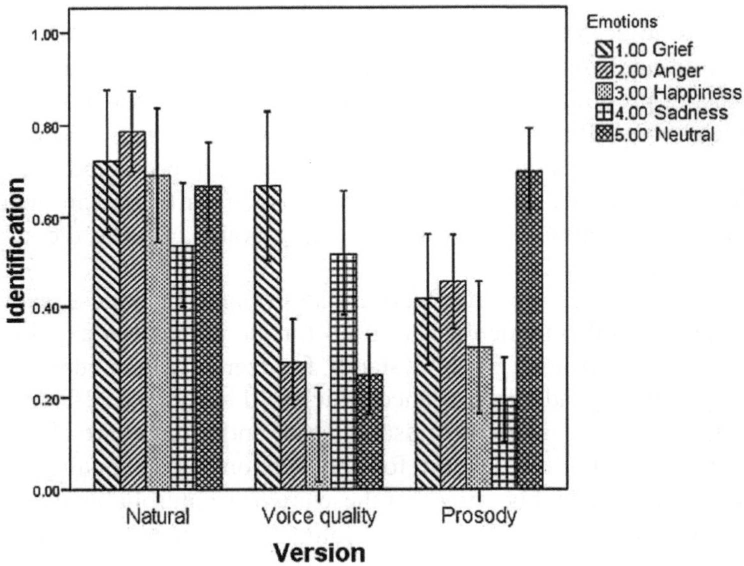

Figure 2: Identification of emotions for 'natural', 'voice quality' and 'prosody' versions (confidence intervals – 95%).

4. Discussion

Testing our main hypothesis according to which usage of non-lexical utterances can be problematic in the study of affective prosody, a series of experiments were conducted. Experiments 1 and 2, which are based on the corpus with affective lexical meaning, show the importance of intonation in the identification of affective states, even if this importance is variable. The presence of natural intonation may even be crucial for the identification of some affective states. Nevertheless, this approach showed another bias: the complete neutralization of emotionally charged words is not possible. The usage of even 'neutral' prosodic contour still retains the amplification of affectively important words, and thus provides better affective identification on the basis of lexical meaning. Another methodological weakness is often present in experiments on the identification of emotions: insufficient number of speakers (1-4). Even if emotional speech is characterized by significant inter- and intra-speaker variability (Scherer 2003, Grichkovtsova 2008), the question stands if such a small sample of speakers covers possible prosodic strategies for affective encoding in a representative way.

Experiment 3 uses a corpus on the basis of the same utterance with purely referential meaning. This experiment allowed us to determine more reliably the perceptive value of intonation and voice quality by avoiding two biases. The first bias is in the analysis of unnatural utterances without lexical meaning, in which the absence of syntactic structure reduces considerably the perceptive value of intonation. In contrast, the second bias relies on the analysis of utterances already connotated by their verbal material. If experiments 1 and 2 show that the presence of affective lexical meaning on its own is not sufficient for optimal identification of emotions, it is difficult to quantify objectively the contribution of prosodic parameters in the process of identification.

The method used in experiment 3 tests our hypothesis concerning the double status of intonation in the language activity: 1) it amplifies informationally important words in the specific emotional context; 2) it contributes to the identification of emotion by its specific prosodic contour. The usage of a lexically neutral utterance allows to evaluate the role of prosodic contour in the identification of emotions by isolating from its amplification function. It is then possible to characterize its acoustic properties on the qualitative and quantitative levels. The results of experiment 3 concerning the role of prosodic contour in the identification of emotions show that this role is predominant in comparison with its amplification function. This observation is not trivial as it confirms strong interaction between prosodic contours and lexical content. Here comes the interest to use utterances with lexical meaning. Non-lexical utterances can only be used for experiments on voice quality. Some limits were observed for the technical quality of prosodic transplantation through our experiments, as it can sometimes damage the voice quality of natural voice, while it does not damage the prosodic contour applied to synthesized voice. Thus, it is possible that results for voice quality are underestimated without questioning our results received for prosodic contours.

Another criticism can be made about the usage of only one lexically neutral utterance. We can reasonably suggest that other syntactically and rhythmically different utterances can give slightly different results. Nevertheless, these considerations do not question the methodology chosen. If it were to prove difficult to use such utterances in the same perception test according to our methodology, it would be possible to start the last experiment over with other types of lexically neutral utterances in order to carry out the comparison.

5. Conclusion

As regards methodology, we highlighted and showed how to overcome three major methodological issues existing in affective speech research: (1) the question of lexical meaning of the utterances used (present or not, affectively charged or not), (2) the question of inter- and intra-speaker variability, (3) differentiation of the specific role of prosody in the expression and identification of affective states.

With the help of our experiments, we showed that voice quality is not the only parameter important in the expression and identification of emotions. Our results underline that prosodic contour plays a significant role in the identification of emotions. This result does not only possess some theoretical value: prosodic contour must play an important part in the modelling of emotions in speech synthesis. The usage of natural prosodic contours by speech synthesis gives access, at least partially, to the expression of affective states. Indeed, voice quality sometimes plays a decisive role in identification, but it is difficult to manipulate this parameter in real time. It is much easier to implement prosodic contours (fundamental frequency, intensity, speech rate) in speech synthesis. The analysis of inter-speaker variability of the corpus and the selection of those strategies which are most adapted for reproduction in speech synthesis constitute the following stage of our project. Detailed acoustic analysis of our corpus in relation with gating points will also be the object of our future work.

References

d'Alessandro, Christophe 2006. Voice source parameters and prosodic analysis. In Sudhoff, Stefan / Lenertová, Denisa / Meyer, Roland / Pappert, Sandra / Augurzky, Petra / Mleinek, Ina / Richter, Nicole / Schließer, Johannes (eds) *Methods in Empirical Prosody Research.* Berlin, New York: De Gruyter, 63-87.

Bänziger, Tanya / Scherer, Klaus R. 2005. The role of intonation in emotional expressions. *Speech Communication* 46/3-4, 252-267.

Chen, Aoju / Gussenhoven, Carlos / Rietveld, Tony 2004. Language-specificity in perception of paralinguistic intonational meaning. *Language and Speech* 47/4, 311-350.

Garcia, Marie-Neige / d'Alessandro, Christophe / Bailly, Gérard / Boula de Mareüil, Philippe / Morel, Morel 2006. A joint prosody evaluation of French text-to-speech systems. In Calzolari, Nicoletta (ed.) *Proceedings of LREC*, Genoa, Italy, 307-310.

Ghio, Alain / André, Carine / Teston, Bernard / Cavé, Christian 2003. PERCEVAL: une station automatisée de tests de PERCeption et d'EVALuation auditive et visuelle. *Travaux Interdisciplinaire du Laboratoire Parole et Language d'Aix-en-Provence* 22, 115-33.

Gobl, Christer / Ní Chasaide, Ailbhe 2003. The role of voice quality in communicating emotion, mood and attitude. *Speech Communication*, 40/1-2, 189-212.

Grichkovtsova, Ioulia 2008. *A cross-linguistic study of affective prosody production by monolingual and bilingual children: Scottish English and French.* PhD thesis. Edinburgh: Queen Margaret University.

Grosjean, François 1996. Gating. *Language and Cognitive Processes* 11/6, 597-604.

Johnstone, Tom / Scherer, Klaus R. 2000. Vocal communication of emotion. In Lewis, Michael / Haviland, Jeannette M. (eds): *Handbook of emotions*. New York: Guilford, 220-35.

Ladd, D. Robert 1996. *Intonational phonology.* Cambridge: Cambridge University Press.

Murray, Iain R. / Arnott, John L. 1993. Towards the simulation of emotion in synthetic speech: A review of the literature on human vocal emotion. *Journal of Acoustic Society of America* 93/2, 1097-1108.

Morel, Michel / Lacheret-Dujour, Anne 2001. Kali, synthèse vocale à partir du texte: de la conception à la mise en œuvre. *Traitement Automatique des Langues* 42/1, 1-29.

Scherer, Klaus R. 2003. Vocal communication of emotion: A review of research paradigms. *Speech Communication* 40/1-2, 227-56.

Yanushevskaya, Irena / Gobl, Christer / Ní Chasaide, Ailbhe 2006. Mapping Voice to Affect: Japanese listeners. In Hoffmann, Rüdiger / Mixdorff, Hansjörg (eds) *Proceedings of the 3rd International Conference on Speech Prosody*, Dresden: TUDpress, paper OS4-4-265.

Appendices

Appendix 1. Examples of utterances from the corpus with affectively charged lexical meaning

Anger: J'ai encore retrouvé ma voiture neuve toute rayée, c'est inadmissible! (I have found my new car scratched, it is unacceptable.)
Doubt: J'ai roulé sans phares en pleine nuit? (I was driving with lights off at night?)

Happiness: Il a appelé sa mère pour lui annoncer la bonne nouvelle. (He called his mother to tell her the good news.)

Irony: J'ai réussi ma chute en pleine rue brillamment. (I managed to fall in the middle of the street very nicely.)

Obviousness: Il a mis un manteau pour sortir! (He put on his coat to go out!)

Sadness: J'ai finalement compris que je ne la reverrais plus. (I finally understood that I would never see her again.)

Appendix 2. Examples of utterances from the corpus with affectively neutral lexical meaning

Anger: Vous appelez ça une chambre d'hôtel? Regardez un peu ces draps! Ils sont ignobles. Vous ne croyez quand même pas que je vais dormir ici! C'est révoltant! *Je vais rentrer à la maison maintenant!* Ce n'est pas un hôtel ici, c'est un élevage de cafards! (Do you call this a hotel room? Look at these sheets! You don't think that I am going to sleep here! It is disgusting! I am going home now! It is not a hotel here; it is a cockroach farm.)

Grief: Tu sais comme j'aimais mon chien? Hier, quand je suis revenu(e) de voyage, j'ai appris qu'il était mort. Je suis bouleversé(e). *Je vais rentrer à la maison maintenant.* J'vais jamais pouvoir le dire aux enfants. (You know how I loved my dog, don't you? Yesterday when I came back from my trip I found out that she had died. I am overwhelmed. I am going home now. How will I be able to tell the children?)

Happiness: Mon frère reviendra demain! Quelle joie! Je suis si content(e)! *Je vais rentrer à la maison maintenant!* Je vais annoncer cette super nouvelle à ma famille! (My brother is coming tomorrow! Such a joy! I am so happy! I am going home now! I will tell this excellent news to my family!)

Neutral: J'ai fini de ranger les boites. Elles sont classées et numérotées. *Je vais rentrer à la maison maintenant.* Je reviendrai demain à dix heures. (I have finished putting the projects in order. They are filed and numbered. *I am going home now.* I will be back tomorrow at ten in the morning.)

Sadness: Ce que tu m'as appris m'a fichu le moral à zéro. C'est vraiment déprimant… *Je vais rentrer à la maison maintenant.* J'ai l'impression que c'est une situation sans issue. (Your news makes me feel so low. It is so depressing. I am going home now. I have the impression that there is no way out.)

Notes on Contributors

VÉRONIQUE AUBERGÉ works at GIPSA-Lab at Grenoble as a senior CNRS researcher in Language Sciences. She is also teaching prosody and automatic language processing in the "Language Industry" master at Grenoble 3 University. She is mainly interested in the modelisation of prosody in human communication. She adopted since years a functional approach of this problem to understand the relative contribution of prosody for each function. Her main contributions allowed the improvement of naturalness and expressivity of prosody for automatic speech synthesis. She currently focuses on emotional expressions in a multimodal and multilingual framework.

NICOLAS AUDIBERT received his PhD in Cognitive Sciences from the National Polytechnic Institute (INP) of Grenoble in 2008. He previously graduated as an engineer in Computer Science from the Technological University of Belfort-Monbéliard (UTBM) in 2002. He obtained a MA in Cognitive Sciences in 2003 (Grenoble INP) and a MA in Language and Speech Sciences in 2004 (Stendhal University Grenoble). He is currently a teaching assistant in Computer Science at University Pierre Mendès-France Grenoble and a research associate in the Speech and Cognition department of GIPSA-lab. His main research interests include Methodology for Acted and Spontaneous Expressive Speech Corpora, Prosody of Expressive Speech, Experimental Paradigms, Voice Quality, and Speech Synthesis.

GREGORY BELLER is a PhD student in Computer Science at the University of Paris VI. A former student of the Ecole Normale Supérieure, he holds an agrégation in applied physics, a master's degree in Music, and a master's degree in Computer Science. He teaches digital music and acoustics at the University Paris-Est Marne-la-Vallée. Since he joined the Analysis/Synthesis team at IRCAM, he has become interested in the musicality of the spoken voice. After working on speech synthesis and prosodic modelling, he is currently working on generative models for expressivity and their applications for speech and music, especially through performance. He has been a member of the VIVOS ANR-project and has co-organized the four conferences of the EMUS project on the Expressivity in Music and Speech. He also takes part in a range of artistic projects as a computer-music designer.

MURTAZA BULUT is a senior scientist in the Digital Signal Processing group in Philips Research Labs in Eindhoven, Netherlands. He received his BSc in electrical and electronics engineering from Bilkent University, Ankara in 2000. He received his MSc and PhD in electrical engineering from the University of Southern California, Los Angeles in 2002 and 2007, respectively. His PhD thesis was on the analysis of acoustic characteristics of emotions and their application for emotional speech synthesis. His work has been regularly published in the major journals and conferences in the field. He serves as a reviewer for IEEE Transactions on Speech and Audio Processing, and is a member of the IEEE Signal Processing Society and the IEEE Computer Society. His research interests are in digital signal processing, speech and image processing, human emotions, human-machine communication and interaction, fuzzy logic, neural networks, and statistical signal processing. His current research is concentrated on audio and speech processing.

CARLOS BUSSO holds a Postdoctoral Research Associate possition at the Signal Analysis and Interpretation Laboratory (SAIL) at University of Southern California (USC). He received his B.S (2000) and M.S (2003) degrees with high honors in electrical engineering from University of Chile, Santiago, Chile, and his Ph.D (2008) in electrical engineering from USC. He was selected by the School of Engineering of Chile as the best Electrical Engineer graduated in Chile in 2003. At USC, he received a Provost Doctoral Fellowship from 2003 to 2005 and a Fellowship in Digital Scholarship from 2007 to 2008. His research interests are in digital signal processing, speech and video processing, and multimodal interfaces. His current research includes modeling and understanding human communication and interaction, with applications to automated recognition and synthesis to enhance human-machine interfaces. He has worked on audio-visual emotion recognition, analysis of emotional modulation in gestures and speech, designing realistic human-like virtual characters, speech source detection using microphone arrays, speaker localization and identification in an intelligent environment, and sensing human interaction in multi-person meetings.

GENEVIEVE CAELEN-HAUMONT is currently a Senior researcher in the Multimedia Information, Communication and Applications Centre, a French-Vietnamese INPG and CNRS laboratory, at Hanoi University of Technology, Vietnam. She is a Director of Research in linguistics at the French National Centre for Scientific Research (CNRS). Her research interests focus on the field of speech prosody with a special emphasis on meaning as the crosspoint between prosody, linguistics and subjectivity. Her work addresses pragmatics and psycho-linguistics and focusses on melodic prominences viewed as an expression of subjectivity, self investment and discourse appropriation. She has published extensively on the subjectivity of prosody, and some of her recent publications include chapters of books, such as «Voice and affect in speech communication» (co-authored with B. Zei-Pollermann 2007), «Prosodic figures of self and collective expression in semi-improvised speech and singing» (co-authored with B. Bel 2008), a book called *Prosodie et sens : une approche expérimentale* (forthcoming), an article in the proceedings of Speech Prosody (2008) «An analysis of the statistical concordances between four French speakers», another article in the proceedings of ASA (2008) «Structures of structures: exploring to what extent speaker variability is spreading». Currently her work is applied to speech recognition, synthesis and human-machine dialogue, both in French and in Vietnamese languages and she has coordinated several international research projects in these fields.

RODDY COWIE is Professor of Psychology at Queen's University Belfast. He studied philosophy and psychology at Stirling and UCLA as an undergraduate (1972), and received his PhD from Sussex (1982) for research on relationships between human and machine vision. He has continued to work on the relationship between computational modelling and visual phenomena where people's subjective experience conflict with 'rational' expectations, including impossible objects, misperception of motion, reading errors, and recovery of structure from simple pictures. He has explored computational methods of analysing deafened people's speech and these methods have generalised to other speech varieties that convey information about the speaker-varieties associated with social class, mental disorder, 'phone voice', and expressive reading. His recent work, arising from EU funded collaborations has focused on the perception of emotion, where both verbal and visual cues function to convey intensely subjective experiences. He led the EU funded Human-Machine Interaction Network on Emotion and is author or co-editor of a wide range of related publications including special issues of *Speech Communication* (2003) and *Neural Networks* (2005).

SOPHIE DE ABREU is finishing her PhD thesis at the University of Paris 7, Denis Diderot (France). She has a double academic training, in linguistics and teaching French as a Foreign Language. Her research interests extend from comparative phonetics, and especially prosody, to discourse analysis. As she is interested in applied linguistics part of her research deals with second language acquisition. She focusses on French and Portuguese speech as a material to her research on communicative functions of language. She is also a lecturer in lexicology, and has taught phonetics and morphology to undergraduate students. Her recent publications include "L'enseignement du français aux Portugais. Prosodie de la lecture" in the proceedings of the conference "La recherche en langues romanes", Paris, 29-30 juin 2007.

HEATH A. DEMAREE, PhD (Virginia Polytechnic Institute and State University), is an Associate Professor of Psychology and Cognitive Science at Case Western Reserve University in Cleveland, Ohio. His research interests involve the genetic, neural, and autonomic underpinnings of emotional experience and emotion regulation. His work also focuses on the emotion-cognition interaction, and especially how emotions impact decisions involving risk. Recent publications have appeared in *Magnetic Resonance Imaging*, *Journal of Affective Disorders*, *Brain & Cognition*, and the *Journal of Personality and Social Psychology*.

ELLEN DOUGLAS-COWIE is Professor of Spoken English at Queen's University Belfast and Pro-Vice-Chancellor for Education and students. A speech scientist, she graduated from the University of Ulster in 1972, and gained her PhD in 1980. Her early work was on social variation in Ulster speech, following which she focused on the way speech changes when people lose their hearing. Over the past decade, she has concentrated on signs of emotion, and has played a leading role in a range of interdisciplinary EU funded projects concerned with the development of emotional interfaces (including the HUMAINE project). In this work, she has focused specifically on creating and labelling databases that reflect naturalistic expressions of emotion. A book *Postlingually acquired deafness: Speech deterioration and the wider consequences* (1992) reports the work on deafness, and her work on emotion is reflected in a special edition of *Speech Communication* (2003).

DONNA ERICKSON is Professor at Showa Music University, Kawasaki, Japan, where she teaches English conversation. She also teaches phonetics at Kanagawa University in Yokohama, and works as a part-time researcher at RIKKEN, Saitama, with the Language Development Team and also the Laboratory for Advanced Brain Signal Processing. Her main research interests are the acoustic, articulatory and perceptual characteristics of prosody, focusing on spoken English rhythm and more recently, of emotional/expressive aspects of spoken language, especially across different languages and cultures. Recent publications include "Exploratory study of some acoustic and articulatory characteristics of sad speech" (2006), "Expressive speech: Production, perception and application to speech synthesis" (2005).

D. ERIK EVERHART, PhD (Virginia Polytechnic Institute and State University), is a clinical neuropsychologist who is board certified by the American Board of Professional Psychology and certified in Behavioral Sleep Medicine through the American Academy of Sleep Medicine. He is an associate professor within the Department of Psychology at East Carolina University and is the director of research the Pitt County Memorial Hospital Sleep Center. His research interests include the neuropsychology of emotion, psychophysiology, and behavioural sleep medicine. He has specific research interests in brain processes associated with the processing of negative emotions. Recent publications have appeared in *Biological Psychology*, *Psychoneuro-endocrinology*, *Neuropsychology*, and the *International Journal of Psychophysiology*.

FLORIAN EYBEN works on a research grant as part of the European Community's Seventh Framework Programme project SEMAINE (FP7/2007-2013) – the Sensitive Artificial Listener project – within the Institute for Human-Machine Communication at the Technische Universität München (TUM). He obtained his diploma in Information Technology from TUM. Teaching activities of his comprise Pattern Recognition and Speech and Language processing. His research interests include large scale hierarchical audio feature extraction and evaluation, automatic emotion recognition from the speech signal, recognition of non-linguistic vocalisations, automatic continuous large vocabulary speech recognition, statistical and context-dependent language models, and Music Information Retrieval. He has several publications in various journals and conference proceedings covering many of his areas of research.

IOULIA GRICHKOVTSOVA received her PhD in Linguistics from Queen Margaret University, Edinburgh. After working as a Research Associate in the CRISCO research centre, University of Caen, she took a contract lectureship position in the Department of Intercultural Studies and Applied Languages at Paris Diderot University. She is specialised in experimental phonetics and psycholinguistics. Her particular research interests include prosody, affective speech production and perception, speech acquisition in monolingual and bilingual contexts. She has recently published a book chapter *Child affective speech: a cross-linguistic perspective* (2007).

SYLVIE HANCIL is Senior Lecturer in English linguistics at the university of Rouen. She holds a PhD in linguistics from the university of Edinburgh. Her main research interests are grammaticalization theory and discourse analysis in relation to aspect and discourse markers, along with the link between prosody and semantic change.

ANNE LACHERET is Research Professor in the Department of Linguistics at the University of Paris X Nanterre and Junior Member of the Institut Universitaire de France (Paris). Her research deals with linguistic modelling of prosodic constructions in discourse. In practice, three domains are analysed: (1) phonetic processing, (2) phonological representations and (3) functional interpretation in terms of syntactic, semantic and pragmatic instructions. Regarding the last point, the question is how expressivity of emotion interacts with constraints of informational packaging in the production of prosodic structure (realisation of prominences, prosodic contours and boundaries in their variability). She has extensive collaborations with scientists from the connected areas: neurosciences, psycholinguistics, computational sciences and text-to-speech synthesis.

PETRI LAUKKA is Associate Professor of Psychology at the Department of Psychology, Uppsala University, and Senior Lecturer of Psychology at the Department of Education and Psychology, Gävle University. His main scholarly interests are emotion research and music psychology. Current research projects include: (a) cross-cultural communication of affect in speech and music, (b) expression of affect in spontaneous speech, (c) functions of music in everyday listening, and (d) individual differences in emotion recognition ability.

SUNGBOK LEE is a Research Assistant Professor of Electrical Engineering at the University of Southern California. He holds a Ph.D. degree in Biomedical Engineering from the University of Alabama at Birmingham in 1991. His main research interests are in the fields of speech production focused on the developmental aspects of speech acoustics and motor control, audio-visual signal processing concerning emotion expression, and speech and language processing for human-machine interaction and assessment. Recent conference and journal publications include "Relation between Geometry and Kinematics of Articulatory Trajectory Associated with Emotional Speech Production" (2008); "Phrase boundary effects on the temporal kinematics of sequential tongue tip consonants" (2008); "Functional data analysis of prosodic effects on articulatory timing" (2006).

QINYANG LI is a PhD Student in the Department of Psychology at the University of Georgia. He obtained his M.S. from Peking University and is now completing his graduate studies in the area of clinical cognitive neuroscience. His research interests center around the role of attention for other cognitive processes such as perception and memory. To elucidate this role, he is currently exploring inhibition in the antisaccade task using electroencephalography and other neuro-imaging techniques.

CATHERINE MATHON, PhD (University of Paris 7), is a researcher in Linguistics and Phonetics in French. She teaches Phonetics and Corpus Linguistics at the University Michel de Montaigne Bordeaux 3 (France). Her research interests target the field of emotions, more specifically the expression of emotions in French. She has published on the linguistic (lexical and prosodic) ways of communicating emotions in French in relation to pragmatic considerations. Her recent publications include "Emotion, from Speakers to Listeners. Perception and Prosodic Characterization of Affective Speech" in C. Muller (ed.), *Speaker Classification II, Selected Projects*, Lectures Notes in Computer Science 4441. She is also interested in discourse analysis and in the specificity of sport comments.

MICHEL MOREL is a Research Engineer at the CRISCO (Centre de Ressources Interlangue sur la Signification en Contexte), where he is in charge of the Kali project (text-to-speech synthesis in French, old French, English and Wolof). His research interests include signal computing, the alphabetic-to-phonetic transcription and a natural prosodic model, including affects, based on automatic syntactic and pragmatic analysis; he is also interested in the applications in voice or vision handicap and some commercial applications.

ALESSANDRA MOSCA is a PhD. student in the History of Grammar at the University of Brescia (Italy) and at the University of Paris 7, Denis Diderot. After finishing her MA degree in French and Swedish cultures and in linguistics at the University of Naples in 2006, she taught Italian at the *Centre culturel italien de Paris* and co-worked with the *Cinémathèque française* as a translator and a subtitler. Her interests include contrastive prosody, translation, teaching and the history of grammar. She is currently writing her dissertation on grammatical terminology.

SHRIKANTH NARAYANAN is Andrew J. Viterbi Professor of Engineering at the University of Southern California (USC) where he holds appointments as Professor of Electrical Engineering and jointly Professor in Computer Science, Linguistics and Psychology. Prior to USC he was with AT&T Bell Labs and AT&T Research, first as a Senior Member, and later as a Principal member, of its Technical Staff from 1995-2000. Shri Narayanan is an Editor for the Computer Speech and Language Journal (2007– present) and an Associate Editor for the IEEE Signal Processing Magazine and the IEEE Transactions on Multimedia. He was also an Associate Editor of the IEEE Transactions of Speech and Audio Processing (2000–2004). Shri Narayanan is a Fellow of the Acoustical Society of America and a Senior member of IEEE. He is a recipient of an NSF CAREER award, USC Engineering Junior Research Award, USC Electrical Engineering Northrop Grumman Research Award, a Provost fellowship from the USC Center for Interdisciplinary research, a Mellon Award for Excellence in Mentoring, an IBM Faculty award, an Okawa Research award, and a 2005 Best Paper award from the IEEE Signal Processing society. He has published over 300 papers and has fifteen granted/pending U.S. patents.

JOHN OHALA is Professor Emeritus of linguistics at the University of California, Berkeley. He specializes in phonetics and phonology. He received his PhD in Linguistics in 1969 from University of California, Los Angeles (UCLA); his graduate advisor was Peter Ladefoged. He is best known for his insistence that many aspects of languages' phonologies (a.k.a. "sound patterns") derive from physical, physiological, and ethological constraints which are independent of language and thus have no place in the "grammar" of a language, i.e., what speakers have to learn inductively from exposure to the speech community into which they are born. He has contributed to an understanding of the phonetics of voice pitch control, speech aerodynamics, the psychological factors underlying speakers' recognition of word relatedness, sound change, and the ethological factors underlying intonation, sound symbolism, and the sexual dimorphism of the vocal anatomy.

OLIVIER PIOT holds a PhD in Phonetics, and his main research project concerns the expression of attitudes by prosody, mainly in French and in English. It involves trying to better understand the meanings and uses of prosody in fields ranging from the expression of emotions to phonology. He graduated in mathematics, which he uses in his research. He has taught general phonetics and phonology as well as prosody at the University of Paris III. He is a member of the Formal Linguistics Laboratory (LLF) of the University of Paris VII (CNRS UMR 7110), where he participates in the PRO-GRAM project (Prosody in French Grammar).

GERHARD RIGOLL is a full professor and head of the Institute for Human-Machine Communication at the Technische Universität München (TUM) in Germany. He received his diploma in Technical Cybernetics, his Ph.D. for his works in the field of Automatic Speech Recognition, and his habilitation in the field of Speech Synthesis from the University of Stuttgart/Germany. He worked for the Fraunhofer-Institute Stuttgart, Speech Plus in Mountain View/SA, and Digital Equipment in Maynard/USA, spent a post-doctoral fellowship at IBM Thomas Watson Research Center, Yorktown Heights/USA, headed a research group at Fraunhofer-Institute Stuttgart and spent a two year's research stay at NTT Human Interface Laboratories in Tokyo/Japan, in the area of Neuro-computing, Speech Recognition and Pattern Recognition until he was appointed full professor of Computer Science at Gerhard-Mercator-University Duisburg/Germany and TUM. He is a senior member of the IEEE and authored and co-authored more than 250 publications in the field of signal processing and pattern recognition. Most of his work deals with Automatic Speech Recognition.

ALBERT RILLIARD is a full-time CNRS researcher at LIMSI (Orsay, France). His research interests are centered around the perception of prosody, and more precisely on expressive prosody. He is currently working on the intercultural aspects of audiovisual prosody, and tries to describe the links between emotional and linguistic expression: how did both impose constraints on the speakers, and how they are perceived and decoded by listeners, amongst languages and cultures. He is also interested in the variability of prosody within romance dialects (inside the AMPER project) and speakers' styles.

ANNETT SCHIRMER is an Assistant Professor in the Department of Psychology at the National University of Singapore. She obtained her PhD from the University of Leipzig and was working for several years as a research scientist at the Max Planck Institute for Human Cognitive and Brain Sciences in Germany. Her research focuses on how listeners process emotional and linguistic cues that are communicated vocally. Moreover, she is interested in what contextual or individual variables might facilitate such processing. To tackle these issues she uses a variety of behavioural, psychophysiological and brain imaging techniques including electroencapholgraphy (EEG) and functional magnetic resonance imaging (fMRI).

BJÖRN SCHULLER received his doctoral degree and diploma in Electrical Engineering and Information Technology for his works in Automatic Speech and Emotion Recognition from TUM (Munich University of Technology), where he currently stays as lecturer. He authored more than 100 publications in books, journals and peer reviewed conference proceedings advancing Speech Processing and Affective Computing. He served as associate editor and reviewer for several scientific journals, including the IEEE Transactions on Audio, Speech, and Language Processing, the Elsevier Speech Communication, Pattern Recognition Letters, and Signal Processing Journals, as invited speaker, special session organizer, chairman, and program committee member of numerous international conferences. Project steering board activities and involvement in research projects related to emotion in speech include SEMAINE funded by the European Community, the HUMAINE CEICES initiative, and projects with companies as BMW, Continental, Daimler, Siemens, Toyota, and VDO. Advisory board activities comprise his membership as invited expert in the W3C Emotion Incubator Group, and his election into the Executive Committee of the HUMAINE Association.

AMY J. SHIPLEY, MA (East Carolina University), is a licensed psychological associate whose research interests include emotional prosody and the effects of sex-related hormones on the physiological responses to emotion. She has served as a lecturer within the Department of Psychology at East Carolina University and is currently seeking a degree in medicine at the Brody School of Medicine at East Carolina University. Her most recent publication appeared in *Behavioral and Cognitive Neuroscience Reviews*.

TAKAAKI SHOCHI completed his PhD at GIPSA-Lab (Grenoble, France) and is currently a post-doctoral researcher at the Graduate School of Social and Cultural Sciences (Kumamoto University, Japan). He spent one year as a research student at the Graduate School of Culture Studies (Kobe University, Japan) and he has taught Japanese Language and Culture at the University of Stendhal (Grenoble, France) in past years. His research interests target the field of cross-cultural perception and production of social affective prosody. He has published extensively on intercultural perception of Japanese, English and French social affective prosody. His recent publications include "Multimodal indices to Japanese and French prosodically expressed social affects" in *Language and Speech* (to appear); "Cultural Specificities and False Friends on Attitudinal Prosody" in T. Sadanobu/M. Nakagawa (eds) *Contrastive Studies on Grammar and Speech*. He currently work on analysis of Infant directed speech.

MARTIN WÖLLMER works as a researcher funded by the European Community's Seventh Framework Programme project SEMAINE (FP7/2007–2013) at the Technische Universität München (TUM). He obtained his diploma in Electrical Engineering and Information Technology from TUM where his current research and teaching activity includes the subject areas of pattern recognition and speech processing. His focus thereby lies on automatic recognition of emotionally coloured and noisy speech and emotion by feature enhancement. His reviewing engagement includes the IEEE Transactions on Audio, Speech and

Language Processing. Publications of his in various conference proceedings cover novel and robust modelling architectures for speech and emotion recognition as Switching Linear Dynamic Models or Long Short-Term Memory Recurrent Neural Nets.

BRIGITTE ZELLNER-KELLER is a senior lecturer in the Department of Psychology at the University of Lausanne, Switzerland. She is active in a Psychological consultation for aged people as well as in academic research and teaching on speech communication. As a psychological counselor, she has been trained to the cognitive and behavioral approach. As a psycholinguist-phonetician, she has been involved in the study of speech prosody (intonation, rhythm, respiration, intensity) in relationship with personality features and psychosocial dimensions in communication (styles of speech, expressivity). She is currently a member of the UNIGER (a gerontology research group) in order to investigate aspects of aging in speech communication. Her previous research was focused on speech prosody modeling, where she demonstrated the importance of the temporal organization of speech such as speech fluency in order to get an agreeable speech flow to listen to. She has contributed to 53 articles and 64 communications at the international level; she is also a member of various international scientific committees and an expert for several journals. She has just edited a text book on the main pathologies and psychosocial issues associated with ageing: "Maladies du vieillissement... un exercice d'indisciplinarité", Actualités Psychologiques, 2008, 21, Institut de Psychologie, Université de Lausanne.

Linguistic Insights

Studies in Language and Communication

This series aims to promote specialist language studies in the fields of linguistic theory and applied linguistics, by publishing volumes that focus on specific aspects of language use in one or several languages and provide valuable insights into language and communication research. A cross-disciplinary approach is favoured and most European languages are accepted.

The series includes two types of books:

- **Monographs** – featuring in-depth studies on special aspects of language theory, language analysis or language teaching.
- **Collected papers** – assembling papers from workshops, conferences or symposia.

Each volume of the series is subjected to a double peer-reviewing process.

Vol. 1 Maurizio Gotti & Marina Dossena (eds)
Modality in Specialized Texts. Selected Papers of the 1st CERLIS Conference.
421 pages. 2001. ISBN 3-906767-10-8. US-ISBN 0-8204-5340-4

Vol. 2 Giuseppina Cortese & Philip Riley (eds)
Domain-specific English. Textual Practices across Communities and Classrooms.
420 pages. 2002. ISBN 3-906768-98-8. US-ISBN 0-8204-5884-8

Vol. 3 Maurizio Gotti, Dorothee Heller & Marina Dossena (eds)
Conflict and Negotiation in Specialized Texts. Selected Papers of the 2nd CERLIS Conference.
470 pages. 2002. ISBN 3-906769-12-7. US-ISBN 0-8204-5887-2

Editorial address:

Prof. Maurizio Gotti — Università di Bergamo, Facoltà di Lingue e Letterature Straniere,
Via Salvecchio 19, 24129 Bergamo, Italy
Fax: 0039 035 2052789, E-Mail: m.gotti@unibg.it

Vol. 4 Maurizio Gotti, Marina Dossena, Richard Dury, Roberta Facchinetti & Maria Lima
Variation in Central Modals. A Repertoire of Forms and Types of Usage in Middle English and Early Modern English.
364 pages. 2002. ISBN 3-906769-84-4. US-ISBN 0-8204-5898-8

Vol. 5 Stefania Nuccorini (ed.)
Phrases and Phraseology. Data and Descriptions.
187 pages. 2002. ISBN 3-906770-08-7. US-ISBN 0-8204-5933-X

Vol. 6 Vijay Bhatia, Christopher N. Candlin & Maurizio Gotti (eds)
Legal Discourse in Multilingual and Multicultural Contexts.
Arbitration Texts in Europe.
385 pages. 2003. ISBN 3-906770-85-0. US-ISBN 0-8204-6254-3

Vol. 7 Marina Dossena & Charles Jones (eds)
Insights into Late Modern English. 2nd edition.
378 pages. 2003, 2007.
ISBN 978-3-03911-257-9. US-ISBN 978-0-8204-8927-8

Vol. 8 Maurizio Gotti
Specialized Discourse. Linguistic Features and Changing Conventions.
351 pages. 2003, 2005.
ISBN 3-03910-606-6. US-ISBN 0-8204-7000-7

Vol. 9 Alan Partington, John Morley & Louann Haarman (eds)
Corpora and Discourse.
420 pages. 2004. ISBN 3-03910-026-2. US-ISBN 0-8204-6262-4

Vol. 10 Martina Möllering
The Acquisition of German Modal Particles. A Corpus-Based Approach.
290 pages. 2004. ISBN 3-03910-043-2. US-ISBN 0-8204-6273-X

Vol. 11 David Hart (ed.)
English Modality in Context. Diachronic Perspectives.
261 pages. 2003. ISBN 3-03910-046-7. US-ISBN 0-8204-6852-5

Vol. 12 Wendy Swanson
Modes of Co-reference as an Indicator of Genre.
430 pages. 2003. ISBN 3-03910-052-1. US-ISBN 0-8204-6855-X

Vol. 13 Gina Poncini
Discursive Strategies in Multicultural Business Meetings.
2nd edition. 338 pages. 2004, 2007.
ISBN 978-3-03911-296-8. US-ISBN 978-0-8204-8937-7

Vol. 14 Christopher N. Candlin & Maurizio Gotti (eds)
Intercultural Aspects of Specialized Communication.
2nd edition. 369 pages. 2004, 2007.
ISBN 978-3-03911-258-6. US-ISBN 978-0-8204-8926-1

Vol. 15 Gabriella Del Lungo Camiciotti & Elena Tognini Bonelli (eds)
Academic Discourse. New Insights into Evaluation.
234 pages. 2004. ISBN 3-03910-353-9. US-ISBN 0-8204-7016-3

Vol. 16 Marina Dossena & Roger Lass (eds)
Methods and Data in English Historical Dialectology.
405 pages. 2004. ISBN 3-03910-362-8. US-ISBN 0-8204-7018-X

Vol. 17 Judy Noguchi
The Science Review Article. An Opportune Genre in the Construction of Science.
274 pages. 2006. ISBN 3-03910-426-8. US-ISBN 0-8204-7034-1

Vol. 18 Giuseppina Cortese & Anna Duszak (eds)
Identity, Community, Discourse. English in Intercultural Settings.
495 pages. 2005. ISBN 3-03910-632-5. US-ISBN 0-8204-7163-1

Vol. 19 Anna Trosborg & Poul Erik Flyvholm Jørgensen (eds)
Business Discourse. Texts and Contexts.
250 pages. 2005. ISBN 3-03910-606-6. US-ISBN 0-8204-7000-7

Vol. 20 Christopher Williams
Tradition and Change in Legal English. Verbal Constructions in Prescriptive Texts.
2nd revised edition. 216 pages. 2005, 2007. ISBN 978-3-03911-444-3.

Vol. 21 Katarzyna Dziubalska-Kołaczyk & Joanna Przedlacka (eds)
English Pronunciation Models: A Changing Scene.
2nd edition. 476 pages. 2005, 2008. ISBN 978-3-03911-682-9.

Vol. 22 Christián Abello-Contesse, Rubén Chacón-Beltrán, M. Dolores López-Jiménez & M. Mar Torreblanca-López (eds)
Age in L2 Acquisition and Teaching.
214 pages. 2006. ISBN 3-03910-668-6. US-ISBN 0-8204-7174-7

Vol. 23 Vijay K. Bhatia, Maurizio Gotti, Jan Engberg & Dorothee Heller (eds)
Vagueness in Normative Texts.
474 pages. 2005. ISBN 3-03910-653-8. US-ISBN 0-8204-7169-0

Vol. 24 Paul Gillaerts & Maurizio Gotti (eds)
Genre Variation in Business Letters. 2nd printing.
407 pages. 2008. ISBN 978-3-03911-681-2.

Vol. 25 Ana María Hornero, María José Luzón & Silvia Murillo (eds)
Corpus Linguistics. Applications for the Study of English.
2nd printing. 526 pages. 2006, 2008. ISBN 978-3-03911-726-0

Vol. 26 J. Lachlan Mackenzie & María de los Ángeles Gómez-González (eds)
Studies in Functional Discourse Grammar.
259 pages. 2005. ISBN 3-03910-696-1 / US-ISBN 0-8204-7558-0

Vol. 27 Debbie G. E. Ho
Classroom Talk. Exploring the Sociocultural Structure of Formal ESL Learning. 2nd edition.
254 pages. 2006, 2007. ISBN 978-3-03911-434-4

Vol. 28 Javier Pérez-Guerra, Dolores González-Álvarez, Jorge L. Bueno-Alonso & Esperanza Rama-Martínez (eds)
'Of Varying Language and Opposing Creed': New Insights into Late Modern English.
455 pages. 2007. ISBN 978-3-03910-788-9

Vol. 29 Francesca Bargiela-Chiappini & Maurizio Gotti (eds)
Asian Business Discourse(s).
350 pages. 2005. ISBN 3-03910-804-2 / US-ISBN 0-8204-7574-2

Vol. 30 Nicholas Brownlees (ed.)
News Discourse in Early Modern Britain. Selected Papers of CHINED 2004.
300 pages. 2006. ISBN 3-03910-805-0 / US-ISBN 0-8204-8025-8

Vol. 31 Roberta Facchinetti & Matti Rissanen (eds)
Corpus-based Studies of Diachronic English.
300 pages. 2006. ISBN 3-03910-851-4 / US-ISBN 0-8204-8040-1

Vol. 32 Marina Dossena & Susan M. Fitzmaurice (eds)
Business and Official Correspondence: Historical Investigations.
209 pages. 2006. ISBN 3-03910-880-8 / US-ISBN 0-8204-8352-4

Vol. 33 Giuliana Garzone & Srikant Sarangi (eds)
Discourse, Ideology and Specialized Communication.
494 pages. 2007. ISBN 978-3-03910-888-6

Vol. 34 Giuliana Garzone & Cornelia Ilie (eds)
The Use of English in Institutional and Business Settings. An Intercultural Perspective.
372 pages. 2007. ISBN 978-3-03910-889-3

Vol. 35 Vijay K. Bhatia & Maurizio Gotti (eds)
Explorations in Specialized Genres.
316 pages. 2006. ISBN 3-03910-995-2 / US-ISBN 0-8204-8372-9

Vol. 36 Heribert Picht (ed.)
Modern Approaches to Terminological Theories and Applications.
432 pages. 2006. ISBN 3-03911-156-6 / US-ISBN 0-8204-8380-X

Vol. 37 Anne Wagner & Sophie Cacciaguidi-Fahy (eds)
Legal Language and the Search for Clarity / Le langage juridique et la quête de clarté. Practice and Tools / Pratiques et instruments.
487 pages. 2006. ISBN 3-03911-169-8 / US-ISBN 0-8388-5

Vol. 38 Juan Carlos Palmer-Silveira, Miguel F. Ruiz-Garrido & Inmaculada Fortanet-Gómez (eds)
Intercultural and International Business Communication: Theory, Research and Teaching.
2nd edition. 343 pages. 2006, 2008. ISBN 978-3-03911-680-5

Vol. 39 Christiane Dalton-Puffer, Dieter Kastovsky, Nikolaus Ritt & Herbert Schendl (eds)
Syntax, Style and Grammatical Norms: English from 1500–2000.
250 pages. 2006. ISBN 3-03911-181-7 / US-ISBN 0-8204-8394-X

Vol. 40 Marina Dossena & Irma Taavitsainen (eds)
Diachronic Perspectives on Domain-Specific English.
280 pages. 2006. ISBN 3-03910-176-0 / US-ISBN 0-8204-8391-5

Vol. 41 John Flowerdew & Maurizio Gotti (eds)
Studies in Specialized Discourse.
293 pages. 2006. ISBN 3-03911-178-7

Vol. 42 Ken Hyland & Marina Bondi (eds)
Academic Discourse Across Disciplines.
320 pages. 2006. ISBN 3-03911-183-3 / US-ISBN 0-8204-8396-6

Vol. 43 Paul Gillaerts & Philip Shaw (eds)
The Map and the Landscape: Norms and Practices in Genre.
256 pages. 2006. ISBN 3-03911-182-5 / US-ISBN 0-8204-8395-4

Vol. 44 Maurizio Gotti & Davide Giannoni (eds)
New Trends in Specialized Discourse Analysis.
301 pages. 2006. ISBN 3-03911-184-1 / US-ISBN 0-8204-8381-8

Vol. 45 Maurizio Gotti & Françoise Salager-Meyer (eds)
Advances in Medical Discourse Analysis: Oral and Written Contexts.
492 pages. 2006. ISBN 3-03911-185-X / US-ISBN 0-8204-8382-6

Vol. 46 Maurizio Gotti & Susan Šarcević (eds)
Insights into Specialized Translation.
396 pages. 2006. ISBN 3-03911-186-8 / US-ISBN 0-8204-8383-4

Vol. 47 Khurshid Ahmad & Margaret Rogers (eds)
Evidence-based LSP: Translation, Text and Terminology.
584 pages. 2007. ISBN 978-3-03911-187-9

Vol. 48 Hao Sun & Dániel Z. Kádár (eds)
It's the Dragon's Turn: Chinese Institutional Discourses.
262 pages. 2008. ISBN 978-3-03911-175-6

Vol. 49 Cristina Suárez-Gómez
Relativization in Early English (950-1250): the Position of Relative Clauses.
149 pages. 2006. ISBN 3-03911-203-1 / US-ISBN 0-8204-8904-2

Vol. 50 Maria Vittoria Calvi & Luisa Chierichetti (eds)
Nuevas tendencias en el discurso de especialidad.
319 pages. 2006. ISBN 978-3-03911-261-6

Vol. 51 Mari Carmen Campoy & María José Luzón (eds)
Spoken Corpora in Applied Linguistics.
274 pages. 2008. ISBN 978-3-03911-275-3

Vol. 52 Konrad Ehlich & Dorothee Heller (Hrsg.)
Die Wissenschaft und ihre Sprachen.
323 pages. 2006. ISBN 978-3-03911-272-2

Vol. 53 Jingyu Zhang
The Semantic Salience Hierarchy Model:
The L2 Acquisition of Psych Predicates
273 pages. 2007. ISBN 978-3-03911-300-2

Vol. 54 Norman Fairclough, Giuseppina Cortese & Patrizia Ardizzone (eds)
Discourse and Contemporary Social Change.
555 pages. 2007. ISBN 978-3-03911-276-0

Vol. 55 Jan Engberg, Marianne Grove Ditlevsen, Peter Kastberg & Martin Stegu (eds)
New Directions in LSP Teaching.
331 pages. 2007. ISBN 978-3-03911-433-7

Vol. 56 Dorothee Heller & Konrad Ehlich (Hrsg.)
Studien zur Rechtskommunikation.
322 pages. 2007. ISBN 978-3-03911-436-8

Vol. 57 Forthcoming.

Vol. 58 Carmen Frehner
Email – SMS – MMS
294 pages. 2008. ISBN 978-3-03911-451-1

Vol. 59 Isabel Balteiro
The Directionality of Conversion in English: A Dia-Synchronic Study.
276 pages. 2007. ISBN 978-3-03911-241-8

Vol. 60 Maria Milagros Del Saz Rubio
English Discourse Markers of Reformulation.
237 pages. 2007. ISBN 978-3-03911-196-1

Vol. 61 Sally Burgess & Pedro Martín-Martín (eds)
English as an Additional Language in Research Publication and Communication.
259 pages. 2008. ISBN 978-3-03911-462-7

Vol. 62 Sandrine Onillon
Pratiques et représentations de l'écrit.
458 pages. 2008. ISBN 978-3-03911-464-1

Vol. 63 Hugo Bowles & Paul Seedhouse (eds)
Conversation Analysis and Language for Specific Purposes.
2nd edition. 337 pages. 2007, 2009. ISBN 978-3-0343-0045-2

Vol. 64 Vijay K. Bhatia, Christopher N. Candlin & Paola Evangelisti Allori (eds)
Language, Culture and the Law.
The Formulation of Legal Concepts across Systems and Cultures.
342 pages. 2008. ISBN 978-3-03911-470-2

Vol. 65–66 Forthcoming.

Vol. 67 Natsumi Wakamoto
Extroversion/Introversion in Foreign Language Learning.
Interactions with Learner Strategy Use.
159 pages. 2009. ISBN 978-3-03911-596-9

Vol. 68 Eva Alcón-Soler (ed.)
Learning How to Request in an Instructed Language Learning Context.
260 pages. 2008. ISBN 978-3-03911-601-0

Vol. 69 Domenico Pezzini
The Translation of Religious Texts in the Middle Ages.
428 pages. 2008. ISBN 978-3-03911-600-3

Vol. 70 Tomoko Tode
Effects of Frequency in Classroom Second Language Learning.
Quasi-experiment and stimulated-recall analysis.
195 pages. 2008. ISBN 978-3-03911-602-7

Vol. 71 Egor Tsedryk
Fusion symétrique et alternances ditransitives.
211 pages. 2009. ISBN 978-3-03911-609-6

Vol. 72 Cynthia J. Kellett Bidoli & Elana Ochse (eds)
English in International Deaf Communication.
444 pages. 2008. ISBN 978-3-03911-610-2

Vol. 73 Joan C. Beal, Carmela Nocera & Massimo Sturiale (eds)
Perspectives on Prescriptivism.
269 pages. 2008. ISBN 978-3-03911-632-4

Vol. 74 Carol Taylor Torsello, Katherine Ackerley & Erik Castello (eds)
Corpora for University Language Teachers.
308 pages. 2008. ISBN 978-3-03911-639-3

Vol. 75 María Luisa Pérez Cañado (ed.)
English Language Teaching in the European Credit Transfer System: Facing the Challenge.
251 pages. 2009. ISBN 978-3-03911-654-6

Vol. 76 Marina Dossena & Ingrid Tieken-Boon van Ostade (eds)
Studies in Late Modern English Correspondence. Methodology and Data.
291 pages. 2008. ISBN 978-3-03911-658-4

Vol. 77 Forthcoming.

Vol. 78 Marta Navarro Coy (ed.)
Practical Approaches to Foreign Language Teaching and Learning.
297 pages. 2009. ISBN 978-3-03911-661-4

Vol. 79 Qing Ma
Second Language Vocabulary Acquisition.
333 pages. 2009. ISBN 978-3-03911-666-9

Vol. 80 Martin Solly, Michelangelo Conoscenti & Sandra Campagna (eds)
Verbal/Visual Narrative Texts in Higher Education.
384 pages. 2008. ISBN 978-3-03911-672-0

Vol. 81 Meiko Matsumoto
From Simple Verbs to Periphrastic Expressions:
The Historical Development of Composite Predicates, Phrasal Verbs, and Related Constructions in English.
235 pages. 2008. ISBN 978-3-03911-675-1

Vol. 82 Melinda Dooly
Doing Diversity. Teachers' Construction of Their Classroom Reality.
180 pages. 2009. ISBN 978-3-03911-687-4

Vol. 83 Forthcoming.

Vol. 84 Maria Grazia Guido
English as a Lingua Franca in Cross-cultural Immigration Domains.
285 pages. 2008. ISBN 978-3-03911-689-8

Vol. 85 Erik Castello
Text Complexity and Reading Comprehension Tests.
352 pages. 2008. ISBN 978-3-03911-717-8

Vol. 86 Forthcoming.

Vol. 87 Carmen Navarro, Rosa Mª Rodríguez Abella, Francesca Dalle Pezze & Renzo Miotti (eds)
La comunicación especializada.
355 pages. 2008. ISBN 978-3-03911-733-8

Vol. 88 Kiriko Sato
The Development from Case-Forms to Prepositional Constructions in Old English Prose.
231 pages. 2009. ISBN 978-3-03911-763-5

Vol. 89 Dorothee Heller (Hrsg.)
Formulierungsmuster in deutscher und italienischer Fachkommunikation. Intra- und interlinguale Perspektiven.
315 pages. 2008. ISBN 978-3-03911-778-9

Vol. 90 Henning Bergenholtz, Sandro Nielsen & Sven Tarp (eds)
Lexicography at a Crossroads. Dictionaries and Encyclopedias Today, Lexicographical Tools Tomorrow.
372 pages. 2009. ISBN 978-3-03911-799-4

Vol. 91 Manouchehr Moshtagh Khorasani
The Development of Controversies: From the Early Modern Period to Online Discussion Forums.
317 pages. 2009. ISBN 978-3-3911-711-6

Vol. 92 María Luisa Carrió-Pastor (ed.)
Content and Language Integrated Learning: Cultural Diversity.
178 pages. 2009. ISBN 978-3-3911-818-2

Vol. 93-96 Forthcoming.

Vol. 97 Sylvie Hancil (ed.)
The Role of Prosody in Affective Speech.
403 pages. 2009. ISBN 978-3-03911-696-6

Vol. 98 Marina Dossena & Roger Lass (eds)
Studies in English and European Historical Dialectology.
257 pages. 2009. ISBN 978-3-0343-0024-7

Vol. 99 Forthcoming.

Vol. 100 Maurizio Gotti (ed.)
Commonality and Individuality in Academic Discourse.
398 pages. 2009. ISBN 978-3-0343-0023-0